CREATIVITY

CREATIVITY

The Art and Science of Business Management

A. Dale Timpe

Series Editor

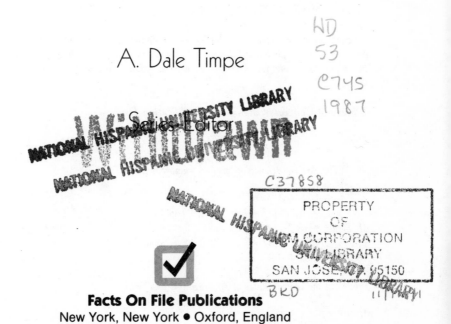

Facts On File Publications
New York, New York ● Oxford, England

This is volume four in Facts On File's series "The Art and Science of Business Management," each volume of which provides a broad selection of articles on an important business topic of our time.
Volume one: *Motivation of Personnel*
Volume two: *The Management of Time*
Volume three: *Leadership*

Creativity

Library of Congress Cataloging-in Publication Data

Creativity.

    (The Art and science of business management)
    Bibliography: p.
    Includes index.
    1. Creative ability in business. I. Timpe, A. Dale.
II. Series.
HD53.C745   1987   650.1   86-29320
ISBN 0-8160-1463-9

Printed in the United States of America

10 9 8 7 6 5 4 3 2 1

CONTENTS

PART III: CREATIVITY AND CONFORMITY

PART IV: MANAGING CREATIVE PEOPLE

PART V: STIMULATING NEW IDEAS

PART VI: RECRUITING AND TRAINING A CREATIVE STAFF

PREFACE

Although psychologists don't know all the reasons why some people are able to think more creatively than others, they have identified certain characteristics that seem to be linked to creativity. Perhaps the three most important are 1) flexibility, 2) persistence and 3) ability to recombine elements to achieve insights. Also key is the ability to break down huge systems into smaller interrelated subsystems and determine how they function together, then recombine these to form a comprehensible "whole picture" framework to work with. A scientist who discovers a new theory usually is guided to his discovery by guesses. He can say only that an explanation that might fit the facts suddenly popped into his mind. As the saying goes, "the mind is like a parachute...it functions only when it is open."

The process that goes on inside the human brain may still be a mystery but, fortunately, we *do* know steps that an organization can take to make the creative process more likely to occur and even flourish. One of the most important of these elements is an organizational climate that is conducive to the free flow of ideas. Several human tendencies affect the creation, development and implementation of the idea. The environment under which people work can act as a stimulant to bring out their innovativeness. Inhibitions and misconceptions act as roadblocks. When people don't worry about making mistakes, even the timid and reticent may come up with some good ideas. Aimless and undirected activity does not bring about innovation. Endeavors must be planned and organized. Motivation is essential to successful innovation, and reward is the single most important motivator. People will go to great lengths to solve problems, but only if they know that their efforts will be recognized and rewarded.

It takes courage to be creative. When you first have a new idea, you're a minority of one. Successful innovators say that ideas that pay off have gone through four steps of development: 1) The idea is conceived. 2) More people become involved as the idea is discussed and examined. This step is considered the most critical to the idea's success, since without general acceptance, the idea is likely to go no further. 3) The idea is publicized and everyone understands its nature and scope. At this time, people investigate its potential, measure its range and evaluate its economic feasibility. Various decisions related to the idea become a part of its development. 4) The innovation represented by the idea is adopted and put into practice.

While certainty is accompanied by security, creativity is accompanied by change—doing things differently. Because change is threatening, many managers resist it. Change evokes resistance, and resistance can be trouble. There is much evidence suggesting that most large organizations are insensitive to the nuances and idiosyncratic work style of the creative personality. A large corporation is a formalized structure that maintains and manages the successes of the past. Procedures have been designed to achieve efficiency in "doing what we do best." Innovation tends to disrupt the stability of the corporate environment. In a large, established organization, innovation thus meets a wall of resistance to change.

Most business organizations operate under the management control concept of "no surprises." But creative development is by its very definition a surprise. Subordinates are penalized if they work on something and they are wrong, but no penalities are attached to missing an opportunity entirely. Rewards do not accrue to those who perform superbly on a failing project. And if successful on high payoff projects, technical people are rarely made millionaires or given rewards perceptible to outside peers. The organization concepts of "chain of command" and "authority must equal responsibility," with their relationships and requirements, need to be reexamined to determine whether they really serve the best interest of the organization and its people. Employees who get things done outside the authority-responsibility and chain-of-command structures should be identified, developed and encouraged.

While large companies are good at coming up with sound ideas, they are generally poor at carrying them out because of the morass of analysis, approvals and politics. Whereas creative thinking is largely positive, judicial thinking is largely negative. Most companies' control systems are predominantly financial. Because other factors like product quality, image and innovativeness are difficult to measure, they do not become bases for rewards. Producing units are held accountable primarily for ROI/profit performance. They have little incentive to undertake longer-term development or investment programs that will not meet these criteria in the short-run. Furthermore, corporate financial results are published monthly and quarterly, forcing top management and all lower levels of management toward very short horizons. Major innovations, such as a breakthrough discovery, often require seven to 15 years before realizing financial success. Also, management must be wary of long-term commitments because of frequent and unanticipated changes in government regulations and taxes. Consequently, there is a search for the one all-encompassing policy (or preplanned solution) rather than tolerance for the chaos of innovative and competing approaches.

Management needs to balance innovation and organizational stability, but unless it also recognizes and exploits creativity, the organization will quickly be left behind by its competition. Unfortunately, it is just when companies need creativity most—during an unstable or fluctuating economy—that they are likely to sacrifice innovative activities for projects with a fast return.

This compendium provides access to a broad spectrum of practical knowledge, research and theory relating to creativity. The diversity of insights, experience and theoretical concepts offers many useful and strategic solutions for encouraging, developing and managing creativity and innovation. The sources represent a wide range of professional publications, including a number not readily available to most business executives. For those wanting to explore a particular aspect in more detail, the bibliography provides a valuable resource tool.

A. Dale Timpe
Series Editor

ACKNOWLEDGMENTS

The articles in this volume are reprinted with the permission of the respective copyright holders and all rights are reserved.

Badawy, Michael K. "How to Prevent Creativity Mismanagement" from *Research Management* by permission from Industrial Research Institute, Inc., © 1986.

Baker, Norman R., Green, Stephen G., and Bean, Alden S. "How Management Can Influence the Generation of Ideas" from *Research Management* by permission from Industrial Research Institute, Inc., © 1985.

Baran, Stanley, Zandan, Peter, and Vanston, John H. "How Effectively Are We Managing Innovation?" from *Research Management* by permission from Industrial Research Institute, Inc., © 1986.

Bauman, Richard. "Don't Let Your Good Ideas Die" from *Supervision* by permission from The National Research Bureau, Inc., © 1986.

Beiswinger, George L. "Why Corporations Stifle Creativity" from *Business & Society Review* by permission from Warren, Gorham & Lahmont, Inc., © 1979.

Blake, Robert R. and Mouton, Jane Srygley. "Don't Let Group Norms Stifle Creativity" from *Personnel* by permission from the American Management Association, © 1985 and The Managerial Grid figure from *The Managerial Grid III*, by Robert Blake and Jane Srygley Mouton, Gulf Publishing Company, © 1985.

Brown, David S. "System for Increasing Inventiveness" by permission from the Journal of Systems Management, © 1983.

Conrath, Jerry. "The Imagination Harvest: Training People to Solve Problems Creatively" from *Supervisory Management* by permission from the American Management Association, © 1985.

Data Management. "Put That 'Better Idea' to Work for You" from *Data Management* by permission from Data Processing Management Association, © 1984.

Ellis, William D. "Creativity: A Path to Profit" from *Nation's Business* by permission from the U.S. Chamber of Commerce, © 1973.

Froman, Robert. "Strengthen Your Reasoning Power" from *Nation's Business* by permission from the U.S. Chamber of Commerce, © 1962.

Gagliano, Caren Calish. "How to Mine and Refine New Product Ideas" from *Business Marketing* by permission from Crain Communications, Inc., © 1985.

Gillis, Jim G. "Creativity, Problem Solving and Decision Making" by permission from the *Journal of Systems Management*, © 1983.

Goldstein, Mark L. "Managing the Goldcollar Worker" from *Industry Week* by permission from Penton Publishing, Inc., © 1985.

Himes, Gary K. "Developing Your Creative Ideas" from *Supervision* by permission from The National Research Bureau, Inc., © 1982.

Himes, Gary K. "Stimulating Creativity: Encouraging Creative Ideas" from *Supervision* by permission from The National Research Bureau, Inc., © 1982.

Howard, Niles. "Business Probe: The Creative Spark" from *Dun's Business Month* by permission from Dun & Bradstreet Publications Corporation, © 1980.

Jantz, Alfred H. "The Encouragement of Employee Creativity and Initiative" by permission from *Personnel Journal*, © 1975.

Kanter, Rosabeth Moss. "Innovation: The Only Hope for Times Ahead?" from *Sloan Management Review* by permission from the Sloan Management Review Association, © 1984.

Kerwin, Robert. "Brainstorming as a Flexible Management Tool" by permission from *Personnel Journal*, © 1983.

Kirkwood, William G. "The Search for Good Ideas" from *Supervisory Management* by permission from the American Management Association, © 1983.

Kottcamp, E.H. Jr., and Rushton, Brian M. "Improving the Corporate Environment" from *Research Management* by permission from Industrial Research Institute, Inc., © 1979.

Lasden, Martin. "Intuition: The Voice of Success?" from *Computer Decision* by permission from Hayden Publishing Company, © 1985.

Luckenbach, Thomas A. "Encouraging 'Little c' and 'Big C' Creativity" from *Research Management* by permission from Industrial Research Institute, Inc., © 1986.

McAlindon, Harold R. "Toward a More Creative You: Unlocking Human Potential" from *Supervisory Management* by permission from the American Management Association, © 1979.

McIntyre, Shelby H. "Obstacles to Corporate Innovation" from *Business Horizons* by permission from Indiana University, School of Business, © 1982.

Mason, Joseph G. "How to Develop Ideas" from *Nation's Business* by permission from the U.S. Chamber of Commerce, © 1958.

Matherly, Timothy A. and Goldsmith, Ronald E. "The Two Faces of Creativity" from *Business Horizons* by permission from Indiana University, School of Business, © 1985.

Merrifield, Bruce. "Stimulating Technological Innovation: Nurturing the Innovator" from *Research Managment* by permission from Industrial Research Institute, Inc., © 1979.

Miles, Mary. "Bright Ideas: 'Sparking'" from *Computer Decisions* by permission from Hayden Publishing Company, © 1983.

Miles, Mary. "Getting Bright Ideas From Your Team" from *Computer Decisions* by permission from Hayden Publishing Company, © 1983.

Myers, Donald W. "How to Nourish the Creative Employee" from *Supervisory Management* by permission from the American Management Association, © 1981.

Nelton, Sharon. "How to Spark New Ideas" from *Nation's Business* by permission from the U.S. Chamber of Commerce, © 1985.

Pollock, Ted. "A Personal File of Stimulating Ideas and Problem Solvers" from *Supervision* by permission from The National Research Bureau, Inc., © 1982.

Quinn, James Brian. "Technological Innovation, Entrepreneurship, and Strategy" from *Sloan Management Review* by permission from the Sloan Management Review Association, © 1979.

Raudsepp, Eugene. "How Creative Are You?" by permission from *Personnel Journal,* © 1975.

Raudsepp, Eugene. "Nurturing Managerial Creativity" from *Administrative Management* by permission from Dalton Communications, Inc., © 1980.

Raudsepp, Eugene. "100 Ways to Spark Your Employees' Creative Potential" from *Office Administration and Automation* by permission from *Administrative Management*, Dalton Communications, Inc., © 1985.

Roberts, Edward B. and Fusfeld, Alan R. "Staffing the Innovative Technology-Based Organization" from *Sloan Management Review* by permission from the Sloan Management Review Association, © 1981.

Rooks, Robin. "Creativity and Conformity: Finding the Balance" from *Management World* by permission from the Administrative Management Society, © 1981.

Rubinstein, Gwen. "Whole Brain Management" from Association Management by permission from the American Society of Association Executives, © 1985.

Sarett, Lewis H. "Stimulating Technological Innovation: The Innovative Spirit in an Industrial Setting" from *Research Management* by permission from Industrial Research Institute, Inc., © 1979.

Schaeffer, Dorothy. "Creativity" from *Supervision* by permission from The National Research Bureau, Inc., © 1980.

Shearring, H.A. "You Can Become More Creative" by permission from the *Journal of Systems Management,* © 1979.

Sinetar, Marsha. "Entrepreneurs, Chaos, and Creativity: Can Creative People Really Survive Large Company Structure?" from *Sloan Management Review* by permission from the Sloan Management Review Association, © 1985.

Studer, Gary A. "Working Creatively" from *Management World* by permission from the Administrative Management Society, © 1982.

Vanden Bergh, Bruce G. and Adler, Keith. "Take This 10-Lesson Course on Managing Creatives Creatively" from *Marketing News* by permission from the American Marketing Association, © 1983.

Vicere, Albert A. "Managing Internal Entrepreneurs" from *Management Review* by permission of the American Management Association, © 1985.

Weiss, Bernard. "Hiring Creative People: Three Opportunities to Make Better Decisions" from *Personnel Administrator* by permission from The American Society for Personnel Administration, © 1986.

Weiss, W. H. "Being Innovative Pays Off" from *Supervision* by permission from The National Research Bureau, Inc. © 1985.

Wheeler, David R. "Creative Decision Making and the Organization" by permission from *Personnel Journal*, © 1979.

Wolff, Michael. "How to Find—and Keep—Creative People" from *Research Management* by permission from Industrial Research Institute, Inc., ©1979.

Zeldman, Maurice I. "How Management Can Develop and Sustain a Creative Environment" by permission from S.A.M. *Advanced Management Journal*, © 1980.

Part 1:
PERSPECTIVES ON THE CREATIVE PROCESS

1.

BUSINESS PROBE:
THE CREATIVE SPARK

Niles Howard

In creativity tests on individuals of all ages, creativity scores invariably drop about 90% between ages five and seven, and by age forty an individual is only about 2% as creative as he was at age five. The hope of creativity research is that what is trained out can be trained back in.

It has long been considered practically an axiom of management that highly creative people get their ideas not through ordinary rational processes like the rest of us, but by some kind of mysterious bolt from the blue. Take the case of John J. Moran, the one-time laboratory technician who made a fortune by inventing an automatic blood analyzer in 1965.

Moran worked for months on the problem before giving up in frustration and setting out on a long-postponed excursion. But on his first day out, as the sun's rays filtered through the hotel window onto his face, he saw in his mind's eye a detailed diagram of a finished machine. Recognizing it as the long-sought solution to the problem, he sprang from bed, hastily sketched it on hotel stationery and flew home, where he spent the next few months building a prototype from the sketch. As it happened, the prototype worked perfectly and Moran built around it a company called Hycel, Inc., which he sold to a West German conglomerate for $40 million.

Although the circumstance of Moran's invention is astonishing to most people, including Moran himself, it is far from unique. Many people who are considered highly creative have described strikingly similar experiences when asked to explain the source of their brilliant notions, and invariably they are at a loss to relate exactly what process they went through to get them. Thus, there is little wonder that practical managers have traditionally held their most creative employees somewhat in awe, commonly winking at the kinds of deviances in everything from dress to office hours that wouldn't be tolerated from other employees.

Over the past few years, however, the notion of the creative genius as some sort of modern-day Merlin has been coming under new scrutiny. A handful of

3

organizational psychologists and scientists have been working with startling success to unravel the mysteries of the creative process. Armed with new knowledge about the functions of the human mind and with a slew of products and techniques ranging from mind-altering drugs to brain-wave reading, these researchers believe they are on the threshold of locating and identifying the origins of the creative spark. By doing so, many are convinced that they will learn to detect that fountain of creative ideas that presumably lies in the minds of us all, and thus learn how to tap it at will. Dudley Lynch, a Dallas, Texas, creativity expert and publisher of *The Creativity Newsletter*, believes that major advancements are near. Says Lynch: "We're beginning to take the brain out of the status of a mysterious black box."

IDEAS AND GROWTH

That this work is of major importance to business goes without saying. It takes no genius to recognize that new ideas are the primary catalyst for growth in any industrial organization, whether they involve coming up with new products and marketing strategies or developing entirely new technologies. It is not surprising, therefore, that executives are following this research closely.

Indeed, since creativity research began in earnest thirty years ago, more than half the 500 largest U.S. corporations, including Procter & Gamble, International Business Machines and Singer, have adopted some sort of formal creativity training, according to a study by Greensboro, North Carolina's Center for Creative Leadership. Given the nature of the activity, it is very difficult to identify what concrete benefits ensue. But among other things, the idea for P&G's Pringles potato chips came from a creativity program, as did the home trash masher and the magnesium-coated bandage used for severe wounds.

Strictly speaking, scientists point out, it is inaccurate to speak of creativity as a trait that some people have and others don't. Everyone is to some degree creative. Even chimpanzees, faced with the problem of retrieving a banana from a high shelf, can assemble an ingenious (for a chimpanzee) collection of chairs, tables and sticks adequate to the task. When psychologists speak of creativity they are actually talking in relative terms. The human mind is taught from birth to accomplish certain tasks in specific ways. Creativity is simply the degree to which one can think of different, more effective approaches.

Why some people have a knack for this while others don't has long stumped the great thinkers. Aristotle, no modest man, futilely pondered the origin of his remarkable insight, and Archimedes, having leaped naked from the bath with the displacement theory fixed in his mind, was at a loss to explain how it got there. Others, from Vincent Van Gogh to Sigmund Freud, concluded that it arose from something other than logical reasoning, but offered little advice on how to achieve it.

Oddly enough, the first person to make much practical progress in this area was not a scientist at all, but advertising man Alex F. Osborn, a principal of New York ad agency Batten, Barton, Durstine & Osborn. An educator by training, Osborn was mystified why some people in his agency were so creative when confronted with a problem, while others could come up with nothing. Drawing on, among other things, the theories of Freud, Jung and Gestalt psychology, Osborn in the mid-1930s decided he had found the answer: Instead of one mode of thought, each person actually had two. One, freely associative, was the idea generator; the other, which worked in a step-by-step logical fashion, acted as a filter. For several reasons, most notably the fear of ridicule by others, the filter had become so dominant in most people that it blocked the release of novel ideas.

THE ART OF BRAINSTORMING

Osborn's theory wasn't exactly original, but the solution was: Eliminate the filter. Gathering his staff in a room, Osborn would toss out a problem and instruct everyone to mention whatever idea came to mind, no matter how ridiculous it seemed. Insisting that ideas thus produced be judged not during but following the session, Osborn quickly silenced any critical remarks that might block free exchange by loudly ringing a bell that he kept close at hand. Before long, the method of deferred judgment was working as Osborn hoped. Instead of the five or six ideas that an hour session had once produced, the group of seven people could now produce up to 150 at a sitting. "Brainstorming," as the technique came to be called, was soon standard procedure at BBDO.

Alex Osborn explained his method in a 1952 book, *Applied Imagination*. It became an overnight best-seller. Newspapers and magazines hailed brainstorming as the long-sought answer to the problem of creativity, and dozens of management consulting companies rose up overnight to teach the ideas to industry. Osborn even set up his own training institute, the Creative Education Foundation, at the University of Buffalo, to promote and improve on the technique. By the late 1950s, it seemed that every group, from church committees to corporate boards of directors, was practicing the craft. But under such intensive use, brainstorming soon showed its faults. Although it worked fine in producing new advertising slogans, it collapsed when it came to big problem-solving tasks, such as the development of financial strategies or new technologies. By the end of the 1950s, the popularity of brainstorming began to fade.

But the notion that ideas might be produced in assembly line fashion under controlled conditions was also being explored by many other researchers. One of them was William J. J. Gordon, an executive of the big Cambridge, Massachusetts, consulting firm Arthur D. Little, Inc. Gordon, a paunchy and flamboyant part-time Harvard engineering professor who at the time sported a flowing red beard, was one of Little's most inventive thinkers, the leader of an elite creative team that was dispatched to clients whenever they had to solve an especially difficult problem, such as coping with a tough new competitor or overcoming a technological snag. Having studied the creative process on the side for years, Gordon was fascinated by the reception given Osborn's theories. But he was convinced that there was much more to creativity than that.

Thus, in the early 1950s, Gordon began tape-recording the sessions of his creative team, and when the team came up with a particularly novel idea, he could play the tapes time and again to discern just how the idea emerged from the group dialogue. Soon a pattern emerged: Whenever someone came up with an idea, Gordon noticed, it was expressed in terms of an analogy with a similar problem found in nature or elsewhere in life. For example, when a farm products company had asked the group to help it come up with a way to insure that seeds were properly spaced in the field, the inventors had come up with the idea of packing the seeds in a dissolvable tape that would be laid in the furrow. The idea arose after a group member thought of a machine-gun belt.

Stimulated by that finding, Gordon, with the help of his Harvard students, began researching some of history's most notable discoveries to determine if the pattern was common. Not only was it common, he soon found, but in virtually every case the analogy had been the key insight that led to the discovery. For instance, scientists had long assumed that infection was caused by internal gases until Louis Pasteur concluded that it came from external micro organisms. Pasteur formed his discovery after observing that grapes would ferment only when the skin was broken.

With this metaphorical theory of creativity in mind, Gordon set about developing a formalized ritual to make use of it, which he described in *Synectics*, a book published in 1960. The technique involved group sessions, during which a problem-solving group was led through a series of steps beginning with the ingestion of background information, followed by a boiling down of a problem to its barest essentials, followed in turn by searching for a natural analogy.

These sessions, often involving Arthur D. Little clients at company head-quarters, had a tendency to become boisterous as clients were encourage to let their minds roam freely in coming up with suitable analogies. One businessman who later studied the techniques was heard to mutter such phrases as "I see a bumblebee in love with an elephant." As word of these sessions spread, Little became dissatisfied with Gordon's methods and in 1960, by mutual agreement, Gordon and several associates left to form a new consulting firm, Synectics, Inc., taking several Arthur D. Little clients with them.

TOO VAGUE?

But while the Synectics methods often proved amazingly good in developing ideas, many clients complained that the methodology was so vague that it only seemed to work when Gordon personally led the sessions. So with the help of a colleague, a former advertising executive named George M. Prince, Gordon set to work to put his theories into more useful form by adding more specific steps. One of the more useful developments in this direction was the observation that every problem requiring a creative solution actually contained at its heart an essential "paradox."

In one of Synectics' most notable assignments, a small company asked Synectics to come up with a way to compress potato chips into a small space. The paradox, of course, was the fact that while potato chips could be compressed, they would be destroyed in the process. Having determined that paradox, the creative group was asked to find an instance in which nature had solved this problem. In the end, the group members found an analogy in leaves. Although fragile, they noted, leaves were often found compressed and undamaged. How? They are moistened. Thus arose the idea of shaping potato chips while moist. The client subsequently sold the idea to Procter & Gamble, which introduced Pringle's potato chips in a can.

By the beginning of the 1970s, hundreds of corporate executives were trooping through Synectics' cluttered Harvard Square headquarters each year in an effort to become creative. But as Gordon and Prince continued to hone their ideas, it soon became clear that they were going in different directions. Although Gordon was convinced that perfecting the metaphorical technique was still the key, Prince had concluded that future progress would come by focusing less on duplicating the step-by-step structure of the thought process and more on jogging loose repressed ideas he was convinced already existed in the mind. Thus, the two parted company—Prince continuing with Synectics, Inc., and Gordon forming Synectics Education Systems (now S.E.S. Associates).

Prince was particularly fascinated by the startling new discoveries being made in brain physiology. It had long been known that the human brain exists in two parts, or hemispheres, and that these hemispheres communicate through a bundle of nerves called the corpus callosum. There was a speculation that the two hemispheres actually constituted the "two minds" referred to in psychological literature, but there was no proof of it. Then, in the mid-1960s, researchers began to publish studies of epileptics whose seizures had been controlled by severing the corpus callosum. Among other things, scientists were able to prove, as had long been theorized, that the left side of the brain controlled the muscles on the right side of the body and vice versa. But most notable was the light shed on the thought process itself.

Through a series of tests, researchers were able to demonstrate that in most people the left side of the brain was the origin of most analytical thought and the source of speech, while the right hemisphere seemed to have no such capacity. Instead, the right hemisphere was apparently a source of dreams, daydreams and other, more intuitive and impressionistic kinds of thought. The discoveries fell like a bombshell on the psychology profession: Here, at last, was the closest thing yet to physical proof of the existence of the two minds.

Prince saw this discovery as a key to unlocking the creative process. The older theories of the two minds were somewhat vague and hard to conceptualize, and were more difficult to communicate to individuals trying to learn how to be creative. Now there existed a superb metaphor for these ideas, and Prince began developing his techniques.

SUPPRESSING THE LEFT

If Bill Gordon's techniques resembled free-for-alls (one cynic called it the "madness method"), Prince's new techniques resembled an encounter session. Reasoning that the key to creativity lay in suppressing the left (or logical) hemisphere of the brain, Prince encouraged his clients to become comfortable with their right brains, the so-called "store house of ideas." Thus, he came up with such techniques as goal-wishes, in which the aspiring inventor would fantasize about how the problem might be solved if there were no fiscal or technical restraints. Having produced a list of such solutions, the client was instructed to review them and try to come up with such an absurd method of achieving them that he would fear dismissal if he seriously proposed it at work. Prince referred to this as the "get-fired solution," but is was one that could in many cases be refined eventually into an imaginative but workable answer.

The work of Osborn, Gordon and Prince has spawned a truckload of creativity training techniques in the past few years, ranging from the highly structured to pure brainstorming. Indeed, Arthur B. Van Gundy, a professor of business at the University of Oklahoma who has spent the past two years trying to track them all down, has found seventy so far. Many of these creativity training groups, Van Gundy says, combine the ideas of all three men so that it is often hard to determine the source.

For instance, North Carolina's Center for Creative Leadership, supported largely by the nonprofit Smith Foundation, uses the basic technique of brainstorming. But in the past years, researcher Stanley S.Gryskiewicz has found that the center can obtain better results by using one of several other idea-stimulating methods, depending on the type of problem and the degree of novelty sought. In one such approach, called "brain-writing," ideas are not discussed openly but written on a piece ofpaper and then passed, minus the writer's name, to another individual, who builds on those ideas and passes the paper on once again. Unlike many other creativity theorists, the center believes that idea generation is only asmall part of creative problem-solving, and thus devotes 90% of its sessions to the logical dissection of ideas.

Others, such as Dallas' Dudley Lynch, believe that the left side of the brain can be repressed by such techniques as playing soft, rhythmic music while gazing at a glass coffee pot onto which a series of colored lights are projected. Even Lynch takes pains to use such techniques in conjunction with more structured methods, such as synectics or brainwriting, if only to allay the fears of his clients, most of whom are used to operating in highly disciplined environments. "They can be very easily turned off," he says.

Some researchers are convinced that the real basis of creativity lies more with the makeup of a given group than with the methods used. For instance, W. E. Herrmann, manager of education operations at the General Electric Management Institute in Croton-on-Hudson, New York, believes there are a number of different kinds of thinking, ranging from iron logic to free association, and that the individual genius is recognized as such by having all of these types. In the past few years, Herrmann has put together a test designed to measure just where individuals fall on that spectrum, and has administered it to more than 2,000 executives attending the institute. By combining individuals of various characteristics, Herrmann believes, it is possible to assemble a group to duplicate the traits of the individual genius.

While a number of corporations have established their own creativity research and training programs, many corporate creativity trainers complain that the new theories are slow to gain acceptance. "Most of the executives around here are highly left-brained," says an official of one corporation. "They don't understand that there is another way of thinking other than in a straight, logical manner. The other day I was explaining these theories to some senior people over lunch, and after ten minutes I could see them giving each other funny looks. They think I'm a nut."

SCIENTIFIC STUDIES

Whether or not such ideas gain wider acceptance in corporations, though, there is a growing suspicion among some creativity experts that the big future progress in creativity will not come through such organizational studies but through more scientific understanding of the brain function itself. Since the important hemispherical findings were made a decade or so ago, there has been an increasing amount of work in universities and other research laboratories aimed at gaining understanding of the chemical and electrical operation of the mind, and how that relates to creativity.

One interesting area of research has been with the use of drugs designed to chemically suppress the working of the left hemisphere, on the theory that with that out of the way, the thoughts of the right brain will come rolling forth. But this research has created more questions than it has answered. While ideas do come forth rapidly, the results are very similar to those obtained by pure brainstorming; many of them are so far removed from practicality as to be of virtually no use at all.

William Gordon, who has studied such tests, contends that they support his theory—shared by many psychologists—that the left, or logical, part of the brain is more involved in the creative process than many researchers believe. In Gordon's view, such research gives strong support to the theory that the formation of creative ideas is actually an oscillation between the right and left hemispheres, with the right hemisphere continuously making free associations and the left performing rapid judgments on them and sending them back to the right brain for more work. This process, Gordon argues further, is precisely what his structured creativity training techniques have been forcing people to do all along.

Other psychologists are convinced that the key to understanding creativity can be found through the techniques of brain-scanning and biofeedback. Colin Martindale, a professor of psychology at the University of Maine, wired students to an electroencephalograph machine and asked them to work out solutions to difficult problems. Martindale noted that highly creative students produced distinctive brain waves when they came up with an answer.

But other researchers are skeptical. "What it sounds like to me is that he has measured only the moment that the student recognized the idea," says Alyce M. Green of Topeka's Menninger Foundation. Green, who along with her husband, Elmer Green, is considered one of the country's leading experts in biofeedback, contends that by the time someone is aware that he has an idea, the idea is already formed.

Over the past few years, the Greens have been working with patients at Menninger in an effort to more precisely pinpoint the moment of creativity, and they have theorized that the critical period is the few moments before one drifts off to sleep at night or the last few moments before one awakens in the morning. During the so-called hypnagogic and hypnopomic states, the consciously analytical or left hemisphere seems to be in closest touch with the subconscious, which dwells in the right hemisphere, where ideas are actually formed. These pre- and post-sleep stages can be clearly identified on electroencephalogram machines by the predominance of theta brain waves, with some alpha waves. In contrast, individuals when fully alert are producing mostly beta waves; when daydreaming, mostly alphawaves; and when sleeping, delta waves.

By using biofeedback techniques, the Greens have been able to achieve and prolong the theta state and stimulate creative ideas. But recently, funding for this experimental work has been sharply reduced, and they have so far been unable to publish details of their work.

FOCUSING ON THETA

Other psychologists, though, believe that the theta state can be achieved without the use of feedback. Professor Eugene Gendlin, a psychologist at the University of Chicago, has developed a technique that he calls "focusing," in which he claims a person can reach a theta state and remain there indefinitely through a process akin to self-hypnosis. By following a series of mental steps, says Gendlin, the subject can make the connection between the conscious and subconscious mind that is the essence of creativity. Dallas' Dudley Lynch calls Gendlin's work "maybe the most important advance in the development of creativity techniques ever."

Yet Lynch and most other creativity experts acknowledge that even the best such techniques have their limits. Numerous studies of history's most creative individuals have shown that while all clearly have the ability to make novel associations, they also tend to have a heavy measure of inborn skepticism, iconoclasm and an almost childlike playfulness of the mind. Indeed, a study conducted a few years ago by one of the country's most prominent industrial laboratories found that one of the most common traits of creative people is a sense of humor. It is doubtful that such things can be taught.

What creativity research and training can do, though, say its supporters, is remove those socially imposed mental barriers to it. In creativity tests on individuals of all ages, creativity scores invariably drop about 90% between ages five and seven, and by age forty an individual is only about 2% as creative as he was at age five. This suggests to many psychologists that the almost total emphasis on logical thought in education may effectively suppress creativity. The hope of creative research is that what is trained out can be trained back in.

2.
HOW TO DEVELOP IDEAS

Joseph G. Mason

All studies to determine what makes a person creative point to four principal characteristics. Experiments have demonstrated that all four of these can be acquired or developed to some degree in any individual.

Ideas are vital factors in business survival today. Business, science, and government need all the ideas they can get. But in any type of organization, creativity must come from the top. Top and middle management executives must set the example.

If an executive himself is not a spectacular idea man, he must at least have enough knowledge and understanding of the creative processes that he does not inadvertently block or discourage fresh or different kinds of thinking within his organization.

This article covers two areas of creative thinking: the factors affecting creativity in you, as an individual; and some practical operational techniques of deliberate creativity—devices and procedures you can use to prime your imagination when you need ideas.

All studies to determine what makes a person creative point to four principal characteristics:

- Problem sensitivity
- Idea fluency
- Originality
- Flexibility

Experiments have demonstrated that all four of these can be acquired or developed to some degree in any individual. This does not mean, of course, that a person who rates low in using his imaginative faculties can suddenly be turned into a creative ball-of-fire. But he can, through application, learn to do more with what he has. At the same time, the naturally creative person can, through experience, learn to raise his already high creative output even higher.

PROBLEM SENSITIVITY

This is basically the ability to recognize that a problem exists; or to be able to cut through misunderstanding, misconception, lack of facts, or other obscuring handicaps, and recognize the real problem.

An example of an initial lack of problem sensitivity occurred during a course in creative thinking being conducted for a major research organization. As a homework exercise, the scientist-students were given six cartoons from magazines and instructed to write new captions for them. One young chemist turned in a particularly good set. After class, the instructor complimented him.

"Thank you," replied the student, "but those were just switches on someone else's ideas. I want to learn to think up new things."

To the instructor, this was a tip-off that the student, who had demonstrated an ability to be imaginative, had not learned to use his imagination to find opportunities for applying ideas. At the next class session, the instructor pointed out opportunities for chemists. Right in the room were the paint on the walls, finishes on furniture, composition ceiling tiles, flooring material, window glass, even the clothing the students were wearing and the textbook materials they were using. All of these represented opportunities for chemical improvements in either basic materials or methods of manufacture. He then gave the students the assignment of bringing in a list of 10 such opportunities the next week.

When, the next week, he asked the young chemist how he had made out on this assignment, he received a self-satisfied smile and the reply: "I've got a couple of ideas that I'm not even going to tell you about—I'm taking them home to work on myself!"

Actually, the easiest way to improve your problem sensitivity is simple to keep in mind that nothing is ever as well done as it could be. Every man-made article, every business operation, every human relations technique can be improved and someday will be. In every situation you encounter as an executive, no matter how many times you have met and handled it before, an opportunity exists to find a better way. If you can once learn to recognize these problems as challenges to your own creative effort, you will be half-way to finding creative solutions to such opportunities.

IDEA FLUENCY

This term simply means that a person can pile up a large number of alternative solutions to a given problem in a given time. The value of this lies in the fact that the more ideas you have, the greater your chances of finding a usable one; the more plentiful your opportunities to get out of the same old ways of doing things.

Idea fluency depends largely upon personal mental habits. It is an attribute that can be developed or improved by nearly every person who will consciously apply himself to it. The theories covering fluency development are simple:

First, remember that it is quantity you are after. Second, don't mix evaluating with your idea gathering. Get your ideas first—worry about whether they are good or not later on.

Devices to aid fluency development are just as simple, but more plentiful. Here are a few of the more common ones. Don't be surprised if you find that you already use one or more of these. Most executives use such techniques from time to time. The value of having them formalized lies in the confidence it gives you to know that these tools exist, that they have a purpose, that you can use them whenever you feel the need of them.

Making Notes. The use of notebooks, or "think books" or "idea traps," as they are sometimes called, is almost universal. Nearly every businessman carries at least one pocket notebook or some substitute such as 3 X 5 index cards or scratch pads. Unfortunately, carrying it is often as far as he gets. Or, if used, it is merely a recording device for statistics such as names, addresses, or what to tell the serviceman about the car next time it goes in.

Note-making can be a big help in idea producing if the right kinds of notes are made and the right uses made of them. The first useful kind of note to make is one that captures any stray idea. Write it down. You have probably had the experience of "going to sleep on a problem," and waking in the middle of the night with a good idea. It was so obviously good that you knew you would remember it in the morning. But came the dawn and disappointment. The problem was still there but the idea was gone. Idea men who really mean it keep pencils and pads all over the house and office to capture those stray ideas immediately, before they have a chance to get away.

Record your observations of circumstances: plant operations when you find yourself with even a few free minutes, you can use such at-the-moment notes as a base for giving the circumstance some thinking time.

Record your conclusions or opinions on problems you have been thinking about. Frequently, a person spends hours, even days, working on a problem. After reaching some good conclusion (an idea or decision), and acting on it, he puts the problem out of his mind to work on the next one. Later, the first problem may recur in the same or a different form. The man may recall that he had thought that problem through once, but without a record of why he did what he did, chances are he will have to do it all again...or else take the risk that all conditions are still the same and the same action is still appropriate.

The statistical note does, of course, have a place. You should certainly form the habit of noting anything that may have possibilities for future use to you, however remote those possibilities may seem at the moment. In this class of notes may be included clippings from newspapers, magazines, books, etc. Psychological tests have established that on information of average interest (i.e., neither slight nor vital), the rate of forgetting is 25 percent within the first 24 hours; 85 percent within a week. In the face of this, pure memory-substitute notes do make sense.

But along with your note-making system, you will have to develop a note-using system to which you transfer your spur-of-the-moment notations at the earliest opportunity. This can be as simple or as elaborate as the problems you are making notes on. Actual systems used by successful and creative executives range from a simple cigar box (which never fills up because the owner constantly pulls out and uses his ideas) to an elaborately indexed and cross-indexed library of loose-leaf notebooks used by a leading physicist. (He does the filing and indexing himself—claims he gets the same pleasure and relaxation out of it that other men get out of arranging stamps in catalogs.)

Whatever system you devise, remember that the objective is to enable you quickly to gather everything you have seen, read, heard, or experienced on a problem or problem area when you need it. Then, when you have the problem, be sure to use the notes. Frequently, the hardest part of solving a problem is just getting started on it. Your notes can provide a take-off or starting point to get you going. They will help stimulate your imagination as you begin the search for ideas.

Picking Your Time to Be Creative. Every individual runs on a daily cycle. Each of us has a time during the day or night when he is most capable of creative or imaginative thinking. Conversely, you probably also have a time when you are most capable of cold-blooded analytical thinking. Your personal cycle is something you will have to analyze for yourself. Once you find it, however, set it aside and guard it zealously for ideating—use it for thinking about problems with a view to getting ideas.

In the same vein, you may find that you create best in some special location. If so, try to use that location for creating. It is probably too much to hope that your day-to-day working schedule can be arranged to let you use both your favorite time and your favorite place for idea collecting, but if you should be fortunate enough to be able to have it this way, by all means do so. You want to give yourself every break in going after ideas.

Set a Deadline. It is human nature to procrastinate on problems. Yet prolific idea men find they are at their most creative in spurts—they get their best ideas when they really go all out to get them. Sometimes, of course, there is a real and practical deadline to supply the urge to push yourself mentally. But you can also simulate such pressure by setting a deadline for yourself. If you really want to get yourself emotionally involved in meeting that deadline, just tell someone else that you are going to come up with 10 or 20 new ideas at such and such a time. This brings up another good individual spur.

Give Yourself a Quota. Remember that the aim of developing fluency is to build up your capacity to generate quantities of ideas. So start shooting for quantity right away. Don't set an impossible task for yourself, but if you can usually think up two or three ways something might be done, try setting a quota of at least five ways. When you can make five, up your quota to 10. When you get to 10, try 15 or 20. You shouldn't have to keep this up long before you will notice that, when a problem presents itself, your mind will automatically begin to run through many different ways of handling it.

You will probably find that the quality of your ideas is improving right along with the quantity. This gets back to the basic advantage of idea fluency: If you have a problem, and you have only one idea as to how to solve it, then good, bad, or indifferent, one idea is all you have. If it happens to fail, then you are right back with no ideas. If you have two ideas, chances are one will be better than the other. If you have 20 or 50 or 100 ideas, your biggest problem may then be to decide which is the best.

ORIGINALITY

In the problem-solver this assumes many degrees. Ideas can range in value from the completely new abstract mathematical theory, down to a way to save 10 cents a day in the mail room. In practical, everyday business problem-solving, complete newness, or pure originality, is usually not what is needed. In fact, it may not even be wanted. The originality required of the business executive is more likely to be that of finding new ways to vary existing conditions, or new ways to adapt existing ideas to new conditions, or a new modification of something that will fit in an existing condition. The difference between a great business executive and an ordinary one is often his ability to produce these original variations to meet existing conditions.

The creative attribute of originality can also be developed, or at least simulated, to the point where it meets the requirements of successful business operation. The secret is in the systematic use of questions.

One of the most noticeable characteristics of highly creative people is their overwhelming curiosity. These people are always asking themselves and others: "Why is this made this way?" "Why do we follow this procedure?" "Is this object really necessary?" "How can we improve the way we do this?" Charles Kettering calls it "systematically challenging the obvious."

The person who does not have this questioning ability will probably never be creative. But such a questioning approach to life, or to business operations, is largely a matter of habit. Therefore, it is something that can be learned. Almost every business organization or business executive makes use of checklists in one form or another. Usually, these are just to remind us not to make any mistakes in an accepted procedure. But another form of checklist can also be used to remind us not to forget to be original. This is made up of operational questions that challenge the obvious aspects of a problem. Using such checklists to spur ideas can be the basis for forming the questioning habit in an executive.

Before going any further on this subject, it should be said that the executive should never forget that his questioning must be done in a positive frame of mind. Too many people use such questions as a way of establishing their presence in an organization. They never go after the answers—they just raise the questions. The object of creative questioning is to uncover new possibilities for better ways of doing things. The person who asks a creative question does so with the intention of trying to find the answer himself.

The best type of checklist is one you make up yourself to fit your own types of problems of a recurring nature. Using such a checklist takes a certain amount of initiative, however. Just a mechanical use of a checklist does not produce originality. The purpose of such questions is to provide challenges to obvious ways of doing things. Therefore, the answers to these questions must be well thought out—even if the final answer is: "No; this is the best we can do right now."

Idea checklists can often be improvised, too. For instance, a sales manager looking for new customers might get real benefits out of just leafing through the yellow pages of a telephone directory with an open mind. An office manager, trying to develop a more efficient utilization of office space, might get some ideas by paging through a trade publication devoted to hotel or kitchen planning. Since you are simply trying to find new or different ways of solving a particular problem, you can never tell when or where you will find an idea you can borrow. The originality may consist in the fact that this has never been used in your particular field before—and if it will solve your problem, settle for that.

CREATIVE FLEXIBILITY

The quality of creative flexibility is largely that of being willing to consider a wide variety of approaches to a problem. This, in turn, is largely a matter of attitude. Rather than obstinately freezing onto one particular idea, or a single approach to a problem, the flexible person starts out by remembering that if one solution won't work, he can always approach the problem from another angle. This is also called "creative expectancy"—meaning, the creative person just plain expects to solve the problem, no matter how many failures temporarily delay the solution.

You can't go far on the subject of creative attitudes before running into the mental blocks that restrict or hamper creativity. Dr. James E. Gates, dean of the School of Business Administration, University of Georgia, has summed up these psychological quirks rather succinctly as "the way we feel about things...the way we see things...the way we think we ought to go about things."

One quick pencil-and-paper demonstration will probably suffice to show how common mental blocks can hamper you in a search for ideas. Let's consider the way we see things. Here are two drawings of an object—the front view and a side view:

Front view   Side view

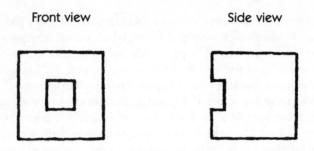

Now, before you read any further, take your pencil and, in one minute, draw the top view of this object.

You will find the top view, and also a cross section view, at the conclusion of this article. Chances are you have drawn the top as a square or rectangular shape. Or, if you suspected a trap, you may have taken a wild stab at some variation of a straight-sided figure. However, this particular object is a cylinder. The square on the front representation and the notch on the side view show a small rectangular area milled off the side of the cylinder. Therefore, the top drawing should be a circle.

Why did you try to make a square or straight-sided figure? Because you were probably hampered by a perceptual block. Because two dimensions of the object appeared to be square, your mind immediately short-circuited to make the third dimension square also. Now translate this simple demonstration into a business problem, where two or three known factors are given to you, and you can easily see why it is sometimes difficult to prevent yourself from being forced into an obvious assumption about a third factor that may completely mislead you as to the course of creative action you should take.

Overcoming such mental blocks to creativity is, again, largely, a matter of developing a healthy skepticism about the obvious. And the necessity to avoid being blocked makes a good case for having a systematic approach to solving problems.

As in checklists, the chances are no one method for processing problems is going to serve every businessman's needs.

Again, the best method you can use will probably be one that you make up yourself to suit your own types of problems. Therefore, the following method should be considered only as an example of what you might consider developing.

Define the Problem. If it is large and complex, break it down. It is much easier to handle a series of small problems than one big problem that may be dismaying in its apparent complexity. Be sure that you yourself sufficiently understand the problem before you try to solve it. Try to state it in 10 words or less. Try to state it several different ways. Try to explain it to someone completely un-familiar with it. Such devices can help clarify your own thinking.

Get the Facts. Study the conditions and relationships of the facts with a view as to how they will affect the value of any solutions you arrive at. You can't know too much about the background of a real problem when you have the job of solving it, but resign yourself—no one ever has all the facts. Sometimes just a good, thorough study of facts will make the problem solution apparent. If so, you can then forget the rest of these steps. But if, after studying the background and conditions of your problem you still don't see a solution, then...

Go After Ideas. Lots of ideas—all you and anyone you can get to help can think up. It is characteristic of any kind of problems susceptible to creative solution that there are many feasible solutions. The only guarantee you have that you will eventually pick the best solution to a problem is to make sure that you have thought of every possible solution. This is where idea fluency pays off. It is in this stage of the problem solving mechanisms already outlined. And remember, don't at this stage let evaluation interfere with your idea collecting.

Use Incubation. If you have labored over a problem and haven't as yet found a satisfactory solution, you run the risk of frustration. The best thing to do then is to get away from the problem—let up on your mind. Your conscious mind is only a small part of the mental powers at your disposal. Back in the memory cells of your mind may be dozens of facts and associations that you have completely forgotten about, and so haven't brought them into use on your particular problem. But they are still there in the subconscious. If you can just give them a chance, they may help you find the solution to your present problem.

Incubation is commonly referred to as "sleeping on the problem." In actual practice, however, it may be just a matter of breaking away from your desk to take a walk to the water cooler, or timing yourself so that you can knock off your concentration to go to lunch.

Evaluate Your Ideas. No collection of ideas, by itself, is worth anything until something is done with them. This means that plenty of cold-blooded judicial thinking has to be exercised and some decisions made. If you follow the proce-dure of starting with a quantity of ideas, it is probably best to do the evaluating in two stages: first, screen the ideas roughly for "possibles," "probables," and outright "impossibles." Then, tighten up your evaluation on the probables and possibles. There is also plenty of room for imagination in this decision-making phase. Often a seemingly impossible idea may be susceptible to a switch to make it usable. Asking creative questions about bad ideas can often develop new ideas or approaches that will be usable.

A final word on evaluating: You must learn to be objective. Too often, a person with a problem will go through all the motions of being organized and methodical in orienting the problem, gathering his facts, collecting literally dozens of ideas, and then will throw all the previous work out the window by adopting the idea he favored in the first place simply because he couldn't maintain his objectivity to the end.

Everything mentioned so far has concerned itself with what the executive can do to promote his own creativity. But no executive operates in a vacuum. A good executive realizes that he must operate through other people. In trying to inspire other people to be more imaginative or more creative, there are a few factors you will have to cope with. Recognizing that these exist is really the key to overcoming them, because an understanding of the situation will help you in planning your approach.

Here are a few of the things that keep the average person from being creative:

Natural Resistance to Change. People get in a rut. They like the ruts they are in because they know them so well.

Laziness. Getting out of a rut requires effort. Creative thinking entails the hardest kind of mental effort. Unless there is some great incentive, and money is often not enough, people prefer the status quo. Life is so much simpler that way.

Lack of Confidence. This comes from lack of experience. The organized effort to promote more creativity is a relatively new force in our culture. You may as well assume that, up to now, no one has ever tried to encourage your workers to use their imaginations; none has ever made them conscious of ideas, or what ideas are, or how to go about having them. You have the job of developing the confidence if you want the creativity.

Fear of Ridicule. This is ingrained in most people through having, at some time in the past, had their ideas laughed at or ignored. It is still common practice today to criticize or laugh at unusual or different ideas before we have taken the time really to think about them and determine whether they are good or not. The executive who wants more ideas from his organization first has to create the atmosphere of encouragement and appreciation of creativity—the climate of safety—the freedom to fail.

No executive can inspire creativity if his own attitude toward it is skeptical.

The creative atmosphere cannot be accomplished through a complete organization overnight—no matter how sold or willing the management. This is even more so in the case of a company that may not have been paying too much attention to workers and their ideas in the past. But one thing we do know: Creativity must come from the top.

It could easily be that the road to success, fame, and fortune for an aspiring executive will be that he has used his own imagination to analyze, develop, and solve the problem of infusing his company with the necessity and the means of getting all-out, imaginative, creative thinking from everyone.

Top view

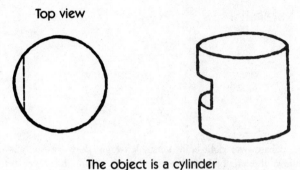

The object is a cylinder

3.
WHOLE BRAIN MANAGEMENT

Gwen Rubinstein

In the debate over right-brain versus left-brain skills, researchers now encourage the use of both sets of abilities. More than ever before, management experts and psychologists encourage managers to trust their intuition, tap their creativity, and rely on "flashes of insight."

In the late 1970s and early 1980s, members of the media began to report on what they labeled a "crisis in American business." The main criticism was that master's of business administration programs and American managers in general had become too analytical, too dependent on numbers and number crunching. They were not fully concerned with people, too short-sighted, and not creative enough. Managers were told they should inject more of their right-brain skills—intuition and creativity—into their management styles.

The accusations and counteraccusations flew from the pages of all types of publications—from scholarly journals to business magazines. Management experts and psychologists argued heatedly about whether managers, their styles of management, and the atmosphere of their organizations could be correctly classified as "right brained," meaning creative and intuitive, or "left brained," meaning logical and rational.

Writing in the May 1985 issue of *Psychology Today*, biopsychologist Jerre Levy, of the University of Chicago, Illinois, reached this conclusion: "Logic is not confined to the left hemisphere [of the brain]...There is no evidence that either creativity or intuition is an exclusive property of the right hemisphere. Indeed, real creativity and intuition, whatever they may entail, almost certainly depend on an intimate collaboration between hemispheres."

The argument has now turned to how managers can meld both their logical and intuitive skills into a holistic approach to management. More than ever before, management experts and psychologists encourage managers to trust their intuition, tap their creativity, and rely on "flashes of insight."

WHICH SKILLS ARE WHICH?

When people speak of left-brain management skills and techniques they generally mean analytical and quantitative methods—using management by objectives, forecasting, and so forth to make the right decisions.

Left-brain-oriented managers, the argument goes, follow rational and logical methods of reasoning: They solve problems by breaking them down into manageable parts, approaching them piece by piece, and relying on logic and data to solve them. They prefer to work in highly structured and hierarchical environments and follow carefully planned decision making methods.

Right-brain management techniques, on the other hand, rely on feelings—intuition and creativity—to solve problems. It follows that right-brain-oriented managers look at problems holistically and reach decisions through flashes of awareness, or insight.

These managers prefer an informal work environment with participatory and horizontal authority structures and make their decisions in an unstructured, fluid, and spontaneous manner.

Managers who integrate these skills are as comfortable dealing with feelings as with facts when making decisions: They let intuition guide decision making after the facts have been scanned and suggestions and recommendations culled from sources on both sides.

What's the key to integrating logical and intuitive skills? Tapping your creative potential, overcoming blocks to innovation, and not letting your logic overrule your intuition.

DEFINING INTUITION

What does intuition mean in practical terms? How can you apply it to your management style and your association's work environment?

In his book *Intuitive Management: Integrating Left and Right Brain Management Skills*, Weston H. Agor, director of the master's of public administration program at the University of Texas, El Paso, uses this image: Think back to an occasion in your life when you thought you understood a person or situation right away but were afraid to act on the basis of that instant awareness. Did you think, "I had better wait, gather more information, and get to know the person or situation better?"

If you did, you're like most people. Not listening to the inner voice that immediately sizes up situations—intuition—is common.

LEVELS OF AWARENESS

Intuition, however, is a highly efficient way of knowing, Mr. Agor believes. "People can process a variety of information on a variety of levels and get immediate cues about how to act," he says. "You can have the answer even though you don't understand all the steps or know all the information you've processed. The more open you are to your feelings, the more secure you become in the ability of your intuition to give you correct cues. The less you project your personal desires for a particular situation or person to be other than they really are, the more efficient your intuitive cues will become."

Executives receive intuitive flashes on several different levels—even if they aren't receptive to those flashes—Mr. Agor believes. He suggests that executives learn through experience which level of intuition works best for them. The four levels he identifies are:

1. *Physical.* At the physical level, intuitive awareness comes as bodily sensations. Just as your body tells you through a headache or stomach ache that you're under stress, for example, it can react strongly to people or situations for no apparent logical reason.
2. *Emotional.* At the emotional level, intuitive signals are transmitted in the form of feelings, Mr. Agor says. For example, have you ever instantly liked or disliked someone you had just met?
3. *Mental.* Intuitive cues can also develop on a mental level. This involves mentally seeing a pattern or order emerge from seemingly unrelated facts. Albert Einstein, for example, attributed his theory of relativity to intuition—a flash of insight helped him see the whole of his experiments and work with objective data.
4. *Spiritual.* At this level, executives come in touch with how their organization's actions and decisions affect the rest of humanity. Spiritual intuition goes beyond individual concerns to emphasize the underlying unity of life.

No matter from which level your intuition comes, you have the ability to develop it further.

TAP YOUR POTENTIAL

Most experts agree that everyone has some intuitive ability. While some people may have more than others, everyone can more fully develop and use the intuition he has. Learning to get in better touch with your feelings and applying them to your work is not an impossible task. As Mr. Agor puts it, "Many managers in many organizations today fall far below their right-brain potential. If they could learn to get in touch with their abilities, they and their organizations would profit enormously."

"People are being creative in millions of mundane and outstanding ways every day," believes Michael Ray, a professor at Stanford University, Stanford, California, who teaches "Creativity in Business," a course in the master's of business administration program.

"We all know how to be creative even if we don't operate that way consistently enough," he says. "The point is that we had better start applying what we know and what research has already told us."

He began teaching the course in 1980 with Rochelle Myers, president of the Myers Institute for Creative Studies, San Francisco, California. The course's goal is to help students "explore the inner creative life and its application to the business world" and examine the nonanalytical side of management through meditation, chanting, observation, dream work, the I Ching, music, and more.

"What we try to do in the course is replicate what you might experience momentarily when you, say, close a particular type of deal, have a meeting in which everything seemed to click, have an insight into a situation that has been keeping you up nights, or start a new job that you have been hungering for and know it's right for you," he explains.

As they developed the course material, he says, they saw increasing concern in the American business community about the failure of its overanalytical approach and growing recognition of how intuition could be incorporated into managerial decision making. At the same time, however, he and Ms. Myers realized that intuition alone wasn't a complete answer.

"An important shortcoming of intuition alone is that it is simply too shallow," he points out. "We had both worked in the area of creativity in business, and we had observed that unless there was the involvement of some very deep personal sources of creativity, idea-generating techniques produced confusion or, at best, short-term gains and long-term dissatisfaction. It was just like the proverbial Chinese meal—an hour later you feel empty."

So they tried to create a course that would awaken individuals to the sources of creativity within themselves. "We knew that in our own experience and in the experiences of businesspeople with whom we had worked, there were amazing moments when ideas flowed effortlessly, when absolutely correct decisions were made quickly without thinking, and when it seemed that some sort of inner power had taken over," he says.

INVOKING YOUR INTUITION

To put your intuition to work for you and to help you trust the impulses you get from the right side of your brain, Mr. Agor of the University of Texas, El Paso, offers these suggestions:

- Examine the process and the means through which insights come to you. For example, you might try recording your insights in a journal: Write down when the insights come and how they come—in dreams, for example—and accuracy. Look for a pattern. "Your journal will give you an overall picture showing whether you seek to implement your intuitive insights or whether you ignore them," he says. "It will also give you clues about how you block your intuition from coming through."

- Share your experiences with others—friends, family members, or coworkers. "Simply taking the risk of sharing your experiences with others can help you unlock and develop your ability," he believes.
- Form a group of peers or friends that will meet regularly to share intuitive experiences. "You might even take a problem you are trying to solve at work or in your personal life as a group project," he says. "Not only will this give you support but it will also help you explore new ways of getting in touch with your intuitive ability."
- Read about the experiences of others. Chances are, he predicts, you'll be surprised to find that what is happening to you has already happened to others.

To develop and encourage creativity in your organization, Mr. Agor suggests the following ideas:

- Create an organizational environment that supports, values, and practices intuitive skills. "People frequently reject innovative ways of solving problems because they become accustomed to one particular way of accomplishing tasks," says Mr. Agor.
- Examine the design of your offices. Seating, color patterns, music, and interpersonal communication play an important part in facilitating the flow of right-brain impulses.
- Where appropriate, keep meeting agendas open and flexible, use no agenda at all, or segment meetings into creative open times. During the open periods, don't allow anyone—particularly left-brain-oriented managers—to evaluate proposed ideas.
- Eliminate the interference that interrupts the flow of intuition—tension, anxiety, fear, and other blocks. Foster a relaxed, positive attitude about letting intuition happen. Common mental blocks include: "Everything is fine"; "Follow the rules"; "To err is wrong"; "Playing is frivolous"; "That's not my area"; "Be practical"; and "I'm not creative."

RUN WITH IT

Sigmund Freud once remarked that the mind is like an iceberg—it floats with most of its bulk hidden below the water. It's the same with your intuitive ability, says Mr. Agor.

To make the most of your intuitive, creative and innovative abilities, he offers these final words of advice:

- Quiet your mind. Learn to relax, don't try too hard, and develop a sense of alert awareness.
- Concentrate. Focus your attention; it might help to visualize your mind as a laser beam.
- Be receptive. Suspend your judgment; be aware of yourself physically, mentally, and emotionally; and listen to yourself and others by holding your ego in check. Think about who you are and what your organization stands for.

And remember: Research shows that people who think they're creative are, while those who think they aren't are not.

Gwen Rubinstein is an associate editor of Association Management.

4.
STRENGTHEN YOUR
REASONING POWER

Robert Froman

Many of us were taught in school that science relies on inductive reasoning, while old-fashioned logic is concerned with deductive reasoning. The history of science and philosophy provides the explanation of this remarkable misconception. Understanding of three basic steps improves performance.

It's possible to reason successfully without understanding just what you're doing. Lack of such understanding, however, can make reasoning a hit-or-miss affair.

The fundamental rules for the kind of reasoning most of us do most of the time in business are fairly simple. To ignore them is to neglect a valuable tool for improving your competitive position.

The basic laws of reasoning can be considered under three headings:

1. Collecting facts.
2. Inductive reasoning.
3. Deductive reasoning.

COLLECTING FACTS

Dr. Ernest Nagel of Columbus University, a leading authority of logic, points out that the scientific method treats facts merely as propositions for which there is considerable evidence. This aspect of the method is readily adaptable to business practice. Its effect is to keep facts hungry and working hard to stay alive instead of letting them get soft, fat, and useless. If you think of facts simply as facts you may find it hard to doubt them. If you think of them as propositions for which there is considerable evidence, it is much easier to look over that evidence and challenge it or try to add to it.

The head of a big city department store once was asked from which part of his area's population he drew most of his customers. He answered that his customers constituted a nearly perfect cross-section of the whole local market. This was for him a plain, hard fact.

Soon afterward, the store's merchandising manager made an analysis of the sales tickets of several preceding months. He was astonished to learn that, although the store was in the central shopping district, the overwhelming majority of its customers were from one comparatively small section of the city. They also were from the lowest third of income.

In the store's early days, when the town was smaller and the population less varied, the chief's "plain, hard fact" may have been a proposition for which there was considerable support. Had he thought of it that way, he would have been able to notice changes. Over the years he would have noticed countless bits of evidence that his clientele was changing. His failure to pay attention to such evidence cost his firm heavily.

An investor once approached an advertising agency for help in marketing a new kitchen gadget. He already had arranged for production and for distribution through sales agents. The advertising agency representative asked whether he had investigated consumer interest in the product. He answered that he had tried the gadget on all his friends and relatives and that they had unanimously assured him it was great. When the agency suggested a more detailed investigation he stalked out angrily.

Some months later the advertising agency learned the gadget had been manufactured in quantity and distributed nationally for sale at $1.49. It had little appeal either for the trade or for consumers. The sales agent then learned that a similar product had been on sale a year earlier at only 39 cents and also failed.

The investor had allowed the item's salability to become for him a fact beyond questioning. He had not really looked upon his friends' testimony as evidence, but reassurance.

The way to avoid such disaster is to give important facts a cold, semi-mathematical treatment. The investor in question could have gone about it this way:

Proposition: This is a salable gadget.
Evidence: A says so and so about it.
          B says such and such. And so on.

This treatment would have made it difficult to miss the point that at least one opinion—that of the advertising agency—was not enthusiastic.

The great advances of modern science stem from the habit of giving all facts this treatment. The word "atom," for instance, is Greek for "the indivisible." Until a couple of generations ago, there was considerable evidence for the proposition that matter was made up of indivisible atoms.

Then new evidence began turning up. Today there is considerable evidence that atoms are made up of dozens of identifiable particles. This enormous change in what once seemed a decidedly hard fact has produced a new era.

INDUCTIVE REASONING

Once you get into the habit of treating facts as propositions requiring supporting evidence you are ready for inductive logic, modern style. This kind of reasoning treats facts and hypotheses much alike. Any proposition may be considered in either category, depending on circumstances.

An hypothesis is, in essence, a guess at the relationship among a number of propositions for which there is considerable evidence. If the guess turns out to be a good one, it graduates to the status of a proposition for which there is pretty solid evidence.

According to Dr. Hans Reichenbach, this often shocks those who think of logic as a series of rigidly prescribed steps in reasoning. Dr. Reichenbach is professor of philosophy at the University of California and a leading authority on inductive logic. The act of discovering a possible explanation for a set of facts, he says, must necessarily be a leap in the dark.

"The scientist who discovers a new theory," he goes on, "usually is guided to his discovery by guesses. He can only say that an explanation which might fit the facts suddenly popped into his mind."

Inductive reasoning, then, is discovering the reasons for a conclusion already known. Deductive reasoning, by contrast, is discovering a conclusion for which the reasons are known.

Ever since Aristotle, logicians have sought to make rules for improving the fruitfulness of such guesses. Not until Sigmund Freud promulgated his theory of the unconscious mind did they have much success.

The human mind is like an iceberg. The greatest part lies below the surface, and it is in interconnections among the many millions of memories stored in the subsurface part of the mind that we must seek hypotheses.

Or rather, this is the way it works when the problem of finding an explanation which might fit the facts is difficult. Sometimes the explanation seems to pop up of its own accord.

For example, a real estate dealer in a small town noticed that the manager of a chain supermarket with a downtown location seemed to have cut down on building maintenance. A week or so later he saw two strangers inspecting a field on the edge of town. The next day he saw the supermarket manager lunching with the two strangers. These bits of evidence almost automatically formed a pattern suggesting the hypothesis that the supermarket was planning a move to the town's outskirts.

THREE RECOMMENDATIONS

Modern studies of the way the mind operates have led to three concrete recommendations on how to seek hypotheses in such cases:

> If you have an hypothesis, check it.
> Don't collect evidence indefinitely.
> After checking, forget the problem for awhile.

The best way to present these recommendations is through an example. A New England metalworking plant was handicapped by a high and growing turnover rate among shop employees. When the owner first tackled the problem, an explanatory hypothesis came easily to hand. This was that his men were being lured away by better pay or highly appealing fringe benefits. It was simple to check. The check revealed that some of the men who left him actually took slight cuts in pay or other benefits in their new jobs.

This brought him to a crucial point involving the first recommendation. Evidence confirming an hypothesis is emotionally satisfying, and contradictory evidence is frustrating. Such frustrations often drive men to look for someone to blame and, in this case, might have led the plant owner to blame his foreman. To steel yourself against this inclination, remind yourself that more than 9 out of 10 experiments in the formal sciences have negative results and that many such disproofs of hypotheses have constituted advances of great importance.

In this case the metal goods manufacturer did not succumb to the temptation to accuse his foreman. Instead, he began interviewing departing employees. As often happens, none of them was articulate enough to explain precisely why he was leaving. The mumbled complaints included frivolities and contradictions, such as that the lunch break was too short or too long.

Among the more serious explanations were one by a comparatively young man who said he had not been taught the capabilities of the machine he operated and one by an older man who said that the equipment he had been assigned was obsolete.

When the plant owner had collected a number of interviews, all he had was a jumble of words and impressions. He had reached the point where the second recommendation applies.

WEIGH THE EVIDENCE

It is not easy to follow this in practice. When the facts do not seem to make sense, the natural inclination is to seek more of them. Some men try to solve many of their problems simply by burying them under great piles of facts.

Unfortunately, there is no formula for prescribing how much evidence will be enough. If you happen to have too little when you stop collecting, however, you can look for more later. For practical purposes it usually is best to try to make do with as little as possible.

Sleep on your problem. This is the technique approved independently by many researchers in psychology and scientific methods for making Dr. Reichenbach's leap in the dark. The technique is to forget the problem for a while.

Practical men often are taken aback when they first hear this recommendation. It sounds a little like something for nothing. It is not, however. Actually, forgetting a problem for a while does not mean doing no more work on it. It means doing no more conscious work. Your unconscious mind goes on working even while you sleep, as you discover every time you dream.

Here is how this worked in the case of the metal goods manufacturer: After about 20 interviews he forgot his problem for a couple of days. When he was alone in his office one morning, it suddenly popped into his conscious mind that the youngster who felt he had not been taught enough and the older man who thought the equipment obsolete had been saying the same thing.

The machines actually were far from obsolete, so the older man clearly had not learned enough about them either. The two things reminded the owner that in his day as a machine operator he, too, had wanted to learn everything possible about his equipment because it had seemed the best way to get ahead.

There was his hypothesis: A considerable number of men might be leaving his plant because they felt he provided insufficient training.

DEDUCTIVE REASONING

Many of us were taught in school that science relies on inductive reasoning, while old-fashioned logic is concerned with deductive reasoning. The history of science and philosophy provides the explanation of this remarkable misconception.

Modern science began its rise in the early seventh century. At that time the teachings of such ancients as Aristotle were considered to be beyond dispute. Those who felt that way insisted that the only way to learn anything was to start with premises established by Aristotle or similar authorities and deduce the consequences of those premises. Those who championed science wanted to forget Aristotle and establish new premises by inductive reasoning.

The premises of modern science, or modern reasoning on any kind of problem, are hypotheses. But once you have your hypothesis it is of no use to you until you deduce consequences from it. Deductive reasoning is every bit as important in modern thinking as inductive reasoning.

The basic form of deductive reasoning, of course, is the syllogism. In its bare bones this consists of a major premise, a minor premise and a conclusion which necessarily follows from the two premises. The usual example is:

Major premise: All men are mortal.
Minor premise: X is a man.
Conclusion: X is mortal.

The most common misuse of the syllogism is a result of failure to state and consider the premises. You have to state premises explicitly in order to be able to consider whether they are valid. Probably the most dangerous kind of syllogism is that in which the major premise states that all so-and-so's are such-and-such. It is the kind we all prefer because it permits certainty in the conclusion. But this understandable but illogical yearning for certainty makes it necessary for us to exert considerable effort to state such premises clearly and examine them carefully.

In the case of the New England metal goods manufacturer with the turnover problem the line of deduction proceeded as follows:

Major premise: His turnover rate seemed unnecessarily high.
Minor premise: Some of those leaving apparently had done so because he provided too little training.
Conclusion: He might be able to cut down turnover by providing more training.

This is the best kind of conclusion that deduction from hypotheses can produce because it indicates a test. The purpose of old-fashioned deduction was to produce certainty. The purpose of this kind of deduction is to produce conclusions that can be tested.

The manufacturer and his foremen began spending an hour or so a day working with each of the men in turn and showing them as much as they seemed interested in learning about what their machines could do. A few of the machines were capable of operations not required in the work of the plant, and the teachers made a point of demonstrating these, too. In the following months the turnover rate dropped.

This is typical of the kind of confirmation that can be had for conclusions deduced from hypotheses. It is never absolute confirmation. In this case other unknown factors could have been responsible for all or part of the turnover drop, and if the added training had been costly, the plant owner would have been foolish not to keep seeking such factors. Since the training was inexpensive, there was little need for questioning its effectiveness.

This is all far from the certainty we desire, but it is the best we can do. Considering the accomplishments of modern science and industry, it is a pretty impressive best.

5.
HOW CREATIVE ARE YOU?

Eugene Raudsepp

Research reveals that creative ability is almost universally distributed. The following test enables you to determine if you have the personality traits, attitudes, motivations, and interests that make up creativity.

In recent years, several task-oriented tests have been developed to measure creative abilities and behavior. While certainly useful, they do not adequately tap the complex network of behaviors, the particular personality traits, attitudes, motivations, values, interests and other variables that predisposed a person to think creatively.

To arrive at assessment measures that would cover a broader range of creative attributes, our organization developed an inventory type of test. A partial version of this instrument is featured below.

After each statement, indicate with a letter the degree or extent to which you agree or disagree with it: A = strongly agree, B = agree, C = in between or don't know, D = disagree, E = strongly disagree. Mark your answers as accurately and frankly as possible. Try not to "second guess" how a creative person might respond to each statement.

1. I always work with a great deal of certainty that I'm following the correct procedures for solving a particular problem. _____
2. It would be a waste of time for me to ask questions if I had no hope of obtaining answers. _____
3. I feel that a logical, step-by-step method is best for solving problems. _____
4. I occasionally voice opinions in groups that seem to turn some people off. _____
5. I spend a great deal of time thinking about what others think of me. _____
6. I feel that I may have a special contribution to give the world. _____

7. It is more important for me to do what I believe to be right than to try to win the approval of others. _____

8. People who seem unsure and uncertain about things lose my respect. _____

9. I am able to stick with difficult problems over extended periods of time. _____

10. On occasion I get overly enthusiastic about things. _____

11. I often get my best ideas when doing nothing in particular. _____

12. I rely on intuitive hunches and the feeling of "rightness" or "wrongness" when moving toward the solution of a problem. _____

13. When problem solving, I work faster analyzing the problem and slower when synthesizing the information I've gathered. _____

14. I like hobbies which involve collecting things. _____

15. Daydreaming has provided the impetus for many of my more important projects. _____

16. If I had to choose from two occupations other than the one I now have, I would rather be a physician than an explorer. _____

17. I can get along more easily with people if they belong to about the same social and business class as myself. _____

18. I have a high degree of aesthetic sensitivity. _____

19. Intuitive hunches are unreliable guides in problem solving. _____

20. I am much more interested in coming up with new ideas than I am in trying to sell them to others. _____

21. I tend to avoid situations in which I might feel inferior. _____

22. In evaluating information, the source of it is more important to me than the content. _____

23. I like people who follow the rule "business before pleasure." _____

24. One's own self-respect is much more important than the respect of others. _____

25. I feel that people who strive for perfection are unwise. _____

26. I like work in which I must influence others. _____

27. It is important for me to have a place for everything and everything in its place. _____

28. People who are willing to entertain "crackpot" ideas are impractical. _____

29. I rather enjoy fooling around with new ideas, even if there is no practical pay-off. _____

30. When a certain approach to a problem doesn't work, I can quickly reorient my thinking. _____

31. I don't like to ask questions that show ignorance. _____
32. I am able to more easily change my interests to pursue a job or career than I can change a job to pursue my interests. _____
33. Inability to solve a problem is frequently due to asking the wrong questions. _____
34. I can frequently anticipate the solution to my problems. _____
35. It is a waste of time to analyze one's failures. _____
36. Only fuzzy thinkers resort to metaphors and analogies. _____
37. At times I have so enjoyed the ingenuity of a crook that I hoped he or she would go scot-free. _____
38. I frequently begin work on a problem which I can only dimly sense and not yet express. _____
39. I frequently tend to forget things such as names of people, streets, highways, small towns, etc. _____
40. I feel that hard work is the basic factor in success. _____
41. To be regarded as a good team member is important to me. _____
42. I know how to keep my inner impulses in check. _____
43. I am a thoroughly dependable and responsible person. _____
44. I resent things being uncertain and unpredictable. _____
45. I prefer to work with others in a team effort rather than solo. _____
46. The trouble with many people is that they take things too seriously. _____
47. I am frequently haunted by my problems and cannot let go of them. _____
48. I can easily give up immediate gain or comfort to reach the goals I have set. _____
49. If I were a college professor, I would rather teach factual courses than those involving theory. _____
50. I'm attracted to the mystery of life. _____

Scoring Instructions: To compute your percentage score, circle and add up the values assigned to each item:

A Strongly Agree	B Agree	C In-Between or Don't Know	D Disagree	E Strongly Disagree
1. −2	−1	0	+1	+2
2. −2	−1	0	+1	+2
3. −2	−1	0	+1	+2
4. +2	+1	0	−1	−2
5. −2	−1	0	+1	+2

A Strongly Agree	B Agree	C In-Between or Don't Know	D Disagree	E Strongly Disagree
6. +2	+1	0	−1	−2
7. +2	+1	0	−1	−2
8. −2	−1	0	+1	+2
9. +2	+1	0	−1	−2
10. +2	+1	0	+1	−2
11. +2	+1	0	−1	−2
12. +2	+1	0	−1	−2
13. −2	−1	0	+1	+2
14. −2	−1	0	+1	+2
15. +2	+1	0	−1	−2
16. −2	−1	0	+1	+2
17. −2	−1	0	+1	+2
18. +2	+1	0	−1	−2
19. −2	−1	0	+1	+2
20. +2	−1	0	−1	−2
21. −2	−1	0	+1	+2
22. −2	−1	0	+1	+2
23. −2	−1	0	+1	+2
24. +2	+1	0	−1	−2
25. −2	−1	0	+1	+2
26. −2	−1	0	+1	+2
27. −2	−1	0	+1	+2
28. −2	−1	0	+1	+2
29. +2	+1	0	−1	−2
30. +2	+1	0	−1	−2
31. −2	−1	0	+1	+2
32. −2	−1	0	+1	+2
33. +2	+1	0	−1	−2
34. +2	+1	0	−1	−2
35. −2	−1	0	+1	+2
36. −2	−1	0	+1	+2
37. +2	+1	0	−1	−2
38. +2	+1	0	−1	−2
39. +2	+1	0	−1	−2
40. +2	+1	0	−1	−2
41. −2	−1	0	+1	+2
42. −2	−1	0	+1	+2
43. −2	−1	0	+1	+2
44. −2	−1	0	+1	+2
45. −2	−1	0	+1	+2
46. +2	+1	0	−1	−2
47. +2	+1	0	−1	−2
48. +2	+1	0	−1	−2
49. −2	−1	0	+1	+2
50. +2	+1	0	−1	−2

80 to 100 Very Creative
60 to 79 Above Average
40 to 59 Average
20 to 39 Below Average
− 100 to 19 Noncreative

*Eugene Raudsepp is president, Princeton Creative Research, Inc., Princeton, N.J.
Further information about the test "How Creative Are You?" is available from
Princeton Creative Research, Inc., 10 Nassau St., Princeton, N.J., 08540.*

6.
INTUITION: THE VOICE OF SUCCESS?

Martin Lasden

When making decisions, listen to your "inner voice." It may be whispering secrets to success. Intuition, as a tool for success, is still, and probably always will be, more art than science.

It's almost embarrassing for executives to talk about the power of intuition. Such talk goes against the grain of what hard-headed management is supposed to be about: pure unadulterated logic—no messy emotions, no leaps of faith, no capricious judgments. Yet time and time again, the role of intuition has been cited as a critical factor to success.

Whether you're trying to decide which strategy to pursue, which vendors or employees to depend on, or how to solve a technical problem, the whispered voice of intuition may call, trying to move you in strange and mysterious ways. Should you listen? First, try to get some hard evidence to back up your feelings. Running with a hunch without the benefit of supporting evidence, especially when much is at stake, can be like jumping out of a plane without a parachute. If disaster strikes, imagine trying to explain your errors by telling your boss that your actions were prompted by a "gut feeling."

For executives heavily involved with computers, there is a paradoxical twist to the role of intuition in decision-making. Computers are governed by precise logic. Yet it is the onslaught of computers on organizations that has engendered the conditions under which intuitive thinking becomes most valuable: conditions such as fast change, turmoil, and leaps into the unknown. Faced with these conditions, mangers may find intuition to be their best resource for decision-making.

Henry Mintzberg, a well-known authority on business management at McGill University, Montreal, alluded to intuition in 1976 in an article in the *Harvard Business Review*. He wrote: "The evidence here is that a great deal of the manager's inputs are soft and speculative—impressions and feelings about other people, hearsay, gossip, and so on. Furthermore, the very analytical inputs—reports, documents, and hard data in general—seem to be of relatively little importance to many managers."

Corroborating support is offered by John Naisbitt, author of the best-seller *Megatrends* (Warner Books, 1983): "Another shift I see that really impresses me is a new respectability for intuition in corporate settings... Now people are willing to say, 'I just feel this is going to work.'"

And Robert Bernstein, chairman of the board at Random House, the New York-based book publisher, has observed: "Only intuition can protect you from the most dangerous person of all—the articulate incompetent."

Intuition gets dicey when there is no time to garner the necessary evidence, when the pace of change is such that future trends cannot be extrapolated from experiences, or when there are not enough facts available to make a rational analysis. Both risks and potential gains are often at their peak at these times: Careers may literally rise or fall on a hunch.

There are no definitive answers to the questions of where intuition comes from and how it works. There are those who ascribe to the intuitive process the most mundane of qualities. Intuition, they attest, is a process of rationalization that happens so quickly that the intuiter is not aware of all the steps his or her mind takes. Others equate intuition with such arcane phenomena as precognition and extrasensory perception.

In a series of experiments conducted during the late 1960s at the New Jersey Institute of Technology, Newark, groups of top executives submitted to tests designed to evaluate their precognitive powers. Of the CEOs who had doubled their companies' profits within a five-year period, 80 percent scored above the levels allowed by chance alone.

In addition, Harvard University researchers have observed that just before making correct intuitive decisions, subjects' hearts beat faster and their palms perspire. When using logic to make decisions, however, subjects revealed no such physiological changes.

Then there's the left-brain/right-brain research that's been pursued recently. According to many of these studies, the left side of the brain is more responsible for logical, linear thinking, whereas emotion and intuition originate in the right side. To determine which half of the brain successful executives rely on more often, Robert Doktor, a business professor at the University of Hawaii, Manoa, working with a neuro-surgeon, several years ago actually wired up 17 CEOs to an electroencephalograph to record which of their brain halves was more active when working on verbal-analytical and mathematical problems. Doktor reported that in every instance, the processing power of the emotion-oriented right side was more heavily relied on.

Admittedly, it would far exceed the limits of the research cited above to suggest that you must be intuitive to be a successful executive. However, intuition—whether you consider it to be fast thinking, ESP, or something in between—is a real phenomenon in the business world that should be taken seriously.

At Mellon Bank in Pittsburgh, George DiNardo, the senior vice president of information systems and research, says he has relied on intuition throughout his career. "I hate the lemming-like behavior banks often exhibit," he declares. "I've taken on many ventures that fly in the face of what others have done."

On what basis were those ventures entered into? "The 'star in the east,'" DiNardo chuckles. Apparently, that star burned brightly for DiNardo in 1970. That was the year he decided it would be feasible to create a central information file on one mainframe that would incorporate all data generated daily by the bank's entire customer base. In 1970, conventional wisdom dictated that three mainframes couldn't accommodate that kind of load, let alone one. However, DiNardo managed to pull it off. He did it by buying the largest mainframe available, which at that time was an IBM System 360, Model 195—the kind of machine bought by agencies like NASA and the London Observatory, not by banks. He then unleashed a dedicated, hand-picked staff on the problem. And he loaded the machine up to 90 percent capacity instead of the conventional 60 percent, and still squeezed satisfactory performance out of it.

DiNardo remembers his boss telling him, "If this doesn't work, you'd better find another job." But it did work. The system functioned for 10 years, yielding all the advantages that accompany maintaining a highly integrated centralized file, putting Mellon Bank considerably ahead of the competition.

How did DiNardo know? "The 'star in the east,'" DiNardo says again. "It's a sense that you can accomplish something without any evidence that it can be done. Other than that, I can't describe it."

DiNardo cites other examples. Once he decided to buy automated terminals from a small vendor hardly anyone had heard of at the time. On another occasion, he woke up in the middle of the night with the idea of selling extra computer capacity to other banks through terminals hooked up via communications lines. And then there was the time he came up with the idea of entering data at the source instead of by a central data-entry group, another idea considerably ahead of its time. DiNardo maintains that in all the years he's been in data processing, when he's had a strong gut feeling about something, he's never been wrong.

Does DiNardo ascribe his enviable record to extrasensory perception? "Come on!" DiNardo responds. "It's not like that at all. I have a trained mind, a qualified staff, vision, and the ability to implement that vision. We're taking the technology and extending its potential five years out. We're not taking any Einsteinian leaps."

In 1960, the late Ray Kroc was offered what his advisors considered a bad deal: buying the McDonald's fast-food chain for $2.7 million. Some years later, when asked to recall the fateful decision, he said, "I closed my office door. I cussed up and down and threw things out the window. Then I called my lawyer back and said, 'Take it!' I felt in my funny bone that it was a sure thing."

For Ray Kroc to stick to that intuitive feeling took courage. All managers need that same courage when making intuitive leaps. At the Chicago Board of

Trade, Robert Jirout, vice president of information services, certainly needed courage when, in the midst of adding a massive amount of new communication technology to the Board, he decided not to go with AT&T's communications services. "We chose an untried vendor," Jirout says. "In fact, we installed the second system they ever built. I had a gut feeling, a sense of where the communications industry was going." The divestiture of AT&T shortly thereafter proved Jirout right.

To say that choosing an untried vendor is risky is an understatement. Although an unknown vendor may offer a better price and more customized service, at least with an established vendor like AT&T, Jirout would have been assured that the system would work—eventually.

"It's hard to pinpoint what turns you on or off about a vendor," Jirout says. "Part of it has to do with the 'chemistry' between the two organizations. Will my technicians get along with theirs?"

Jirout hastens to add that if this vendor had fallen flat on its face, he had a backup plan ready. But, he acknowledges, that would have been uncomfortably embarrassing. Fortunately, the backup plan was never needed.

Just as there is room for intuition in vendor selection, there is also room for intuition when deciding whom and whom not to hire onto your staff. Of course, there will always be attempts to quantify the process—administering tests to systematically compare qualifications, conducting highly structured interviews. But, as many managers readily admit, a strong gut feeling—one way or the other—can immediately circumvent any standardized procedure. As Bill Synnott, the senior vice president of information systems at the First National Bank of Boston, says, "Intuition is always more valuable in managing people than in dealing with things." He acknowledges that on several occasions he has hired people whose qualifications were not very impressive on paper, but who subsequently performed well nevertheless.

During a face-to-face meeting, an intuitive manager may observe a thousand different subtle cues. As Mintzberg of McGill University points out, "Oral communication enables the manager to 'read' facial expressions, tones of voice, and gestures." Thus, Mintzberg says, it is not surprising that of the managers he's studied, all display a marked preference for oral, face-to-face communication.

However, insists Robert Umbaugh, vice president of information systems at Southern California Edison Co., Rosemead, CA, this doesn't mean reacting to potential employees on the basis "of how your hormones are flowing that day." He says, "It's your total experience that tells you whether or not that person will fit." Umbaugh admits that he, too, has shunned the objective "evidence" on several occasions when hiring new employees.

In addition to choosing among clearly defined alternatives—such as whom to hire, which vendor to use, what strategy to pursue—You should also heed the voice of intuition when you have to solve problems that don't offer any clear-cut choices. In both art and science, anecdotes abound about great thinkers whose insights came as flashes of revelation, a kind of "Eureka!" syndrome.

Some of these accounts can be almost spooky. For example, the 19th-century German chemist August von Stradonitz Kekule struggled for months trying to determine the molecular structure of certain organic compounds. Then, one day, according to Kekule's recollections: "I turned my chair to the fire and dozed," he wrote. "Again the atoms were gambolling before my eyes. This time the smaller groups kept modestly in the background, my mental eye rendered more acute by repeated visions of this kind, could now distinguish larger structures of manifold conformation: long rows, sometimes more closely fitted together, all twining and twisting in snakelike motion. But look! What was that? One of the snakes had seized hold of its own tail, and the form whirled mockingly before my eyes. As if by a flash of lighting, I awoke..."

In that instant Kekule realized that certain organic compounds are not open structures but closed rings. Kekule had literally dreamed the benzene ring—one of the cornerstones of modern chemistry.

Examples like this demonstrate intuition's close association with creativity. Both intuition and creativity represent a breaking away from conventional lines of logic to arrange data in new and innovative ways. Creativity theorists claim that this is more than a process of stubborn persistence. Indeed, they believe the contrary is true. For example, in the process of problem solving, theorists refer to the need for "incubation"—periods when the problem solver must mentally "walk away" from the problems at hand to allow the mind to subconsciously wander and slip away from the blinders that excessive persistence may bring. The late Arthur Koestler alluded to these periods in his book *The Art of Creation* (Macmillan, 1964) as times when the mind is actually engaged in quiet rebellion against itself. "This rebellion against constraints which are necessary to maintain the order and discipline of conventional thought, but an impediment to the creative leap, is symptomatic both of the genius and the crank," he observes. "What distinguishes them is the intuition guidance which only the former enjoys."

For pragmatists who would like to be able to rely on such gifts, there's one obvious question: Can the intuitive process somehow be tapped on demand, perhaps even instilled into an organization? At Tektronix Inc., Beaverton, OR, Steven Rogers, decision-systems project leader, sought to answer that question. Five years ago, he headed a team to design an interactive, color-graphic simulation of a production-control system. Employing visualization techniques, Rogers had team members close their eyes during brainstorming sessions to try to visualize solutions to the problems before them. The process was described in a paper, co-written by Rogers, published in the 1980 conference proceedings of the American Institute of Industrial Engineering. "[One] guided-imagery exercise was employed to 'take' the participants to a place where they could 'see' [the system] in use. Important things to focus on included the physical appearance, the user, the kind of information being selected, and the environment in which the output was to be used. Based on this experience, the team's sharing of impressions and discussion formed the first series of graphic records... The records, in turn, led to a working definition of the system being designed and pointed to areas that needed a more careful analysis in order to be understood."

What were the project's results? It was not an unqualified success. The system never came to fruition. Its development was halted as a result of other problems outside the team's control. However, Rogers admits that there were members within the group who were highly skeptical of these meditative practices. "It's true that software engineers may have more problems with this approach," Rogers says. Still, he insists, there were many team members who were enthusiastic about these techniques and found them helpful in examining system alternatives.

Are Rogers' methods a harbinger of things to come? Perhaps. The Stanford University Graduate School of Business (Palto Alto, CA) offers a course, "Creativity in Business," that seeks to put students in better touch with their intuitive voices. A company called Innovation Associates in Framingham, MA, offers a similar seminar for executives, and boasts among its instructors a professor from the Sloan School of Management at the Massachusetts Institute of Technology. The seminar costs $1,350 and has graduated some 1,000 executives, including many CEOs.

Despite attention from respected sources like these, intuition is still fraught with tremendous ambiguity. For those who would delve into its inscrutable intricacies, a tendency to over-mystification must be guarded against. Some must be wary of elevating intuition to the status of divine revelation, in which the intuiter is seen as beyond reproach, above the dicates of reason. Consultant Philip Goldberg, in his book *The Intuitive Edge: Understanding and Developing Intuition* (Jeremy P. Tarcher Inc., 1984), cites a study in which 83 percent of the scientists surveyed admitted to having assistance from their intuition. However, Goldberg continues, what is frequently not mentioned by those who cite the study is that only 7 percent of these scientists said their intuition was always correct. Other estimates ranged from as high as 90 percent to as low as 10 percent.

Thus, although managers may wish to enjoy the benefits of listening to their intuitive voices, it is the flaws in those voices that remind us that intuition, as a tool for success, is still, and probably always will be, more art than science. Managers should listen to their inner voices, but heed them judiciously.

Martin Lasden is the western editor for Computer Decisions *magazine.*

7.

WORKING CREATIVELY

Gary A. Studer

The small company's greatest advantage is that the personnel are gener-alists who know overall company operations better than do employees of large firms. Plus, if someone has an idea for improvement, he or she usual-ly can just walk into the president's office and offer it.

One of the best ways to plan long-range strategies is to properly encourage creativity within companies. While this is being done increasingly in large institutions, primarily in the manufacturing arena, it has not been applied as widely in the service sector, especially in small firms.

There are several reasons for this. Firms, understandably, are preoccupied with short-term goals due to high interest rates, increased bankruptcies, and a more competitive environment. This leaves little time, except at the highest executive levels, for long-range creative thinking. And, when employee turn-over is high, creativity is stymied at the lower levels.

In the largest companies, creativity flourishes best either through an in-ternal think-tank group charged with plotting the future or by contracting the work.

The internal approach, of course, has an advantage in that no one knows the company better than its own personnel. The group should be quite small, since it should not be difficult for members to meet.

Since meetings are expensive, they should only be called when absolutely necessary. The time spent working on a think-tank project should not detract from a person's normal job hours. Truly creative people will be willing to spend extra hours conceiving an idea. If an employee complains about the additional time commitment, he or she doesn't belong in the group.

The death knell of creative thinking is rigidity, and the activities of the group members in this job assignment should not be regimented. In managing creativity, the best way to manage it is not to manage it at all. The rigidity will come when an idea is presented to management. It is counterproductive in prior stages.

Unstructured people are usually best for this group. They are the visionaries capable of designing strategies. However, they are also the most difficult to motivate and satisfy in their traditional positions, since this creative spirit is probably being constrained.

The people chosen should be interested in creative thinking for its long-term corporate impact and internal personal reward, not for possible political gain. Political infighters and climbers are detrimental to any creative group. The people should be at a high enough level to know what is going on in the industry and the company, yet not too oriented to what they view as built-in constraints.

ACTIVITIES AND RESULTS

Creativity is not a day-to-day activity. A creative person may go for weeks without an idea when a totally non-connected occurrence will stimulate an idea. Progress may be extremely rapid after this, often a matter of days until a plan is formulated and ready to be presented to management. Catalysts for a creative idea could be reading an article or talking to a colleague.

Management should expect a wide range of ideas, some sound, some impractical, some insignificant and some very profound. The ideas in total should represent several functional areas.

Management's responsibility is to decide whether to study the idea further. In any case, management should communicate with the group member. Inaction by management at this point is a disruptive demotivator with long-term impact.

Nearly as fatal as a blow to creativity as rigidity is insistence on quantifying results. This can be minimized by making sure that this creative exercise does not interfere with performance of the participant's normal job.

The trouble with measuring the activities of the think tank is that facts are much more quantifiable than ideas. Therefore, the performance of individual members of the group should not be measured, since it only is of little value but can be a demotivator and generate undesirable competition. The sole measuring device should be a periodic report of what ideas the group has had and what became of them.

To truly creative people, being chosen for such a group is an important reward in itself. The interaction with other people with similar characteristics is also a reward.

Access to top management to present, and possibly discuss, an idea is an even greater reward and a powerful motivator, regardless of whether the idea is accepted. Recognition by management is the ultimate reward, and coupled with a quantifiable expression of satisfaction, results in a very loyal, productive employee.

Small companies have certain built-in problems in tapping the creative talents of their people. Yet, their need for it is just as great due to their high bankruptcy rate.

Too often, small companies "follow the leader," not realizing that what is good for the leader may not be good for the follower. However, small companies cannot spare the people to do creative thinking. They run lean ships.

The small company, however, has certain advantages in encouraging creativity. Employees in the small company are usually more permanent, more loyal, and are not fast track. Small companies also have a less regimented environment.

The small company's greatest advantage is that the personnel are generalists who know overall company operations better than do employees of large firms. Plus, if someone has an idea for improvement, he or she usually can just walk into the president's office and offer it.

A creative think tank will not work in a highly charged political arena where ideas become political footballs. It will also not work where management is totally interested in the short term and the bottom line.

In the absence of these constraints, within realistic expectations, a creative group can provide low-cost vitality, with the promise of new ideas rather than no ideas.

Gary A. Studer is director of management services with Form Systems, St. Louis, Missouri.

8.
TOWARD A MORE CREATIVE YOU: UNLOCKING HUMAN POTENTIAL

Harold R. McAlindon

> Most of us so underestimate our ability and our potential that we go through life without ever sensing what we could have accomplished. Underestimating our own potential causes us to underestimate the potential of others.

Dr. Dudley Calvert tells a true story of a railway employee in Russia who accidentally locked himself in a refrigerator car. Unable to escape, he resigned himself to his fate. As he felt his body becoming numb, he recorded the story of his approaching death in sentences scribbled on the wall of the car.

"I'm becoming colder," he wrote. "Still colder, now. Nothing to do but wait." Finally, "These may be my last words..." And they were, for when the car was opened, they found him dead. Yet the temperature in the car was only 58 degrees! The freezing apparatus was, and had been, out of order. There was no physical reason for his death. There was plenty of air. He hadn't suffocated. He had been the victim of his own illusion.

A subject in a hypnotic trance is told that his arm will be touched with a red-hot rod. The experimenter then touches him lightly with a pencil. What happens? A heat blister appears. It is exactly the same sort of blister that would have appeared had the subject actually been burned.

These two incidents dramatically illustrate the power of the human mind. It is so powerful that it can determine the quality of a person's future. Many people, particularly those in business, have not grasped this important truth. But the way we think about ourselves and our potential has a vital effect on our view of the realm of possibility. In fact, it creates the realm of possibilities for us.

MIND-STIFLING INERTIA

Most of us so underestimate our ability and our potential that we go through life without ever sensing what we could have accomplished. We don't appreciate how much more we're capable of contributing or how we may have inhibited the lives of other people.

Abraham Maslow, whose research on self-actualization has contributed much to changing our views about the capacities of people, used to try to inspire learning in his pupils by asking them, "Which of you is going to write the next great novel? Who is going to be the great senator or President? Which of you is another Schweitzer? When his students were faced with these questions, they would blush, squirm, and giggle. Then Maslow would challenge, "If not you, who will?"

Maslow points out that there are times when each of us has flashes of inspiration—the desire to do something of real magnitude—but, after giving it serious thought we inevitably develop a "Who, me? Who am I kidding?" attitude. What we don't realize as individuals is that everyone who has ever done something for great numbers of people had this same kind of self-doubt and humility. But each of them relentlessly continued on.

Like Maslow's students, many people in positions of responsibility within organizations fail to realize that they have within them the power to change that organization for the better. You may be one of these people. You have more creative resources than you may have ever perceived. Your responsibility to yourself and to your organization is to unleash your thinking processes and to consistently and positively assert your creativity.

A friend of mine once advised me, "Harold, watch out for people who try to lower your goals. There will be teachers, business associates, and friends who will say, 'Don't set your goals too high; we don't want you to be disappointed.' They'll tell you to be realistic and not to set your goals beyond your potential." Then he chuckled, "Of course, they don't have any idea as to what their own potential is, yet think they can judge yours."

Today's top priority message is to make the most of your potential. It's a cause that I feel absolutely evangelical about because we're spending our entire lives using only one-half of our talents and energies. Once we recognize this, we can experience the challenging, fulfilling accomplishments for which we were created. Belief in your own potential will result in your setting stretching goals.

LEVELS OF CREATIVITY

When a group of university psychologists tested creativity in various age groups, it found that about two percent of the 45-year-olds tested out as creative according to the criteria set. When they tested a 44-year-old group, the figure was the same, as it was for those 43 years of age. But when the same test was given to children, the number of seven-year-olds ranked highly creative jumped to 10 percent and of five-year-olds in that category to 90 percent. The psychologists concluded that nearly everyone is born creative, but somehow this spark is lost in the growing-up process.

In order to keep this natural creativity alive and productive, our task is to grasp, nurture, and channel our creativeness into positive, constructive pursuits. If we then integrate and relate our creativity with the creativeness of others, we can channel this effort toward some of the foremost challenges in the world. This can best be done in an organizational setting. However, our organizations must be structured in a way that will encourage this interrelation-ship of skills, knowledge, and creativeness. It begins with us, as managers, to overcome the feelings of inadequacy and to link our strengths with the strengths of others.

UNDERESTIMATING POTENTIAL

Dag Hammarskjold confessed to a feeling of personal unworthiness that went so far it led him to undervalue and even doubt the reality of the friendship and sympathy that must always have been offered him in abundance.

When businessmen underestimate their ability and potential, they often rely on artificial stimulants to gain feelings of being "adequate." These recourses, of course, are false, short-lived, and self-destructive. Alarming reports inform us that the use of alcohol and drugs are at an epidemic level in the United States.

In the business environment itself, managers fail to delegate authority and responsibility, whether out of fear of being replaced or because they don't know how to delegate. Consequently, they suppress the potential of the entire organization. They seem to be afraid to try something innovative and creative, because they fear the possibility of failure and the bursting of their balloon. It would be impossible to calculate the cost to organizations of good ideas that have never been developed or implemented.

In education, when human potential is underestimated, curriculums are developed that offer no challenge to the students. Many mandatory courses aren't relevant to the world or to the individual lives of the students. Teachers and professors who underestimate their own ability fear change and feel threatened by suggestions for more creative methods of learning and participa-tion by the class. In the last decade, especially, we have seen the results of this on our campuses.

Politicans who underestimate people's potential fail to come up with programs that will help to inspire man to climb up out of his habitual rut. Those with false images of themselves and their ability are unwilling to persist in the arena of human progress where laws are made and real progress can at least be initiated. Too often, they resort to means other than their own competence. The last few years have begun to put the ineffectiveness of this method on display.

Even more disastrous is when you, as an individual, underestimate the potential of the people around you. If you are a father or a mother, you could be inhibiting the growth of your children without ever realizing it. Realization of human potential and personal growth and development is not accomplished passively. It's a process that involves constantly confronting, encouraging, sharing, reevaluating, and adjusting your view and perspective of life. Discipline is not enough. Creativity, courage, individuality, and the perception of beauty and love must be continually reinforced.

THE STONE AGE OF DEVELOPMENT

What is your personal potential? How much talent do you actually have? How good are you capable of feeling? Joseph Batten, author of the book *Tough Minded Management*, believes that only one person in ten thousand feels as good as he possibly can. I agree with him. And this is probably a generous estimate. The truth is that we're just beginning to understand and grasp the tremendous potential of people. It is almost as if people as individuals, in groups, and in organizations are literally in the stone age of their development.

Ivan Yefremov, an eminent Soviet scholar and writer, says that man, under average conditions of work and life, uses only a small part of his thinking equipment. "If we were able to force our brain to work at only half its capacity," he claims, "we could, without any difficulty whatever, learn 40 languages, memorize the large Soviet encyclopedia from cover to cover, and complete the required courses of dozens of colleges."

Engineers have estimated it would take a building several acres in size to house the computers that would match the dullest human brain.

In his book *Self Renewal*, John Gardner noted that "most people stop growing in a spiritual sense by the time they finish high school. Most people stop growing in virtually all areas of our existence. This is tragic because research has shown that the capacity to think, to learn, and to innovate continues to grow well past middle age. The mature person's richer background of experience is advantageous in the special work of creative problem-solving. In truth, more than 64 percent of the great achievements of the world have been made by people over 60."

Only two things keep "old dogs" from performing new (creative) tricks: negative attitudes and the failure to try. There is a tremendous sleeping giant in each person that only you, the individual, can awaken.

UNLOCKING HUMAN POTENTIAL

How do we tap the reservoir of human creativity?

Arnold Toynbee, the famous historian, believed that civilizations (people) develop "in response to a challenge of special difficulty that rouses man to unprecedented effort." This concept is supported by the work of the famous psychologist Dr. Henry Link. In his research of "fully successful" people, Dr. Link found this common denominator: "They had developed the habit of trying something difficult, challenging, and stretching every day."

I want to present you with a personal challenge. A challenge that can have a far-reaching effect on future generations of people. The commitment is to the pursuit of a concept that I will call "actualization"—the actualization of our organizations through the actualization of our people. Because organizations can do what individuals cannot, the key to a better society and a better world lies within the framework of our organizational functioning.

Dr. Abraham Maslow, as he developed the concept of the self-actualized person, was convinced of this. In his book *Eupsychian Management*, he stated, "I gave up long ago the possibility of improving the world or the whole human species via individual psychotherapy. This is impractical. As a matter of fact, it is impossible quantitatively. Then I turned for my utopian purposes to education as a way of reaching the whole human species ... But as important as education is, perhaps even more important is the work life of the individual, since everybody works. If the lessons of psychology, of individual psychotherapy, of social psychology, and so forth, can be applied to man's economic life, then my hope is that this, too, can be given an eupsychian direction, thereby tending to influence in principle all human things."

What I am proposing is a process for "organizational actualization." I will provide a model for integrating individual talents and helping organizations reach toward their ultimate potential. I believe that it is impossible for man to achieve his true potential without such a model.

Much has been written about organization development and renewal. These are important concepts, but the result of such processes is a return to, and reinforcement of, mediocrity. Examine the cycle. A company is begun. It is full of vitality, excitement, and hope. As it goes through its growth processes, organization, control, and other management concepts begin to strangle the vitality of the people. It's at this point that a company tends to try to regain what it originally had through a renewal or an O.D. program. It is regaining the status quo, but where are the sensations of its original growth?

I believe that man is finally awakening to the tremendous capacity that lies dormant within him. We are seeing this awareness in the popularity of such writings as *Jonathan Livingston Seagull*. The individual is still the most important inhabitant on earth. However, reality tells us that man works and lives in groups. Since groups and organizations can do things that individuals cannot, we need to go beyond self-actualization to group actualization and to organizational actualization.

Organizational actualization will accelerate self-actualization throughout the organization. The reverse is not always true because behavior is not always constructively channeled. Working to improve the world by improving ourselves and our organizations is the most practical way of creating a better tomorrow.

HOW TO MAXIMIZE HUMAN POTENTIAL

- Visualize what you want to become. Hold fast to that vision.
- Make a list of your strengths, values, and goals in life. Get in touch with who and what you really are.
- Double the potential you think you have and others have.
- Do something difficult every day. Keep stretching, learning, and growing.
- Learn more about the nature of people and try to understand it.

Remember...

- No person has ever fully fulfilled his or her potential.
- Every person has far more ability than he or she realizes.
- Our perception of what is possible actually determines what is possible.
- Underestimating our own potential causes us to underestimate the potential of others.
- The era of human development has just begun.

Harold R. McAlindon is Director of Human Resources and Organization Development, The Institute of Financial Education.

Part II:
THE DEVELOPMENT OF CREATIVE POTENTIAL

9.
HOW MANAGEMENT CAN INFLUENCE THE GENERATION OF IDEAS

Norman R. Baker
Stephen G. Green
Alden S. Bean

Can idea generation be managed? Not if we mean that it can be strictly controlled by management. If, however, we mean that it can be strongly influenced by management, then the answer must be a strong "yes."

- Is the type of technical idea generated related to the individual(s) who first suggested it? Which sources tend to produce what kinds of ideas? Which source is most likely to generate new product ideas? New process ideas?
- Is the source of first suggestion influential in determining whether the project will succeed or fail? Does this influence vary by type of project? Who is most likely to suggest successful new product projects? Successful new process projects?
- Do the relationships vary according to the line of business toward which the project is directed? If yes, how?

These questions have been examined using a database developed by The Study of Industrial Innovation, conducted over the past eight years in cooperation with the Industrial Research Institute (IRI) and the National Science Foundation. The study collected data on 211 R&D projects carried out by 21 companies in four lines of business: low carbon, flat rolled steel; agricultural chemicals and pesticides; packaged foods; and industrial chemical intermediates.

This article reports what we learned from the database about the generation of ideas, where an idea is defined to be a potential proposal for undertaking new technical work which will require the commitment of significant organizational resources such as time, money, people, energy.

A number of previous studies[1,2,5] have described the idea generation process as the coming together of an organizational need, problem, or opportunity with a means for satisfying the need, solving the problem, or capitalizing on the opportunity. More recent literature[3] has described idea generation in terms of performance gaps or in terms of discrepancies between what the organization could do because of a goal-related opportunity and what it is actually doing in terms of exploiting that opportunity. A performance gap may be either a need, problem, or opportunity awaiting a technological means or a technological means awaiting an appropriate need, problem, or opportunity. In this study we were interested in the role played by the individual(s) who first recognizes and articulates the performance gap.

WHAT WE FOUND

Result 1. The type of idea generated is related to the source of first suggestion for some sources, but not for all. Some sources are more likely to generate certain types of ideas than others.

Table 1 presents the total number of times a source was cited for each of four types of projects. Only four of these sources exhibit a statistically significant relationship with type of project. It is interesting that three of these sources—marketing/distribution/sales, production/engineering/technical services, customers—are the three most closely linked to the eventual users of R&D project outcomes. Further, they are more likely to suggest projects of the type associated with the users with which they are linked; i.e., both marketing/distribution/sales and the customer are more likely to suggest product projects and are less likely to suggest process projects while production/engineering/technical services are more likely to suggest process projects and less likely to suggest new product projects.

Technical sources, inside or outside the firm, are not statistically related to the type of project.

Result 2. The source of first suggestion is related to the success/failure outcome of new product projects. Sources that are likely to suggest successful R&D projects tend to vary according to type of project. The relationship was statistically significant only for new product projects, however. It was not statistically significant for product modification, new or modified process, or product/process projects.

Tables 2A and 2B summarize the relationships between source of first suggestion and type of project for new product and process projects respectively. New product projects were least likely to succeed when R&D was the sole source and most likely to succeed when marketing/distribution/sales and/or the customer were involved as a source of first suggestion. The likelihood of success for new products was 53 percent when marketing/distribution/sales and/or the customer were involved, but only 35 percent when R&D alone was the source.

Table 1—Total Number of Times Each Source Was Cited by Type of Product

Source of first suggestion that project be undertaken[1]	Type of Project				Row Total	Statistical Significance[2]
	New Product	Product Modification	Process	Product & Process		
R&D staff	64	11	18	49	142	NS
R&D first-level management	42	9	18	23	92	NS
R&D middle management	58	8	29	36	131	NS
VP of R&D	13	1	7	14	35	NS
General management	10	4	7	17	38	.05
Marketing/distribution/sales	53	13	10	39	115	.009
Production/engineering/ technical sales[4]	5	3	20	13	41	.000
Customer	37	9	5	26	77	.02
Government representative	1	1	1	2	5	(3)
Vendor/supplier	2	0	3	9	14	(3)
Technical, outside firm[4]	13	4	3	16	36	NS
Column Total	298	63	121	244	726	

[1] More than one source could be cited per project. [2] A X^2 test was performed on the 2 × 4 table where the rows are "source cited" and source "not cited" and the columns are "type of project". Each source is tested independently. "N.S." indicates that the X^2 test was not statistically significant at .05. [3] X^2 not calculated due to insufficient number of observations. [4] These categories are combinations or original items. "Technical, outside the firm" includes consultants and colleagues outside the firm.

Table 2—Mutually Exclusive Sources of First Suggestion and Success/Failure of R&D Projects

A. New Product Projects

Source	Number of Successes	Number of Failures	Total	Percent Successful
R&D alone	29	55	84	35%
Marketing/distribution/sales and/or Customer	18	16	34	53%
R&D *and* Mktg./dist./sales and/or Customer	23	16	39	59%
Total	70	87	157	45%

Statistically significant at .0025 by X² test. 157 out of 169 (93%) of the new product projects were suggested by one of the three sources listed in Table 2A.

B. Process Projects

Source	Number of Successes	Number of Failures	Total	Percent Successful
R&D alone	24	13	37	65%
Production/engineering/ technical services	7	1	8	88%
R&D *and* Prod./engin./ technical services	8	1	9	89%
Total	39	15	54	72%

Not statistically significant at .05 by X² test. 54 out of 78 (69%) of the process projects were suggested by one of the three sources listed in Table 2B.

While the relationship concerning process projects is not statistically significant, it is clear that the likelihood of success was higher when production/engineering/technical services was involved than when R&D alone suggested the idea (89 percent vs. 65 percent). There was no discernable pattern concerning product/process ideas and, therefore, the data are not presented.

When these results were discussed at an IRI Meeting, two questions were raised. First, did the ideas suggested by R&D alone result in highest contributions than the ideas for which marketing/distribution/sales and/or the customer were sources? If not, were they different in any way? Statistical analyses to address these questions lead to two additional results.

Result 2a. When only those new product projects which succeeded were examined, the amount of contribution actually realized by the firm was not statistically related to the source of first suggestion. Successful new product projects suggested by R&D alone contributed just as much, on the average, as successful new product projects for which marketing/distribution/sales and/or the customer were a source.

Result 2b. New product projects for which R&D was the sole source of first suggestion differed from other new product projects in a number of ways, including the following:

- Lower initial probabilities of achieving technical or business objectives (.02). (Numbers in parentheses are levels of statistical significance associated with one-way analyses of variance.)
- Less well-defined and less widely recognized initial technical and business goals and objectives (.008).
- More costly, longer times to completion, involving more scientific and technical areas (.007).
- Less well-developed (.01) and more costly (.004) scientific and technical areas.
- Less pressure from the user of the project's results to get the project started (.001).
- Higher likelihood of being protected by patents (.0007).

Thus, a clear, consistent pattern is suggested. The new product projects for which R&D was the sole source of first suggestion were riskier, more technically complex and less well understood at the time they were initiated. For these reasons, they were less likely to succeed than projects for which marketing/distribution/sales and/or the customer were a source, either with or without the joint involvement of R&D. When they did succeed, however, they contributed just as much as other new product projects. In addition, their results were more likely to be protected by patents. (The data also suggest that source is not related to short- vs. long-term contribution.)

Table 3—Total Number of Times Each Source Was Cited by Line of Business

Source of first suggestion that project be undertaken[1]	Line of Business				Row Total	Statistical Significance
	Flat Steel	Agricultural Chemicals	Processed Foods	Industrial Chemicals		
R&D staff	42	48	17	34	141	.000
R&D first-level management	20	27	15	28	90	NS
R&D middle management	32	23	37	41	133	NS
VP of R&D	12	7	8	8	35	NS
General management	3	16	9	11	39	.05
Marketing/distribution/sales	24	19	43	36	122	.001
Production/engineering/ technical sales	11	6	8	10	35	NS
Customer	32	11	7	29	79	.000
Government representative	0	3	0	2	5	(2)
Vendor/supplier	9	4	1	1	15	(2)
Technical, outside firm	5	23	4	7	39	.000
Column Total	190	187	149	207	733	

[1]More than one source could be cited per project. (2)X^2 not calculated.

Result 3. The involvement of certain sources of first suggestion varied across the four lines of business.

Table 3 presents the detailed results concerning the variation across lines of business. In general, the results can be summarized as:

Source	Flat Steel	Agricultural Chemicals	Processed Foods	Industrial Chemicals
R&D Staff	M	H	L	M
General Management	L	M	M	M
Mktg/Dist/ Sales	M	L	H	M
Customer	H	L	L	H
Technical, outside	L	H	L	L

where "H" denotes relatively high level of involvement; "M" denotes moderate level of involvement; and "L" denotes relatively low level of involvement.

These results appear to be consistent with the characteristics of the underlying line of business. For example, processed foods is a classic example of a consumer business, and one would expect marketing/distribution/sales to be most heavily involved in this business. Similarly, flat steel and industrial chemicals are industrial markets and the heavy involvement of the customer should be expected. Since agricultural chemicals is neither a consumer nor industrial market and since new products are based on technical advances, the heavy involvement of technical sources, both inside and outside the firm, can be explained. The relatively low involvement of R&D staff as sources of first suggestion for new product projects in processed foods is less easy to explain.

PRACTICAL IMPLICATIONS

The source of first suggestion is a potentially important managerial concern, especially for new product projects. It affects several project characteristics, including both type of project initiated and likelihood of success. The extent to which particular entities are involved as sources varies according to characteristics of the line of business.

The following interpretations of the previously presented data appear to be valid:

- Increased involvement of production/engineering/technical services in the idea generation process is likely to lead to ideas for process projects. These projects can be expected to have high probabilities of success and to result in significant contributions to the firm. (Process projects were more likely to result in high contributions to the firm than either new product, product modification, or product/process projects.)
- Increased involvement of marketing/distribution/sales and/or the customer in the idea generation process is likely to lead to ideas for new product projects. These projects can be expected to have relatively high probabilities of success, have relatively well-defined technical and business objectives, and not be technologically complex.
- R&D is the most frequently cited source of first suggestion that a project be initiated. This is true for all types of ideas and all lines of business. When R&D is the sole source of first suggestion for new product projects, the projects are likely to have relatively low probabilities of success, have relatively uncertain business and technical objectives, and be technologically complex.

Given that the source of first suggestion appears to be such a key variable, it is incumbent upon R&D management to manage the process of idea generation and the resulting mix of sources. Earlier work by Baker, Siegman, and Rubenstein[2] provides additional insights on how to approach this task. They offered a systems description of why high-quality ideas may be generated but never submitted for formal consideration as R&D projects. They note that R&D staff are required to perform two distinct activities: 1) carry out R&D effort on currently approved projects and 2) generate ideas for new projects. In most organizations, the rewards associated with good performance on approved projects (e.g., salary increases, promotion) tend to be highly visible and given on a regular basis. In short, they are relatively predictable and certain. In addition, failure to perform may lead to punishment (e.g., lack of advancement, firing). Thus, strong organizational pressures exist for doing well on the approved projects.

In contrast, the rewards associated with idea generation and submission (e.g., recognition, opportunities to publish, opportunities to determine future assignments, awards, bonuses) are far less predictable, visible and certain. Moreover, they are less likely to be given on a regular basis. Further, the time taken for (the more uncertain) idea generation is time taken from (the more certain) performance on current activity. Thus, idea generation effort can be viewed as jeopardizing the more certain rewards. The net is that idea generation is not viewed by R&D staff as an effective strategy for obtaining organizational rewards such as salary increases and promotion[4].

One might suspect, therefore, that there are ideas which are generated, but which are never submitted for formal consideration as new R&D projects. Indeed, this was demonstrated in the earlier study[2]. Moreover, once these unsubmitted ideas were brought to the attention of R&D management, they were more likely to become projects than other ideas being considered at the same time. Included in the unsubmitted ideas were a disproportionately high number of ideas that lead to approved, funded projects when compared to ideas that were submitted during the same time period.

WHY IDEAS WERE NOT SUBMITTED

The author then examined the unsubmitted ideas in detail in order to discover why the ideas were not submitted. Their findings were:

- Ideas will be submitted only if the individual who originated the idea believes that: 1) the idea's business and technical objectives would be perceived as relevant by management; 2) the rewards expected from idea submission would be at least equal to the "lost opportunity" associated with the time and effort which could have gone toward working on current projects.
- Idea submission occurred when the idea originator believed that both the reviewer and the time were appropriate. An idea judged as not relevant at one point in time was judged as relevant at another point in time by the same reviewer. Also, an idea perceived as not relevant by one reviewer was viewed as relevant by another reviewer at the same point in time. Thus, relevance of business and technical objectives was both time and reviewer dependent. Mixed signals and perceived unfairness were the predictable consequences.

It was common for ideas to be submitted which were sufficiently incomplete that management felt objective evaluation was not possible. Why? Time pressure on the current projects, uncertainty concerning type and magnitude of rewards and the regularity with which they were given, and uncertainty concerning how relevant the idea would be considered by management, all discourage the idea originator from investing the time and effort necessary to fully develop an idea. Yet, the R&D staff was told to generate and submit new ideas. The result was the submission of ideas perceived by management as incomplete.

What happened in these cases? Often, the "must be logical and rational" myth was invoked and management had a reason for not reviewing the idea for project status. A common response was to "shelve" the idea and tell the idea originator to develop it more fully "on his free time." This response was seen as negative by the idea originator—time and effort were invested with no perceived reward being received. As a result, expectations concerning organizational rewards were modified downward for the next cycle.

Individuals learned about organizational goals, rewards, and processes in three ways: first-hand experience, second-hand from veterans who had traversed full cycle, and what was communicated to them by management. Thus early first-hand and second-hand experiences were crucial, important factors in determining the attitudes and behaviors concerning idea submission learned by new employees are whom the new employees learned from and what message they learned.

Most of the first-and second-hand learning involved ideas that were submitted and reviewed some time in the past and most of the lessons learned were outdated by the time the learning was taking place. Moreover, the idea originators placed more credence on the early first- and second-hand experiences than on what management was communicating. Thus there was a substantial time delay between the time when change occurred and management communicated the change and the time when the change was recognized and believed by the idea originators.

The findings from this study, coupled with the findings concerning source of first suggestion, translate into action steps which R&D management can use to manage idea generation.

ACTION STEPS

Management can influence the type of idea generated by:

• What is communicated and to whom.

The content of the communication, e.g., needs, problems, opportunities, goals, objectives, priorities, resources, etc., influence what will be perceived as relevant. These all function as focusing mechanisms and tend to focus idea generation activity on what is communicated.

Each recipient of the communication is a possible source of first suggestion. Thus, recipients should be selected with particular needs in mind and in light of the results concerning source of first suggestion. If more product projects are sought, make sure marketing/distribution/sales are involved. For more process projects, involve production/engineering/technical sales. R&D should be involved in any case.

• Its behavior and actions.

All of these outcomes of management behavior and actions serve to focus idea generation: Which ideas are selected as projects; which activities (e.g., current project activity, idea generation, idea submission) are emphasized during performance reviews; which activities have time pressures or deadlines imposed on them; and which rewards in what quantity are given for idea generation and/or submission.

• Which sources of first suggestion are made accessible to the R&D staff.

Make sure that the readily accessible sources and the kinds of R&D projects most needed by the firm are consistent. The findings concerning sources of first suggestion provide clear guidance in this regard.

Management can enhance and sustain idea generation and submission by:

- Telling the potential sources of first suggestion, especially R&D staff, that new project ideas are desired.
- Telling them what kinds of ideas are desired.
- Communicating goals, objectives, needs, priorities, etc.
- Making idea generation and submission a part of the job description.
- Making idea generation and submission part of the performance appraisals.
- Rewarding individuals who do well at idea generation and submission.
- Exerting time pressures—set short-term goals and expectations for idea generation.
- Periodically updating and communicating the information that the R&D staff must have in order to: 1) assess whether the idea will be positively and enthusiastically received by management; 2) evaluate the nature and quantity of rewards likely to be received if the idea is a winner and the losses if it is not. Minimize the extent to which relevance is seen as reviewer dependent.
- Positively recognizing idea generation and submission when they occur and publicly recognizing ideas when they become a project or part of a project.
- Allowing for and considering the submission of incompletely developed ideas by providing the support necessary to develop them more fully.
- Rewarding the idea originator when the project results in value to the organization.
- Providing, when possible, the idea originator with the opportunity to research, develop, transfer, and implement the project and its consequences.

In summary, the number of ideas generated and submitted is determined by both how many of these 12 steps are implemented and the extent to which they are implemented. The mix of ideas—e.g., product vs. process, level of technical complexity, likelihood of success, etc.—depends upon which sources are encouraged to participate in idea generation and how the sources are focused by managerial action, behavior, and communication. Finally, a cautionary reminder when planning and assessing change: do not overlook the time lag between when change occurs and when the changes are recognized and believed.

Can idea generation be managed? Not if we mean that it can be strictly controlled by management. If, however, we mean that it can be strongly influenced by management, then the answer must be a strong "yes." It is clear that learning will take place with or without management's attempt to manage the process. Doing nothing concerning idea generation appears to be a much riskier management practice than judicious use of the findings and action steps presented in this paper.

ACKNOWLEDGMENT

This paper is based on research supported by the National Science Foundation under Grant ISI 7921581. Any opinions, findings, conclusions, or recommendations are those of the authors and do not necessarily reflect the views of the National Science Foundation.

The authors are grateful to the individuals in each firm who approved and/or participated in this study, especially the liaisons. The IRI's Research-on-Research Committee was actively involved continually since 1977 in study definition, design of data collection methods and questionnaires, and interpretation of results, and we thank the many committee members who helped us. We also are grateful to several of our graduate students, especially Warren Blank, Kathleen Verderber, Kumar Suresh Tadisina, and Venkatesan Srinivasan.

References

1. Baker, N. R., and J. R. Freeland, "Structuring Information Flow to Enhance Innovation," *Management Science,* Vol. 19, No. 1, September 1972.
2. Baker, N. R., J. Siegman, and A. H. Rubenstein, "The Effects of Perceived Needs and Means on the Generation of Ideas for Industrial R&D Projects," *IEEE Transactions on Engineering Management* Vol. EM-14, No. 4, December 1967.
3. Baker, N. R., E. P. Winkofsky, L. Langmeyer, and D. J. Sweeney, "Idea Generation: A Procrustean Bed of Variables, Hypotheses, and Implications," *Management of Research and Innovation,* B. V. Dean and J. L. Goldhar, editors, North-Holland Publishing Company, New York, 1980, pp. 33-51.
4. Kerr, S., "On the Folly of Rewarding A, While Hoping for B," *Academy of Management Journal,* Vol. 18, 1975.
5. Utterback, J. M., "The Process of Technological Innovation Within the Firm," *Academy of Management Journal,* Vol. 14, March 1971.

Dr. Norman Baker is acting senior vice president and provost at the University of Cincinnati. Dr. Stephen Green is associate professor of organizational behavior in the University of Cincinnati's Management Department. Dr. Alden Bean is the William R. Kenan, Jr., Professor of Management and Technology at Lehigh University.

10.
THE ENCOURAGEMENT OF EMPLOYEE CREATIVITY AND INITIATIVE

Alfred H. Jantz

Employees who demonstrate creativity, initiative and resourcefulness, and who get things done outside the authority-responsibility and chain of command structures, should be identified, developed and encouraged.

One of the aspects of organizational behavior, sometimes overlooked, is the relationship of the traditional classical concepts of "chain of command" and "authority must equal responsibility" to employee creativity and initiative. It is proposed that these concepts be questioned or challenged to determine if a modification of them would contribute to better results for management and greater development of potential and self-actualization for employees.

It is suggested that greater emphasis, in the administration of these concepts, should be placed on the behavior, attitudes and initiative of non-supervisory salaried employees. These are the people who are expected to "get out production," regardless of whether they are providing a service, or producing a product, paperwork, reports, records, etc. Basically, they are the people who are expected to do what they are told by their superiors, within the framework of the relationships and rules manifested in the existing or organizational structures.

The organizational concepts of "chain of command" and "authority must equal responsibility," with their relationships and requirements, need to be reexamined to determine if they really serve the best interests of the organization and its people. Such questioning or challenging might yield innovations or changes which may utilize more completely the potential of employees in accomplishing the goals of the enterprise and creating a more satisfying working life for the people in industry who look at the job as something more than the source of a paycheck.

Realistic modification of the organizational concepts being considered could yield new approaches which recognize that power within organizations also comes from sources other than authority. This modification requires recognition of the creativity, initiative, influence and potential accomplishments of those people in industry who do not have formal authority or status.

In an article on "Sources of Power of Lower Participants in Complex Organizations," David Mechanic states that frequently low-ranking employees in an organization have more power and influence than officially given to them by the authority structure. The sources of this power are largely independent of the chain of command or formal authority.

Lower participants, according to Mechanic, acquire power in an organization when they are able to gain access to sources of information, to people, and to instrumentalities. This closeness to the above three factors gives lower-level employees knowledge that others do not have, puts them in a position to influence higher-level participants, and gives them greater control over facilities.

Personal characteristics of individuals also give them greater power. A person's attractiveness or personality will cause higher participants to enjoy contacts with the person, thus giving him or her a greater degree of closeness to and influence over higher participants. A person's expertness will also give him or her greater influence and power. Other personal attributes which also help to account for the power of lower participants include effort, interest and willingness to use power.

It is the control over access to persons, information and instrumentalities, however, which provides lower participants with the most effective way to achieve power. This control makes other members of the organization dependent on the lower participants. Those dependent on these "power-packed" people may be on a higher, lower or associate level. These other people look to the influential lower participants to provide information, advice and service which may be more difficult or impossible to obtain through regular organizational channels. These lower participants frequently operate outside of the traditional authority and responsibility system and "get things done" regardless of and sometimes in spite of the normal chain of command. For example, a manager's secretary, through one telephone call, may be able to obtain a service or favor from the facilities or maintenance department that a foreman could not obtain without much paperwork, several approvals (or disapprovals) and lengthy delays. If a foreman, faced with an actual or impending breakdown of machinery or equipment on the production line, were to go through formal channels, he would be faced with a considerable time delay or possible disapproval of the request by the general foreman or superintendent in his own department, or by two or three levels of supervision in the maintenance department. Skipping channels and using the power and influence of the secretary to the manager of production enables the foreman to achieve his goal of keeping the production line in operation, and saves the company unnecessary expense resulting from production-line shutdown and idle production workers.

This lower participant power concept is, of course, not in harmony with the traditional authority, responsibility and chain of command concepts. The classicists hold that authority and responsibility is the realistic system for distributing resources, keeping track of them and directing them. Mechanic holds that the authority and responsibility system may not reflect reality. Reality must recognize the power of lower participants in order for companies to achieve optimum use of physical and human resources.

This point of view becomes more plausible and acceptable when we consider the positions of influence occupied by many lower participants in industry. Without a doubt, certain lower-level positions in industry are power-laden, and give their occupants a great deal of influence. Such positions as secretaries, administrative assistants and technical specialists frequently give these people more power and influence than those with formal authority. An incident from personal experience demonstrated the real power and authority of an administrative assistant. In a casual and informal conversation with an administrative assistant to the director of production, a training supervisor, in response to a question regarding the status of a future training program, stated that the program was not progressing very well because the production superintendent had been too busy to provide the information and data necessary for preparation of the training course materials. The necessary cooperation was forthcoming in an hour's time as a result of one two-minute telephone call from the administrative assistant (salary grade 7) to the superintendent (salary grade 11), in which the superintendent was threatened by a low-level "bawling out" from the administrative assistant whose power and influence with the superintendent's superior posed a threat resulting in immediate cooperation and fast action, which could not be achieved by recourse to the usual channels. Such examples as this lend support to the conclusion that people in the organization who occupy such positions without formal authority frequently become the "power behind the throne."

A study conducted by the author reinforces this point of view in relation to opportunities to exercise initiative, problem solving ability and creativity of business college seniors who, in most cases, become lower-level participants in organizations upon graduation. In this study, conducted at Eastern Michigan University, an attempt was made to determine whether an employer's attitude toward recognition of employee initiative, problem-solving ability and creativity are significant factors in the decisions of above-average students regarding employment upon graduation. In the course of this study, data was gathered which strengthened the view that new college graduates are strongly in favor of opportunities within the organization to exercise initiative and creativity in jobs which permit them to apply lower level influence and power within the organization.

In this study of 96 students, most of whom (56) were management majors, students were asked to evaluate 25 factors as to the relative importance of each in their decision to accept employment with a prospective employer. Only five of the total were chosen by students as being "of great importance." Two of the first three factors were related to an employer's programs and attitudes toward promoting or recognizing initiative, creativity and resourcefulness, and for providing opportunities for participation by lower-level salaried employees. While the opportunity to participate in a suggestion or proposal program, and interesting and varied work were "of great importance" to two-thirds of the students (66.7 percent each), ranking third and chosen by 56.4 percent of the students was the opportunity to apply one's creativity, initiative and resourcefulness. Ranking third in the "quite important" category was the opportunity to contribute ideas to solve departmental and company problems, selected by 47.4 percent of the students.

From this study, it can be concluded that companies wishing to maximize the effectiveness of the recruiting efforts among business college graduates should place greater emphasis on the management attitudes and programs which promote and encourage employee initiative, resourcefulness and creativity. This may well be one of the key factors in making the best use of a company's most precious asset—its employees. This also may be a key factor in attracting business college graduates who are superior, creative and dedicated to the achievement of company goals as well as their own. The creative employees within the organization are the ones who conceive new and better ways of doing things, devise cost-saving shortcuts, suggest means of increasing productivity, think up new products ideas, and offer ideas for greater sales and profits.

The concepts reviewed in this article point to the need for taking a new look at the formal organization, with a view to changes and innovations that might be necessary to bring about a more effective realization of both organizational and individual goals. With greater attention and consideration to individuals, organizations might realize that their own goals or objectives are more easily attainable.

If the abilities and potentialities of employees are recognized, encouraged and developed, organizations will be in a better position to fully utilize their lower-level management personnel. Behavior is greatly determined by the attitudes of employees themselves, and management. If employees believe that the organization is concerned with the full development and realization of employee potential, then employee attitudes toward the company, supervision and the job will significantly improve and be reflected in behavior that is in the best interest of both the organization and the individual.

Too rigid observance of the formal or organizational concepts and requirements may lead to stagnation and frustration of employees. The need for revisions and changes in organizational programs and relationships should be given more consideration. Particularly, the typical authority and responsibility system needs to be challenged. Recognition should be given to the fact that people frequently can and do operate beyond the authority-responsibility system, and that the results obtained are often superior to the formal method in terms of efficiency, saving of time and effects on people.

It is frequently found that lower-level employees who operate outside of the formal authority-responsibility system are superior employees with a high degree of creativity, initiative and resourcefulness. But these qualities are frequently not recognized or tapped by management. So these people look for other outlets for their ingenuity and initiative, and use them to get things done outside of the authority-responsibility structure. This creativity, without a legitimate outlet, may be directed by the individual at things other than organizational goals.

The creativity, initiative and resourcefulness of employees may be used to help realize the goals of management by "getting things done" outside of the authority-responsibility structure. People with a high degree of creativity see many alternatives, and are able to go over, around or under obstacles in attaining their goals. Frequently, however, these creative individuals are looked upon as mavericks, and attempts are made to hold them in check. Employees who demonstrate creativity, initiative and resourcefulness, and who get things done outside the authority-responsibility and chain-of-command structures, should be identified, developed and encouraged. Their creativity should be developed and channeled so that it will better serve the best interests of both the individual and the organization.

Alfred H. Jantz is an assistant professor of Management at Eastern Michigan University College of Business. He holds an M. B. A. degree from the University of Detroit.

11.
DEVELOPING YOUR CREATIVE IDEAS

Gary K. Himes

Change is a way of life for today's supervisor—adapt or perish. It is very unlikely any organization can do today's job with yesterday's methods and be in business tomorrow.

Jim Edwards, production supervisor of the Heavy Metals Department, was hanging up the phone when he heard a knock on the open door.

"Hi, Jim," said Gene Rogers, the area maintenance supervisor. "Just stopped to say we finished. The pump was repaired, and the small line replaced with a large pipe. As you requested, we didn't use any bailing wire or chewing gum."

"Thanks. I'll have to hand it to your crew. They are really creative," replied Jim.

"True. Our crew has some original ideas, but they also have a supervisor who gives them the opportunity to be creative." said Gene.

"Explain."

"I believe creativity has provided everything enjoyed today," responded Gene as he sat down and removed his hard hat. "The ability to think, judge, reason, imagine and originate has produced everything used. My thinking time is very important."

"Wish I could find the time. Look at all this paperwork," exclaimed Jim as he waved his hand over his desk.

"Years ago, I was bogged down by detail, busy doing things and handling too much," replied Gene. "But an experienced superintendent set me straight. I now delegate some responsibilities along with the necessary authority and organize my time."

"Sounds good, tell me more," said Jim.

"Plan. Train people. Think about how to improve your job. A few people accuse me of sleeping when I'm actually daydreaming. I close the door, put my feet on the desk and actually daydream or think about job improvement methods," explained Gene.

"I've heard a few comments about that."

"That superintendent said time used each day for thinking leads to a much richer and more productive life. I think he is correct as he is now a vice president." Standing, Gene continued, "I'll see you. I have another problem to think about."

"I would like some more ideas along these lines." said Jim.

"Sure, any time." A smile crossed Gene's lips. He would gladly provide a production supervisor better work ideas mixed in with the proper maintenance philosophy.

Are you like Jim, always busy with details and doing things? Do you want more creative thinking time?

If bogged down by details, train and delegate. What details or parts of a job can be delegated? Who can have expanded jobs through training? Can some details be simplified, consolidated or eliminated? . . . how?

Spend time deciding how to properly use the hours in a day. Read a time management book. How much waste is in your daily effort? Any wasted motions? How can you better organize your time?

Be concerned with doing the right things; not with doing things right. When this is achieved, time will be available for creative thinking.

Creativity...that nebulous process which transform a series of abstract ideas closer to reality—the application of mental ability and curiosity to an area resulting in the creation or discovery of something new.

As a supervisor, how can you be more creative? How can one's potential creative abilities be directed toward department goals? What hinders creativity?

Your creative ability can certainly be expanded if it is nurtured and allowed to grow. Creativity seems to require the ability to see things with a fresh viewpoint. This is critical! It's been said, "The mind is like a parachute. . . . it functions only when open."

Most creativity doesn't produce dramatic discoveries that soar forward in a gigantic leap. In practice, creative steps usually produce small changes, and major innovation is the sum of routine improvements. Very few people achieve the highest creativity levels; most can show more originality in regular activities.

Different work requires the use—to various degrees—of different types of creativity. Principle creative methods are duplication, extension, innovation and synthesis. Frequently, the methods are combined.

Duplication. Substantial progress is made when successful practices of leaders are quickly adopted. The wise supervisor screens other work methods/ procedures; appropriate ideas are altered or modified for your use.

Extension. A basic innovation is taken, and its usefulness is increased by expanding its applications.

Innovation. Something new is produced. A person develops an idea which is a sharp break with traditional practice. This major change may cause serious difficulty in getting an idea accepted.

Synthesis. Ideas from diffeent sources are used. Seemingly unrelated concepts are combined into a valuable product or service. Managers often use synthesis as the talents of people combined with resources create products.

THE CREATIVE PERSON

In an area where the ground remained frozen during the summer, one person observed that scraps of food thrown outside were preserved and didn't rot. His name was Clarence Birdseye. A new industry developed because his observation was followed up.

What sets the creative supervisor apart from other individuals? Few people, if any, use their entire creative potential. Everyone has some amount of creative ability, but individuals considered to be creative simply better utilize their abilities. Creative people are not geniuses. Instead, creative people are flexible and seek solutions in unexplored areas.

Among the distinctive characteristics of the so-called creative people are the following:

Sensitivity to Surroundings. There is an ability to see things, note problems or areas of need and be aware of promising situations. There is an knack for making unusual and detailed observations.

Flexible, Open, Curious and Selective. Adjustments to new developments and changes are quickly made, unique solutions to problems and remote relationships can be seen and previous assumptions are dropped in the face of new evidence. There is an intensive curiosity about everything. Problems are broken into their component parts, relationships among variables are understood and fundamental aspects and critical parts of a problem are grasped.

Independent Judgment. There is a willingness to be different and deviate from past practices even if it means standing alone against pressures to conform. Risks are taken if they appear to be worth chancing failure. Mistakes are viewed as situations from which better ideas may arise.

Tolerance of Ambiguity. Creative people tolerate uncertainty, complexity and apparent disorder since these conditions may produce desirable answers. There is little need to impose a premature and simplified structure.

Mental Flexibility. The creative mind shows mobility as related and unrelated data and ideas are rearranged, modified and redefined. When no significant thoughts occur for a problem, work is stopped. Upon returning, a fresh approach comes with greater ease. This incubation period, just a few minutes or days, gives a person's memory time to recall many forgotten facts and associations which may provide the keys to solving a current problem.

As stated long ago, "It takes courage to be creative. Just as soon as you have a new idea, you're a minority of one."

STIMULATING IDEAS

Like any individual skill, your creative potential can be developed to a high degree of proficiency. However, certain techniques insure a fuller development of this potential.

For the mind to produce, it needs challenge, stimulation, exercise and action. But ideas do not come from a vacuum; instead ideas come from borrowing and improving, combining, modifying, and associating new facts and trying to apply techniques and ideas from other fields. Some techniques which insure fuller development of creative potential include:

a.   Determine the problem to be solved, not just symptoms. Write down the problem to be solved, the product/equipment to be altered, or the process to be improved. A large and complex problem should be broken down, as a series of small problems is easier to solve.

b.   Using a pencil/pen, write down ideas as they occur. Don't stop to analyze or evaluate; just write down the ideas immediately. Keep a writing tool handy to record ideas before they get lost.

Possibly you've had the experience of waking up at night with an excellent idea to solve an earlier problem. It was so obviously superior you felt sure it would be remembered in the morning. But disappointment and only a forgotten idea came with the dawn.

c.   Record your observations: plant operations, production problems, bottlenecks, personnel conflicts and work procedures. Later, when you have a few minutes, use these notes to channel thinking to the most critical/important problems.

d.   Ask questions to stimulate idea flow. Put something to use? Other uses if altered? Adapt? Modify? Change size, speed, or weight? Substitute? Rearrange? Reverse? Combine? Ask yourself who, what, when, where, why and how.

e.   Select a time and place for thinking. While ideas can and do occur everywhere and anytime, experience shows certain surroundings are more conducive to idea creation. Make thinking a part of the daily routine in an appropriate place during a time when you are most productive.

f. Set a goal and a deadline. A realistic, quantified goal and a time schedule provide the driving force to produce ideas. When attending to daily matters, creativity suffers. Procrastinating on a problem usually wastes time and produces more serious problems.

SELLING IDEAS

A company must sell its products to a customer before there is any benefit. In like manner, an idea that is not sold or used has little value.

Obtaining acceptance of your idea by others is often the critical problem. If approval is not obtained, an idea withers and dies just as a young plant dies without water, sunlight and nutrients. For approval, care must be taken in presenting ideas.

Prepare. The future of any idea depends largely on the thoroughness of its development. Have all aspects been studied? Is the idea good but impractical because of cost or circumstances? Are the facts accurate and logically developed? Do you thoroughly know the idea? Can you communicate to your supervisor the company benefits of this idea?

Present. During a time free of distractions, make an effective presentation. Schedule the meeting in advance if a large block of time is required. Be prepared to answer all pertinent questions and know more than you will present. Prove the advantages of the idea and discuss ways to overcome the disadvantages. Depending on the firm's management style, you may want to "plant the seed" by briefly mentioning the subject and its highlights a week or so before the formal presentation. If pressed for more explanation, just say the details haven't been worked out.

Test. If practical, ask for approval to test the idea on a small scale. This provides the opportunity to discover what the idea can accomplish with minimum cost. Also any "bugs" can be discovered and removed.

Do Not Give Up. If the idea is a good one, stick with it. Another time, place or supervisor may be more appropriate. Ideas and their development are based on facts accumulated from experience and work. Keep at it; the passage of time will be beneficial.

Your leadership role as a supervisor requires making your department and company more successful. This requires idea creation which enables more to get done and makes your job easier. Some ideas are easy to implement; others hard. Whatever the degree of difficulty, putting new methods into practice requires change.

While ambitions and talk come easy and are cheap, genuine commitment to change is hard. Many people like to retain the status quo. Change means being willing to take reasonable and realistic risks.

When management gives approval to try a new idea, consider the forces that are likely to resist change and those that are likely to be receptive to the change.

Just as you sold the idea to management, it is necessary to clearly and carefully explain the benefits of the change to subordinates. Stress the WHY and the benefits to individual workers to fully gain their cooperation.

Your ideas will be more successful when you follow a realistic plan of action, which is modified as required. Ask for help since new ventures need support, not obstructions. Persuading subordinates to accept change can be ongoing; just as one change is sold and implemented, you may face the challenge of yet another change.

Change is a way of life for today's supervisor—adapt or perish. New ideas and solutions to problems are creative by modifications, by processing or by manipulating old methods.

It is very unlikely an organization or its supervisors can do today's job with yesterday's methods and be in business tomorrow. Combine old methods in new ways; review methods in different situations; add or take away other ideas; change their color, speed, size or purpose and substitute.

By being totally aware of your surroundings and being receptive to new ideas, you can increase your creativity.

Develop and implement your creative ideas or lose ground to competitors. The choice is yours.

12.
ENCOURAGING "LITTLE C" AND "BIG C" CREATIVITY

Thomas A. Luckenbach

> Management's role should be to remove roadblocks, expedite effort, and provide resources, catalysis, and encouragement. Management itself should be innovative and learn how not to impede creative effort.

Big C and little c are terms which have been used to distinguish between creativity levels: creativity with a little c for innovative but not very impactful problem solving; creativity with a capital C for the big breakthrough innovation. Big C is a scarce commodity, but little c is within reach of any organization, for it is often merely a matter of improving employee attitudes. A deliberate program to encourage more little c can be an effective first step in developing an entrepreneurial spirit. This, in turn, could spawn Big C.

One low-risk approach is to compile a list of specific, important, current problems which have defied solution by the regular staff in the normal course of events. The compilation should be given to all employees to enlist their ingenuity in solving them. Meaningful incentives should be offered to encourage active effort, and safeguards should be built in to avoid rigging. A coordinator should compile the list and accept written proposed solutions. Problem-posers should be obliged to evaluate the proposals and respond within a reasonable time. Modest rewards and recognition for acceptable solutions should be granted to both solver and poser. A catchy name for the program might be helpful, but avoid those which might generate embarrassing acronyms, such as Problems in Search of Solutions.

ORGANIZING OF BIG C

In a tightly managed business, employees seldom have time for more than the normal demands of their job. As a result, creative inventing does not happen often enough.

Lately, some companies have tried to remedy this by copying the 3M Company's approach—allowing technical people to devote 15 percent of their office time to working on their own ideas. Maybe this works for 3M (the $100 million/year product Post-it, the yellow notes with not-so-stickum, is claimed to have roots in this program) and maybe not. It's hard to tell, since aside from this, 3M has long had an enviable reputation for innovation.

If a company is truly serious about making a "pull ahead" effort, this 15 percent approach may not be enough. After all, it amounts only to 72 minutes a day per person. However, there is another 15 percent approach which may be more productive of invention.

Don't allow everyone to devote (some would say fritter away) 15 percent of their time to creative pursuits. All are not interested, many are not creative, and some will abuse the privilege. Don't spread the allowed effort evenly among all the employees. Instead, concentrate it among the creative few. Permit up to 15 percent of your staff to take a *creative sabbatical.* Allow creative employees the opportunity to set aside what they are doing and work on their new product ideas full time for a year (and more, if needed).

Don't pale at the number. Look at it this way: right now you may have no new product ideas, nor a mechanism to foster any. This "intrapreneurial" approach is way to change your organization and beget ideas. If you have a technical organization of 500 people, it means you could have up to 75 new ideas being worked on. If the historical pattern holds and one in ten new product ideas pans out, you will have seven or eight new products to sell. What did you have before? Of course, you don't have to start with 15 percent—it depends on how entrepreneurial you want to be. Just remember, the product Post-it generates annual sales of $100 million. That's *BIG C.*

And don't worry about getting done the work your inventors were doing previously. One way or another the really important things will get done: some less important things may be delayed, some things won't get done at all. But maybe they didn't deserve doing in the first place.

Who should participate? Anyone who wants to, regardless of training, position, seniority, etc., so long as they either have a reasonable idea to work on or have demonstrated creative talent and will likely generate some ideas, given the time and freedom. Above all, be open-minded: all inventors do not look alike; you couldn't pick one out in a crowd. And you don't have to pick them all in the first year. The program should be a continuing one with people regularly entering and leaving.

Remember, nine of ten new ideas won't work out; and not all successful inventors are repeaters. So it is important to have a regular flow of new talent trying new ideas. Considering this, it is vital that participation in the program be considered an honor and that no stigma be attached to failure. Tangible evidence of participation (a plaque, etc.) should be provided and this should be the same regardless of whether or not their idea became a product. Besides, a generous, publicized reward should be given for successful new products developed in the program.

How do you manage such a diverse group and effort? As little as possible. Management stifles creativity. Don't demand weekly or monthly reports; don't have program reviews, performance appraisals; in short, don't get in the way. Management's role should be to remove roadblocks, expedite effort, provide resources, catalysis, encouragement. Management itself should be innovative and learn how not to impede creative effort. Remember, managing the other way did not produce much *Big C*; given a chance, intrapreneurship will.

CONSIDER FORMING A PEER PARTNERSHIP

If entrepreneurship and corporateness are antithetical, it is because companies are structured for control. Since way back when, the hierarchical business structure (HBS) has been the norm, imposed on all departments regardless of function. And clearly it works—if control is the goal; it even works in technical areas.

The HBS is effective for managing a wide range of technical activities, such as measuring, testing, instrumenting, and product/process development. In short, the HBS works with any activities which involve standardized techniques and available technology.

But research and inventing transcend these, and, for that reason, the HBS is counterproductive in a research department. Therefore, a company wanting to be intrapreneurial must recognize this and organize the conduct of its research differently, avoiding the HBS and its layers of technically unproductive managers. Instead, it must adopt a structure that will foster, not discourage, creativity.

One approach (there are others) is to reorganize into a *peer partnership*, operating in much the same way as a law firm or a partnership of physicians (only lawyers and physicians working in government or private business seem to tolerate HBS's). Ranking scientists and inventors (perhaps from a sabbatical program) would comprise the partners. Others not yet qualified to be elected full partners would be junior partners. Technicians and other support personnel would comprise a group of associates. All this would be under the leadership of a director, whose chief responsibilities would be to determine corporate needs, to communicate these to the entire group, and to devote himself to expediting his organization's creative effort. And he must achieve and maintain a sense of urgency, for, after all, it is a business endeavor, not an academic exercise.

Yes, large companies can become entrapreneurial and reap the benefits of *little c* and *Big C*. It just takes guts, imagination, determination, and patience.

Should your company take the bold step? Don't take too long to decide— the '90s are just around the corner. But remember this: what you decide may determine whether your company will be among the leaders of the '90s, or trailing along with the also-rans.

Thomas Luckenbach is a specialist in textile fibers and fabrics with more than 25 years of R&D management experience at three major corporations.

13.
THE TWO FACES
OF CREATIVITY

Timothy A. Matherly
Ronald E. Goldsmith

There's more to creativity than most people realize. Though often mis-
trustful of one another, adaptors and innovators are both creative. By
being aware of the forms that creativity can take, managers can match the
abilities of their personnel to the needs of the organization.

Whenever academics or managers discuss the characteristics which they feel
are essential for the long-term success of business organizations, they are
certain to put creativity near the top of the list. Creative individuals assume
almost mythical status in the corporate world, as tales of an Edison or a
Steinmetz transmit the culture of the organization to new members. An
organization with a reputation for creativity inevitably is considered a good
place to work.

Nothing testifies quite so well to the corporate concern with creativity as the
plethora of techniques designed and sold to enhance creativity in the decision-
making process. From the Madison Avenue razzle-dazzle of brainstorming to
the sedately systematic Nominal Group Technique, there has been neither a
supply shortage of tips, techniques, and systems to enhance creativity nor a
lack of demand for these products.

While creativity long has been assumed to be of value in such areas as
marketing and product development, there is a growing feeling that its impact
on the strategic planning process makes creativity desirable at the highest level
of the firm. The strategic decision process within the firm may be inhibited or
blocked because of an absence of the ability or inclination to engage in the
necessary creative process. One leading textbook, in discussing reasons why
the strategic planning process often fails to come to fruition, notes that
strategic decision making is fundamentally a creative process that is difficult. It
demands a type of thinking and breadth of knowledge that many executives
who have arrived at top management levels have neglected as they rose in the
ranks because they devoted themselves to solving short-range problems in their
narrow functional areas of expertise.[1]

Traditional efforts to enhance creativity, whether from the perspective of a firm desiring improvement or the individual offering techniques, tend to suffer from at least two basic deficiencies. First, they tend to be vague and imprecise in defining creativity. Post hoc judgments decree that those actions which subsequently result in radical improvements in organizational performance must have been creative. Secondly, they tend to emphasize creative *processes* to the neglect of creative *persons*. The first deficiency is not significant if one is in the business of creating legends. However, it provides little help for the manager concerned with identifying and nurturing creativity in its embryonic stages. The second deficiency stems, perhaps, from a democratic (or perhaps self-aggrandizing) belief that we all possess great stores of creative potential just waiting to be released. However, it ignores the readily observable fact that the majority of creative ideas in any organization are generated by a handful of people.

Another puzzle emerges when creative behavior is examined from the perspective of the organization. There is often a significant difference between what organizations say they value and what their common *practice* indicates.[2] Although organizations persistently endorse open communication, flexibility, risk-taking, trust, and innovation, standard practice often seems to discourage these behaviors and to reinforce evasion, rigidity, caution, suspicion, and stability.

THE NATURE OF CREATIVITY

A portion of the difficulty in identifying and encouraging creative management can be traced to unclear, imprecise, or inadequate conceptualizations of the nature of creativity. Too often, creativity is seen as the generation of unique solutions to problems through the discovery of previously unobserved relationships between know factors of the insightful revelation of solutions to previously unsolvable problems. While the activities in this definition certainly may be desirable, by themselves they fail to identify the total scope of an organization's demands for creativity or even the role of creativity in the functioning of the organization.

This view of creativity, from a practical perspective, is by no means guaranteed to pay off in any way that substantively benefits the organization, its members, or its constituents. As Theodore Leavitt observed, "A powerful new idea can kick around unused in a company for years, not because its merits are not recognized, but because nobody has assumed the responsibility for converting it from words into actions. What is often lacking is not creativity in the idea-creation sense, but innovation in the action-producing sense, i.e., putting ideas to work."[3]

A further inadequacy of the traditional notion of creativity is that it places a premium on revolutionary change precipitated by identifiable discontinuities in the operations of the firm. There are certainly situations where this sort of turnaround is probable—and, indeed, some situations in which it is absolutely necessary. Most firms, however, are rather competent at what they do, having invested considerable effort, experience, and intelligence in mastering their respective crafts. Managers in these firms may recognize the desirability of radically improving the organization's performance. They also understand that the probability of winning this sort of creative lottery is quite low and that the best odds for enhancing the company's fortunes lie in small increments of improvement, arduously obtained.

A more useful definition of creativity is the generation of ideas that result in *the improvement of the efficiency or effectiveness of a system.* The advantages of this conceptualization of creativity are that 1) it is results-oriented, thus establishing some objective criteria for the evaluation of creative input; and 2) it opens the door to a proper valuation of creative activities that may be overlooked because they are not spectacular.

ADAPTORS AND INNOVATORS: TWO PROBLEM-SOLVING STYLES

Insight into the influence of personal characteristics on creativity comes from Michael Kirton's research into the nature of the creative process.[4] Basically, Kirton posits a continuum of decision-making styles. Where individuals are located on the continuum depends on whether they tend to be *Adaptors* or *Innovators*. Adaptors are those who seek to solve problems by "doing things better." They prefer to resolve difficulties or make decisions in such a way as to have the least impact upon the assumptions, procedures, and values of the organization; they seek to improve the existing framework and do not "rock the boat." Innovators, on the other hand, are inclined to "do things differently." They are likely to see the solution to problems in the alteration of the basic approaches and framework of the organization; a certain amount of disruption may contribute positively to the achievement of the organization's goals.

Individuals differ, then, not only in their *levels* of creativity but also in the *form* that creative expression takes. Thus there are both qualitative and quantitative differences in individual styles and levels of creativity. Table 1 summarizes some of the characteristics of adaptors and innovators.

In reality, of course, most people do not fall strictly and exclusively into one of these two personality types. Rather, this typology represents opposite ends of a continuum, with most people representing some combination of these two extremes and incorporating elements of both styles in their approaches to problem solving. Individual problem-solving styles normally are distributed across almost the entire range of possibilities, with women tending to be more adaptor-inclined than men and with younger adults tending to be somewhat more innovative than older adults.[5] Interestingly, neither intelligence, level of education, nor occupational status appears to be significantly related to adaptation/innovation style.

Table 1.
Two Approaches to Problem Solving

Adaptor

Employs disciplined, precise, methodical approach
Is concerned with solving, rather than finding, problems
Attempts to refine current practices
Tends to be means-oriented
Is capable of extended detail work
Is sensitive to group cohesion and cooperation

Innovator

Approaches task from unusual angles
Discovers problems and discovers avenues of solutions
Questions basic assumptions related to current practice
Has little regard for means
Has little tolerance for routine work
Has little or no need for consensus; often insensitive to others

Adapted from Michael Kirton, "Adaptors and Innovators: A description of Measure," *Journal of Applied Psychology*, 61, No. 5 (1976): 623.

Each of these basic problem-solving styles has its own strengths and weaknesses and makes its own contribution to the function of the organization. For some problems the methodical, detailed application of the existing organizational methods yields the most effective result. Some problems, on the other hand, cry out for the original, innovative solution that gives the organization a totally new direction. The presence of different approaches to problem solving within a single organization or operating unit may lead to disagreement over the desirability of solutions, disagreement that ranges beyond simple discussion of technical merits. Adaptors and innovators may not see eye to eye and may not understand that their differences lie at a fundamental psychological level. Thus, the potential for considerable interpersonal conflict arises, with both individuals and organizations paying the price.

To adaptors, innovators may seem to be neurotics, grandstanders, and misfits, bent on upheaval and destruction within the organization. Innovators, on the other hand, may view adaptors as dogmatic and inflexible "organization types" who serve as insurmountable obstacles to fundamental change in the organization. Although objectively inaccurate, such pejorative stereotypes tend to polarize decision makers and prevent objective evaluation of the merits of individual ideas.

A PLACE FOR EVERYONE

In their own ways, adaptors and innovators may be equally creative. Each cognitive style may lead to solutions that increase organizational effectiveness.

Adaptation/innovation is a distinction between styles of creativity, not levels of creativity. Although most theory, research, and discussion of creativity stress the generation of novel ideas, adaptive solutions may cope well with new situations, new information, or new problems while preserving the essential values, assumptions, and equilibrium of the organization. The opposite of creativity is not the generation of conventional ideas, but rather the failure to generate ideas at all.

Indeed, there are often sound reasons for an organizational bias toward adaptive solutions to problems. Not only do adaptors tend to be better suited for the prolonged, routine activities involved in implementing a decision, but the fact that adaptive solutions tend to minimize institutional disruption also makes them more palatable to most organizations.

Innovators, too, have their place in the organizational process. The importance of their contribution may be illustrated by an analogy to Kuhn's model of the progress of science.[6] According to this model, the development of scientific theory tends to be organized around and directed by a dominant paradigm or conceptual model. However, when a mass of evidence accumulates that is inconsistent with this model, a "paradigm switch" occurs, in which the old model is precipitously abandoned in favor of a new paradigm that better accommodates existing data and impels productive inquiry.

In a similar sense, innovators are inclined to challenge the prevailing view of how the organization operates and how it defines its mission. For the organization that is functioning well under its existing paradigm, this may be neither necessary nor desirable. For the organization in which the paradigm is being invalidated by contradictory data—declining profits or market share, loss of technological leadership, or other deteriorating performance criteria—or for those aspects of operations in which a successful mode of performance is not established, innovation may range anywhere from being valuable to being critical for the survival of the firm.

MANAGING FOR CREATIVE RESULTS

Concern for creativity in management is perhaps well founded. However, with an awareness of the alternative forms that creativity can take, management can target specific areas for improvement. Some specific suggestions are offered here.

Matching Creative Styles to Organizational Needs. As previously noted, there are some situations in which stability is highly valued, and others in which flexibility is essential. For example, six categories of managerial personalities (management archetypes) have been identified for six basic strategic directions.[7] For three of these directions—Explosive Growth, Expansion, and Retreat-Reposition—a flexible, divergent individual with an innovative bent is desired. For the other three—Continuous Growth, Consolidation, and Harvest—a stable, adaptive personality is more appropriate. Similarly, the stage of the company's life cycle may influence the requisite capabilities of a management team, with entrepreneurial (that is innovative) skills and administrative and integrative (that is, adaptive) abilities shifting in importance at various stages.[8]

Matching Creative Styles to Job Requirements. One of the most critical tasks for any organization is that of matching the skills of people to the demands of the jobs they are to perform. Considerable attention is devoted, therefore, to screening, testing, interviewing, and evaluating both potential and current employees to select those whose aptitudes best suit them to the requirements of particular jobs. This matching process is not less important in the case of managers, whose skills, especially in communication and problem solving, are deemed of critical importance. It is no easy matter, however, to identify the salient characteristics of managers or potential managers.

Creativity style may prove to be especially important to certain positions; for example, in product development. There is increasing evidence that firms must be able to develop and market new products or services in order to ensure long-term survival. Innovative problem solvers may be ideally suited to the task of creating and developing new products, where the emphasis is upon novel solutions or ideas. Adaptors may be better suited to administering existing product lines, where the usual demands involve maintenance, administration, and improvement of existing systems.

Training. An awareness of the Adaption/Innovation continuum may benefit organizational training programs in three areas. First of all, judgmental barriers need to be overcome. If managers are to interact on a more objective, less psycho-emotional plane, they need to put aside the pejorative stereotypes adaptors apply to innovators and vice versa. A second possibility lies in the potential for expanding individual creative repertoires. Adaptors can be encouraged to introduce greater novelty in their problem solving; innovators, on the other hand, can be encouraged to develop more systematic ways of approaching problems and implementing solutions. Finally, knowledge of their own creative styles can help individual managers adapt to specific problems and situations and adopt appropriate problem-solving behavior.[9]

The ability of a firm to generate internal changes in procedures, to produce new products or to react to new competitive situations is often essential to its long-term survival. Change may take the form of radical departure from the organization's established operations, or it may involve less sweeping modifications in behavior of and in the organization. Though they differ in styles, both the innovative and the adaptive contributions are creative. The truly creative firm is one where both types of creative input are recognized and valued for what they can offer, and where each is encouraged in those situations in which it is appropriate. By recognizing the potential contributions of both of these creative personality styles, organizations can build balanced, creative management teams and enhance organizational effectiveness.

References

1. George A. Steiner, John B. Miner, and Edmund R. Gray, *Management Policy and Strategy: Text, Readings, and Cases*, 2nd Ed. (New York: Macmillan, 1982).
2. Chris Argyris, "Interpersonal Barriers to Decision Making," *Harvard Business Review*, March-April 1966: 84-97.
3. Theodore Leavitt, "Creativity Is Not Enough," *Harvard Business Review*, May-June 1963: 72-83.
4. Michael Kirton, "Adaptors and Innovators: A Description and Measure," *Journal of Applied Psychology*, October 1976: 622-629.
5. Ibid.
6. Thomas S. Kuhn, *The Structure of Scientific Revolutions*, 2nd Ed. (Chicago: University of Chicago Press, 1970).
7. J.G. Wissema, H.W. VanderPol, and H.M. Messer, "Strategic Management Archetypes," *Strategic Management Journal*, January 1980: 43.
8. Ichak Adizes, "Organizational Passages—Diagnosing and Treating Lifecyle Problems of Organizations," *Organizational Dynamics*, Summer 1979: 3-25.
9. Stanley S. Gryskiewicz, "Creative Leadership Development and the Kirton Adaption-Innovation Inventory" (Greensboro, N. Carolina: Center for Creative Leadership, 1982).

Timothy A. Matherly and Ronald E. Goldsmith are assistant professors in the departments of management and marketing respectively at The Florida State University.

14.
DON'T LET YOUR GOOD IDEAS DIE

Richard Bauman

> Every idea you have that involves changing the way things are done, manufacturing a new product or providing a new service you will have to "sell" to someone else. Unfortunately, an awful lot of good ideas die young.

How many of your good ideas have been killed off lately? Undoubtedly you have come up with some clever, innovative ideas on how to improve a product, do something better or faster or provide a service that's been needed for years. You've probably had ideas for businesses, products or services that could have been real moneymakers. But nothing ever came of those ideas.

Unfortunately, an awful lot of good ideas die young. They are strangled, figuratively speaking, before they ever have a chance to develop. The thing that kills many good ideas is words. To have ideas evaporate before your eyes, all you have to do is tell them to someone—a friend, a co-worker, even your boss—and you'll likely hear several "good reasons," why your idea isn't viable.

"That's been tried already," is an old standby, discouraging phrase. "No one in upper management will buy it," is another stock line. "It can't work because…" followed by any number of opinions as to why your idea will never make it.

With these or similar words echoing in your ears, it's easy to believe you have been shortsighted and not very practical. So you toss out your idea and go back to doing whatever it is you normally do. The worst thing about discarding your ideas on the say-so of self-appointed critics is they are possibly, even probably, dead wrong.

Before you consign an idea to limbo, it's important to remember that every business, every manufactured item, every successful service started out as an IDEA. Not one modern convenience, product or service miraculously appeared. Someone thought it up, developed it and somehow put it on the market where it has survived or failed.

The reactions others have to your ideas probably aren't that much different than the reaction a lot of now famous people endured when they first suggested an idea of theirs not only had profit potential, but was just what the world needed. It's a good thing people like Edison, Bell, the Wright brothers and virtually thousands of others had open minds, but closed ears when it came to critics of their ideas. Many of their critics were experts of their era.

For instance, the Wrights faced nearly unending ridicule after they suggested a self-propelled heavier than air contrivance could fly. Experts and non-experts had a great time being pompous on the possibility of flights.

There was Professor Simon Newcomb, a respected American astronomer, who took delight in saying the Wright brothers were wasting their time and money. "There is no known combination of substances and machinery and forms of force (that) can be united in a practical machine…which man shall fly long distances through the air," said Newcomb.

They had critics not only amongst scientists, but in the clergy, too. Bishop Milton Wright said, emphatically, "Flight is reserved for angels and to think anything different is blasphemy." The bishop's statement also proves that family members don't always support good ideas—he was Wilbur and Orville's father!

Long after the Wright brothers had succeeded and airplanes were being built by dozens of companies, the doubters persisted. Marshall Ferdinand Fach, in 1910, said the airplane was interesting but of no use to the Army. Even as late as 1939, Rear Admiral Clark Woodward scoffed at the idea of airplanes sinking battleships. "As far as sinking a ship with bombs, it just can't be done." That was a mere two years before the Japanese attack on Pearl Harbor which started World War II and nearly destroyed the U.S. Pacific Fleet.

Rarely is an idea marketable as it is first conceived in someone's mind. It generally takes some research, refining and a lot of hard work. Sometimes years of hard work.

An item you probably use everyday, the zipper, took literally decades to go from idea and crude model to common usage. Yet today it is used in everything from clothing to keeping artificial turf on sporting fields together.

DESIGNING A ZIPPER

Whitcomb Judson invented the zipper in 1891 when he grew tired of having to lace his shoes. Along with his partner, Lewis Walker, they set up a factory to produce zippers in 1894. They soon learned it was easier to design a zipper than to produce one.

Equipment capable of making zippers couldn't be found. They made numerous attempts to build their own machinery. All ended in failure. Discouraged, Judson abandoned his partnership and left the company. Walker, on the other hand, became even more committed to the zipper. He hired a Swedish engineer, Gideon Sundbeck, who eventually did create a machine for manufacturing zippers cheaply and in large quantities.

In 1921, Goodyear Rubber produced rain galoshes using Walker's and Sundbeck's zippers. The public loved them. By the end of the decade, zippers were being used in a variety of garments. It had taken nearly three decades for an idea to become a reality, and another 10 years before the product found common usage.

Edison and his lightbulb fought an uphill battle, even after he had proven it was not only feasible, but a tremendously useful item. His detractors, nevertheless, continued to voice the opinion, "It will never work."

Henry Morton, the president of Steven's Institute of Technology, said of the lightbulb: "Everybody acquainted with the subject will recognize it as a complete failure." Had Edison listened to his detractors someone else would have invented the lightbulb.

Even Edison made mistakes about the value of a good idea. Edison invented the phonograph and is credited with inventing the motion picture projector, too. Yet after trying to create talking motion pictures he gave up, rationalizing his failure by saying of talking pictures, "They are a hopeless novelty the public will not support."

When you have an idea for a way to do something better, faster, more cheaply or more productively, don't let others discourage you from pursuing it, whether it is something that will benefit the company you work for or something you want to market yourself. Before you give up on it, be sure you have really researched it and are satisfied it's not going to work out.

Henry Ford was assured by Alexander Dow of the Dow Chemical Co. that the internal combustion engine would never work out as a means of propelling automobiles. "Electricity is the coming thing," Dow told Ford, "but gasoline—no." How many millions of electric Fords have you seen?

George Westinghouse, on the other hand, was called a fool by Commodore Vanderbilt when he tried to sell the idea of airbrakes to the railroad magnate. Vanderbilt couldn't grasp the concept of rubber hoses and air pressure replacing mechanical, hand-set brakes on trains. It was not because Vanderbilt was stupid. It was more a case of "we've done it this way for years," or "don't confuse me with facts, my mind's made up."

Every idea you have that involves changing the way things are done, manufacturing a new product or providing a new service you will have to "sell" to someone else. Whether you're trying to convince corporate upper management that you have a great idea that will be profitable for the company or you're trying to obtain financial backing for your idea, you can't avoid having to sell it. You'll be most successful if you really prepare your sales pitch.

DOCUMENT YOUR CLAIMS

This means having done your research thoroughly and carefully. You'll need to anticipate questions and objections and be equipped to give facts, not opinions. Document your claims not only for what you propose to do, but why it is better than what is currently available or being done. Charts, photographs, statistical evidence and even working models impress and convince others. They will all help sell your idea to those in a position to authorize it or back it.

What if your idea is turned down? You might want to take it elsewhere, especially if it is a concept you are trying to market.

Charles Darrow's idea wasn't overwhelming in the sense that the world would have stopped turning had he not pursued it. Yet literally millions of people in the United States, Canada, South America, Europe and even Asia loved his idea. It made him a lot of money. What did Darrow do? In 1932, he invented the game Monopoly.

Darrow created the game on his kitchen table and tried to sell the idea for it to Parker Brothers Inc. They turned him down. Supposedly, experts at Parker Brothers told him the game was too complicated and took too long to play. They recommended numerous changes. If he made those changes, they agreed to take another look at the game. Darrow, on the other hand, liked his game the way it was and chose to leave it alone.

Instead, he began selling it door-to-door and then through a Philadelphia department store. Sales were so good that the experts at Parker Brothers decided to take another look at it. They bought the rights to Monopoly and paid Darrow a royalty on every game sold. In the last 42 years, over 80 million copies of the game have been sold. The game is virtually unchanged from the way Darrow designed it, except for the foreign versions where street names have been changed to reflect native streets and locales.

Some of your ideas won't be practical and will probably deserve to be turned down. But others will be terrific and should be pursued. In either case, don't just listen to those who should know but are too quick to turn it down. Your ideas are yours and only you should bury them.

15.
STIMULATING CREATIVITY: ENCOURAGING CREATIVE IDEAS

Gary K. Himes

> It is up to the manager to coordinate, nurture, direct and control employees' creative activities. The problem often is not in producing creative ideas, but in achieving the disciplined activity required to convert thought to practical usefulness.

It was almost past the end of the customary lunch period for the second shift of the Hoffmann Metals Co. when the three line supervisors of the assembly department sat down together for their delayed lunch.

Outside, the wind continued to blow rain against the windows of the old, red brick assembly plant. Considering the severity of the storm, the downtime due to electrical problems was short. Hoffmann Metals was an old company, but its management strongly believed in preventive maintenance.

"I've only been here a short time, but I am impressed," said Ed Graves, the assistant shift supervisor. "A buddy at my previous employment phoned and said they have had electrical problems all evening."

"Yes, our engineering and plant maintenance groups are really creative when it comes to protecting utility lines and outlets," said Phil Brooks as he tilted his red hard hat back on his forehead. White strands of hair, mixed with the black, were quite evident.

"At the company I used to work for, management made it well-knowm through its actions that ideas originated at the top," explained Pat Stowe. "That company had a bunch of barriers against creativity by middle managers and hourly employees. You could write a book about their problems in leadership, communication breakdowns and lack of decision making skills."

While only a recently promoted assistant shifter, the experience and observations as an hourly employee and leadperson gave Pat an excellent understanding of management practice—both good and bad.

"Sounds like you're talking about my former employer," laughed Ed Graves. "They had those problems and some more...like poorly defined goals, no information sharing, excessive daily job pressures and uneven participation.

Some people were always busy but others should have reached for the paycheck with a hand behind their back."

"How did they continue to make a profit and stay in business?" questioned Brooks.

"I've wondered that myself but I can't give you a good answer. Maybe one of their products was selling creativity barriers to backward companies," responded Ed Graves as he softly laughed at another one of his corny jokes.

"Talking about the lack of creativity makes me glad I stayed with Hoffmann," said Brooks. "We had some of those problems years ago, but things changed when we got our current top managers. I thought of leaving, but I'm glad I stayed."

"I know Hoffmann is a better company and shows a greater interest in employees than my former employer," responded Pat.

"Speaking about creativity, look at this sandwich my spouse packed for me," exclaimed Ed. "It has two types of meat, cheese, lettuce, pickle, mustard..."

Would you like to work for Hoffmann instead of your current employer? Why are some crews or departments more effective? Why do some groups have a flair for accomplishing things in unexpected, original ways? How can creativity be stimulated in groups and companies?

The need for creative people, effectively working together, is evident everywhere. Progress makes it essential to accept and adapt to new challenges and the complexities of life. Competition makes it critical for a firm to have creative managers.

The company that fails to develop its creative resources is soon forced out of business by competitors. These other firms have a better product, lower cost, better marketing, or a more imaginative and forward-looking management.

THE CREATIVE MANAGER

One's personality and mental abilities determine only potential creative skills. The utilization of that potential is strongly determined by the firm's climate or environment.

It is up to the manager to coordinate, nurture, direct and control employees' creative activities toward achieving organizational objectives. If this is not done, truly creative people will seek other outlets—community groups, unions, hobbies, other work—for their skills.

A manager needs to continually promote a work situation in which originality is encouraged rather than inhibited. Creative management is needed in setting objectives, motivating group members and changing organizational goals. If this is not achieved, the manager has neutralized or inhibited creative efforts.

The desired organizational climate which encourages creativity is characterized by:

Good Supervisor—Subordinate Relationships. A manager should strive to build an atmosphere which encourages change and new ideas. Design a positive individualized approach to stimulate and encourage creativity. Give recognition for all new ideas and a special thanks when deserved.

Open Communication. Creative success usually builds upon the work of others. This building depends on the free flow of information and access to data. Contact with outside sources should be encouraged. Blocking communications seriously hampers creativity.

Active Support and Cooperation. Establish a definite procedure for the fair and consistent consideration of ideas conceived by subordinates. Communicate the results of implemented ideas to the entire company. Privately discuss ideas which cannot be used, and explain why. Bring together workers who have a variety of skills and experiences to create a mix in which creative borrowing prospers. Diversity stimulates the development of new ideas.

Attention to Highly Creative Personnel. If possible, partly isolate the creative person from daily operating pressures. Provide an environment conducive to study and work. Assign work carefully by stressing how the work meets the objectives of both the individual and the company.

Time to Think. Moderate slack time provides the opportunity to think and engage in creative work. This time may not be possible in a constrained setting or when employees are continually engaged in handling crises or immediate problems.

Avoidance of Premature Criticism. Premature criticism, impatience and saying "we tried it before" or "it will not work" can easily destroy almost all ideas. A manager should protect creative people from untimely pressures to produce results. Ideas should be evaluated on their merits.

"Loose-Rein" Management Style. Operations tend to be decentralized, autonomous and independent. Idea people are given freedom to choose, pursue problems and discuss ideas. Management tolerates and expects risk taking as they do not run an "extremely tight ship."

STIMULATING CREATIVITY IN ORGANIZATIONS

The creative manager realizes that he/she does not have all of the answers. It is certainly desirable, when appropriate, to seek help from a group or an individual.

If you work for a firm in which ideas have for years come only from the top, getting subordinates to think creatively can almost be a mission impossible. Possibly something could be done individually within your department.

If you work for a forward thinking firm, the sharing of thoughts already exists. It should be easy to stimulate creativity.

While a variety of methods have been used to stimulate group creativity, several methods are more useful in a manufacturing environment. The methods are: brainstorming, circular approach, value analysis and check list techniques.

Brainstorming is extremely valuable for problems that need creative solutions. Ideally, the problem is defined and specific in scope. Several days before the session, give a subject, cluster of subjects or a problem to each participant. This gives people an opportunity to think about the matter and write down any ideas in advance. During the session, the leader's role is to keep ideas flowing and centered around the announced topic. Get participation from everyone; do not let one person monopolize the conversation. Ideas are written down on a pad or chalkboard as they are generated.

The rules for brainstorming are: no criticism until later screening period; encourage free-wheeling ideas, the wilder the better; obtain a large quantity of ideas to increase the possibility of good ideas; and combine ideas or otherwise improve the suggestions of others.

Sometime after the session is over, the entire group or just several people can review the ideas generated and select the best ones. The ideas could be typed and distributed so participants can conveniently study them at their desk and select the practical ideas.

The *circular approach* to problem solving uses five steps: define, gather facts, determine alternatives, decide and take action. With this circular concept, one can start at any point, stop anyplace and continue around several times. This allows things to be examined and reexamined and the problems and alternatives to be restated.

When frustrated at any point, stop. Hopefully an insight will help solve the problem. Also as more facts are discovered, the problem may become better defined.

The objective of *value analysis* is to find a method of performing a job which achieves only the necessary functions at a minimum cost. Six questions are asked about each working component in order to increase its value: What is it? What must it do? What does it do? What did it cost? What else will do the job? What will that cost?

A method of obtaining leads is to use the *check list technique*. Items on a previously prepared list are checked against the problem or subject being considered. This method produces a number of general ideas for follow-up purposes.

Some items on the check list are eliminated since they apparently do not contribute to the difficulty.

Once the check list or a series of lists has been developed, the individual employee can easily use the appropriate list during either normal operating conditions or emergencies.

OBTAIN WORKERS' IDEAS

Employees who are actually doing the work eight hours a day plus any overtime can be a valuable source of ideas. Don't spend all of your time in the office; instead, walk around the production floor and start brief informal conversations with employees at their work stations. To encourage new employee ideas you should do the following:

Be Receptive. More and better suggestions occur if you offer encouragement. Convince subordinates of your sincere interest by promptly recognizing deserving employees. If you are impatient, too busy, or indifferent, a high wall is built between yourself and crew members.

Give Credit Freely. Recognizing an employee's contribution to your boss marks you as a good supervisor. Your reward will be worker loyalty, respect and more ideas.

Be Appreciative. Only minor improvement may result from an employee's idea, but even a small improvement is certainly a step in the right direction.

Help Prepare Suggestions. Some individuals lack the necessary technical, mechanical or writing skills to put an idea on paper. Offer your help in expressing the idea.

Respect an Employee's Idea. Any idea is of significant importance to the person who thought it up. Regardless of your opinion about the idea, it is important to someone; show consideration and be courteous. When an employee devotes time and effort to improving operations, it is only natural for the individual to expect credit and recognition. If you take the idea as your own, you probably will never receive another idea from that person.

Look for a Related Idea. A worker's idea may not be practical, but it can reveal another idea which helps solve a problem. If so, give the employee credit for the alternative solution.

Encourage Suggestions. Your continued support and help will spur employees to think constructively and develop better ways to do their jobs. Build enthusiasm and team work by sharing improved work methods.

Explain Any Rejection. When an idea is not adopted, the worker deserves an explanation of why the idea will not be used. This may require a careful and thoughtful answer, but you will gain the employee's confidence. Many good ideas are not economical or are impractical for a given situation, time or place. As Alexander Graham Bell said, "Great discoveries and improvements invariably involve the cooperation of many minds. I may be given credit for having blazed the trail, but when I look at the subsequent developments, I feel the credit is due others rather than to myself."

An excellent idea is not automatically transformed into action and results. Many ideas are developed by people who do not have the authority or responsibility to implement them.

Ideas may be impractical for a variety of reasons. Some examples include: management style and the belief that ideas originate only at the top; an insufficient number of people with the right skills to convert the idea into practice; economic conditions; implementation costs; marketing considerations and the company's political environment.

The problem often is not in creating ideas, but in producing the disciplined activity required to convert thought to practical usefulness. An idea which survives these three questions is a good prospect for practical applications:

a. Can the firm make available the resources (employees, money, time, materials, supplies and space) to implement the idea?
b. Will the environment (political, economic, social and government regulations) within which the firm operates permit the idea to be carried out?
c. Will the idea, if utilized completely or partially, be worth the cost?

Yes, there is opportunity for everyone in an organization to use his or her innate creative ability in some manner to improve work output.

Most people can use creativity to determine how to do things better. But leaders with responsibility for an area have the obligation of using creativity to determine what things will be done.

Be assured that your competitors—other supervisors and firms—are creative and implement appropriate ideas. If you fail to do likewise, you will slowly but surely fall behind.

Part III:
CREATIVITY
AND
CONFORMITY

16.
ENTREPRENEURS, CHAOS, AND CREATIVITY: CAN CREATIVE PEOPLE REALLY SURVIVE LARGE COMPANY STRUCTURE?

Marsha Sinetar

The creative personality and creative thinking can cause chaos in a well-oiled organizational process. The author demonstrates how management can identify and cultivate creative talent while still maintaining the orderly functions of the company.

"I love chaos: it is the mysterious, unknown road. It is the ever-unexpected, the way out: It is freedom, it is man's only hope. It is the poetic element in a dull and orderly world."—American artist Ben Shahn, 1966.

Suddenly, big business is in love with creativity. With the same fervor with which it courted MBAs in the 1970s, American industry is now trying to lure entrepreneurs into managerial positions. It has discovered that survival in today's volatile, global marketplace means finding, developing, and sustaining the very mavericks it rejected only a few years ago.

Why this dramatic shift in focus? One of the reasons is apparent as soon as we examine the entrepreneur's instinctive intelligence: entrepreneurs are better able to spot options and create new directions for an industry. Typically, they deal well with ambiguity and change, and that is a prerequisite for success in today's fast-paced business world. They can distinguish real from imaginary pitfalls, and the brightest among them can turn error into opportunity. Small wonder then that industry is scurrying to acquire creative thinkers.

Even current buzzwords point to the important place creativity holds in business. Intrapreneurial describes entrepreneurial characteristics when these turn inward, for organizational benefit. Entrepreneurialize is jargon used to describe any business activity that allows large, calcified organizations to internalize the advantages of smaller, more nimble companies. But, whatever the terminology, progressive corporations are hiring entrepreneurs, sending managers to creativity seminars, and bringing in creativity specialists to teach executives how to think in original ways.

However, just because big business wants entrepreneurs doesn't mean it is prepared to accept or appreciate their way of working. There is much evidence suggesting that most large organizations are insensitive to the nuances and idiosyncratic work style of the creative personality. In reality, a substantial number of creatives are strangled within the orderly, systematic cultures of large companies: they can't work in these structured environments. Sometimes they leave, and sometimes their ideas just die, unused and unnoticed. But because business needs creative people, it must learn to understand—and support—this inventive breed of worker.

WHO AND WHAT IS A CREATIVE ENTREPRENEUR?

It is possible to distinguish two types of creative entrepreneurs: the activist and the creative thinker. Actually these two categories are not at all clear-cut, since all entrepreneurs if successful possess healthy doses of business acumen and original/resourceful thinking skills. What distinguishes one type from another is a subtle, almost elusive difference in thinking mode and in the manner of getting a job done. The activist is a doer. He has an innate understanding of what it takes to run, expand, reconceptualize, or create a business. This person's thought processes—the steady, incremental way of thinking, doing, communicating—fits into and naturally complement the core of organizational life. The activist is a natural dance partner to business, and activists have an intuitive, sixth sense when it comes to motivating personnel, marketing new products, and dealing with financial issues. They know, without having to learn through academic institutions or books, how to put business principles to use within organizations so that both principle and organization succeed.

Victor Kiam, president of Remington Products, Inc., serves as an excellent and well-known media model of the activist entrepreneur. With effectiveness and energy he participates in all facets of his company's operations. He markets and even sells the product: his ad campaign, "I liked this shaver so much I bought the company," is now nationally familiar. He meets regularly with employees to motivate and inspire them. Kiam has built an impressive, clear corporate identity. In fact, if media reports are accurate, this activist entrepreneur is doing so well he is currently moving his products into the Japanese marketplace, thus reversing a global trend of Japanese products encroaching on U. S. markets. An impressive achievement.

The creative thinker, on the other hand, is more like an artist or inventor. Primarily a thinker, he derives his greatest pleasure from the act of thinking itself, from the creative process in action. Achievement for him comes when mental abstractions are transformed into concrete forms —when idea becomes reality. Indeed, the creative thinker loves the conceptional work of his technical specialty so much that sometimes practical business needs get overshadowed by the images of his professional frame of reference (e.g. engineering, computer technology, genetics, mathematics, etc.). This person is totally absorbed in experimentation, investigation, and innovation. Money, status, the outcomes of business are secondary to the act of creation. It is thinking itself which provides deep, visceral satisfaction: a fact industry must not overlook or misinterpret.

For the creative thinker, problems are sorted out in a stylized, unpredictable, and often disorganized manner; herein lies the greatest conflict that creatives have within organized corporate structures. Often, creative thinkers are hard to get to know. As managers they frustrate and surprise people in their departments; as employees they don't conform. In any role their habits contradict organizational expectations and mores.

One such manager, a nationally respected visionary known best for his grasp and application of computer technology, arrives at work early each morning and makes coffee for everyone. Accustomed to working late into the night, he then cleans up the coffee room before the custodians can get to it. He is oblivious to his company's unwritten social law that says senior executives must not engage in such activities. Thus he unknowingly thwarts lower level employees' ego needs to do a job they feel is rightly theirs.

Another creative thinker, a corporate vice president, upsets subordinates and superiors alike by refusing all clerical help, including a secretary to answer his phone and type his letters. Instead, he scrawls all memos on yellow legal pads, unaware that his colleagues get irritated because of this and because they can't get in touch with him when he's away from his office.

For all that, the creative thinker is not a wild-eyed nonconformist. With respect to most of the small customs of life, innovators may be very ordinary, even boring, people. But these personalities thrive on freedom in three important areas of life:

- Freedom in the general area of their work and the way in which the work gets done
- Freedom to ask novel or disturbing questions
- Freedom to come up with unusual solutions to the things they're thinking about (sometimes in the form of what seems, to others, to be impractical ideas)

In other words, these types must have lots of room for experimentation and "play." Such license is like air for breathing to the bright, inventive mind, yet it is only the rare organization that can provide this.

CREATIVITY MEANS DISTURBING THE STATUS QUO

Creativity means bringing into existence something that has never existed before. For the person who creates, thinking is play, and this becomes both his motive ("I desire to think") and his goal ("so that I can think some more"). Part of his recreation is experimentation: this is unsettling to others, and disruptive to organizational life. Courting error, taking a "let's see what happens" stance, is natural to the creative thinker, but anathema to large organizations.

Because of size and structure, big companies are risk-averse, even though they may give lip service to being otherwise. Errors, mistakes, failures: these must be avoided because they destroy careers, departmental efficiency, record keeping, and the like. *Organizations are designed to administer, maintain, and protect what already exists; creative thinkers are designed to bring into existence that which has never been before.* The creative's need to think and invent disturbs the well-oiled machinery of organizational process; thus, creativity is experienced as chaotic in most business environments. Some examples will help illustrate this fact.

The head of a technical unit of a prosperous, multinational corporation thinks nothing of spending vast sums of money to experiment with state-of-the-art systems equipment. Colleagues who are responsible for the corporate bottom line wonder if he is sane. "Just buy something reputable and stop playing games," they plead in an effort to keep expenditures down, but he continues to load his offices and theirs with a variety of experimental equipment and spends freely. While his associates think he's irresponsible, he thinks about the future, and electronics, and how to bring his company into the forefront of technology. Because he cannot (or will not) communicate in terms familiar to others, a knowledge and goals gap grows between himself and those important to his success.

Another entrepreneur, hired to help a corporation reconceptualize itself into new markets, spent the majority of his first year wandering about the halls, asking people vague, unanswerable questions. His incomprehensible approach alarmed fellow executives; more action-oriented business colleagues considered his constant probing a waste of time. Months passed without formal meetings or the development of a strategic game plan. This creative thinker appeared to lack the logic and discipline of a businessman.

In time, the man successfully accomplished what he'd been hired to do. His style of handling the project, however, put him on thin ice even with those who'd hired him in the first place, again underscoring the difficulty that creatives have in a structured setting and the difficulty structured organizations have with the creative process.

WHAT DO CREATIVE ENTREPRENEURS HAVE IN COMMON?

Every truly creative individual is a minority of one. There is no one else like him or her. It is difficult to group such persons into neat descriptive categories, except to say, as we have, that they don't fit the stereotypical way of doing business. However, the broadest area of their thinking skills and style of pursuing goals can be codified:

- They are easily bored, and would rather move into untried areas,
- They are comfortable with ambiguity, at least when it comes to work,
- They are neither risk-averse nor troubled by ambiguity,
- They may be uninterested in social matters, and thus may not be socially "well-rounded,"
- They need to use their minds to solve difficult, personally fulfilling problems,
- The healthier their personalities, the more likely it is that they experience their work as a calling or dedicated vocation.

When working in unexplored problem areas, creative entrepreneurs are able to cope without support or approval from others. According to research done by Paul Torrance, creativity researcher at the University of Georgia, Athens, creative people are happy with solitude, and they are less in need of discipline or order. Their dominant need may be to use their brains on complex problems, and this often overshadows their dependency on the approval or opinions of others.[1]

One such individual expressed his need to use his mind this way: "I love to use my brain...it actually feels good in a physical sense. The best times for me are when I'm working, uninterrupted, on something that needs a solution. My ideal job would be if I could sit in a room with the door shut with no one to bother me, and the company would just slide problems it needs solved under the door."

Such attitudes are disruptive to, if not disrespectful of, others. An all too familiar example is the creative entrepreneur who walks away from a successful business to work on a new project. His actions confuse family and colleagues alike. The energy, money, and time he must put into the new venture could so easily go into expanding the existing, profitable business. But, for a creative mind, moving on to a new challenge is natural, perhaps necessary. As a creative friend once told me, "Show me something easy, and I'll show you something dull."

Figure 1.

Common Challenges Facing the Creative Entrepreneur

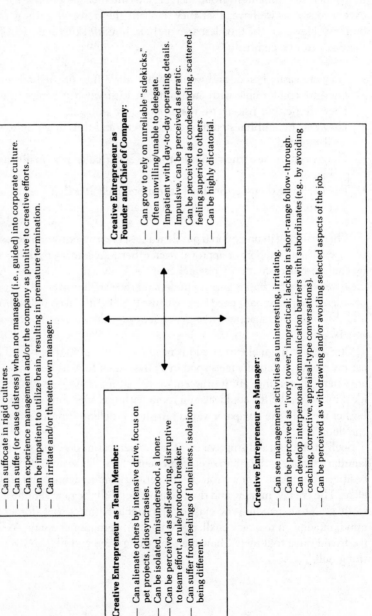

Creative Entrepreneur as Subordinate:

— Style, thinking, expectancies can clash when reporting to logical, linear thinker.
— Can suffocate in rigid cultures.
— Can suffer (or cause distress) when not managed (i.e., guided) into corporate culture.
— Can experience management and/or the company as punitive to creative efforts.
— Can be impatient to utilize brain, resulting in premature termination.
— Can irritate and/or threaten own manager.

Creative Entrepreneur as Founder and Chief of Company:

— Can grow to rely on unreliable "sidekicks."
— Often unwilling/unable to delegate.
— Impatient with day-to-day operating details.
— Impulsive, can be perceived as erratic.
— Can be perceived as condescending, scattered, feeling superior to others.
— Can be highly dictatorial.

Creative Entrepreneur as Team Member:

— Can alienate others by intensive drive, focus on pet projects, idiosyncrasies.
— Can be isolated, misunderstood, a loner.
— Can be perceived as self-serving, disruptive to team effort, a rule/protocol breaker.
— Can suffer from feelings of loneliness, isolation, being different.

Creative Entrepreneur as Manager:

— Can see management activities as uninteresting, irritating.
— Can be perceived as "ivory tower," impractical; lacking in short-range follow-through.
— Can develop interpersonal communication barriers with subordinates (e.g., by avoiding coaching, corrective, appraisal-type conversations).
— Can be perceived as withdrawing and/or avoiding selected aspects of the job.

HOW CAN ORGANIZATIONS SUSTAIN CREATIVE TALENT?

After all has been said about creative entrepreneurs, it must be clear that there are no instant answers, no quick-fix formulas that large organizations can use to harness the potential of creative people. There are, however, a few basic principles that can help businesses utilize the ideas and energy of entrepreneurs with more probability of success. (See Figure 1 for analysis of the creative entrepreneur as subordinate, team member, manager, and founder of company.)

First of all, management must be able to identify creative talent, then it must know how to use it. To accomplish this task, it should ask itself the following questions:

1. Who are our creative people, and how do we know they are creative? (This implies setting criteria for identifying innovators.)
2. What opportunities exist for creative people within this organization?
3. What barriers have key managers placed in the way of creative thinkers?

Once the organization knows who its creative people are, it must become introspective and ask itself:

1. In what way do we reward creativity?
2. Do we punish—that is, do we negatively reinforce, reject, or embarrass—those in the organization who look different or experiment freely?
3. In what specific ways do we encourage or promote experimentation and independent thinking?

Finally, in order to cultivate more independent, inventive thinking practices, organizations should audit thinking time. An expert isn't needed at this juncture, but opportunities to think are. An organization can ask itself:

1. What problem-solving opportunities exist for nonmanagers?
2. Do managers usually make all important decisions? What types of decisions are nonmanagers encouraged to make?
3. Are staff meetings, round table discussions or small group meetings agenda bound, tightly structured, or time restricted? Or are these used, on occasion, as brainstorming sessions?

THE CHALLENGE TO BUSINESS

One of the greatest challenges facing business today is encouraging creative people to express themselves innovatively while still maintaining the orderly functions of the company. If this is not done, creative entrepreneurs will leave generous salaries, incentives, and fringe benefits for more exciting and personally meaningful ventures.

In the words of one executive who left a large corporation to start his own company, "I needed the basic kick of using my brain on things that really mattered. I was bored in my other job, even though I was handsomely paid. There was no way of really thinking through the tough issues, no accountability or feedback in any immediate way. What I needed was the chance to use my mind. The company was too generous, but they didn't give me what I needed most—a real challenge."

Reference

1.   E.P. Torrance, *Guiding Creative Talent* (Englewood Cliffs, N.J.: Prentice-Hall, 1962).

Marsha Sinetar is president of Sinetar & Associates in Santa Rosa, California. She has a PhD from California Western University and is the author of many business articles.

17.

HOW MANAGEMENT CAN
DEVELOP AND SUSTAIN
A CREATIVE ENVIRONMENT

Maurice I. Zeldman

The corporations that will survive and thrive in the future are those that foster creativity today. Many companies are "taking the creativity cure," but are they really sincere?

Creativity for corporations, like vitamins for people, is essential for good health and growth. Though older businesses involved in slowly changing markets or technology need not necessarily "take a creativity cure," companies whose share of the market is constantly shifting or those that are dependent on high technology ought to take creativity seriously.

It doesn't require a great deal of probing to determine whether a company is sincere about creativity. There is a simple acid test—how does the company deal with failure in a creative endeavor? If failure means loss of a job or never being given an opportunity to lead another creative project or activity, the company has delivered its message loud and clear. That message is: Don't try anything difficult or challenging if you value your job. Besides discouraging further creativity, that company may be training its competitors' best people by discharging a team leader after a failure. The significant point is that the team leader may have learned how to succeed. The better approach is to review the failure and if a sincere effort was made on a difficult assignment, give the project leader a "purple heart" for valor in battle. Such an approach trains and stimulates creative leaders. A company that has such an attitude toward failure will find people willing to take intelligent risks. This is not an appeal to reward failure; it is an appeal for companies to dissect failure and learn how to win. After all, though there have been thousands of scientific failures, we still spend money on cancer research, knowing that the reward for one success far outweighs the cumulative failures.

CREATIVITY ON THE DECLINE

How has creativity fared in most corporations? Since the turn of the century, there have been more engineers and scientists produced by universities than the world has cumulatively seen from the beginning of time. Yet the scientist-entrepreneur was a more frequent phenomenon at the beginning of the 20th century than in recent times. Unfortunately, in the last ten years, U.S. patents by American inventors have declined. This fact is an indication of a general decline in U.S. corporate creative output and can be explained by the following factors:

1. Restrictive company policy creates an atmosphere where "breakthrough" will not be attempted for fear of failure.
2. All-encompassing pre-invention disclosure agreements in vogue in most U.S. companies discourage innovative people from pursuing new concepts. These agreements are illegal in most Western European countries and Japan.
3. The effects of inflation on long-term research projects have caused many companies to look for fast-return projects.
4. The unpredictable nature of true innovative activities encourages MBA-indoctrinated managers to emphasize fast payback projects at the expense of long-range growth activities.
5. U.S. Government regulatory requirements have turned a large segment of development funds away from innovation.
6. The drive toward narrower specialization has limited the scope of professionals.
7. In recessionary periods, companies cut growth and innovative technical activities more severely than any other sector of the business.
8. Corporate acquisition is often used to replace internal growth.

HOW TO FOSTER CREATIVITY

If a creative environment is important to a company, the following steps can be taken.

1. Evaluate the areas where risk is a factor in growth. Set up a special set of ground rules for this sector of the business, rules that permit entrepreneurial managers and technical specialists to function in an atmosphere where they won't fear being fired if they fail. (3M, in its new-business activities, does this by setting up ventures in the same way that Junior Achievement businesses are formulated.)
2. Examine corporate policy concerning pre-invention disclosure agreements. Limit the agreements to company business or to the direct work

assignments given to an individual. When in doubt, examine the patent laws used in Germany, Great Britian, Scandinavia, and Japan.

3. Develop corporate long-range objectives for areas of internal growth, and fund these areas on a coherent industry basis. Bear in mind that generalizations based on all industry averages are useless, since each industry segment has specific requirements based on product life cycles, competition, customer needs, and resource requirements. Remember, too, that one-product companies go out of business when their product becomes obsolete, so a good rule of thumb is the introduction of three successful new products per product life cycle.

   People working on long-range new products are generators of future profit and growth. Such funding is particularly important to companies that are in medium to high technology areas, for historically they tend to grow in greater proportion to the money spent in development than others. Statistically, in the long term, a policy of developing long-range new products is also a hedge against inflation.

4. Most modern corporations calculate their investment opportunities in new activities with concepts that involve the time value of money such as net present value, internal rate of return, or profitability index. Although the concepts are good, it is difficult to get accurate input data, so these calculations should be used primarily as a guide to sort out the real "dogs." If too much weight is given to these computations, only fast payback projects will pass the test, and a large corporation will inadvertently kill its long-range growth potential.

   Successful entrepreneurs always have a gut feel about new areas of growth. If your corporation is lucky enough to have an entrepreneur with the drive and desire to undertake new and challenging projects, try to keep that individual, and use the financial-analysis models as a cross-check. Remember that most film companies felt that instant pictures were an insignificant market. It took a man with guts and persistence like Dr. Land of Polaroid Corporation to prove that the instant picture market was real.

5. In these days of overregulation, it is necessary for a growth-oriented company to keep its perspective. In many industries development funds must be expended on regulatory activities to keep the company out of court and in compliance with regulations. If, however, all growth funds are used in regulatory activities, new business development will cease. Thus a balance between regulation and development is necessary. Where the proper balance rests is dependent on one's industry segment. For example, high technology requires more development funds than medium technology. In determining what should be the balance between regulation and development, be guided by the old saying, "Render unto Caesar that which is Caesar's, and render unto God that which is God's."

6. Many studies on creative individuals show that creativity declines with age and too much education. Unfortunately, too many companies have

become degree- and specialty-happy; in some companies you almost need a Ph.D. to sweep the floor! But not all members of a team need to be creative; usually, one creative individual goes a long way. What is necessary for real creativity is a balanced team of Ph.Ds, scientists, engineers, technicians, and people who came through the school of hard knocks. The specialists are essential for analysis and concept documentation, but the generalists and the driven inventor with or without education are also necessary.

7. Recession is a cyclic phenomenon in our society. During these downtimes CEOs and GMs often cut all innovative activities out of their budgets. The result is corporate loss of the best, most creative people. And even if they are not on the layoff list, they become nervous and look around.

    Companies should recognize that creative, driven people are generally the most marketable employees they have, and they should do everything feasible to keep them.

    In cutting research budgets during recessionary times, companies can also be deferring, if not severely damaging, their future. What happened in the textile industry recently is a case in point. The producers of textile machinery went through fairly rapid recession-boom-recession periods in the late 60s and early 70s. Manufacturers, in order to cut costs, phased out or drastically reduced their engineering activities. During this period, Sultzer of Germany developed a bullet loom and Poland developed a water jet loom. When one of the recessionary periods ended, new OSHA regulations were beginning to be implemented, and some of the old American looms did not meet specifications. The shuttle-cock looms that did were slow, noisy, and produced dust, a factor in white lung disease. When the recession ended, fabric manufacturers who started purchasing looms again opted for the more modern equipment, which resulted in a loss of sales and market resegmentation for the older U.S. loom manufacturers. The only road left for them was through licensing the newer technology and attempting at considerable cost and risk to catch up. Had there been a consistently more creative environment in this industry, the large business losses may have been prevented.

8. Some companies feel that it is possible to acquire all of their creative requirements. Acquisition of companies or concepts can certainly be used to improve a company's position in an industry, a technology, or a market. The problem occurs when companies take an all-or-nothing position about acquisition when they should strike a balance between creative internal development and externally infused growth through acquisition.

To develop a creative environment in a company we must start at the top. The CEO sets the pace. Desirable internal growth areas should be outlined and then supported with funds, tenacity, and a willingness to take reasonable risks. The companies that fail to use current finances for long-range potential future gain may be putting themselves out of business, for the great corporations of the future will be those that are or become creative today.

Maurice I. Zeldman is president of EMZEE Associates, a management and technical consulting firm that specializes in the management of product development and related areas.

18.
OBSTACLES TO CORPORATE INNOVATION

Shelby H. McIntyre

It is difficult for large corporations to be innovative because of characteristics inherent in their structure. But, with determination and the proper emphasis from top management, it can be done.

Robert J. Mayer, a vice president at Booz, Allen and Hamilton management consultants, recently noted that the lack of innovation "poses a significant threat to U.S. dominance of world wide markets in the 1990's."[1] It has also been suggested that the lag in U.S. productivity behind such world market competitors as West Germany and Japan can be traced, at least in part, to sagging American innovativeness, a phenomenon which has been called "the graying of America."[2] These observers seem to feel that the U.S. needs more innovation if our economy is to prosper. Where is such innovation to come from? Can it be expected from the large corporations with vast resources?

First, I should make clear the distinction between "innovations" and "inventions." Whereas an invention is the creation of a new idea or new knowledge, an innovation is the commercial exploitation of such knowledge.

And where do innovations originate? Perhaps surprisingly, large industrial enterprises, with their vast resources and huge research laboratories, are frequently not the source of the innovations which one might most expect from them. Large corporations turn out their fair share of patents, but do not seem to excel in the commercial exploitation of those patents. For instance, granola was introduced by the back-to-nature movement of sixties, not by General Foods, General Mills, or Quaker Oats; instant photography was introduced by the then fledgling Polaroid Corporation, not by giant Eastman Kodak; computer-based switchboards (PBXs) were introduced by the then tiny Rolm Corporation, not by huge A.T. & T.; micro-computers were introduced by the entrepreneurs at Intel and not by mammoth IBM or Fairchild; Xerography was introduced by the Haloid Corporation (later named Xerox), and not by Addressograph-Lithograph; start-up company Federal Express introduced the overnight package delivery service, via a special jet fleet, even though Emery

Air Freight and United Airlines were much better equipped to make such a move; Tandem Computers, a new start-up company, established an extremely successful commercialization of a fail-safe computer with dual processors running in tandem, even though IBM and the other computer giants had toyed with this idea for years. This list could be greatly extended.

Such examples suggest that large industrial enterprises do not have an edge with respect to being innovative, even though they devote more resources to research and development than do all the smaller firms combined. In fact, Henry E. Riggs states:

"To an amazing extent, major new products incorporating new technology have been brought to the market by new companies, rather than by those companies with large investments in fundamental research...Indeed, it is difficult to name any major new industry that has been created by large companies."[3]

Recognizing these facts, many large corporations have put together venture teams in an effort to stimulate innovation within existing organizations. However, a 1977 survey reveals that corporate-based venture teams may not be a panacea either. Out of ten major corporations contacted, Dan T. Dunn, Jr. found that: "The venture groups at the sample companies were, at best, ineffective and, at worst, embarrassing failures. In fact, none of these companies continues to use venture groups."[4] From the case histories discussed by Dunn, it seems that even the venture teams set up to avoid the corporate hierarchy were not able to escape substantial organizational interference. As Donald A. Schon foresaw:

"The large corporation has created a race of entrepreneurs without authority. The entrepreneurial task has been delegated to those below but not the independence to carry it out...The essence of the problem is that in order to justify investment, the subordinate must bring his ideas to the boss before they have proved themselves, and at that early stage he can never adequately defend them."[5]

The relationship between rate of innovation and size of firm is still being explored. Early economists argued that bigger firms possessed inherent advantages over the smaller ones.[6] But later inquiries revealed that industrial concentration was not on the increase, that the big firms were not supplanting the smaller ones.[7] Some have argued that there is an optimal firm size somewhere in the midrange, which may vary from industry to industry, for maximal innovativeness.[8]

OBSTACLES TO INNOVATION

With such clear advantages—the vast resources and sophisticated labs, experienced marketing departments, economic media buys, well-known corporate names, existing channels of distribution, and so on—why aren't large corporations developing more of the successful and innovative new products and services? Why are large organizations continually beaten to the marketplace by smaller firms with many fewer resources? The obstacles to innovation stem from the nature of large corporations, whose principal purpose and strength is to manage and maintain an already achieved base of success. The conservatism and inertia in large organizations give rise to the following difficulties.

1.   Very large organizations foster resistance to change.

A large corporation is a formalized structure which maintains and manages the successes of the past. Procedures have been designed to achieve efficiency in "doing what we do best." Innovation disrupts the stable state of corporate society, interfering with the corporation's vigorous and continuing efforts to be efficient at what it does and, therefore, to stay as it is. In a large, established organization, innovation thus meets a wall of resistance to change.

2.   Innovation may threaten current successes.

Frequently, large corporations are reluctant to innovate in areas which would compete with their already existing products, markets, and/or technologies. Honeywell, for instance might not be expected to develop a digital thermostat because it currently commands the dominant position in the mechanical thermostat market. In addition, huge sums have been spent to automate the production of its mechanical thermostat. The company is not likely to risk losing market share and its capital investment for the sake of innovation.

3.   The corporate hierarchy breeds conservative subordinates.

The relationship of boss and subordinate may lead to conservatism. Subordinates who take risks are exposed to the possibility of bad outcomes. Since bosses tend to spend more time worrying about problems than thinking about successes, bad outcomes are more likely to be noticed and remembered than good outcomes. The subordinate who takes risks thus may turn up as the one who seems to cause the most problems. When the subordinate and the boss are not in daily contact, it is difficult for the boss to evaluate the appropriateness of the subordinate's risk-taking. At higher levels, where subordinates and bosses have even less frequent contact, negative consequences of risk-taking by subordinates may be more pronounced. To the extent that this observation of corporate life pertains, truly innovative people are not as likely to be promoted and rewarded in a large corporation as are their more conservative counterparts. As a result, large corporations tend to be staffed with more conservative people.

4.   Product/market boundary charters sometimes preclude innovation.

When development work goes on within a corporate divisional structure, division business charters sometimes cut off potentially successful innovations because they do not match the current narrow objectives of that division.

5. In a large organization, the separation of power constitutes a "weakest link" constraint on innovation.

Innovation requires both development and marketing of the product. These functions are usually separated in large organizations because specialization is believed to enhance efficiency. As a result, coordination is more difficult, and inflexibility is likely. The separation of development and marketing leads to a "propose and dispose syndrome,"[9] where each function is free to propose something which must be disposed of, or acted upon, by the other function. Since enthusiasm and vision are critical to innovation, it is difficult for one function to sell its idea to the other. The result is conservative moves that satisfy the minimal vision of both functions.

6. The politics of large organizations can lead to compromises that decrease the effectiveness of attempts at innovation.

The balance of organizational power can lead to other difficulties, ones ex-emplified by the old adage that "a camel is a horse designed by a committee." V. Stefflre observes that new product champions sometimes try to form a coali-tion of committed advocates to a project by delegating out selected components of the development process so that each group involved gets something that they personally want. Stefflre recounts the following hypothet-ical example as being representative of what he has sometimes encountered during his career as a new product consultant to various consumer packaged goods companies.

"Suppose R&D has built a milder product. The president may have been bugging marketing management about the company's failure to sell to children; the agency may have been working out a new campaign focusing on strength; and the packaging group may have some plastic packaging techniques they wish to try out and the market research department some new data collec-tion devices. Then, the new product will be researched using the new data collection devices and soon appear as aimed for children, exhibiting a new and improved packaging, with a strong advertising campaign to compensate for the unusual mildness of the product itself. The product will then move successfully through the organization as each major group sees it as satisfying some need. The product may then fail in the market (hopefully only in the test market) through what will be counted for within the organization as an 'act of God.' Products of this type fail to achieve a proper 'fit' between the product and its packaging, advertising, and marketing plan. The net result is a product seen by consumers as a nothing product—not because it doesn't have striking components but rather because they point in different directions and cancel each other out. Each member of the coalition can then, with justification, blame participants other than himself for the product's failure and everyone, but the man responsible for profits, is left happy."[10]

7. The largest firms tend to emphasize short-run efficiency.

Large organizations use management control systems which emphasize financial measures. Short-term profits, the bottom line, and return on investment become the objectives. These are measured on a yearly basis. But the payoff from innovation is typically at least five or more years.[11]

8. The rotation system of training managers at large corporations develops a short-run perspective in managers.

Large enterprises train their managers by rotating them through the organization. Assignments for fast-track, bright managers are seldom made for more than two years. Thus, these individuals do not see innovations as being within their horizons on any particular assignment.

9. Large organizations can only get excited about something big.

Frequently, large corporations view a given market opportunity as too small to be interesting. However, these small market niches sometimes mushroom into sizable markets over time when proper market development is practiced (as happened, for instance, with the markets for granola, fiber optics, and lasers). Spin-off firms are often started by individuals who leave a large firm because it does not allow them to pursue an innovative project. Sometimes these spin-offs become very successful. The Control Data Corporation is a prime example. CDC was a spin-off from the Univac division of Sperry Rand in 1957; now CDC dwarfs its parent organization.

10. Large firms have marketing departments that follow, rather than lead, the market.

Narrow and inappropriate application of the marketing concept has sometimes led companies to be driven by market needs which are extant and to ignore latent or potential needs. If too much reliance is placed on market surveys, consumer questionnaires, and test panels for new product ideas, the tendency is to develop incremental product improvements or changes in existing products rather than to develop new products for which there may be no readily perceived or existing market.

11. For large organizations, growth opportunities exist through acquisition.

Sometimes large organizations think in terms of achieving growth through acquisition. Such a strategy is essentially evidence of the greater difficulty of being innovative within the existing corporate structure. But the decision to emphasize a strategy of absorbing already successful innovations may discourage new developments at home.

OVERCOMING OBSTACLES

The typical entrepreneurial business, which has brought us so many innovations in the past, suffers far less from the above problems. The entrepreneur is an individual who does not answer to a given boss on short-run outcomes, who can appreciate and thus integrate both the capabilities of the firm and the need of the market, who sees beyond the short-term financial figures, and who does not rotate through the organization and thus can develop a long-run perspective. Furthermore, the entrepreneur, by definition, has a vision of what could be, rather than what is, and sees the rewards of going after a small, fledgling market. Finally, the entrepreneur has no vested interest in the existing technology or market due to fear of cannibalization.

It should be remembered that many of the weaknesses of large corporations, from the point of view of innovation, are the very strengths which generate economic efficiencies in managing already developed products, markets, and technologies. As H. I. Ansoff and R. G. Brandenburg point out, performance objectives for business are often inherently incompatible. For instance, it is not possible to maximize both current operating efficiency and strategic responsiveness.[12]

Does all of this mean that large corporations should avoid innovation? Certainly not. But it does suggest that large organizations must be cognizant of the fact that innovation will not happen easily; it must be fostered, nurtured, and actively pursued. There are a few large corporations which have been successful over the long term at being innovative, such as 3M, Texas Instruments, Hewlett-Packard, International Harvester, and Wang Laboratories. These exceptional corporations have a spirit of innovation at the top of the organization, and this spirit is communicated and reflected down the hierachy. To overcome the obstacles to innovation, these companies use the following techniques:

1.   Goals are set for innovative achievement.
At 3M, for instance, every division is expected to get 25 percent of its sales each year from products that did not exist five years earlier. As Daniel J. Mac Donald, general manager of 3M's Occupational Health and Safety Products Division, comments: "Our top executives are never interested in what you've already got on the market. They want to know what's new."[13]

2.   Managers are encouraged to take a long-term perspective.
As Dr. J. Elder, General Manager of the New Business Ventures Division of 3M, notes: "We only think of Cinderella on the night of the Ball, but we tend to forget she was around being formed for eighteen years before that. So it is with new technology and new ventures."[14]

3.   Successful innovation is rewarded.
At International Harvester, inventors are given large cash bonuses and lavish praise. An $11,000 banquet was recently thrown for one inventor.

4.   Failures are accepted as part of the game.
Managers and researchers who spawn a loser often are given a second and

third chance by companies which realize that even the most effective innovator faces a high risk of failure in the extremely complex and competitive business of innovation.

5. Engineers and research scientists are encouraged to meet the customer.

A recent survey of high technology firms noted that business units managers in successful, high-technology companies encourage their product development engineers to get out into the field. These managers want their designers to meet users directly in their own environment rather than having user's needs communicated to designers via the marketing department. Hank Gauthier, a division manager at Coherent Corporations, notes:

> There is a danger that the marketing identification of an opportunity will not get translated down to the lab inventors in a way that they can completely appreciate. To overcome that, you have to have the lab people get out to see the customer, to appreciate his point of view. These are things that are very difficult to communicate through a written report. These customer interactions can trigger creative thought on the part of the design engineer that may never really come to the mind of the marketer. This relationship between the design engineers and the customer also has a motivational component. The marketing department doesn't have to work as hard to sell the designer what features and characteristics the product needs to have.[15]

6. Special unrestricted funds are made available to explore innovative ideas without upper-level approval.

For instance, Texas Instruments has a program called IDEA which allows forty program representatives throughout the company to finance long-shot projects without any higher-level approval.

7. Customers are carefully screened to identify new ideas.

User groups and customer conferences are continually held to identify customer reactions, problems, ideas, and innovative suggestions. Hewlett-Packard and Wang Laboratories have institutionalized these procedures.

Large corporations face substantial obstacles to innovation. If top management is not vigorous enough at encouraging and stimulating innovation, it is unlikely to occur. But the obstacles to corporate innovation can be overcome, and some leading corporations have created the appropriate climate. There appears to be no panacea, such as the much touted corporate-venture groups approach. It takes creative, planned, long-term determination and emphasis by top management to generate the innovative results.

References

1. "How Four Companies Spawn New Products by Encouraging Risks," *The Wall Street Journal*, September 18, 1980.

2. Robert H. Hays, "Return to Risk Management Attitude Essential," *The Challenge*, 1977: 6-9.
3. Henry E. Riggs, "The Case for Technology Entrepreneurs," *The Stanford Engineer*, Spring-Summer 1980: 11-19.
4. Dan T. Dunn, Jr., "The Rise and Fall of the Venture Groups," *Business Horizons*, October 1973: 32-41.
5. Donald A. Schon, *Technology and Change* (New York: Delacorte Press, 1967).
6. J. A. Schumpeter, *Capitalism, Socialism and Democracy*, 3rd Ed. (New York: Harper and Row, 1950): Chapters VII and VIII.
7. J. Jewkes, "Are the Economies of Scale Unlimited?" in *Economic Consequences of the Size of Nations* (New York: Macmillan, 1963): 102.
8. F. M. Schere, *Industrial Market Structure and Economic Performance* (Chicago: Rand McNally, 1970).
9. Schon, *Technology and Change*: 126.
10. V. Stefflre, *New Products and New Enterprises: A Report on an Experiment in Applied Social Science*, University of California, Irvine, March 31, 1971.
11. Norman D. Fast, "New Venture Departments: Organizing for Innovation," *Industrial Marketing Management*, 1978: 77-88.
12. H. I. Ansoff and R. G. Brandenburg, "A Language for Organizational Design: Part I and Part II," *Management Science*, August 1971: B705-31.
13. "How Four Companies..."
14. "Minnesota Technology Wellspring," *Scientific American*, October 1980: M-4.
15. A. V. Burno, S. H. McIntyre, and T. T. Tyebjee, "The Marketing Concept in High Technology Firms," *Marketing Science Institute Report*.

Shelby H. McIntyre is an assistant professor of marketing at the University of Santa Clara in California. He is the author of numerous articles.

19.
DON'T LET GROUP NORMS STIFLE CREATIVITY

Robert R. Blake
Jane Srygley Mouton

> Group norms—shared attitudes or opinions—can be changed to promote
> group creativity. If group members participate in making the change, the
> payoff will be well worth the effort.

Two months ago you assembled the six most talented individuals you could
find for your new project team. They were bright, eager, and quite knowledgeable in their fields of expertise. The project seemed to get off to an enthusiastic
start; three or four members had several innovative ideas worthy of considering
for the project.

At first there were heated arguments about the best direction to take. After a
few weeks, however, you noticed that the were settling into fairly routine
actions and that, in fact, all six of them were agreeing on conventional
solutions to the problems. Most of the "new" ideas offered were not new at all
but, rather, rehashed programs that had proven inadequate. The plans they
presented do not seem to exhibit any of that innovation and talent you were
counting on. What stifled it?

TARGETING INDIVIDUALS OR THE GROUP?

This very question has been asked by forward-looking managers in many
companies at one time or another. Answering it is particularly important when
new conditions demand that changes be made—when the traditional solutions
no longer lead to bottom-line progress.

In searching for an answer, the most natural place to look is at the individuals involved. Are most of them bright but lazy? Are they "loner" types
whose best "style" is to work independently? Maybe the particular mix of
people has some "personality conflicts" and can't agree on anything. The
attitudes of individuals, then, become the target. Efforts to change them in-

clude such actions as replacing the laziest members, instituting democratic "rules" for reaching agreement so that everyone can be heard and appreciated, or even dividing up tasks so that each member can solve his or her own piece of the problem.

GROUP NORMS

While some or all of these explanations provide some insight into problems of individuals, the key point is overlooked: Our attitudes arise from an "invisible" influence—the *norms* of the groups in which we participate.

A norm is an attitude, opinion, feeling, or action shared by two or more people—that guides their behavior. Groups are characterized by the norms their members share. The *norms* of a group regulate and coordinate interactions among its members. If norms were absent, we might refer to the individuals physcially assembled in the same place as an *aggregate*, but not as a group.

We can understand the project group's low level of creativity by first examining the role of norms and traditions operating within groups. Second, we can look at how norms arise. Finally, understanding how group norms can change from a stagnant status quo to productive problem solving provides the key to unleashing maximum creativity.

The concepts of norms, standards, and traditions are not often used to describe individuals. Groups have norms, but individuals usually are not pictured that way. We may speak of someone as having an attitude or values, but it is more customary to speak of a group as having norms or traditions. Even though it is individuals who transmit the norms of the group, the norms and traditions themselves belong to groups, not individuals.

The project team above, then, may share certain behavioral regularities: 30-minute coffee breaks, getting started late, or waiting for a certain member to read over the plans from the last meeting. These habits, which are reinforced over time, become the group's norms and traditions. Other norms can center on such operating modes as avoiding conflict so that no member's feathers are ruffled or requiring a majority vote on each idea adopted. Traditions, precedents, and policies also constitute norms that may either stimulate or stifle creativity.

GROUP COHESION IN THE WORK PLACE

Common interests, values, and attitudes among group members contribute to a group's *cohesion*. At the outset, people are attracted to those with similar backgrounds and interests; as they share experiences over time, they come to develop common feelings, norms, and customs. Psychological studies have demonstrated repeatedly that members of a cohesive group tend to conform to group norms even if it means contradicting a previously held opinion not shared by the group.

THE TWO SIDES OF CONFORMITY

The process by which group attitudes and behavioral norms are adopted is called *convergence* toward the norm. Social forces powerful enough to influence members to conform may influence them to perform at a very high level of quality and productivity. All too often, however, the pressure to conform stifles creativity, influencing members to cling to attitudes that may be out of touch with organizational needs and even out of kilter with the times. As a result, important innovations are not made, and there is a heavy price to pay.

The managers you handpicked on the project team converged toward a norm of low productivity and routine thinking. Whenever a member pressed for an innovative or bold approach to the problem at hand, others in the group ignored or opposed his or her position. The member who persisted with a "deviant" viewpoint would have been promptly rejected by the others. An understanding of how convergence toward the group norm and conformity operate can be seen in the fate of a General Motors executive who challenged the "big car" norm. For a while, the other members tried to swing the executive around to their point of view. When they were unsuccessful, the manager was ignored but not forgotten and, eventually, terminated.

Once a norm is established, conformity pressures keep it in use. In many respects, this is basic to the exercise of cooperation. But this cooperation may no longer be in tune with the needs of the time—when cooperative employees in a "smoothly running" status quo operation are not enough to meet the demands of new competition, regulation, cutbacks, or other environmental forces.

WHY MOST CHANGE EFFORTS FAIL

Unaware that norms exist, many managers who want to increase creativity rely on the exercise of unilateral power to compel shifts in behavior. Such a manager may say to a lethargic group, "I demand that this group get hopping right away. We need some solutions around here fast. Furthermore, we need to move in a completely different direction. What we've been doing is no good anymore." These statements rest on the assumption that the command itself is strong enough to produce the desired behavior.

The method is sometimes successful, but far more often it fails because the people who are supposed to "get hopping" usually resist. They would rather act according to the prevailing norms set by their colleagues' behavior than to follow a boss's directives—though they may not realize this specifically and consciously. Change-by-decree not only provokes resistance, but also may alienate those expected to shift their behavior.

Using a different strategy, you may decide to take a "go slow" approach to change. Over a period of time, you know what the norms are and you discourage an "overnight" approach to change. But without a systematic effort to evaluate norms and develop a change strategy, you may become merely the spokesperson for the group's normative culture and fail to influence any real change.

SHIFTING THE NORMS IN YOUR ORGANIZATION

After prevailing norms are identified and understood, specific steps can be taken toward shifting to norms that better serve corporate objectives. In examining a work group's existing attitudes and values, new norms can be explored for increasing productivity and creativity. The key to achieving such a norm shift, however, is to involve those who are controlled by a norm in changing the norm. Let's examine the conditions for accomplishing this:

1. Organizational members who need to shift their behavior should become active participants in the systematic change process. A first step is to help decision makers identify the assumptions they make as they work to achieve results with and through others. The Managerial Grid® framework (see Exhibit 1) has been useful in this respect. After studying theories of leadership, conflict management, and the role of group norms and culture, team members openly discuss and evaluate prevailing norms before adopting new ones.

2. The managers responsible for ultimate decisions lead the change effort. If you, the project team leader, are not involved in the process of thinking through the limitations of existing norms, you can't support and approve the development of new, more appropriate norms. Quality Circle (QC) and Quality of Work Life (QWL) approaches to change, for example, have often been hampered by the absence of the leader whose behavior and attitudes strongly influence subordinates. Project team managers who examine their own leadership approaches and receive feedback from other managers in a seminar setting can examine their own behavior in light of theory-based leadership.

3. Because group norms are rarely self-evident, the development of a strategy by which participants can identify and address problems is essential to managing norms and standards. One way to do this is to formulate an open, direct, and unbiased statement that identifies the problem. Then ask participants what can be done to solve it. Applying this strategy to your project team, you and the team members would discuss dissatisfaction with the low quality of your output and diagnose the problem. Only after

the group focuses on the problem can the norm become visible and commitments be made toward solutions.

4. Facts and data to clear up misconceptions that hold an unproductive norm in place are provided. With 9,9-oriented communication (see Exhibit 1), a free and open exchange of information facilitates the rejection of an old norm and the acceptance of one that squares better with the facts in the situation.

5. Opportunities are provided to ventilate feelings and emotions. In this way negative attitudes that prevent constructive problem solving are dissolved and new norms developed.

6. Casual agreements made during the process are crystallized to prevent misunderstandings later on. Clarification, written recordings, and repeated communication of group agreements about change prevent confusion from diluting the effectiveness of planned norm shifts.

7. Follow-up is essential to support changes in norms. Because new norms are always weaker than those they replace, people tend to backslide toward the norm that previously prevailed. After the project team has adopted new norms, the manager and team should regularly review them for slippage.

8. Although the above steps can lead to effective changes in any work group, the best results occur when they are consistent with organizationwide efforts to merge attitudes toward productivity with high organizational performance.

MOVING OUT OF THE PREDICAMENT

A large regional utilities company was able to solve problems arising from the norms that were hampering a project team's progress in making key decisions. Pressures were mounting after unexpected fuel cost increases and new technological developments triggered staggering first-quarter losses.

The engineering division manager faced a number of tough decisions concerning the newest plant. His project team began to flounder, even though he had handpicked the members who, he thought, were the best people around. After he and another division manager discussed these problems and began to examine the norms and culture of their company, they realized that operations were conducted primarily on a "compromise" basis. Few people wished to "rock the boat" by suggesting plans or programs that departed from past precedents. On the Grid framework in Exhibit 1 they identified this as 5,5, or "Organizational Man" management, because a moderate level of concern for production balanced a moderate level of concern for people.

The project team manager and team members decided to spearhead an effort to raise the quality of the team's recommendations. They developed a norm-shifting action plan that included several facets. First they discussed their drift toward mediocrity and then wrote a short description of the problems as they saw them.

As it turned out, there were several misconceptions about the reasons for the needed plant changes. Once these were cleared up with some relevant cost data and an open discussion, productive plans were made with the full commitment of the team members.

Another serious problem had been the manager's lack of involvement with the group. Although he expected top-quality results, it appeared to the team that they would have to take all the "heat" from any off-beat or risky recommendations they made. As the manager became involved with the team in identifying the problems and prevailing norms, they were able to move toward adopting the norms that promoted rather than retarded innovation in the company. Follow-up activities included the team's making a short weekly re-

Exhibit 1.

The Managerial Grid ®

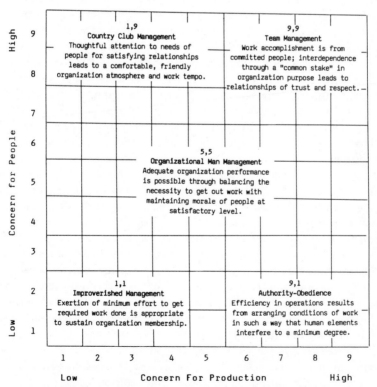

Source: Blake, Robert R. and Mouton, Jane S. *The Managerial Grid III: The Key to Leadership Excellence*. Houston: Gulf Publishing Company, 1985, P. 12. Reproduced by permission.

port on Monday morning and tracking their progress during the past week. Backsliding was also recognized and addressed in these sessions.

Team members began feeling freer to entertain ideas that had not been tried before. The 9,9 Grid theory of principled management offered a model for team members to use in giving one another feedback and critique. Even though they spent some time in heated debate about the efficacy of one or another proposal, the quality of the recommendations improved dramatically. After several of their plans were successfully implemented in the new plant, they began taking pride in their identity as innovative trouble-shooters.

NORM SHIFTING FOR PRODUCTIVITY: ANOTHER EXAMPLE

Employees in a large plant had gotten into the habit of slacking off during the last hour of the day's shift. Supervisors were aware of the problem and felt pressure from their managers to take action. However, the problem seemed so entrenched that they considered it virtually insoluble. Instead, the supervisors avoided the problem by burying themselves inside their offices with paperwork during that hour of the day. After management confronted the supervisors with the issue, the 4 managers and 20 supervisors began meeting together to diagnose and remedy the problem. Previous attempts to solve it were evaluated so that ineffective plans could be understood and avoided in the future. In a discussion of the underlying reasons for the problem, supervisors zeroed in on their own feelings about who was to blame for the problem. Finally, it was agreed that none of the managers had felt any responsibility for turning the problem around. A group norm of allowing the problem to continue arose from the distrust the supervisors had felt toward one another.

At the next several meetings the discussion opened up. Solutions were developed and plans made. An action plan was formulated. It was agreed that during the first few weeks all supervisors would meet with their employees about the new plans, and the supervisors *themselves* would become visibly active in their work area. During the next few weeks the supervisors talked to anyone seen slacking off and interviewed them to see if they understood the new plan. If the behavior continued, disciplinary actions were to be taken. It turned out, however, that no disciplinary actions were needed. The supervisors' commitment to solving the problem was enough to clear the air and improve morale among supervisors and employees alike. The supervisors reconvened twice to review progress.

This approach to the problem of slacking off is a good example of how norm shifting can be used to replace a "do nothing" norm that had been held in place by the distrust the supervisors felt toward one another.

CONDITIONS THAT PROMOTE CREATIVITY

Although many approaches aimed at reducing the effects of conformity have been developed, the more genuine solution is for group members to understand and *themselves* counteract the constraints exerted by these pressures. Brainstorming and other techniques that involve "rules" aimed at reducing convergence or conformity effects may be useful. Ultimately, however, creativity will be heightened to the greatest extent when members acquire discussion skills that enable them to retain independence in the face of pressures. When problems and proposed solutions depend on an objective, critical examination of the facts at hand, it is particularly important that group participants be able to monitor and modify the influence of group norms.

THE MANAGEMENT OF NORMS

Recognizing and observing the effects of norms as an "invisible web of control," then, is essential to managing the dynamics of norms and conformity in the work place. The process of leading a norm-changing effort involves managers in a systematic study of the role of norms in their own operational units. All employees who share prevailing norms must be involved in examining and redirecting them if any productive change is to occur. Through strategy-development sessions in which data are shared, emotions ventilated, and agreements clarified, the negative attitudes and misunderstandings that block progress can be overcome. Finally, an organizationwide focus on development and strategic change prevents the adoption of "patched on" solutions that can slip under pressure.

Dr. Robert R. Blake is chairman of Scientific Methods, Inc. of Austin, Texas. Jane Srygley Mouton is the president of Scientific Methods, Inc. These two have co-authored more than 30 books. The Managerial Grid, published by Gulf Publishing Company, has sold more than one million copies.

20.
TECHNOLOGICAL INNOVATION, ENTREPRENEURSHIP, AND STRATEGY

James Brian Quinn

Historically, western societies have largely relied on the individual inventor/entrepreneur for many of their most startling innovations. In order to meet the enormous challenges of our times, large institutions must understand and exploit the individual entrepreneurial system.

Innovation—creating and introducing original solutions for new or already identified needs—must be one of the central themes for society and for technological management during the next few decades. The challenges are new and on a scale never before attempted by mankind. If one believes the most prevalent projections, the U.S. and world must within the next fifteen to twenty years:

- Feed a new population as large as the world's entire population in 1940,[1] but with less massive use of chemical fertilizers and biocides.
- Develop and deliver as much new energy as has been produced in all history to date[2]—with each increment harder to find and develop—and yet eliminate acid rains like those which have reached pH3 levels in Sweden and New England.
- Meet additional demands for foods, raw materials, and products 100 percent greater than today's,[3] with land resources ever more marginal and safe waste disposal ever more difficult.
- Generate net real capital at an annual rate at least twice as high as today's despite governments' preemption of capital for social redistributions.
- Genuinely improve the living, working, educational, urban, and environmental habitats of people in both industrialized and developing countries.
- Simultaneously increase each nation's health standards, shift from disease

cure to morbidity prevention systems, and restrain population growth within reasonable bounds.

- Employ 30 to 50 percent more people, many in service industries, while increasing productivity enough to halt inflation.
- Accomplish all this without fatally disturbing natural equilibria or creating resource crises that lead to war.

Although some elitists might choose to ignore them, these demands represent the genuine needs of the world's population. Despite some claims to the contrary,[4] we cannot accomplish these aims using today's technology, much less yesterday's. To live even as well tomorrow as today, in real material and social terms, is impossible without significant changes. Because of the massive investments needed for many solutions, much of this innovation will have to occur in large institutions.[5]

Unfortunately in the past, although some large institutions have been quite innovative, most have not. Historically, western societies have depended on the individual inventor/entrepreneur for many of their most startling innovations.[6] In fact, this "individual entrepreneurial system" has proved history's most successful method for meeting new human needs. Policy makers should try to understand why this system has worked so well and what problems and potentialities exist in adapting its approaches to larger organizations and the huge-scale problems of the future. In my experience, I have had the opportunity to observe and study scores of technical/entrepreneurial ventures. While one could select from many specific examples, two well-documented classics typify successful individual technical/entrepreneurial patterns.

Mr. Howard Head

Starting in 1947-8, Mr. Howard Head, then an aerospace designer, metals expert, and ski enthusiast, began to design, build and test metal skis. Working in his home shop he would create a ski, produce a few, and then beg ski professionals to test them. Despite their disparaging comments and three years of broken and twisted skis, Mr. Head persisted. He was described as "possessed by his idea," a "fanatic" on the subject. After each test—and failure—he would redesign the ski, make some more, and take them out for tests. Head worked night and day out of his own home. He ran out of his own money and his company, incorporated with only $8,000 of Head 's capital, almost went under. An infusion of $60,000 (for 40% of the company) at the right moment saved the concern. Only after six to seven years and scores of design failures did Head finally begin to make some money from his enterprise. Hundreds of others had tried to design metal skis, but had failed. Head's skis worked so well they were called "cheaters" by the trade. They sold for $100 in a market used to paying only $25, and helped create the ski boom of the 1950s.[7]

Mr. Chester Carlson

Around 1935, Mr. Chester Carlson, former carbon chemist, printer, and patent lawyer, was working in the patent office of Mallory Company. He was disturbed by the cost and errors involved in typing and copying patterns for transmission to outsiders. Carlson began to work nights and weekends, at home and in the public library, to create a copying process. He experimented with various photoelectric plate surfaces and adhering black powders. Working with very simple equipment and a part-time employee in a rented room, Carlson got his first image in October 1938. With a crude demonstration device, he agonizingly went from company to company seeking development support. But they all turned him down. No one could visualize the potential of the process; there was no significant copying business then. By 1942, Carlson had obtained patents on basic concepts in the process. But by then Carlson was, in his words, "in desperate straits" financially, although he only had some $3,000 invested in the process. Finally, in 1944, a "vest pocket" division Battelle had set up to sponsor new ideas agreed to use some of its own money for development in return for a share in potential royalties.

In 1947, as a result of seeing a write-up of one of Carlson's patents, a small company named Haloid investigated and agreed to license and develop the process. The company's existing products were stagnating, and its president, Joseph Wilson, was willing to take risks to develop an entirely new market. Although xerography became one the of the great success stories of all time, it was not profitable until the early 1950s, thirteen to seventeen years after its conception.[8]

These and many other similar examples reveal clear patterns as to why this form of entrepreneurship has been so effective.

FANATICISM/COMMITMENT

The system allows talented fanatics a way to pursue their ideas without the personality pressures and second guessing typical in large organizations. For success, the individual must be fanatically committed in order to endure the pain, frustration, and effort of overcoming the technical and market obstacles that always confront a new idea. The system permits the match-up of personalities, opportunities, and incentives under which such people thrive. It frees the innovator to interact flexibly with other experts and users without intervening bureaucracies.

CHAOS ACCEPTANCE

The inventor/entrepreneur is not bound to formal plans or PERT charts of progress. Progress on a new innovation typically comes in spurts among unforeseen delays and setbacks. He accepts and even enjoys the essential chaos of development. And he does not have to waste time explaining his progress—or lack thereof—to a board or legislature with less commitment and with false expectations concerning the speed and orderliness of progress.[9]

LOW EARLY COSTS

Because the inventor/entrepreneur works out of his own home, his overhead cost is minimal. He invents to avoid costs. He uses sweat capital instead of dollars for materials or equipment. As a result, failure cost is low and not publicly visible. Although many failures occur, there are no formal inquiries when the entrepreneur is wrong. Future progress is not inhibited by past failure or fear that such failure could be represented as a fraud against the public or stockholders.

NO DETAILED CONTROLS

In the early stages, detailed market estimates are costly, inaccurate, and perhaps misleading. Early estimates of such things as computers, xerography, and metal skis were all misleading. No market existed for such products. Consequently, market estimates both seriously understated potentials and entirely missed the products' opening market niches. For example, Head skis were first successful for beginning, not expert, skiers; xerography started as a method for making cheap lithographic originals. Early market estimates repeatedly indicated: that only 5,000 Xerox machines would ever be sold; that the total computer market was limited to 30-300 units operating at millisecond speeds; and that "metal skis were no good and would never sell," especially at a $100 price.

INCENTIVES/RISKS

The individual inventor/entrepreneur can satisfy his personal desires for money, achievement, or recognition, and is motivated to do so. Because he is a committed expert in the field, he perceives the risk as less than any review group would. He does not panic when others might. This becomes especially important when risking money on very large-scale systems.[10]

LONG TIME HORIZONS

The inventor/entrepreneur is undeterred by the seven to fifteen years that typically elapse between invention and financial success.[11] He does not make detailed financial calculations of such matters. He defines success as of the time of exploitation, and he provides a continuity of interest and support for the entire development cycle.

FLEXIBLE FINANCIAL SUPPORT

The inventor/entrepreneur is not dependent on any single financial source. If one source will not satisfy, others may. At crucial times there are specialized venture capitalists used to taking "one out of twenty" development risks. They are not bound by the bureaucracies or the inflexibilities of large organizations or government agencies. They do not rely on detailed analyses of financial projections to make their judgments. They evaluate the concept of the business, the capabilities of the entrepreneur, and the broad dimensions of the opportunity rather than the details of its finances. They recognize that, in any new venture, forecasts are so inaccurate that they must trust their judgment of people much more than numbers.[12]

MULTIPLE COMPETING APPROACHES

For every success there are hundreds of failures. Thus, although the probability of any one individual succeeding is low, the large number of contenders actually makes the probability of satisfying any real need very high.

NEED ORIENTATION

Because the only solution that survives is the one that will sell, the individual inventor/entrepreneur keeps his eyes glued to the market need. He gets as close as he can to the marketplace and opportunistically snatches anything that will help solve his problem. The entrepreneur's lack of resources and risk of his own property force invention and rapid adoption of any new solutions. There is a minimum of the NIH (Not Invented Here) complex. The entrepreneur's loyalties are to the idea and its success—not to promotion in a vertical organization.

Unfortunately the individual entrepreneur is unlikely to resolve completely many of the large-scale technological problems now facing our society and the world. But he is likely to help in their solutions. Thus, as policy makers approach today's major problems, they should both maintain the health of the individual entrepreneurial system and try to design its most important success characteristics into any new institutions formulated. Similarly, large existing institutions should try to learn from such experiences and adapt the best characteristics of this remarkable system.

LARGE INSTITUTION PROBLEMS

Instead, many large organizations operate in a mode which actively discourages entrepreneurial innovation. Their most common shortcomings are outlined below.

Fanatics versus Organization. The kind of entrepreneur described above is neither political nor power oriented. He is obnoxious, impatient, egoistic, and perhaps even a bit irrational in organization terms. As a consequence, he is not hired. If hired, he is not promoted or rewarded. He is regarded as "not a serious person," "embarrassing," or "disruptive." He quickly builds up political resistance in the organization. He rarely stays long enough to complete his innovation, often preferring to go it alone after his large organization frustrations.[13]

Expect Orderly Advance. Various groups within large organizations expect technological advance to be orderly. They insist on PERT or CPM methodologies to plan or track the innovation. When, as predictably happens, the innovation does not follow plan, it is deemed a failure. Consequently, the technical group begins to work to prove the plan rather than to achieve innovation on the shortest and least costly cycle. By definition, the things that go wrong are the things the planner could not anticipate. This is why Murphy's Law works. It is also the reason why projects constantly run behind schedule, cost more than anticipated, and bring technical groups under fire for "low productivity." One well-known organization even went so far as to charge its technical management for failures to achieve anticipated profits on products not yet invented.

Spend Too Much. In many organizations, as soon as a new technical project is identified, it is charged with its full personnel, materials, overhead, and backup costs. The innovator cannot lower his cost by using his sweat capital. No one is encouraged to work all night because all speed-ups lead to increased charges for overtime or doubletime. As a result, progress is slow, and early stage costs soar. The project quickly becomes unattractive in present value terms. As costs mount, the political exposure of the project becomes ever higher, as does its criticism. Consequently, much of the really innovative technical work in such organizations is hidden from management and carried on "underground," for fear it will be killed.

Detailed Control Too Soon. As soon as a project is defined, professional managers seek market research information to justify its potential returns. They ignore the facts that an adequate market research study might actually cost more than the risk of carrying the project ahead, or that the market information may be positively misleading. Chaos or parallel approaches to the same goal are unacceptable; such things appear "wasteful" or "duplicative" to orderly professional managers. Formal procedures become necessary to make up drawings, get model shop work, obtain equipment, or utilize technicians. As a result, the time between experiments lengthens, the cost of each experiment soars, and innovative productivity plummets.

Don't Reward Risk. Most organizations, business or political, operate under the management control concept of "no surprises." But development is by its very definition a surprise. Subordinates are penalized if they work on something and are wrong, but no penalties are attached to missing an opportunity entirely. Rewards do not accrue to those who perform superbly on a failing project. And if successful on high payoff projects, technical people are rarely made millionaires or given rewards perceptible to outside peers.

Time Scale Conflict. As noted, the typical major innovation takes some seven to fifteen years from first discovery to profitability.[14] At any reasonable rate of return, present value calculations decrease future returns to extremely low levels. Because of long time horizons, uncertain market information, and high early cost, major innovations appear essentially irrational if analyzed by standard financial techniques. Consequently, many companies purposely undertake a "strong second" posture, letting others undertake the initial innovation. They then try to move powerfully with their established marketing, large-scale manufacturing, or finance capabilities to take over the already proven market. Unfortunately, if a whole industry follows this policy, that industry is likely to become strongly second rate, and the nation's trade suffers.

Control Systems. Most companies' control systems are dominantly financial. Because other factors like product quality, image, and innovativeness are difficult to measure, they do not become bases for rewards. Producing units are held accountable primarily for ROI-profit performance. And they have little incentive to undertake longer-term development or investment programs which will not meet these criteria in the short run. Corporate financial results are published monthly and quarterly, forcing top management and all lower levels of management toward very short time horizons.[15] This is compounded when managers are not penalized for underinvesting in crucial nonmeasurable areas like skills development, plant maintenance, and technological innovation. Since a manager is likely to move from his existing job within three to four years, he is unlikely to be there when the results of his underinvestment take place.

Top Man Problems. If only one out of twenty advanced development projects really pay out, how can an organization reward a manager who, in his investments, is right even twice as often as one would expect? After all, he will still be wrong 90 percent of the time. Large enterprises tend to make decisions based on forecast data, rather than the venture capitalists' criteria of "the concept, the people, and (only then) the finances." And people willing to take venture capital risk rarely survive the financial controls of these organizations. Hence those who make capital allocations in large enterprises are seldom intuitively comfortable with true "venture financing."

Because of such difficulties, many organizations have tried to centralize risk, taking on new ventures in "development," "entrepreneurial," "new enterprise," or similar groups. Although some such approaches have been successful, most have failed. The main reasons were: 1) corporate time horizons were not long enough to play the probability game and wait for results, 2) venture teams were staffed with professional managers balanced as to their marketing, financial, and technical skills, [16] rather than infused with the deep-seated expertise and personal commitment a real entrepreneur needs, and 3) full costing of ventures (including all overheads) made those ventures difficult to justify in financial terms and excellent targets for cutbacks during short-term economic or organizational crunches.

LARGE-SCALE INNOVATION

Nevertheless, some major enterprises have an extremely fine record in large-scale innovation. We investigated many successful organizations and their practices to see if any clear patterns did appear. We will focus our illustrations here on a few well-documented organizations and innovations know to most technical audiences: The IBM 360 introduction, [17] the practices of Bell Telephone Laboratories, [18] the Xerox 914 introduction, development of synthetic rubber and catalytic cracking by the oil/chemical industry, and the innovation of float glass at Pilkington Brothers, Ltd. [19]

Many formal management techniques can assist in planning and controlling the continuous small-scale innovations that are characteristic of almost any successful enterprise. [20] Some of these are also useful at various stages in managing major large-scale innovations. However, for the latter, other processes seemed to dominate. The following patterns—not surprisingly, quite similar to those found in smaller-scale enterprises—applied to most of the major innovations studied:

1. A strong incentive existed for successful development. Each private company had at risk millions to billions of dollars. However, if successful, IBM or Xerox would achieve powerful positions in their expanding fields; Pilkington would make millions in royalties and control access to important work markets; the oil/chemical industry would meet urgent wartime demands; and Bell-AT&T could defend its monopoly position, expand its revenue base, and defend from obsolescence the largest privately held asset base in the world.

2. A clearly defined need was specified in economic/technical performance

terms for the whole system, each important subsystem, and the interaction of various subsystems. Great care was taken at the outset not to define these needs in terms of particular technologies or solution sets. IBM and Bell at first defined their needs in terms of "user needs," "functions to be performed," "systems architecture," or "black boxes" of input/output characteristics. Pilkington decided early that, to be introduced, its float process must "perform to obsolete existing plate technologies."

3. Multiple competing approaches were encouraged at both the basic research and development levels. This technique serves a different purpose in large company development programs. It a) creates a positive competitive spirit among the people on each program team, b) stimulates scientists' and engineers' commitment to their programs, c) instills a sense of urgency to the work, d) allows the discipline of knowledgeable people critiquing each other's approaches, e) encourages people to invent and to use basic research knowledge to improve their approach to the problem, and f) prevents premature commitment to any single approach. Final system choices can be made as late as possible consistent with the information available. Multiple competing approaches, by being more effective, ultimately end up being more efficient. For such reasons, almost all large-scale innovating companies consciously encouraged parallel development.

4. User guidance and participation in programs insured that specifications remained current and that people who would manufacture, install, service, or use the system had a hand in its development. This interface occurred at all levels of the organization, not just at the technical or top level alone. To facilitate this interface, development groups were placed in physical proximity to research, production, and, when appropriate, marketing groups. People were often moved to locations where face-to-face contacts could more easily occur.

5. High expertise and research discipline were maintained by assembling first-rate people and supplying them with a leader possessing extensive knowledge about programs and their underlying art.[21] Nonperformers were removed from programs. Bell Laboratories, for example, conducted peer reviews of its highly selected basic researchers' performance, and over a decade some nine out of ten of these researchers moved on to other tasks. IBM reassigned its most talented technical people to head its 360 programs and systematically weeded out nonperformers.

6. Time horizons in successful innovative enterprises were longer than those common in their fields. Bell, Xerox, and IBM all had planning and advanced systems groups looking decades ahead, and their top managements began major innovative programs even when product lines appeared solidly positioned for seven to ten years into the future. Pilkington was privately held, was not concerned about short-term stock movements, and was headed by a vigorous chairman in his mid-forties. Each company was

willing to absorb the fiscal drains associated with significant developments. Pilkington, for example, experienced negative cash flows for eleven years on its float glass introduction.

7. Committed champions were encouraged to carry forward major developments. Chairman Vincent Learson created this style at IBM during that company's most innovative period. He encouraged different groups to bring forward proposed designs for "performance shoot-outs" against competing proposals. At one time it was, in fact, difficult to find a successful major IBM innovation that derived directly from formal product planning rather than this championship process. Similarly, Alastair Pilkington, who championed float glass, is now chairman of Pilkington Bros.—the first person outside the direct lineage of the founder to hold that position. And Bell Labs fostered its own breed of Nobel Prize winners and champions (like Shannon, Shockley, and Pierce) for various products and causes. Each system found appropriate ways to reward such champions, sometimes even for extraordinary contributions on projects which failed in the marketplace.

8. Top level risk-taking support. For large-scale innovations to reach fruition, some top executive must be willing to take risks. At IBM, Messrs. Watson and Learson, successive chairmen of the company, were behind the 360 development and maintained close contact with both the program and its potential customers during crucial periods. Pilkington established a special Directors' Float Glass Strategy Committee at the Board level to coordinate float's introduction.

9. Morale-discovery mode. Two common elements in highly productive innovative programs were that objectives were clear to all and identified as genuinely worthwhile by those on the program. High morale occurs when team members intensely share a common goal.[22] "Making more profits" rarely achieved such identity in larger organizations. But creating a significant technical advance did prove energizing. For example, at Pilkington, "people would literally work until they dropped of fatigue and then come back for more" because they saw their innovation as exciting, challenging, and capable of making St. Helens "the creative center of their industry." In successful programs there was a fervor to solve a problem, to genuinely invent, or to create something new for a purpose. Challenging goals stimulated people to look beyond the feasible to the possible.

A CONTRAST TO TODAY

It is fascinating to contrast these characteristics and those in the preceding section with the nation's approaches to today's major problems in energy, environmental improvement, health care, public transportation, productivity, or even urban housing. Sanctions are substituted for incentives. Two to four years' political horizons dominate. There is a search for the one all-encompassing policy (or preplanned solution) rather than tolerance for the chaos of multiple competing approaches, each vying for its piece of the action. Productive fanaticism and commitment are alien to many of the institutions working on such problems. Instead, researchers and technologists are offered civil-servant-like security. And bureaucracies rather than markets or potential users guide major programs.

Political policies discourage top level risk-taking by establishing price controls or "windfall profits" taxes in areas where needs are high. Regulations change too often and on too short a time horizon to develop significant new technologies or to get a payback on them. The media pillory those who do take risks (as in auto exhaust or mpg innovations) by calling them "foot draggers" if they are not successful and "liars" if they said the task was difficult and then succeeded. Incorrect predictions of doom are lionized while successful problem solvers' patents are taken away. Whole programs, like that for controlled fusion, are laid out to the year 2000 on the assumption that little new will be discovered in the future, that nothing will be invented, and that the innovator must solve every problem his technology might possibly create before it can be introduced or even tested. There is no assumption that future inventions might resolve problems if they do appear. Far form encouraging much needed solutions, today's institutions and practices frequently discriminate against the very innovations which are essential to a constantly improving future.

MAJOR ORGANIZATIONAL STRATEGIES

Nevertheless, major organizations can develop real strategies to respond to the large-scale challenges ahead.[23] The process must start at the very top of the organization. People of courage and vision do head many of the nation's largest organizations. These people have such credibility that, if they were willing to take the risks, they could convince both the financial and press communities to report their cases in favorable terms. The response to GM's "downsizing" decisions provides an excellent example. Despite the negative effects of financial controls and reporting, such efforts can be made worthwhile to the companies themselves. After all, favorable P/E ratios are really premiums for anticipated future earnings. Further with a challenging vision of the future, organizations can more easily attract valuable people committed to solving major problems and willing to put forth the entrepreneurial efforts that characterize great enterprises—like IBM, Xerox, Pilkington, Intel, Control Data, or Texas Instruments—in their most productive years. However, this vision must be backed by a number of specific practices which stimulate invention and entrepreneurship throughout the entire organization.

Unlimited Access Concept. Most corporate managers approach the planning-budgetary process as if they were rationing a limited available stock of capital or resources. Venture capitalists and financial houses take another approach—that there is no real limit to available capital. They simple seek ideas or business opportunities of sufficient quality to attract capital at the current price. Even when capital was most scarce, capable people like Gene Amdahl and Seymour Cray were able to quickly obtain backing for ventures where they had sufficient expertise. Similarly, corporations can develop an "unlimited access" attitude and be willing to seek outside capital if necessary to support ideas of adequate quality. The real task, then, is to challenge the organization to produce high quality ideas directed toward its goals and market needs.

Opportunity Planning. To accomplish this, the whole planning process must be converted from a "resource rationing" process into an "opportunity seeking" process. Essentially, the enterprise can define its major areas of expertise and interest broadly. It can then encourage and evaluate proposals to achieve these in the same way the venture capitalist does: first in conceptual terms only, using very broad figures; then through a careful appraisal of the individual or team making the proposal; and finally by considering the company's capacity to support the concept if it is successful. Only if the concept passes muster as a high potential idea would more detailed numerical analysis be used. Then the process must purposely allocate resources to major new innovations as a portion of a "total portfolio." For example, the organization can protect itself by investing the bulk of its resources in traditional, less risky, cash-generating ventures. But overall strategy could purposely define a portion of its total portfolio as investable in longer-term, higher-risk ventures and thus yield new concepts.

Portfolio Planning. Many companies have found such portfolio planning to be an effective way to break out of the short time horizons and risk-averse tendencies of normal control systems. In essence the corporation's total product/business strategy is broken out into its most important thrusts. Each of these thrusts is defined as a coordinated "mission"[24] cutting across all of the several groups or divisions which must support it. For example, the development of a second generation of products might require support from marketing, production, engineering, research and development, and/or specific geographical groups. Figure 1 illustrates how planning in each of several existing divisions could be laterally coordinated toward "mission goals."

Planning within each of the functional groups must insure that sufficient resources are committed behind each mission and that these commitments are coordinated laterally among divisions. Some missions, such as technical work to build the quality leader for a product line or to take care of anticipated environmental requirements, might have negative or very low present values for specific divisions or functional groups. Nevertheless, these investments might be crucial to the success of the total strategy. In short, the requirements of the major missions with a strategy must override the raw ROI or PV rankings of projects within a particular function or division. Otherwise, "current product lines" and "cash cows" obtain all of the organization's attention. Long-term, developmental, and growth-related activities will be systematically driven out of the technical mixture, and the future of the enterprise can be jeopardized. The strategy's major thrusts define the components for the portfolio of missions. These can be segmented by criteria, such as time horizon to payout, risk category, product life cycle, product or geographical area supported, or other criteria appropriate to the specific strategy.

Control System. Clearly, the control system must then be adjusted to measure performance along mission lines. Within each mission, it might be appropriate to rank projects by ROI, PV or other similar criteria. However, the control system should be dominated by the strategy. It must ensure that all of the important goals of the enterprise are served in the patterns intended, not just current profitability. With sophistication and care, this end can be accomplished.

Motivation Systems. Motivation systems must then reward performance toward these goals.[25] In most corporations and government laboratories, the motivation for research and development personnel quickly becomes the completion of publishable papers, the expansion of budgets, and "the carrying

Figure 1.

Schematic Diagram—Missions Crossing Divisions

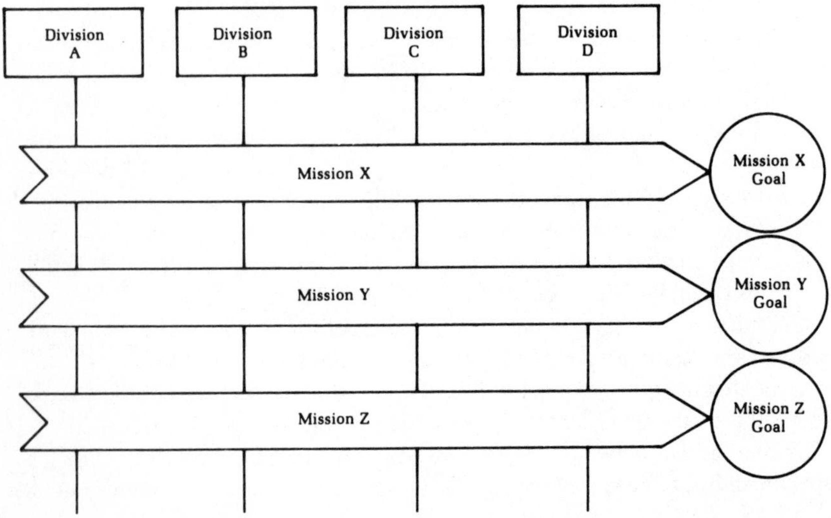

out of investigations." Rarely do such organizations make their technical entrepreneurs into millionaires or give them other perquisites representing
success. A few conglomerating concerns, however, have learned that they
need to reward richly the people who headed their intended growth divisions,
or those people will grow similar enterprises elsewhere. Similarly, outstanding
technical entrepreneurs have been recognized, even if belatedly, by some large
enterprises. Although admittedly tricky to implement, such awards do have
stimulating effects.

Skunk Works. Many companies have found that a most effective way to stimulate truly innovative development is to place a highly talented team of engineers, technicians, and model builders "in a shed" where they can work
closely and informally together—without the formal procedural structures of
larger units. This was the approach used by Cray at Control Data, the
Pilkington float glass development team, Kelly Johnson at Lockheed, Issogonis
at British Motor Corporation, Bruekner at KMS, and numerous other
successful innovative groups in large companies. The approach tends to orient
the group toward its tasks, rather than toward organizational promotion. It
speeds turn-around time, increases the number of experiments, and encourages
all technical, design, and shop personnel to join in the venture as productive
coequals.

Goal Identity. The organization must then recruit people with the necessary
entrepreneurial, inventive outlooks. Often, in recruiting, research-technical
groups squander enormous time checking the applicant's course work, publications, and detailed technical knowledge, and neglect the question of
whether he might really invent something or have the will to see it introduced.
The organization must make clear that its major objectives include innovation
and the directions toward which those innovations should lead. Goals must
appeal to and stimulate technical people, and the organization must seek to
promote identification with these goals by ensuring that employees: 1)
participate in goal establishment, 2) make their own proposals for specific
technical approaches, and 3) are measured and rewarded against challenging
performance goals. The more people can understand, identify with, and internalize stimulating goals, the more likely they are to work productively on
their own, create in relevant directions, and follow through to ultimate uses of
their results.

Win a Few. Finally, managements must allow a sufficient number of projects
and a long enough lead time for the "one in twenty" success ratio to have effect.
Initially, entrepreneurial managers may need to undertake projects with
somewhat lower risk ratios in order to build management confidence. Once top
managements develop a "comfort factor" with a few entrepreneurial investments, they tend to be more willing to accept venturesome risks farther from
traditional approaches, and innovation flourishes.

CONCLUSIONS

There are, of course, no panaceas leading to instant innovativeness. However, such broad guidelines do seem to increase the probability of entrepreneurial action in larger organizations. They are consistent with current knowledge about the entrepreneurial process and, given the enormous challenges of our times, such practices would seem to offer the opportunity for large institutional, national, and profit yields at minimal risks to sponsors. It is essential that technological managers and policy makers learn from past successes and failures those patterns that lead to important innovations. Only then may there be hope that we can reverse one of the tragic trends in our current national posture. There is little doubt that innovative large institutions could solve many of the huge-scale problems of the late twentieth century. But they must be consciously managed to do so.

References

1. This projection assumes a population growth rate of 1.8 percent.
2. This projection assumes an energy growth rate of 4-5 percent.
3. This projection assumes world GNP growth at 4-5 percent.
4. E. Schumacher, *Small Is Beautiful* (New York: Harper & Row, 1973).
5. For some of the national policy issues that this article poses, see J. B. Quinn, "National Policies for Science and Technology: New Approaches for Public Needs," *Research Management*, November 1977, pp. 11-18. Presently, in this article I approach problems at the individual enterprise level.
6. J. Jewkes, D. Sawers, and R. Stillerman, *The Source of Invention* (London: Macmillan & Co., 1985); J. Schmookler, *Invention and Economic Growth* (Cambridge, MA: Harvard University Press, 1966); E. Mansfield, *Industrial Research and Technological Innovation* (New York: Norton, W. W. & Co., 1968).
7. "Head Ski Company" (case study, President and Fellows of Harvard University, 1968); *Wall Street Journal*, 16 January, 1968, p.1.
8. See J. Dessauer, *My Years with Xerox* (New York: Doubleday & Co., 1971); J. Ermenc, "Interview with Chester Carlson, December 1965" (Hanover, NH: Thayer School of Engineering); J. B. Quinn, "Xerox Corporation (A)" (secondary source case, Amos Tuck School, 1978).
9. See D. Schon, *Technology and Change* (New York: Delacorte Press, 1967).
10. For effects of risk perception by the financial community, see: U.S., Department of Commerce, *Technological Innovation: Its Environment and Management*, 1967; "The Consequences of a Worsening Shortage," *Business Week*, 22 September 1975, p. 62.
11. R. C. Dean, Jr., "The Temporal Mismatch—Innovation's Pace vs Management's Time Horizon," *Research Management*, May 1974, pp. 12-15.

12. J. A. Timmons, L. E. Smollen, and A. L. M. Dingee, Jr., *New Venture Creation: A Guide to Small Business Development* (Homewood, Il: Dow Jones-Irwin, 1977).
13. See G. Bylinksy, *The Innovation Millionaires* (New York: Charles Scribner's Sons, 1976).
14. See Dean (May 1974).
15. See L. Beman, "Why Business Ran Out of Capacity," *Fortune*, May 1974, pp. 260-271; "The Breakdown of U.S. Innovation," *Business Week*, 16 February 1976, pp. 56-68.
16. For example, see M. Hanan, "Corporate Growth through Venture Management," *Harvard Business Review*, January-February 1969, pp. 43-61; K. H. Vesper and T. G. Holmdahl, "How Venture Management Fares in Innovative Companies," *Research Management*, May 1973, pp. 30-32.
17. T. A. Wise. "IBM's $5,000,000,000 Gamble," *Fortune*, September 1966, pp. 118-124; T. A. Wise, "The Rocky Road to the Marketplace (Part II: IBM's $5,000,000,000 Gamble), *Fortune*, October 1966, pp. 138-152; G. Bylinksy, "Vincent Learson Didn't Plan It That Way, But IBM's Toughest Competitor Is—IBM.," *Fortune*, March 1972, pp. 33-61.
18. See Quinn (November 1977).
19. L. A. B. Pilkington, "Review Lecture: The Float Glass Process," (London: The Royal Society, 1969); J. Ermenc, "Interview with Sir Alastair Pilkington, 25 June 1968" (Hanover, NH: Thayer School of Engineering); J. B. Quinn, "Pilkington Brothers, Ltd," (unpublished case, Amos Tuck School, 1977).
20. See E. Roberts, *The Dynamics of Research and Development* (New York: Harper & Row, 1964); E. Pessemier, *Managing Innovation and New Product Development* (Cambridge, MA: Marketing Science Institute, 1975); J. B. Quinn, "Long-Range Planning of Industrial Research," *Harvard Business Review*, July-August 1961, pp. 81-102.
21. For a classic description of Oppenheimer as such as manager, see N. F. Davis, *Lawrence and Oppenheimer* (New York: Simon & Schuster, 1969).
22. See J. B. Quinn, "Strategic Goals: Process and Politics," *Sloan Management Review*, Fall 1977, pp. 21-37.
23. See Quinn (July-August 1961); J. B. Quinn and J. A. Mueller, "Transferring Research Results to Operations," *Harvard Business Review*, January-February 1963, pp. 49-66.
24. For an example, see D. J. Smalter and R. L. Ruggles, Jr., "Six Lessons from the Pentagon," *Harvard Business Review*, March-April 1966, pp. 64-75.
25. The OST system of Texas Instruments, Inc., contains many of the detailed characteristics. See Texas Instruments, Inc., 9-172-054, ICCH, Harvard University.

Dr. James Brian Quinn is the William and Josephine Buchanan Professor of Management at The Amos Tuck School of Business Administration, Dartmouth College.

21.
CREATIVITY AND CONFORMITY: FINDING THE BALANCE

Robin Rooks

> With proper handling and supervision, the creative individual's pecu-
> liarities, which are often diagnosed as symptoms of a problem employee,
> can be highly productive. Combining firmness and permissiveness will
> motivate the creative employee to do his or her best work.

"Entrepreneurial innovation will be as important to management as the
managerial function...and will be more important in the years to come." So
says well-known business author Peter Drucker in *Technology, Management, and
Society*. Organizations, he goes on to say, will have to learn to regard change as a
challenge and an opportunity to make innovations and seek out productive
creativity.

Proper management of creativity is perhaps the most potentially rewarding
challenge facing business today. With change so rapid, the creative process is
essential for keeping up with new trends, thoughts and tools. Creativity can
result in new, improved products, streamlined procedures and waste reduction.

Management needs to balance innovation and organizational stability, but
unless it also recognizes and exploits creativity, the organization will quickly be
left behind by its competition. Far-sighted, progressive and open-minded
management can maximize creativity by understanding and recognizing what
it is, nurturing it, and capitalizing on it. Unfortunately, it is just when they
need creativity most, during an unstable or fluctuating economy, that
companies are likely to sacrifice creative activities for projects with a fast
return.

Attempts to scientifically research and measure creativity began in the 19th
century with Sir Francis Galton. Although a pioneer in the field of the systematic measuring of human mental abilities, Galton's theories were often
naive, off the mark and inconclusive. His attempts to align creativity with
heredity and/or intelligence floundered. He did, however, sow the seed of
measuring and testing people for their mental capabilities. World War I and
World War II escalated worldwide attempts at mental testing.

Most of this research has consisted of attempts to identify the characteristics of those who have already been labeled as creative, to isolate the processes of language and imagination, and to compare the activities of groups described as "normal" and "creative." The process of validating test results is beset with more complex problems. Without a standard definition for creativity, how can a reliable test be constructed for it? And once there is a test, how can the results be verified?

Currently, much creativity research is subject to dispute and, scientifically at least, the concept is still elusive. Like much psychological and behavioral testing, creativity testing has not been unconditionally successful. It has not failed totally, however, if only because of the variety of effects it has generated.

Who are creative people? One myth is that creative people are born creative and are only found in the art department, design studio or research lab. The truth is that people learn to be creative, that these talents can be developed, and are found in the lowest and the highest echelons of any organization. Creative potential is a Sleeping Beauty, awaiting only the opportunity to awaken and be aware.

Although psychologists do not know all the reasons why some people are able to think more creatively than others, they have identified a few aspects that seem to be very involved in creativity. Perhaps the three most important are 1) flexibility, 2) persistence, and 3) the ability to recombine elements to achieve insights.

Flexibility is the ability to transcend rigidity. While most people solve problems using old, familiar paths, the creative person can quickly and successfully approach a problem from a completely different angle. This fresh look rejects patterned responses and premature conclusions. An organization that usually makes rigid, inflexible decisions will find its employees generating pat, uncreative solutions—or no solutions at all.

The persistent application of trial and error, to the point of preferring intuition over logic, is part of the creative process.

Persistence can overcome stagnation by prompting the use of various strategies to seek out new and unusual hypotheses.

When the elements of a problem are familiar but need a solution that is original, a mental rearrangement or *recombination* of the elements may facilitate success. This ability to recombine appears to be particularly vital. Taking information that has been accumulated by others or by oneself and reassembling it in a totally new way can produce insights that open up a whole new field of thought.

Insight from recombination usually follows a pattern of intense concentration, great frustration, temporary abandonment of the problem and then sudden attainment of a solution. Apparently, the unconscious continues to work out, or mull over, a problem during sleep or relaxation in the "abandonment" stage. This is also the stage of judgment and decision-making. Although care should be taken that ideas are not prematurely rejected as impractical, they should be relevant to the company or solve a significant problem.

A mystique about creativity may be justified in the art world, but not in business. More and more, creativity is being recognized as essential and valuable to change, progress and prosperity in the office. Management should regard creativity as a compelling way of using the minds of its people. A dynamic management system requires comprehensive and escalated creativity as one of its management objectives.

Rapid growth increases an organization's complexity and the number and seriousness of its change-related problems. Inherent in large systems is the tendency for order and prediction to crush flexibility and creativity.

In any organization, creativity and creative thinking run along a continuum from high to slightly creative. There are those who actually create new ideas and products, those who manipulate old ideas and old products and put them in a new perspective, and those who stimulate creativity in their peers and subordinates. Therefore, creativity or the creative process can actually be an ongoing activity throughout all levels of an organization.

With proper handling and supervision, the creative individual's peculiarities, which are often diagnosed as symptoms of a problem employee, can be highly productive. Most authorities would agree that the crucial aspect in managing a creative individual is good supervision; therefore his or her relationship with the immediate supervisor is most important. If the supervisor understands how vital time and freedom are to the employee, the manager and the company can reap the harvest of innovation. These concepts of time and freedom include:

- freedom of expression;
- job satisfaction;
- effective communications; and
- mutual respect and encouragement from management and fellow workers.

Freedom of expression can be fostered by providing a creative atmosphere both emotionally and physically. Pressure should be specially directed towards attaining goals. Tread a middle ground between firmness and permissiveness to enable a creative employee to work at his or her own pace, but give the individual definite goals to accomplish and an approximate deadline to meet. Allow him or her some time alone for intense concentration, reflection and insight.

To increase a creative employee's *job satisfaction*, recognize his or her creativity both publicly and monetarily. Make him or her feel secure. Tolerate failures—failures may eventually lead to success. Nothing kills true initiative faster than fear. You could inadvertently be handing over to your competitor your best employee by unnecessarily dismissing him or her for failure.

Foster *effective communications* by encouraging an employee or simply listening sympathetically. Help him or her verbalize his or her thinking and reach conclusions. Always let him or her know just how he or she stands, and evaluate work quickly. Individuals need constructive criticism and praise. They also need to know the results of their work so that they can either move on or elaborate on what they've already done.

Attain *mutual respect and encouragement* by defending a creative employee from unnecessary attacks by others. Respect his or her outside activities and sources of stimulation. Some creative individuals keep unusual time schedules or outside associates. Tolerate some short-comings, as long as they don't interfere with work.

Innovation and creativity do not happen in a vacuum or in a predictable order. But innovation and creativity are essential for the successful manufacturing of an organization's products or rendering of its services, the capturing of its market, the development of its technology, and the best and fairest use of its people. Understanding, planning, organizing, motivating and controlling the creative process in an organization takes courage, the same courage found in the truly creative individual—a personal courage of mind and spirit.

According to Jean-Jacques Servan-Schreiber, "Management is, all things considered, the most creative of all arts. It is the art of art. Because it is the organizer of talent."

22.
MANAGING INTERNAL ENTREPRENEURS

Albert A. Vicere

Bureaucracy and red tape can discourage creativity and entrepreneurship. Often, attitudes and the general gestalt within a group can be more important than policies or pronouncements by management, but translating intangibles into concrete results is a mystery to many managers.

We see and hear a lot about creativity and entrepreneurship today, especially when the topic is American management practices. Critics lament our lack of vision, deplore our loss of competitive zeal, and search for the misplaced "Yankee ingenuity" that helped to make the United States the most prosperous nation on earth.

Many experts have proposed techniques for reviving creativity and entrepreneurship in this country. They involve things like searching for excellence, creating cultures, and focusing on quality. And companies are trying them all—with varying levels of success. Still, critics say, American management is not doing enough to spur productivity and economic growth.

I recently read an article by advertising agency president Malcolm MacDougall in the trade publication *Adweek*, in which MacDougall discussed the qualities of good and bad advertising clients. In effect, he also described the characteristics of corporate clients that encouraged entrepreneurship and creativity within their respective agencies.

Advertising is a business that demands creativity and entrepreneurship of its practitioners. Their job is to find and capitalize on their clients' competitive advantages. Ad people need to stay fresh, current, and ahead of the competition—their pay-checks depend on it. To be successful, they must do it every working day of every year, throughout their careers.

It seemed to me, then, that advertising people should have a pretty good feel for the organizational traits that encourage creativity and entrepreneurship, which after all aren't much different from those that encourage the same attitudes among any other organization's employees. So I intently read through MacDougall's article, with an eye toward its application to management.

He noted that good clients don't make things easy on an agency. In fact, "they are tough, demanding, and absolutely intolerant of mediocrity, of anything less than the very best effort and the very best work." He went on to list the qualities of a good client, some simple, basic powerful ideas that got me thinking about the way we manage people in a business organization and how we might unleash the untold creative potential of those people.

I then made my own list of the qualities of good management—the type of management that builds organizations where creativity is a way of life, and every employee can be an entrepreneur. Here goes:

1.   Good management gets excited. Within a framework that demands quality, good mangers get excited about ideas, developments, concepts, theories, and products. They realize that innovation demands experimentation, and show genuine excitement for ideas, before and after they are tested, whether or not they work.

Sound crazy? Try this yourself the next time a subordinate brings you an idea: Look him or her in the eye and say, "That's great! I'm behind you all the way!"

After your subordinate gets over the initial shock, you'll probably hear, "Do you really mean it?" To which you retort, "I like new ideas, and I value people who produce them. Let's give it a shot. What do we have to lose? "

Suddenly, the creative juices will start flowing. Within your demanding, quality-focused structure, you've given your blessing for innovation. Just compare this attitude with the typical response: "That's an interesting concept. Let me get back to you on it." Creativity and entrepreneurship demand the spontaneity that excitable management generates.

2.   Good management builds pride. As MacDougall says, "Good [managers] seem to have a consistent style that somehow makes everyone involved with their business feel like one of the Chosen Few." They are quick to give credit to specific individuals. When they like something, they praise it and the people who developed it; when they don't like something, they criticize the development, not the people who worked on it.

Good managers should also exhibit loyalty. Loyalty is infectious. These managers make employees feel appreciated, wanted, successful, and effective. They make people happy to come to work, happy to give a little bit extra, and determined to reach a goal. Most importantly, they generate mutual respect.

3.   Good management doesn't butt in. The real pros provide input when asked and have ultimate responsibility for approval, but they stay out of the creative process. They are aware that it is their subordinates' job to develop, plan, and execute products and ideas—and they respect their subordinates' ability.

4.   Good management starts from the top. Andrew Grove, the president of Intel, is a good example. A busy man running a very successful company, he values creativity, entrepreneurship, and peak performance. He also understands managerial leverage—how two management heads can be better than one. Why is he so successful? He believes in his people. He coaches them, prods them, and helps each of them fulfill his or her potential. He knows that his role is to make decisions and provide general direction. He also understands that his employees do the work, know the ropes, and are eager to demonstrate their competence.

During its 15 years of existence, Intel has been extremely successful. The company invented both the memory chip and the microprocessor, among other innovations. Obviously, Grove is doing something right. His attitude creates a culture which says, "Okay, folks, we're good and we know it, but we can be better. If we all work together we can create, invent, succeed, and surpass. And it'll be exciting to do it."

5.   Good management appreciates mistakes. Fletcher Byrom once said that to be successful, you should make sure you generate a reasonable number of mistakes. Andrew Grove likens management to sports—over time, he says, we're bound to lose 50 percent of our games.

What are these heretics referring to? To the freedom to experiment, explore, test, and create without fear of punishment or embarrassment. Good management knows that innovation, entrepreneurship, and creativity only thrive in an open environment.

Ask 3M about this concept. It works because each of us, deep down, has a great idea we'd like to try. A feeling that we can do something better than anyone else. We just need an opportunity to let it out without fear. Once we do, it's like a fountain—creativity just bubbles up. You know the feeling; it's happened to you. You have a stroke of genius, and everyone loves your idea. Doesn't it feel great? Think of that on a regular basis. Pretty exciting, right?

6.   Good management is downright demanding. I've mentioned this before, but a reminder never hurts. All this creativity and entrepreneurship must occur within an environment where only the best will do.

Conflicting objectives, you say? Wrong. I'm talking here about a culture that says, "We want to be the best. And to be the best, we've got to be innovative, stay ahead of the competition, and be creative and entrepreneurial. If we are to accomplish our goals, we can't stand still. We need new ideas, new products, and new processes. And we can't develop them without experimenting, playing out our hunches, shaking up the system. Our ultimate objective is to be the best, and to have fun doing it."

7.   Good management pays well. In dollars, of course—but also in recognition, freedom, opportunity, and environment. Creative entrepreneurs want to climb mountains, bridge the unknown, and beat out the competition—be recognized for it. Good managers create a supportive environment for these folks and acknowledge their contributions, both in public (in the form of recognition and promotion), and in private (in the form of higher pay).

8.   Good management encourages experimentation. Good management doesn't get bogged down in detail. They have a "bias for action." They know that problems require careful analysis, but they don't overanalyze. They're willing to test, on a small scale, any idea that seems good to the person who developed it. If the idea pans out, that's great; on to the next stage. If it doesn't, then they go back to the drawing board. You never really know unless you try.

9.   Good management listens. By now this point should be obvious. Creative and entrepreneurial people need sounding boards—people to present ideas to, to help put things into perspective, and to support them. People to gently guide them, to listen to their problems and help translate their ideas into usable formats, to acknowledge their successes, and to put failures into perspective.

Good mangers do all those things, by being open and supportive, but also by being demanding and goal-directed. As the saying goes, "If you don't know where you're going, you'll probably end up somewhere else." Good management makes no bones about the organization's direction, nor about its belief in the abilities of its members.

10.   Within its demanding framework, good management encourages individuality. In effect nothing is sacred. Everything's up for discussion, every idea has merit, and every concept is worth exploring. Sure, most ideas will fall through the cracks. But, every once in a while, some champion will burst forth from his or her cocoon with a "Eureka!" that rattles the rafters. And that's what makes it all worthwhile.

Albert A. Vicere is associate director of executive programs and assistant professor of business administration at the Pennsylvania State University.

23.
WHY CORPORATIONS STIFLE CREATIVITY

George L. Beiswinger

What if Michelangelo had spent five years painting the ceiling of a Burger King? Today, the nature of the corporation is incompatible with the requirements of true creativity. Elements inherent in the corporate concept (hierarchy, consensus, compromise) are the antithesis of those that spark a work of art.

If Vincent Van Gogh had been employed by a produce broker, his Potato Eaters would have had countenances of satisfaction and contentment. They might even have been smiling to show their approval of potatoes. And if Van Gogh's graphics had not possessed these attributes, his employer would not have permitted their release. This illustrates a fundamental truth about all creative work produced under the sponsorship of a corporate organization: The work is expected to portray the sponsoring entity in a favorable manner, or it isn't allowed to portray it at all. All other considerations, including those of an aesthetic nature, are of secondary importance.

Have you ever witnessed the introduction of a new consumer product, amid saturating advertising—perhaps a can opener, a lawnmower, or even an automobile? And have you wondered how its maker, a giant corporation, could have overlooked a basic design flaw that even a first-year art student would not have made?

Doesn't a big company have competent designers on its staff? Doesn't it have marketing advisors that should have anticipated the product's poor balance, incompatible colors, or obviously "dated" appearance? Don't they have access to top-notch consultants? Of course, you can be sure that all such resources were fully deployed. But when the final design was submitted to the corporation's executive committee, one of its members, perhaps an accounting vice president or the corporate legal advisor, thought that the product's appearance should be modified; furthermore, he had enough clout to enforce the changes, regardless of the outcome.

The person ordering the change may have a valid reason for his decision—one that may even be good for the corporation and its stockholders. Perhaps the manufacturing method for the better-designed product is too expensive, or perhaps the better design uses a material that may soon be in short supply. But the reason could simply be a matter of personal preference.

A major New York publishing house recently asked a leading design firm, specializing in corporate identity, to help it create a new image. The professional designers were thorough and painstaking in studying the big publisher and in fitting the new identity to the company's needs. Uniformity and consistency would be maintained in every application of a newly designed logotype, whether it be stationery, book jackets, packing cases, building signs, or rolling stock. However, when the corporate identity manual was being created—the guide for the new program's implementation—the firm's chairman insisted that his own personal business card design be included in the new logotype. The chairman's design, which was in the style of the late nineteenth century, subsequently appeared side by side with the more contemporary elements.

The truism illustrated by these examples: Corporate creative endeavors are often a function of the corporate hierarchy, and the person who is responsible for final approval may have little or no knowledge or feel for aesthetically oriented concepts.

Several years ago the president of a large corporation was asked to review the material to be included in the firm's annual report to stockholders. Included was a photograph of a new frozen food case being used by the company, but it wasn't just any photograph. This one included a very appealing small boy who on tip-toes was reaching into the case in an apparently unsuccessful effort to retrieve a frozen tart. Although the photograph had not been planned, it was an art director's dream, the kind that a producer of television commercials would have worked for hours to obtain. It tugged at the heart strings of everyone who saw it. Well, almost everyone. The company president, after studying the photo, proclaimed: "This would be a pretty good photograph if it didn't have that kid in it."

The hierarchical organization of the corporation has a tremendous effect on the aesthetics of corporate-produced art. In a hierarchy, every superior is constrained to comment on and modify every inferior's work, whether such comment or modification is indicated or not. Here's a familiar dialogue: "Has the vice president of marketing seen this ad layout yet?"

"No, but you can be sure he'll make several changes when he does. Perhaps he'll switch the position of the body copy, or call for an Old English headline, instead of the Helvetica." (If he didn't make a few changes, he wouldn't be doing his job.)

Artistic preference at the top of an organization chart lays a heavy hand, knowing or not, on preferences at lower levels. For there are many ways to the chief's heart. When a former admiral became the president of a large chemical company several years ago, sailing ships soon adorned the walls of company offices, even at the plant level. Later when a new president showed an interest in the preservation of wildlife (especially ducks), the ships came down and up went mallards. In pointing out some of the practices that restrict or limit aesthetic considerations in connection with corporate artistic endeavors, I do not mean to imply that these changes were not desirable in their contexts. My objective is to show that the nature of the corporation is incompatible with the requirements of true creativity. Elements inherent in the corporate concept (hierarchy, consensus, compromise) are the antithesis of those that spark a work of art.

If the corporate artist wishes to accept the rewards of the corporation (and they are great), he or she must be willing to permit compromise. Those who insist on doing their own thing must, of course, generally support themselves in whatever manner they can. Perhaps that is why the true artist is traditionally depicted as somewhat of an ascetic, living in a garret. For example, the famous Boston portrait painter Gardner Cox was recently retained by the federal government to produce a portrait of Henry Kissinger. The government rejected the final result, but offered to support the painter while he made requested changes. Mr. Cox refused, saying he liked the painting as it was. Exercising his independence cost him the $12,000 fee. With that attitude, Mr. Cox could never work for a corporation.

ARTIST AND SLAVES

Today's corporate entities (companies, government bureaus, nonprofit institutions) are major employers of artists. How do they react to corporate restrictions? Not favorably! Some work at the same job for years, but only because they are bound by the golden handcuffs of compensation; artistically, they consider themselves as shackled as the galley slaves of another era. Many more work a short time at one place, quit, go to another, then another. Corporate creators are today's modern gypsies. Every issue of their professional newsletters is filled with news items of resignations and new assignments. Normally, a creator (artist, art director, advertising copywriter, public relations director, corporate communicator) accepts a number of compromises in connection with his or her work, until their cumulative effect creates a conflict which results in termination.

Here's another familiar quote: "Did you know that Bill Smith has left XYZ Corporation as creative director? He's now at the ABC Agency as an account executive. And did you hear what happened to Mary Jones at Ajax Widgets? She resigned to become a consultant." Unemployed corporate creators are known as consultants or freelancers. For in matters of corporate creativity, tenure is directly related to willingness to compromise.

A FEW CONCESSIONS

Some companies recognize an artistic temperament or personality and make certain accommodating concessions. When one of the Big Three auto makers wanted to lure the chief designer of a competitor to its design studios, it reportedly agreed to install a garden with a working fountain in his office. During the time I was at one of these companies, designers were permitted, if they preferred, to grow beards and long hair, and to report for work in such attire as sweat shirts and sandals. Other executives were required to wear conventional business apparel. Furthermore, the designers were encouraged to "do their own things" off the job; each year, the company sponsored a giant art show, where the artists could display and sell the results of the creative efforts they had pursued elsewhere, unfettered and on their own time.

George L. Beiswinger is a writer in the fields of business and the social sciences.

24.
IMPROVING THE CORPORATE ENVIRONMENT

E. H. Kottcamp, Jr.
Brian M. Rushton

Innovation must have the understanding of top management, and must be managed as a total system in which diverse functions are effectively coupled.

Although innovation is inevitably affected by forces outside direct control by the corporations concerned it is nevertheless felt that industry should allot more of its time and effort to managing the elements of the innovative process that are under its control. In this connection, the following areas are of prime importance within the corporation:

1. Top management's attitude toward innovation.
2. Functional coupling within the corporation.
3. The effect of organizational structure.
4. The management of change in corporations.

TOP MANAGEMENT'S ATTITUDE TOWARD INNOVATION

The demands of society are constantly challenging the existence of any system or enterprise. The lessons of history are quite clear that in order to survive, every enterprise must respond to societal values and expectations. Key to the survival of a corporation is its capacity for self-renewal and sustained momentum, and the stimulation and channeling of this capacity are a principal responsibility of senior corporate management and particularly the chief executive officer. In the case of high-technology corporations, self-renewal is almost synonymous with innovation. The fostering of innovation, then, is not an option but a vital necessity for the top leadership of a technology-oriented enterprise.

Corporate leaders recognize innovation to be one of their most important responsibilities. However, a host of internal and external factors affecting the life of corporations have tended to force attention away from an energetic pursuit of technological innovation and can vitiate top management's readiness to mobilize corporatewide cooperation. Such factors include increasing government regulation, a burdensome tax structure, the deepening problems of capital fund creation, and rising labor, materials and energy costs. All of these, and more, represent urgent problems that corporate leadership has been forced to cope with in terms of a logical ordering of priorities, and innovation may have lost ground in that prioritization.

The formal training of corporate leadership has perhaps played a hand in the ordering of the above priorities. There has been a natural need to deal first with those issues that lend themselves to more rapid solutions and promise to yield solid returns immediately or in the near term. This attitude has both called for and been reinforced by courses in the business and management curricula of universities as well as special programs and seminars that stress traditional business skills. Only recently have executive training programs begun to systematically address the problems and techniques of managing change and technological innovation. There is a need to accelerate the development and dissemination of such training programs at the highest levels in U.S. industry.

In many cases heightened awareness of the critical importance of technological innovation may be needed to bring about a change in the way corporations and their governing boards assess the long and difficult process that results in successful innovation. Technological innovation should be accorded the same day-to-day attention and support as has traditionally been give to corporate funding, share of market, plant operations and the like. In short, corporate strategic plans must include more of the alternatives based on technological innovation and stress a dedication—or rededication—to the correct stewardship of that complex process.

Two concrete recommendations geared to improving this stewardship are:

- Top leadership must assume the responsibility for studying, understanding, and implementing the techniques of innovation, above all in the high-technology corporations.
- Management training curricula should pay more attention to courses designed to sharpen the skills of corporate leadership in the area of technological innovation.

FUNCTIONAL COUPLING WITHIN THE CORPORATION

The management of innovation requires a balanced attack on many centers of uncertainty, whether technical, economic or social. Innovation must be managed not as an agglomeration of individual segments but as a total system in which diverse functions and attitudes are correctly coupled. Some key elements in a system aimed at technology innovation are:

- The technology itself, including a feasible manufacturing approach.
- The vision of desirability in the marketplace.
- Appropriate financial management, including capital formation and the allocation of risk capital.

Barriers to innovation, especially in the corporate environment of very large organizations, often arise because of problems inherent in coupling many diverse requirements, outlooks and function. Some examples of these problems as they relate to the three key functions are:

Function 1: Technology. Innovation encompassing high risk but high reward often results from major technical advances, e.g., the transistor, synthetic fibers, antibiotics, xerography, the digital computer, and instant photography. Problems arise in this type of innovation because of the seemingly excessive time it takes to couple the gathering of fundamental knowledge to a vision of the marketplace or acceptable financial rewards. Thus, high-risk innovation meets with various degrees of opposition in the modern corporate environment. Attention to short-term gains often gets in the way of developing a balanced portfolio of short-term and long-term overall corporate strategies. If high-risk, high-reward breakthroughs are to be achieved, there will have to be a more tolerant, patient attitude toward the process of technology innovation.

Function 2: Market Desirability. Many important innovations address latent market needs. Since they create markets, the market cannot be quantified in advance. The vision relating what can be done—in invention —to what is worth doing—i.e., what is potentially marketable—is perhaps the most important element in the process of innovation. Failure to establish this coupling is a distinct barrier to innovation.

Senior corporate management must provide guidance as to how comfortable they are with selected fields and business areas and declare what they are willing to allow the corporation to engage in. Although much has been said about the desirability of champions who will push a development, it is equally necessary that a corporation have tough, practical leadership that can pull differing functions and attitudes together and move them forward toward clearly defined goals. This push-pull mechanism is an extremely powerful coupling force. Failure to create the environment where the technologist works together with the marketing visionary and where both interface with top management is certainly a formidable barrier to innovation.

Function 3: Financial Management. Failure to properly assess financial resources is cited as a major cause of failure for individual entrepreneurs and

small businesses. In contrast, large corporations often overdo financial evaluation and analysis of the prospects of a new idea. Indeed, the new-idea
champions in a corporation rightly complain of "paralysis by analysis" and feel
that few innovative ideas can get through these corporate filters.

Rigid application of classical financial analysis is not well suited to the early
stages of innovation, where it can sometimes create an insurmountable barrier.
As opposed to the control-oriented mode more generally applicable to mature
business operations, a financial attitude that is supportive over the longer term
is what is needed to stimulate innovation.

A more subtle financial barrier is the practice of placing responsibility for
innovation on the research department but keeping financial control in the
hands of profit-center management. To hold one function responsible for long-
term results while financially controlling it via a corporate unit answerable
primarily for short-term gains is counter-productive. In terms of the attitudes of
top management, such an approach can only be looked upon as a "mixed
signal" from above. The question then becomes: Do those in top management
really support innovation or are they abdicating this particular responsibility in
favor of other selected higher priorities?

Nothing is more effective in pulling down barriers to innovation than a
management committed to all-out corporatewide functional cooperation for
innovation. The converse can be devastating. Here are some recommendations for functional coupling aimed at enhancing innovation:

- Recognize that innovation is a complex series of events taking place
  within the corporation as a whole. Failure to couple any of the functions
  in this series can make the whole system fail. Consistency of support is
  required by the long-time horizons of technology innovation. On/off support discourages risk-taking or personal commitment at the technical innovative level.
- Realize that there is no such thing as relying on an isolated function to be
  solely responsible for creativity. The whole corporation must share this
  responsibility.
- Be aware that classical financial analysis rigidly applied to the early stages
  of the innovation process can seriously inhibit or even totally stifle the
  process. A sustained level of funding over long periods of time is a critical
  requirement.
- Encourage the co-existence of technology development champions and
  the kind of top management that is supportive yet forceful. These two
  elements create the push-pull action needed to move innovation forward.

THE EFFECT OF ORGANIZATIONAL STRUCTURE

It is probably impossible to arrive at a consensus on the precise character of
the perfect organizational structure for maximizing innovation. Each industry

has its own specific characteristics, and these characteristics determine how best to create such a structure. However, certain principles are noted:

- Modern technological innovation within large corporations seems to demand a critical mass that contains a sufficient array of specific basic skills, both technical and nontechnical. If the scope is too narrow in terms of resources, individuals perceive very limited horizons.
- Every interface crossed in the process of technological innovation necessitates a technology transfer, and hence problems of acceptance, ownership and control arise. Each interface can become a potential barrier to innovation unless managed and coordinated with great skill.
- A profitable operation usually has the resources available to provide for the future. An unprofitable one often does not and is forced to focus on only short-range needs.

THE MANAGEMENT OF CHANGE

Innovation is a fragile process; and when rapid or significant changes in total environment take place, the process can suffer severely if not managed in an empathetic manner. The turbulent seventies are probably a harbinger of things to come, and we must get accustomed to managing innovation in periods of continuous change. Examples of changes in the total environment that will particularly influence innovation are given below.

Perceptions of the People. For the solution of problems such as inflation, energy shortages, pollution, urban blight and strife, and racial tension, the population looks mainly to two institutions—the government and big business. As big business shoulders an ever-increasing portion of the responsibility for providing such solutions and allocates more of its resources to them, corporate management may find itself being forced toward more conservative, risk-free positions—and the innovation process will suffer.

Government-Business Interaction. Increased government regulation of business is causing disturbing changes in the general business environment. Business leaders are becoming reactive instead of proactive. The expectation that government will add to the list of imposed and sometimes arbitrary rules and regulations is causing short-term tactics to take precedence over the longer-range, more strategic postures. If our tradition of innovation is to survive, a better balance of long- and short-term considerations must be achieved.

International Competition. Our national prosperity will be tied more strongly in the future to how well American corporations can compete internationally, either as multinational partners or entrepreneurs in world markets. This trend requires that appropriate risk-benefits analyses be continually performed to decide on the current balance between satisfying desirable social goals and achieving the necessary economic competitiveness. If the funding of high social goals drains too many of our resources away from technological innovation, not only will our world position be penalized but eventually our ability to fund these desirable social programs also will lessen.

Changing Work Ethic. The traditional work ethic is undergoing significant change. Personal desires such as job satisfaction, freedom of dissent, and discretionary time are becoming essential items in the minds of the labor force. Business managements are finding increasingly that they must sacrifice profits to satisfy these needs of their employees.

Increasing Female Representation. The impact of more women in our labor force will continue to cause great changes. Management and scientific ranks in the male-dominated technological industries are prime areas for female participation. The effect of women on the innovation activity in the corporations in such industries is likely to be quite significant. How to take maximum advantage of these new inputs for the process of innovation is still another challenge in the management of change.

No one can prophesy the precise scenario of the future, but we have highlighted some key problems and challenges in what is emerging as one of the most dynamic periods in America's socioeconomic history. The top priorities of American corporations must embrace actions aimed at maintaining our ability to innovate in an atmosphere of constant change.

In closing, the Industrial Research Institute joins others in making a strong appeal for rededication to technology innovation with and by American corporations. In a world of increasing competitiveness and rapid, often drastic socioeconomic change, corporations must continue to identify emerging needs and innovative directions and deal with them proactively. Techniques for guiding a complex array of talents and functions through the often long process of technological innovation are based on, among other things: (1) a receptive attitude toward the champions of new technology and the requirements of various departments involved in the innovative process, and (2) an ability to keep these various elements in balance and make certain they continue to be functionally coupled with each other and with factors from the marketplace, government, and society as a whole.

Finally, to be successful, innovation, particularly of the break- through type, requires longer-term financial support. Boards of directors, as the final arbiters of corporate strategy, must be willing to authorize this kind of support in the face of pressures to put the major part of a company's effort into projects geared to current or near-term returns.

Dr. E. H. Kottcamp, Jr. is assistant to the vice president and manager, Product Research and Chemical Process Research, Bethlehem Steel Corporation. Dr. Brian M. Rushton is president of Celanese Research Company.

Part IV: MANAGING CREATIVE PEOPLE

25.
MANAGING THE
GOLDCOLLAR WORKER

Mark L. Goldstein

The need to encourage and effectively manage innovation is becoming an
increasingly important part of the corporate challenge. Managers are
aware that their own experience may not yield adequate answers.

Every Thursday afternoon at the Kansas City, Mo., headquarters of
Hallmark Cards, Inc., nearly 100 employees file into a small theater to watch
cartoons. But not always cartoons. Sometimes it's Laurel & Hardy or the Three
Stooges; occasionally it's film classics, depending on the projectionist's mood.
And it's all on company time.

As members of Hallmark's 800-strong creative department, these writers
and artists are actually doing their jobs—searching for ideas and visual scenes
to use on cards, wrapping paper, and other products.

"Thursday Theatre," as it's called, is one of the tools Hallmark uses to
motivate its most-talented employees—the people who give birth to the
company's products. Indeed, without innovative concepts or eye-catching
card designs, Hallmark would attract little attention on gift-shop shelves.

Besides showing movies, the company also regularly sends key employees
across the country, even to other continents, with instructions to wander in art
galleries, watch plays, or window-shop—hunting for ideas and trends that
might translate into sales.

Sometimes it pays off handsomely. Several years ago, while viewing the King
Tut exhibit at Washington's National Gallery of Art, one roving employee
suddenly pictured the famous gold death mask as a puzzle for children. "That
one trip has brought more than a $500,000 return," says Garry Glissmeyer, vice
president of Hallmark's creative department.

BEYOND THE "FORTRESS"

While few companies are willing to invest as heavily as Hallmark in fostering
creativity, the need to encourage and effectively manage innovation is becoming an increasingly important part of the corporate challenge. Historically,

company R&D centers have been the fortresses of innovation. And R&D managers have long understood that creative employees should be motivated and rewarded differently than other workers. Firms like 3M Co., for instance, have long had reputations for operating research centers in a way that allows creative people to follow their intuition. And the result often has been revolutionary new products—including masking tape and wet/dry sandpaper.

Until recently, though, the philosophy guiding such operations rarely has spread beyond the laboratory door to other departments. Managers have dictated by virtue of their advance education, lengthy experience, and corporate clout. But times have changed. An energy crisis; the deregulation of transportation, banking, and telecommunications; an exploding computer age; and a tidal wave of imports have shaken U. S. companies. In the struggle to survive, managers are searching harder for innovative solutions, aware that their own experience may not yield adequate answers.

Moreover, given the fast pace of change today, many managers have no more expertise—perhaps even less—in specialized areas than the people they supervise, particularly when they're managing "goldcollar" workers—those whose jobs require a high degree of creativity and/or special skills, and who often are engaged in projects that significantly affect the company's future. Besides product-development personnel, their ranks include such employees as financial managers, computer programmers, advertising copywriters, and engineers with critical skills.

INTIMIDATED

Not only are manufacturing companies putting more emphasis on developing goldcollar workers, but their numbers are also swelling geometrically in the service sector.

"The rapid growth of the service industry has created many jobs in management, finance, marketing, and computer software. The people attracted to these jobs are smart, motivated people whose goals tend to be different from those of traditional workers," explains Robert F. Kelley, senior consultant at SRI International, Menlo Park, Calif., and the author of a recent book which identifies this type of employee—*The Gold Collar Worker.*

Today, the challenge for many companies is to find managers who know how to motivate goldcollar workers (Mr. Kelley lays claim to coining the term) and to identify employees with unusual potential for innovation. Many traditional "top-down" managers are intimidated by members of this highly educated, creative "company brain trust," suggest several experts, including Mr. Kelley.

Insecure managers feel threatened by the newfound importance that these employees have gained in a world where seniority and experience carry less weight. "They don't know how to handle goldcollar workers," Mr. Kelley says. "They're afraid of what they don't understand; so instead of helping creative people flourish, they clamp down. It's the worst thing they can do."

Other managers, however, are unwilling to take the responsibility that comes with encouraging innovation, preferring instead to toe the line for the boss. Still a third type of manager refuses to treat employees differently, convinced that there is no such thing as goldcollar workers. (Even if there is, he reasons, there is still no need to give that worker special attention.)

"Creative people rock management's boat," declares Lester C. Krogh, director of R&D at 3M. "Managers are too afraid to go out on a limb for an idea," he says. Indeed, employees constantly pushing extravagant ideas, creating different operating methods, or pursuing independent hunches on company time rarely have been tolerated in the past. Managers pressed by higher up executives for short-term results aren't about to allow deviance from set goals or procedures. Yet Mr. Krogh warns, "When management refuses to be supportive of its workers, productivity goes way down."

SPECIAL TREATMENT

But management styles are changing with the times—especially in fiercely competitive high-technology companies where ignoring innovation is tantamount to economic suicide. Being first, faster, or better is crucial to success in the computer business. Consider Interleaf Inc., a three-year-old Cambridge, Mass., company that creates software for workstations. To stay competitive, Interleaf must regularly reissue its software and offer new capabilities—which makes its software engineers classic examples of goldcollar workers.

"We have people who are making major contributions, so the company needs to pay special attention to them," explains David A. Boucher, president of Interleaf. "If you don't recognize their creative potential and learn to use it, you're not going to get the same results. The difference can be critical. Mr. Boucher estimates that the best programmers produce nearly 50 times as much code as an average programmer.

This understanding is slowly finding its way into other businesses as well. Whether it's a Hallmark employee with a new theme for card designs, an oil-company financial executive checking currency prices at dawn to save the firm $70 million in international debt exposure, or a young manager charged with developing mortgage-banking products, each plays an important role requiring creative thinking and risk-taking.

WEIRDOS?

The nature of their work, in a general sense, identifies who the goldcollar employees are. But as with any group, some deserve the label more than others—those who exhibit a real genius for what they do. And identifying the most promising innovators isn't always easy. "The myth of weirdos running around wearing plaid shirts and no socks just isn't true," insists Carl Hakmiller, professor of social psychology at the University of Connecticut. Most gold-collar workers lead outwardly "normal" lives, making it difficult to detect un-usual creativity early on. There are other problems: although high-quality work might seem to be a reasonable indicator, some veterans don't consider consistent performance as a measure of exceptional creativity. "There's nothing wrong with people whose work is always first-rate, but that doesn't mean they're innovative," says 3M's Mr. Krogh. "The ones producing patents all the time may not have that flash of brilliance."

Brain trust employees capable of special achievement usually exhibit common traits. Experts agree that the driving force behind most creative workers is a need to feel that they are making a contribution, that what they do adds value to the company. Most are also career-driven, rather than job-oriented; they are constantly evaluating their current role and future prospects with the company.

"Goldcollar workers view their talents as an asset, as their own best invest-ment, and they decide when the return isn't good enough," SRI's Mr. Kelly says. "In their own way they've become company customers—only they are buying management style." Indeed, they are better able to make choices about where they'll work than any other employee group.

An equally important characteristic is independence. Most innovators tend to focus on projects or goals, and have little patience with the distractions of paperwork, company politics, or strict regulations. " To these people, work is an extension of themselves, and they don't take well to trivial interference," warns Prof. Hakmiller. A strong corporate bureaucracy or inflexible organiza-tional structure is likely to send most creative people packing—or, at the very least, substantially reduce their productivity.

TOLERANCE NEEDED

Old-line managers may view goldcollar workers as glorified trouble-makers—petty egoists with insubordinate tendencies. "But run that depart-ment like an army and you'll have a rebellion," warns Rowland W. Schmitt, senior vice president for corporate research at General Electric.

One key to motivating creative workers is tolerance. The experts recom-mend lots of communication—and the ability to tolerate dissent. Executives who are unwilling to consider new ideas and alternative ways of doing things may be shutting the door on their best resources. Companies best known for innovation find ways to avoid managerial autocracy and to increase communication with supervisors, between co-workers, between departments, and even between innovators and customers.

Both Hallmark's creative department and 3M's researchers, for instance, have regular brainstorming sessions on product ideas and development. Hallmark frequently sponsors seminars with successful writers, artists, and photographers to spur ideas. 3M sends its researchers to customers' sites to evaluate products and consider new applications. Interleaf physically integrates its departments (by strategically locating offices) to encourage code writers to interact with sales and marketing employees, as well as customers.

Improving product-related communication, though, is not enough. More than any other employee, the goldcollar worker demands feedback on his performance. And he may want it from peers as well as supervisors. In some companies, managers are even taking a backseat to peer evaluations; when managers do conduct employee reviews, the discussion focuses mainly on the employee's aspirations.

At Interleaf, peers not only review each other's work, but all new applicants—code writers and software managers—are interviewed by members of the department. Mr. Boucher, the president, notes that only one out of every 100 candidates is asked to join the 30-member software staff. "Their quality has to be so good that they tend to expel anyone who doesn't measure up," he says. While he admits that the scrutiny of supervisors by the department is unusual, he defends it, declaring, "The work they perform is so important that if the staff feels an individual (supervisor) is inadequate, we'll react."

LEAVE THEM ALONE

Of all the keys to managing goldcollar workers, autonomy may head the list. "The best thing you can do for creative people is just get out of their way. Give them a task and leave them alone," counsels Peter F. Drucker, recognized management authority and professor of social science at the Claremont Graduate School, Claremont, Calif.

However, they shouldn't be given just any job. Brain trusts should be assigned major projects, but one of their own choosing whenever possible, experts say. A deadline should be imposed, the resources allocated, and then—importantly—the supervisor should walk away.

If the manager has done a good job matching the worker with the task, the project will be a success. At least that's how it's supposed to work. Veterans like 3M's Krogh point out, though, that there must be a reasonable tolerance of failure. "Probably 60% of the things we try don't work, but success takes some gambling," he says.

Because of the risk level, 3M has developed a project-sponsorship tack that lines up an interested executive with a specific research effort. In theory, the executive's support helps shield the reseacher from bureaucratic skirmishes and from the pressure to produce short-term results.

Most goldcollar workers who achieve their goals do so because the work and its environment motivate them. If given the freedom to pursue ideas, make contributions, and see immediate results as well as access to state-of-the-art equipment, innovative employees will usually live up to their promise.

In Data General Corp.'s "Eagle" project, for example, a special team of engineers was assembled by the Westboro, Mass., computer maker in the late 1970s to build a powerful minicomputer. The result was Data General's successful MV/8000 mini. "The chance to be part of an entire new project from the ground up was exciting," recalls James Guyer, a senior engineer on the project and currently a senior section manager. "The thrill is being able to see what you've been working for so hard actually function. It's knowing that you've helped make a difference."

MONEY HELPS

Satisfaction is obviously a powerful reward for creative people, but attuned managers are starting to ensure that rewards for innovative work are linked to something more tangible—bonuses, for example. In fact, the Hay Group, Philadelphia-based compensation consultants, reports that nearly one-half of the high-technolgy companies it recently surveyed paid bonuses to non-executive employees. In technology companies, especially, incentive-compensation programs are being structured to complement product-development cycles, offering goldcollar workers bonuses or stock as certain project objectives are met.

Some start-up firms offer brain trust workers substantial blocks of stock when they join the company, which not only motivates them to work hard—since they're working for themselves—but also makes it financially attractive to stick around. "Where once it was simply labor for money, management is recognizing the strategic value of sharing profits and using bonuses, royalties, and stock as motivation tools," says Mr. Kelley at SRI.

Ironically, the rewards goldcollar workers want most—even more than money—is peer recognition. Traditional annual achievement awards are given at many companies, 3M and General Electric included; and Hallmark encourages its most-creative workers with additional field trips. To some, being assigned to a special project is an award in itself. "People on the [Eagle] project had a definite feeling of self-importance, and it helped keep us going. There was a mystique that we were the best design engineers in the company," Data General's Mr. Guyer admits.

ELITISM

Sometimes, however, goldcollar workers push the limit. Inflated by their self-importance, they have a tendency toward elitism. When faulty air conditioning at the Data General labs pushed the temperature into the 90's, the Eagle engineers walked off the job, refusing to return until it was fixed. "We didn't give management much choice—but it was fixed by morning," chuckles

Mr. Guyer. Understandably, such testiness worries managers. Elitism not only breeds arrogance; it also can undermine authority. "Regardless of how talented or valuable some workers are, like it or not, there are some guidelines they must adhere to," declares 3M's Mr. Krogh.

Whether treating certain workers as elite benefits a company is keenly debated. Steven Jobs, chairman of Apple Computer Inc., exploited the idea while developing the Macintosh computer. During breaks, engineers assigned to the project enjoyed a stereo system, video games, and a Ping-pong table supplied by the boss. Meanwhile, engineers working on the Apple II computer grew resentful.

Even proponents of elitism as a motivating force recognized its potential for abuse. "I don't think any organization can tolerate a large number of completely independent, creative types," says Prof. Hakmiller. "Managers have to know when the means are defeating the ends."

As well, they have to know which workers will respond to the style of management recommended for talented, innovative employee groups. Some of the methods for coaxing the brain trust to new heights may also motivate "average" workers—although it may take more time and effort on the manager's part.

Is the result worth it? "You never know," says SRI's Mr. Kelley, "when a whitecollar will turn gold."

26.
HOW TO PREVENT CREATIVITY MISMANAGEMENT

Michael K. Badawy

> Many managers do not apply what behavioral scientists have learned about creativity and creative environments. One reason for this mismanagement is the assumption that creativity alone will lead to productive results. Not so!

Many technical managers try to inspire creativity, only to find that the creative performance declines. Understanding creativity, how the creative process works, some of the misconceptions about it, and how to handle creative staff can prevent this.

Many managers do not apply (or even sometimes misapply) what behavioral scientists have learned about creativity and creative environments. This leads to mismanagement and poor results.

One reason for this mismanagement is the assumption that creativity alone will lead to productive results. Not necessarily so! In order to be effective, creativity needs to be buttressed by organizational support and good managerial leadership and interpersonal skills. Bear in mind that while creativity implies bringing something new into being, innovation implies bringing something new into use.

Another reason is that while many engineers and scientists can think of imaginative ideas for new products or services, few have the skills and/or motivation to carry these ideas through to fruition. Since it takes a creative person to recognize one, it is necessary to have creative managers in order for creativity to flourish.

A third reason for mismanagement relates to the nature of creativity itself. Raw creativity alone is a mixed blessing in that the creative idea may be something that has been unsuccessfully tried in the past. Unless you are familiar with other peoples' past experience in your field, valuable time can be wasted pursuing ideas that have already proved unworkable.

Another reason for creativity mismanagement is the poor organizational practices adopted by many technical managers which end up blocking and

Table 1.

Twelve Ways to Kill Creativity

1. Drag your feet. Who can argue with the painstaking manager who wants to run it through again?
2. Say yes, but do not do it. This touch of diplomacy leaves almost everyone pleased—for a while.
3. Wait for full analysis. Logic seems to be on your side.
4. Do not follow up. Drop the idea among your associates and let them worry about it.
5. Call many meetings. This will kill time and the interest of others.
6. Put the idea into channels. That way you can forget about it.
7. Boost the cost estimates. A hero's role is guaranteed for saving the company money when the idea is vetoed.
8. Wait for market surveys. They take time—maybe too much.
9. Stick to protocol. Red tape will be around a long time after the dead idea.
10. Worry about the budget. Why spend money when things are going well?
11. Lack a sense of urgency. Your business has existed and will exist for a long time, so why rush?
12. Cultivate the "Not Invented Here" syndrome. If a good idea is someone else's, do not be guilty of pushing it.

Adapted from S.J. Fraenkel, "How Not to Succeed as an R&D Manager," Research Management, May 1980, pp 35.

hampering creativity. Managers seem to do (and know) more to stifle creativity than to induce it. They do not give creative people the freedom they need to hatch their creativity, often chaining them to the rules and regulations of the organization. Table 1 provides some "advice" for those managers who do not want to see creative ideas blossom in their organizations.

While certainty is accompanied by security, creativity is accompanied by change—doing things differently. Because change is threatening, many technical managers resist it. In their quest for coping by maintaining the status quo, they end up behaving in ways that block creativity. Worse yet, the psychological process is so intense (consciously or subconsciously) that they believe in the legitimacy of their actions without knowing that what they, in fact, are doing is mere rationalization. Table 2 provides a sample (representative!) of ways that some technical managers block creativity.

Finally, a frequent source of creativity mismanagement is a lack of understanding of the cost of creativity. For example:

• Time spent on creativity is diverted from the time available for other

Table 2.

Sixty-One Ways to Block Creativity

A good idea but...
Against company policy.
Ahead of the times.
All right in theory.
Be practical.
Can you put it into practice?
Costs too much.
Don't start anything yet.
Have you considered...
I know it won't work.
It can't work.
Too many projects now.
It doesn't fit human nature.
It has been done before.
It needs more study.
It's not budgeted.
It's not good enough.
It's not part of your job.
Let me add to that...
Let's discuss it.
Let's form a committee.
Let's make a survey first.
Let's not step on toes.
Let's put it off for a while.
Let's sit on it for a while.
Let's think it over for a while.
Not ready for it yet.
Of course it won't work.
Our plan is different.
Some other time.
Surely you know better.
That's not our problem.
The boss won't go for it.

The new people won't understand.
The old timers won't use it.
The timing is off.
The union won't go for it.
There are better ways.
They won't go for it.
Too academic.
Too hard to administer.
Too hard to implement.
Too late.
Too much paperwork.
Too old fashioned.
Too soon.
We have been doing it this way for a
    long time and it works.
We haven't the manpower.
We haven't the time.
We're too big.
We're too small.
We've never done it that way.
We've tried it before.
What bubble head thought that up?
What will the customers think?
What will the union think?
What you're really saying is...
Who do you think you are?
Who else has tried it?
Why hasn't someone suggested
    it before if it's a good idea?
You are off base.

purposes. A typical manager's attitude is: "I wish my people would spend less time dreaming up new ideas and more time getting the work out."

• Some creative suggestions are resisted because they are politically unwise—when, for example, they are antithetical to the values and beliefs of key executives.

• Creative individuals, generally, tend to be high turnover risks and can be lured away by other companies that desire their talents and skills.

• Highly creative organizations tend to be less predictable and more chang-

ing than those emphasizing efficiency and productivity. Some managers find these conditions distressing.
* Highly creative people can be an economic burden on the company. It is expensive to carry people on the payroll whose ideas may not pay off for years. Many organizations choose to purchase creative ideas from the outside rather than turning their R&D laboratories into intellectual "parking lots."

IDENTIFYING CREATIVE INDIVIDUALS

Creativity is like height, weight, and strength. People vary considerably in these dimensions, but everybody has some height, some weight, and some strength. Likewise, there is a certain amount of creativity in all of us but some of us are obviously more creative than others.

Creative scientists and engineers can be identified by learning about their traits (what they are) and their behavioral styles (what they do). Bear in mind, however, that there are many variations with and between creative technical people. Research can only provide us with a set of stereotypes at this time.

From the standpoint of traits, creative individuals are generally characterized as self-stimulating, independent, sensitive, goal oriented, and capable of giving direction to their own efforts. They are also more emotionally open and flexible than their less creative counterparts. Their multi-level thinking can be characterized by both freshness and a strong tendency to see the forest but not individual trees. Research data clearly suggest that creative individuals are different in terms of their personality structures, values, and trait orientation. Consequently, the most common mistake technical managers make is to attempt to manage highly creative individuals using the same standards applied to the more conventional members of the work team.

The other requirement for spotting creativity is to understand and learn about work patterns and behavioral styles of creative people. Two predominant characteristics of these styles are: the courage to be different, and a dedication to long hours and hard work.

Typical behavioral patterns of creative individuals include persistence, tendency to ignore or pay scant attention to the everyday demands of society, a rigid regularity in the allocation of time for work, and an approach to work that can never be described as casual. Table 3 shows a practical stereotype of the creative person and illustrates the extent of differences between creative and less or non-creative individuals.

Table 4 presents a behavioral stereotype of the creative individual at its best. The creative person is introverted, non-conforming, autonomous yet adaptive, and striving. Furthermore, creative individuals have sustained curiosity, dedication, intuition, and willingness to work. Research, in fact, shows that morning, noon, and night are all the same to creative people; they don't work by the clock. Problems may take years to solve: time has a personal, not social meaning.

CREATIVITY AND INTELLIGENCE

In spotting genuinely creative engineers and scientists, it is important to understand the difference between creativity and intelligence. Psychologists generally agree that while a creative person is an intelligent person, high intel-

---

Table 3.

The Creative Person: A Practical Stereotype

Creative people are especially observant, and they value accurate observation (telling themselves the truth) more than other people do.

They often express part-truths, but this they do vividly; the part they express is the generally unrecognized; by displacement of accent and apparent disproportion in statement they seek to point to the usually unobserved.

They see things as others do, but also as others do not.

They are thus independent in their cognition, and they also value clearer cognition. They will suffer great personal pain to testify correctly.

They are motivated to this value and to the exercise of this talent (independent, sharp observation) both for reasons of self-preservation and in the interest of human culture and its future.

They are better able to hold many ideas at once and to compare more ideas with one another—hence to make a richer synthesis.

In addition to unusual endowment in terms of cognitive ability, they are by constitution more vigorous and have available to them an exceptional fund of psychic and physical energy.

Their universe is thus more complex, and in addition they usually lead more complex lives, seeking tension in the interest of the pleasure they obtain upon its discharge.

They have more contact than most people do with the life of the unconscious—with fantasy, reverie, the world of imagination.

They have exceptionally broad and flexible awareness of themselves. The self is strongest when it can regress (admit primitive fantasies, naive ideas, tabooed impulses into consciousness and behavior), and yet return to a high degree of rationality and self-criticism. *The creative person is both more primitive and more cultured, more destructive and more constructive, crazier and saner, than the average person.*

---

ligence is not a prerequisite for creativity. In general, intelligence is a measure of an individual's ability to understand a circumstance and to get to a conclusion rapidly and efficiently, be it an arithmetic calculation, an engineering problem, or some form of social behavior.

An intelligent person arrives at his goal directly by ignoring irrelevancies in his analysis. While the intelligent mind concentrates and directs toward an efficient solution, the creative mind, on the contrary, wanders in every possible direction—relevant or irrelevant. In short, the intelligent mind is measured by the ability to store and recall information with speed and accuracy. The outcome is a predetermined expectation. The creative mind is different. The information is used to come up with the unique and the unexpected. Thus, it

---

Table 4.

How to Identify and Recognize Scientific Creativity

A high degree of autonomy, self-sufficiency, self-direction.

A preference for mental manipulations involving things rather than people: a somewhat distant or detached attitude in interpersonal relations, and a preference for intellectually challenging situations rather than socially challenging ones.

High ego strength and emotional stability.

A liking for method, precision, exactness.

A preference for such defense mechanisms as repression and isolation in dealing with affect and instinctual energies.

A high degree of personal dominance but a dislike of personally toned controversy.

Relatively little talkativeness, gregariousness, impulsiveness.

A liking for abstract thinking, with considerable tolerance of cognitive ambiguity.

Marked independence of judgment, rejection of group pressures toward conformity in thinking.

Superior general intelligence.

An early, very broad interest in intellectual activities.

A drive toward comprehensiveness and elegance in explanation.

A special interest in the kind of "wagering" which involves pitting oneself against uncertain circumstances in which one's own effort can be the deciding factor.

---

seems that creativity and intelligence tests are interdependent within a certain range of IQ's. The crucial point here is that there is a positive relationship between the two variables, and above a certain level of intelligence being more intelligent does not guarantee a corresponding increase in creativeness.

MEASURING CREATIVITY

Although no available test can determine with any reliability who will perform creatively in the future (Shapero), there are at least two ways to measure creativity: puzzle problems, and creativity questionnaires.

Solving puzzle problems measures an individual's ability to overcome routine or conventional thinking. Therefore, a scientist or engineer capable of solving these puzzles is probably more creative than one who cannot solve many of them.

One of the problems in using puzzles to measure creativity, however, is that many of them correlate too highly with intelligence (general mental ability) or other abilities. It follows that many engineers or scientists who perform well on these puzzles are, therefore, intelligent, but not necessarily creative.

Two general types of questionnaires can be used. The first requires solving a series of small problems. One of the difficulties with these tests is that although they measure creativity, they are also highly correlated with inductive reasoning ability and abstract thinking.

The "Creativity Personality Test" is the other type of creativity questionnaire. It attempts to measure the potential for creative thinking through an individual's attitudes toward important issues related to creative behavior and thinking.

These two instruments should, of course, be supplemented by your personal observations—as a technical manager—of your subordinates' behavior under actual job conditions. Close and frequent observation of how the scientist or engineer goes about problem-solving can give you some general clues for assessing his creative potential. The fact remains that the only valid and reliable way to identify individuals with a high probability of future creative performance is through evidence of past creative performance (Shapero). The more recent and continuous the past creative performance, the greater the likelihood that there will be future creative performance.

MANAGING CREATIVE PEOPLE

You can't motivate your engineers and scientists to be creative. To be creative, one must have a creative mind. Your task as a technical manager, then, is to create the "right" environment where creativity can grow and flourish. Broad generalizations for boosting creativity won't work since specific environments must be tailored to fit specific situations. However, here are three categories of tips and guidelines which will help you in handling creative team members.

1. SELECT CREATIVE INDIVIDUALS

Spot Creative People During Job Interviews. In addition to the general traits and behavioral stereotypes of creative people discussed above, here are several research-based pointers to help you generally differentiate between creative and less creative job candidates. The more creative individuals:

- Are less anxious than less creative individuals
- Are more autonomous, more dynamic, and more integrative than their less creative colleagues.
- See their own attitudes as being different from those of others
- Have fewer authoritarian attitudes than do their less creative colleagues
- Place higher values on practical matters and utility, more emphasis on harmony and form, and less emphasis on elusive values.
- Are more oriented toward achievement and acceptance of their own inner impulses; less creative individuals are more oriented toward avoiding situations in which they might be blamed for their activities or in which they might feel inferior
- Give greater evidence of psychological well-being
- Appear to take fewer unwarranted risks than their less creative colleagues
- Work slowly and cautiously while analyzing a problem and gathering data. Once they obtain the basic data and approach the point of synthesis, they work rapidly. The less creative individual spends less time in analyzing the problem but more time in attempting to synthesize the material.

Understand Expectations of Creative People. Research shows that the most important environmental factors in stimulating creativity as rated by engineers and scientists are (in decreasing order):

- Recognition and appreciation.
- Freedom to work in areas of greatest interest.
- Contacts with stimulating colleagues.
- Encouragement to take risks.

The lowest rated factors (in decreasing order) are:

- Nonconformity tolerated.
- Opportunity to work alone rather than on a team.
- Monetary rewards.

- Criticism by supervisors or associates.
- Creativity training programs.
- Regular performance appraisals.

2. ADOPT CHARACTERISTICS OF LEADERS WHO ENCOURAGE CREATIVITY

Research shows that leaders who encourage creativity have unique behavioral characteristics which you should consider adopting. Some useful clues include:

Willing to Absorb Risks Taken by Subordinates. Managers who encourage creativity allow subordinates considerable freedom to be creative. One cost of such freedom is mistakes which are sometimes expensive. In contrast, managers who are afraid of mistakes restrict the freedom of subordinates to experiment, hoping to eliminate most errors.

Comfortable with Half-Developed Ideas. Managers of productive research laboratories do not insist that every t be crossed and every i dotted before supporting an idea. They are willing to listen to, and support, "half-baked" proposals and encourage subordinates to press on. Creativity-inducing leaders will not graciously welcome every preposterous idea since they have good intuitive sense about what might work. Yet they are hesitant to discourage the creative flow of ideas or to kill innovation in the bud.

Willing to "Stretch" Organizational Policy. Creativity-inducing leaders do not normally disregard rules and policies, but they do know when the rules need to be stretched for the greater good.

Able to Make Quick Decisions. Leaders who foster creativity have good track records in recognizing which half-processed idea is worth betting on. They are also courageous enough to immediately commit resources to carrying it out. The creativity-discouraging manager is predisposed to calling for further studies, or putting the suggested idea in the hands of a committee.

Good Listeners. Productive managers listen to their subordinates and build on their suggestions. They seem to have the ability to draw out the best in their people and then add to it. A manager who encourages creativity will listen to an idea and then ask a question such as "how might your idea be applied on an even wider scale?"

Don't Dwell on Mistakes. Creativity-inducing leaders are "willing to begin with the world as it is today and work for a better future." They learn from experience, but do now wallow in it.

Enjoy Their Jobs. Managers who induce creativity among subordinates are enthusiastic, invigorating individuals who like what they are doing. They exude a contagious enthusiasm.

Note that perfectionism is supposedly important in order to be creative yourself while this same characteristic could inhibit creativity in subordinates. What you should remember, however, is that while this duality may be true, highly creative engineers or scientists may not be perfectionists. They are, in fact, "loose" or at least they are not obsessed with details. Bear in mind also that general descriptions of creativity are simply valid trends and should not be taken too literally—they are true much of the time, but not always.

3. ESTABLISH A CREATIVE WORK CLIMATE

Creativity is the combined influence of creative people working in a creative environment that encourages (or at least does not discourage) creativity. In handling creative team members, good supervision is critical. The engineer's or scientist's relationship with you overshadows every other influence. Here are 16 specific guidelines for managing that relationship.

Focus and Gear the Pressure to Goals. Many creative people need the reassurance of just enough gentle pressure on the reins to keep them aware of their objectives. Setting definite goals and an approximate time limit will help provide the necessary sense of urgency. You need to make your presence felt, but without the slightest trace of oppressiveness.

Foster Interpersonal Contact. Contact must never be lost between you and your staff. Frequent communication, coupled with freedom to make certain decisions alone, is the ideal compromise. A creative person needs a sympathetic ear—a sounding board for his ideas.

Give Continuous Feedback. Creative people are eager for evaluation of their efforts. Since real results may be long postponed, appraisal of creative efforts is often difficult. Therefore, it is important to be alert for signs of frustration and resentment. Talk informally with your people and demonstrate your interest. Indicate your understanding of their goals, and let them know the importance of their results and the positive reactions of other managers as soon as possible.

Defend Against Attackers. Because of the unique nature of his job, it might be wise to tolerate the scientist or engineer's idiosyncrasies and impatience. In defending his behavior, the focus should be on his accomplishments. Managers should understand that some inconsistency in behavior may be necessary for creativity, and also that impatience may come from deep absorption in a task—not personal animosity.

Allow Ample Time to Think. While the creative engineer or scientist does not necessarily want to be isolated, he does want to have periods of mental seclusion and separation from real world pressures. Many of the best creative ideas come during an idle period immediately following intense concentration. That is when the unconscious presents the conscious mind with new insights. Sometimes, ideas have to be put in the oven to bake for a while.

The individual whose creative effort is part of a group project often develops ideas when he is alone, but the reverse is also true. Remember that the bottom line, however, is that creativity is basically an individual act, and that creativity solely on a group basis does not work, with the possible exception of an occasional brainstorming session. In short, allow freedom but don't let go. Never take the attitude "Charley, you're on you own!" The creative person doesn't want to be ignored, and you must keep contact, with discretion.

Build Confidence. Any individual whose contribution is principally ideas rather than actions is normally at his best when only his mind is challenged—not his security or ego. Encourage him in order to build his self-confidence to the maximum. Job security, good pay, and a high degree of job satisfaction go a long way toward bolstering the creative individual's self-confidence and security.

It should also be noted that the compelling force in the creative professional must be a positive attitude, in contrast to the defensive attitude of the fearful or frustrated person. An individual motivated by fear is more likely to play it safe than to create. It follows that if you are trying to make your subordinates more creative, be sure they don't feel threatened by project demands. Threats generate resistance, not results.

Know How to Handle Failures. Learn to control your own fear of failure by showing tolerance for your subordinates' failures. A creative atmosphere requires that an engineer or scientist be able to present radical, even unworkable ideas without being harshly judged. The best product your company produced may have sounded silly when first proposed.

You must give your subordinates a wide margin for error in order for them to be able to experiment, create, and innovate. Without this, their fear of failure will destroy true initiative and stifle creativity. Note that fear of failure is more intense in large bureaucratic companies than small entrepreneurs' settings. While the possibility of failure is part of the entrepreneur's "culture" and can consequently be lived with, it is largely discouraged (or worse, denied) in complex corporate structures because "one failure brands you as a loser."

Recognize the Need for Outside Stimuli. Creative individuals should be given freedom to communicate with peers outside the organization. The creative engineer or scientist needs the professional status acquired through identification with technical societies, meetings, conventions, local universities, and other professional groups. It is a mistake to discourage these activities.

It is also wise to defer to the creative individual's source of stimulation. As there seems to be a tradeoff between conformity and creativity, some conformity may be well sacrificed as the price for creativity. Examples include allowing some divergence from the usual business hours, dress code, coffee breaks and so on. Letting him do "his thing"—whether it is yoga, meditation, or jogging—without forcing your own values and philosophies on him can help stimulate his creativity.

Provide Appropriate Direction. Be tolerant but don't pamper. You must distinguish between an inventive individual's legitimate impatience with unrealized possibilities and his petulance over failure. You are not, however, expected to perform as a nurturing parent, nor is he to play the enthusiastic child. When necessary, you must be tough—the stern adult who resorts to logic, breaking through emotional barriers without becoming emotional.

Provide a Comfortable Climate. Few individuals can produce new ideas and creative solutions in an uncomfortable environment. Relieve creative people, as much as possible, of routine chores and supply them with office assistance.

Recognize Creativity—Publicly. Many creative people regard themselves as a different breed worthy of special consideration by management. Management should recognize and respond, within reason, to this feeling. Recognition is vital food for the soul of the creative person. His high energy level is directed toward satisfying his feeling of self-esteem. Therefore, all of his accomplishments should be given full recognition by bringing them to the attention of peers, superiors and upper management.

Understand That Creativity Is Not Enough. When hiring, don't seek those who are only creative. Someone with additional talents is to be preferred, even if his creativity is slightly less than that of another candidate. For example, in addition to being an original thinker, a creative person must be able to sell what he created. Management does not usually recognize a good idea unless it is presented by a good salesman.

Provide Instant Evaluation and Feedback. Creative people are impatient and expect their ideas to be evaluated quickly. Even though premature decisions are to be avoided, the creative person should be given a quick reading on his progress, even if you only indicate that his ideas are under study.

Put Up With Some Innocent Foibles. Do not deny creative individuals a few harmless quirks. Special furniture or decor and window views may be crucial to the creative function. Tolerate such personal idiosyncracies as: always making tea and never drinking it; never lighting the pipe that is constantly in his mouth; drinking soda continuously; having a messy office and cluttered desk.

Such foibles are innocent, and serve some purpose. They will also prevail over all efforts to eliminate them. The creative individual will inexorably march to his own drumbeat. As a manager, you should monitor the "beat" but don't try to change it.

Maintain an Intrapreneural Climate. This essentially means creating an entrepreneurial organization within a large bureaucracy. While large companies are good at coming up with sound ideas, they are generally poor at carrying them out because of a morass of analysis, approvals and politics. Instead of risking losing creative scientists and engineers who have caught the entrepreneurial fever, encourage them to become "intrapreneurs." Intrapreneurship seems to work best in companies (e.g., 3M) with a long tradition of encouraging employee independence and innovation within independent business units which essentially operate as separate organizations. Intrapreneurship has been adopted or tried by such companies as IBM, Hewlett-Packard, GE, Data General, Du Pont, Texas Instruments, AT&T, and General Motors Saturn Corporation.

Balance the Need for Freedom and the Necessity of Structure. At times freedom is required for creativity; at other times structure; and sometimes a combination of the two. Remember that the "playful" organization enables people to be more creative; the structured enables the creative to be more productive. The former may be more appropriate for research, the latter for business, but each has elements of the other and neither could succeed without embracing its opposite.

Michael Badawy is professor of technical management and applied behavioral sciences at Virginia Polytechnic Institute, Falls Church, Virginia. He is the author of Developing Management Skills in Engineers and Scientists, *published by Van Nostrand Reinhold.*

27.
NURTURING MANAGERIAL CREATIVITY

Eugene Raudsepp

The key to creativity is knowing how to generate new ideas. However, there's a lot more involved than sitting around waiting for inspiration to strike. Creativity is a highly "personal" process that can be encouraged or inhibited by the attitudes of management.

We are now confronting an accelerated rate of change in new technologies, socio-economic trends, and new attitudes and values. The near future promises to bring us, among other challenges: 1) economic uncertainty, 2) rising cost, 3) scarcity of resources, 4) sharper competition, 5) the specter of more government regulation, 6) a greater influence of international events in U.S. domestic affairs, 7) rising consumer discontent, 8) quicker-paced demographic changes, 9) greater emphasis on quality of work life, 10) growing discontent on the part of creative individuals with the corporate world of work.

The growing discontent is due to a number of factors: lack of proper recognition of the creative innovator and feedback to him or her, lack of understanding as to what motivates and fuels the innovator, improper managerial (non-specialist or non-technical) interference in decisions of purely technical nature, inadequate rewards structure for the innovators, lack of equitable parallel managerial and specialist promotion structures, disenchantment with fancy job titles with little or no substance, poor direction and management of creative employees. All this, at least for the early 1980s, will show itself in further faltering and deterioration in productivity and innovativeness.

To cope with these trends and problems, management urgently needs to use more creativity, imagination, and resourcefulness.

Creativity, of course, involves a lot more than merely sitting around waiting for inspiration to strike. An administrator must learn how to tap his or her subconscious for new ideas, capture the most promising ones, and develop them into feasible solutions. Much has been written about the nature of the creative process and of the means for measuring creative potential. But little is available about how to actually use creative powers to forge original and useful solutions.

The key to performing creatively is in knowing how to generate and work with new ideas—the creative mood must be nurtured, novel ideas captured when they occur, and the most valuable ideas developed in the light of the particular purpose or objective at hand.

STRATEGIES

Novel ideas cannot be induced at will, but you can encourage their appearance by fostering conditions that are conducive to creative thinking. Although these conditions will depend on your particular personality and habits, the following strategy will help you discover and apply them.

Pick the Right Time of Day. For many individuals, night is the best time for creative reflection. Daytime—with its practical orientation and bustling activity—can act as an obstacle to the emergence of original ideas. Of course, there are individuals who prefer the early morning hours for their creative labors. Others need bustling activity around them in order to stimulate their creative powers.

Whatever time is found to be most conducive to creative thinking, you must be able to close out the external world—to detach yourself from the surrounding commotion so that your inner world of ideas can come alive. This ability to become inwardly isolated is not necessarily conditional on outward isolation. Many creative people can tune in on their private selves in the noisiest of environments.

Inward isolation is the primary requirement for significant creative work. Without such detachment, you cannot fully exploit your creative potential. Moments of such detachment can be more productive than hours of merely physical isolation.

Learn How to Relax Mentally. Every creative person has his own peculiar ways of putting himself into the relaxing, expectant frame of mind that facilitates creativity. The composer Debussy used to gaze at the golden reflections of the setting sun on the river Seine to establish an atmosphere for writing music. The philosopher Schiller kept rotten apples in his desk-drawer; their aroma helped him get into the right mood for creative thought. Dostoyevsky found that he could dream up his immortal stories and characters best while doodling.

The point of these and similar peculiarities is to develop the free-floating concentration necessary to encourage new ideas and "see" their implications. These peculiarities are also necessary for restraining over-active thought patterns and for shutting out distractions. As one focuses on only a single scene or object, environmental distractions are muted or eliminated. This is essential, for the ringing of the telephone, a conversation down the hall, or some other momentary interference could shatter the protective bubble of the creative mood.

Left Hemisphere

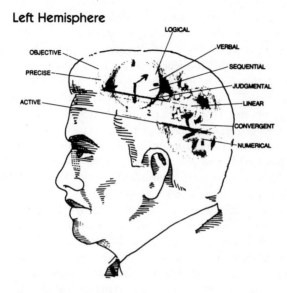

Right Hemisphere

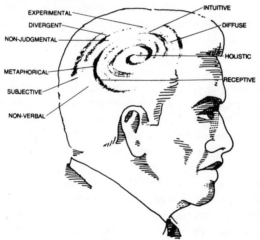

Perhaps the strongest support for the value and validity of intuitive thinking comes from recent scientific research which shows that the two hemispheres of the human brain mediate and process different kinds of tasks and problems. The left hemisphere (in our culture the more dominant and overdeveloped) specializes in verbal and numerical information processed sequentially in a linear fashion. The left hemisphere is the active, verbal, logical, rational, and analytic part of our brain. The right hemisphere is the intuitive, experimental, non-verbal part of our brain and it deals in images and holistic, relational grasping of complex configurations and structures. It creates metaphors, analogies, and new combinations of ideas.

For some people, physical activity promotes the flow of imaginative ideas that can bring a creative insight. This activity might consist of pacing the floor, hiking, or exercising. The outward rhythmic activity relaxes the conscious mind so that the unconscious can function freely.

What, then, is the best time to work? What habits are most conducive to creative thought? Too much variation exists to make any firm rules. Suffice to say, the optimum times and conditions for the production of new ideas are the occasions when you attain an uncluttered rapport with your subconscious and you feel free from the practical demands of the environment. You should be free from the stereotyped frame of mind that governs your noncreative periods, as well as from the conservative, established ways of thinking that crowd your consciousness during those periods.

This need for "inner relaxation" accounts for the frequent claim of many creative people that their most valuable ideas occur during periods of passivity, relaxation, or even fatigue. For example, Newton is said to have solved many of his problems when his attention was suspended by complete relaxation. Edison, when he was confronted with a seemingly insurmountable problem, would stretch out on a couch in his workshop trying to fall asleep.

Be Alert. Although the creative mood will encourage creativity, new ideas may appear at the most unexpected and inconvenient times. Thus, you must have a part of your mind on "standby" so that these ideas will not be overlooked.

Being open to creative thoughts means that you must be prepared to respond to them whenever they appear. For example, Newton regularly interrupted whatever he happened to be doing to follow up on an idea that had just occurred to him. Once, he had a particularly illuminating idea on the way to the cellar to get some wine for his dinner guests; he promptly forgot his errand and was found some time later hard at work in his study.

Maintain Productive Work Habits. Since creativity cannot be turned on at will, there will be periods of sterility in every creative person's life. For most individuals, the sterile periods greatly outnumber the creative ones. Some people find it hard to cope with such periods. They lapse into apathy and indolence, finding numerous excuses for postponing creative tasks. This is a sure way to develop poor work habits, and, perhaps, stifle future opportunities for insight.

Rather than give up or wait for what may never come, you should continue to think and work productively. By working even when you don't feel the presence of a driving inspiration, you will still be able to come up with solid solutions. While the quality of these solutions may not be earth-shaking, they will get the job done.

Above all, you should allow for a steady input of fresh information, experience, and points of view. These inputs serve as stimuli for your own creative thoughts.

CAPTURING NEW IDEAS

Creative ideas can be elusive and transient. At the moment when such an idea occurs, you may feel that it is unforgettable. Yet, only moments later, you may have forgotten it. If the idea is worthwhile, it should be put into some tangible form for later reference.

Precisely when an idea should be recorded depends on the individual and on the idea itself. People who have not had much experience with the creative process should commit new ideas to writing as soon as they appear. People with more experience should jot down firm ideas immediately, but allow the less-developed ideas to remain fluid and out of conscious focus for as long as possible. As a general rule, the more complex the idea, the more advisable it is to postpone recording it until its possibilities are explored.

There is a prevalent notion that the first ideas that emerge in the course of finding a solution to a problem are valueless. While this may be true with relatively unfamiliar problems or with problems on which no conscious effort has been previously spent, it is not true with problems that have been "stewing" for a long time. With these problems, the first ideas are frequently the best. Therefore, it is advisable to pay close attention to first ideas, even though the effortlessness with which they appear may make them suspect.

You should resist the urge to critique the idea while you are mulling it over or writing it down. Nothing will inhibit the creative process more than being critical of a new idea when it first emerges. This does not mean that criticism, judgment, and evaluation have no place in the generation of new ideas. But they should come into play only at the conclusion of the creative process, when an objective assessment is called for.

During the idea-capture stage, you should be aware only of the "suggestions" and "directions" that emerge from your subconscious. No single thought that occurs to you should be pinpointed as being most important, for this inhibits further development of the idea. In a sense, the creative person often first "feels" his idea, rather than thinks it.

HANDLING NEGATIVITY

Although creativity is a highly "personal" process, it can be encouraged or inhibited by the attitudes of management and other staff members. When a person's suggestions are subjected to immediate criticism, he is likely to conclude that the attack on his idea is an attack on him personally, and to develop hostility toward the person initiating the attack. He soon refrains from suggesting anything at all, or he resorts to second-guessing in an attempt to suggest something that will be accepted and approved.

One way to lessen the harmful effects of negative criticism on others is by learning to apply tact and diplomacy when criticism is necessary.

When a valuable new idea emerges, it is usually accompanied by a "global theme"—an inkling of the direction that the overall solution to the problem must take. You should hold onto this theme firmly because it will serve to guide the idea through the countless possibilities and pitfalls that will develop.

Because of this global theme, selectivity is exercised almost unconsciously. The feasibility of the idea is tested. Refinements and revisions are accepted and rejected. Apparent obstacles become opportunities for further development. At every stage of the development process, the global theme acts like a magnet that draws on the proper facts and experience to shape the original idea into its final form.

Occasionally, elements that are incorporated into the idea will later be seen to be irrelevant. But such revisions will be made in the light of the global theme. Only when you have a firm grasp of this theme will you be able to assemble the appropriate data that will contribute to the idea's development. This intuitive guidance should continue until you cannot improve the idea further.

Of course, idea development does not always go so smoothly. Sometimes the process is marked by many false starts and blind alleys. In such cases, only dogged persistence will succeed in clearing away the obstacles to success.

On rare occasions, you may feel that you can give in to the "white heat" of the creative mood. You may sense the implicit theme of the emerging idea so clearly that you can work straight toward the end result, without being hampered by the strain of having to sift through a maze of details and alternatives. Under these conditions, you should do whatever your subconscious promptings lead you to do. When the task is done, you will feel that your idea has grown effortlessly and almost spontaneously. Ideas developed in this fashion need, as a rule, very little revision.

The most likely possibility, however, is that the development of the new idea will go smoothly at first, only to give way to mounting frustration later on. As tension increases beyond some optimum point, you will find that you are forced to spend more and more effort, with less and less to show for it. Errors will start to pile up and the path of development will seem confused. At this point, it is important to stick to your work, calling upon all your reserves of energy and using all the methods of problem solving that have worked for you in the past.

Eugene Raudsepp is president of Princeton Creative Research Inc., Princeton, NJ. He is the author of More Creative Growth Games, *published by G.P. Putnam.*

28.
CREATIVE DECISION MAKING AND THE ORGANIZATION

David R. Wheeler

> Creative thinking is an intangible factor and difficult to use in improving the firm's bottom-line position, but without creative thinking among the employees, it is doubtful that a firm can remain competitive.

Creative decision making and problem solving are two of the most important talents that employees can posses, talents that are necessary for the financial health and prosperity of any firm. Unless a firm can respond with unique products/services, innovative marketing strategies and creative responses to complex problems, it may find itself losing sales, shares of the market and profits.

Creative thinking occurs at all levels of the firm. Good ideas for improvements and original insights into operations can arise in any group, from the hourly workers to the president.

The trend in education at business schools has been toward analytical reasoning to the almost total exclusion of intuitive reasoning. Formal statistical methodologies, quantitatively structured operations research techniques, and management science approaches have replaced subjective thinking. The result has been computer-like, "insulated" managers—and less understanding of the consumer.

The demise of creative business thinking has been noted by industry publications, the federal government and concerned workers. An article in the February 16, 1976 *Business Week*, "The Breakdown of U. S. Innovation," called it the "MBA syndrome," noting that the emphasis on scientific decision making has contributed to the decline in technological innovation. Risk is not to be taken unless the decision can be supported with objective facts, not subjective feelings. The emphasis in business has been directed toward current products and away from the invention or development of new products for the future.

Outside the area of product invention, creative employees are still an important aspect of a firm's success. Job success has been related to several factors, including nonverbal reasoning, judgment, intuition, intelligence and the ability to perform systematic analysis. Managers are needed who can temper logical and rational thinking with creative insight and intuitive understanding (judgment).

Creative thinking is needed in the sales department, for example. Successful salespeople are sorely needed who can interpret the buyers' wants and financial abilities and then translate these judgments into a persuasive campaign to convince the customer to buy the product. It has been found that salesclerks in department stores who have scored high on tests of creativity are also more likely to be in the top third of sales in their departments.

The most successful firms are those that recognize the value of their employees' creative talents and have found ways to use those creative talents to the best advantage of both parties.

THE FRAGILE COMMODITY

While the need for creative employees may be recognized, there has not been much progress made in teaching creative thinking. Most researchers in the area tend to believe that a person can be born an artist, a poet, a writer, a creative problem solver, but that teaching those talents is impossible. However, it has recently been shown that an enriched environment, practice and the proper attitude can be used to actually increase IQ scores.

In an evaluation of over 400 studies of managerial development programs, Robert J. House concluded that the results of such programs were sadly disappointing. So far, we do not know what creativity is or how to measure it, nor do we teach our employees to think creatively.

The process that goes on inside the human brain may still be a mystery, but fortunately, we do know there are certain things that an organization can do to make the creative process more likely to occur and even flourish. One of the most important of these elements is an organizational climate which is conducive to the free flow of ideas. It is crucial for managers, administrators and the employees themselves to recognize the need for the continual infusion of unique ideas into the business firm. Every employee's unique cognitive contribution must be recognized and rewarded if continued business interaction in the market is to be expected.

Creative decisions are a fragile commodity. They are easier to destroy than to develop. Just before the outstanding bankruptcy of the New York-based chain of department stores, W. T. Grant, managers were put through some strange training procedures to help "improve" their decision-making abilities. Those managers that did not meet their assigned store sales quotas, reported the *Wall Street Journal* (February 4, 1977), were hit in the face with pies during monthly "improvement sessions," had their ties cut in half, pushed peanuts around the floor with their noses or had to wear diapers in public. In such an oppressive environment as this must have been, business failure was almost guaranteed.

Creativity must originate from within the individual. Attempts to program creativity into an employee will only inhibit those processes which are essential for originality and innovation.

SETTING THE STAGES

In 1926, Joseph Wallas described the three stages of the creative process as preparation, incubation and illumination (insight). The creative environment of the firm must be constructed so that these stages can occur.

Preparation occurs in school, in life and on-the-job. It includes the skills of reading, writing, talking, listening and thinking. We learn these with practice. Incubation occurs as the subconscious mysteriously arranges various inputs into unique patterns of thought. Unable to "find" a solution, many people find that an answer will suddenly pop into their heads while their conscious attention is directed to some other task. Some creative people have learned how to relax their bodies, play golf, jog or turn to another project as soon as they find themselves "blocked" and unable to come up with a solution to a complex problem. Firms have discovered that employee decision making has been improved as the result of having exercise rooms, physical fitness programs and relaxation areas.

The third stage of the creative process, illumination, occurs when a solution or idea suddenly flashes in from the subconscious mind. Archimedes experienced this flash of insight during his attempts to discover the amount of impurities in the king's golden crown. Archimedes had consciously struggled with the problem for days before falling into his tub exhausted. While relaxing in the hot water, the answer appeared to his conscious mind: the law of specific gravity.

Several firms have devised ways to tape the creative resources of their employees. McDonald's, the hamburger chain, has installed special soundproof rooms with water beds where tired executives can go and relax while allowing their creative, subconscious minds to search for solutions. Prudential Insurance Company has found that its employees think better after only a couple of weeks of using the physical fitness centers. Consequently, employee turnover and absenteeism have also been reduced, since the employees who use the centers are sick less often. Prudential supervisors have reported that the quality of work, as well as the quantity, has increased significantly.

Creative thinking is an intangible factor and difficult to use in improving the firm's bottom-line position, but without creative thinking among the employees, it is doubtful that a firm can remain competitive. Intuition, subjective thought, creative ideas and decision making are difficult to measure and to teach. They come from within an individual, from that person's self-motivation. However, the conditions necessary for the growth of individual creative self-expression can be established within the organization by removing threats, negative sanctions and coercive influences. Every employee can be creative, even in the most routine of jobs, and every organization should try to establish a climate where original thinking can grow and flourish.

David R. Wheeler is assistant professor of Business Administration, University of Houston, Downtown College, Houston, Texas. He is the author of a book on the use of behavior modification techniques in self-development programs.

29.
TAKE THIS 10-LESSON COURSE ON MANAGING CREATIVES CREATIVELY

Bruce G. Vanden Bergh
Keith Adler

Managing a creative advertising staff is a balancing act. You must provide a structure for solving creative problems and identifying the most sensitive stages of the process. Getting to know your creatives takes time, but the rewards more than pay for this effort.

Here is a short course on managing creatives creatively. Its goal is to illustrate the creative process and identify places where you can improve your relationships with the creative people you manage or work with.

Lesson 1. The creative process is primarily perceptual, not analytical. Thus, the way your creative people see the problem at hand will affect the outcome more than anything else. Knowing this, be careful to paint a clear picture of what you expect from the creative process. The clearer the presentation of the problem, the better the solution can be.

Lesson 2. Recruit and hire talented creative people, and be willing to invest in them. You must have good writers, artists, and production people working on your projects to get good results. Talent can provide you with unlimited problem-solving possibilities; a lack of talent will seriously limit what you can accomplish.

Lesson 3. Know your creative people's styles, moods, interests, etc. Since certain problems require certain talents, match your people to the problems by determining who is most likely to be motivated by the specific challenge. Knowing your creative personnel takes time, but the rewards more than pay for this effort.

Figure 1.

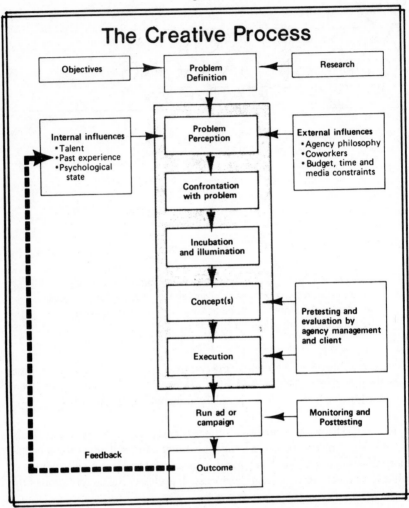

The Creative Process

Objectives → Problem Definition ← Research

Internal influences
• Talent
• Past experience
• Psychological state

→ Problem Perception ←

External influences
• Agency philosophy
• Coworkers
• Budget, time and media constraints

Confrontation with problem

Incubation and illumination

Concept(s) ← Pretesting and evaluation by agency management and client

Execution ←

Run ad or campaign ← Monitoring and Posttesting

Feedback

Outcome

Lesson 4. Once the problem is clear, the talent is good, and the people are matched to the problem, turn your attention to nurturing the right environment. A good fit between talent and surroundings can have a synergistic effect. Convey confidence and encourage risk-taking. Once you've turned the problem over to your creatives, let go. Defer your judgment of the process until later.

Lesson 5. Observe from a distance and don't interfere, but be willing to help if problems surface, such as creatives not working together as a team. You're now a socio-emotional leader, not a taskmaster, so smooth the ruffled feathers and encourage them to move forward. Be a good listener.

Lesson 6. At this stage it's necessary for the creatives to get a little crazy (that's how they get their ideas). First, they will attack the problem with a vengeance. Some will get irritable, others will gnash teeth, still others will appear placid. This stage is idiosyncratic and unpredictable, but let it unfold. If you want unique ideas that solve the problem differently and better than before, let their minds race from one possibility to another.

Lesson 7. Let it simmer. Many creatives need a period where they can get away from the problem and let it incubate. They need time. Give your creatives a free rein, but demand that the work get done on time. This a balancing act. It takes experience to know when you've reached the point where the reins need to be tightened.

Lesson 8. Get back to reality. There's still a problem to solve. Now is the time to judge and evaluate. Ideally, you'll have more than two good ideas to compare. Do your critical thinking out of range of your creatives. Then, carefully prepare your evaluation of their work. Be clear and specific, but also considerate. Massage their egos, but get the solution you want.

Lesson 9. The creative process is dynamic. Although you might be near the end of the project, your reaction to their creative work will affect how well the process works in the future. Always be constructive, and make sure the process ends with a sense of self-fulfillment for the creatives. Point out good aspects of all alternatives and let them know the final ideas are theirs.

Lesson 10. The process we've just described is diagramed in Figure 1. It provides a structure for solving creative problems and identifying the most sensitive stages of the process.

Bruce G. Vanden Bergh is associate professor of advertising and Keith Adler is assistant professor of advertising at Michigan State University, East Lansing, Michigan.

30.
BRAINSTORMING AS A
FLEXIBLE MANAGEMENT TOOL

Robert Kerwin

Brainstorming as a problem solving technique was developed in the 1930s. In this era of high technology it is still an effective technique to solicit ideas to meet a specific list of goals.

Recent experience has show me that brainstorming is a useful management tool not just to solve problems but also the help develop employees, establish policy, improve communication, and determine new business activities.

Having recently accepted the responsibility of managing a department that employs many creative engineers—who have diverse interests and backgrounds and work in four largely autonomous areas of technology—I was faced with various challenges. The most critical of these were to develop a personal understanding of the department's capabilities, to establish technical direction for the department, and to develop the next year's internal research and development plan. Although I did not want to change the basic character of the department, there were certain operational modifications that I felt would have long-term benefits. One area I wanted to improve was communication among the four technology areas. I believed that each area could benefit and grow from an understanding of the problems, limitations, and capabilities of the other areas.

This could certainly be achieved over a reasonable period of time, but next year's internal research and development plan was due in less than three months. This deadline posed a particular challenge because my background did not include significant experience in any of the four technologies.

I looked on the task of generating next year's plan as a vehicle for gaining a better understanding of the capabilities and interests of the department's senior staff. This understanding I believed would be invaluable in guiding the development of the department's product lines and the pursuit of new technologies. It was this belief that led me to tap the potentials of brainstorming as a flexible management tool.

THE BRAINSTORMING CONCEPT

The concept of a brainstorming session seemed tailormade to begin the process of improving interarea communication and begin deepening my own understanding of the unique character of the department and its personnel.

Brainstorming as a problem solving technique was developed in the 1930s by Alex F. Osborn. Several authors have described brainstorming as a technique to solve problems, generate new product ideas, and help develop a team spirit. Over the years it has been used, and possibly misused, to accomplish many other ends. My intent was to use the brainstorming technique to solicit ideas that would help meet the following goals:

- determine the department's capabilities and interests
- trigger interarea communications
- generate a shopping list of potential new products or technologies
- suggest approaches to improve marketing prowess
- improve the professional environment of the department
- identify policies, procedures, and operations that should be reviewed and improved
- improve productivity.

With these goals in mind I set about planning a brainstorming program. Ground rules for creating an atmosphere that will stimulate and maintain the free flow of ideas needed for a fruitful brainstorming session exist plentifully in the literature. Summarized below, in order of importance, are the rules I believe are essential for successful brainstorming:

1. No criticism or value judgments can be allowed during the sessions.
2. The quantity of ideas is more important than the quality of any single idea.
3. The number of participants should be between six and 10, including the leader. This number is large enough to keep the ideas flowing, but small enough to let everyone participate.
4. Participation, not ideas, should be complimented. If the leader compliments specific ideas, an atmosphere of reward seeking develops. What you are after is a freewheeling outpouring of ideas.
5. The leader should record each idea as it occurs, but these notes should not identify the author with the idea. Failing to observe this precaution can make the more sensitive participants clam-up because they don't want to say anything stupid. Remember, even bad ideas can and will generate good ones.
6. Each session should embrace at most four topics, and about one hour per topic should be allotted. (Even though the sessions I will describe covered five topics, the technique is just as effective when used for only one. In fact, five topics was at least one too many. I believe the limit should be three or four.)

FIND A PRIVATE PLACE

To free the brainstorming sessions from the constraints and interruptions of the normal workday environment, I decided to hold them off company premises. To promote a more relaxed and innovative atmosphere, I decided on a private residence rather than a hotel conference room.

There were about 14 people I wanted to involve in the brainstorming, so I planned two sessions. Once the decision was made to hold the sessions off site, the number of topics per session was increased from three to five, to insure that each group could devote a full day to brainstorming without running out of areas to explore.

Very little was done in the way of formal preparation. The participants were given one week's notice of the sessions and asked to give some thought to and do some selective reading about future hardware advances that might interest our customers—and that might add focus to our internal research and development plans. They were also told that the first topic for discussion would be technology-related. However, they were not informed of other specific topics to be discussed. During the sessions, I wanted them always to focus on the current topic and not be distracted by looking ahead to future topics.

Two groups were formed; each group represented a cross section of the four technical areas. The groups were scheduled on consecutive days to cut down the chances that the first group's ideas and discussions would bias the second group. Once a group arrived, I briefed them on the six ground rules listed above.

SESSION FORMAT

The discussion focused on the first topic until it became obvious that ideas were drying up and the conversations were beginning to drift. Then the next topic was opened for discussion.

I used a stand-up flip chart to log the ideas as they were generated. When one page was filled, I tore it off and taped it to the wall so that everyone could review what had been suggested. Toward the end of each day's session, as the flow of ideas slowed, we reviewed the lists, topic by topic, and each person selected two or three ideas he or she was willing to write about.

In the following week I assigned the ideas no one had selected to appropriate participants, so that each idea would be supported by at least a brief explanatory paragraph. I hoped these backup paragraphs would clarify the brief entries on the flip chart for readers who had not been part of the brainstorming sessions. (In fact, this proved not to be necessary since those who took interest in the results of the sessions grasped the ideas readily without recourse to explanatory paragraphs.)

OUTCOMES AND OBSERVATIONS

I found that a leader cannot contribute as much to the second group as to the first, mainly because of his or her knowledge of the previous day's activities. Several times, the second group's discussions appeared to parallel the first group's thoughts only to result in a totally different idea. In addition, there was not any significant statistical difference between the two groups with respect to the number of ideas on any single topic.

Each idea was evaluated as to which product line it might impact and which of the four sections within the department would be involved in its implementation. The ideas were also reviewed to determine if they should be candidates for the upcoming research and development plan. Each idea was assigned a priority that reflected its potential impact on the department's business plan. Those ideas with high priority that also qualified for research and development funding were added to the plan.

Those high priority items that did not qualify for the plan were given increased attention by myself and other senior members of the department. The non-technology topics were reported, without editing, to management.

Most of the ideas presented warranted follow-up and did aid in establishing direction for the department. Significant progress was made toward the goals we set out to accomplish. My understanding of the capabilities and interests of the people who attended the session was enhanced and, as was expected, communication among participants improved.

A major factor in this improvement was that each participant developed a better understanding of each intradepartmental area and its principal area of interest.

A COMPLETE SUCCESS

Many of the ideas raised have been given more focused attention than they would have received without the benefit of the brainstorming session. Many of the thoughts and suggestions that were generated during the two one-day brainstorming sessions are now a matter of policy in the daily operation of the department. Brainstorming surfaced several ideas that have been and will be useful in establishing technical direction for the department. Many of the technical ideas will be useful in determining future research and development planning. Useful suggestions surfaced in all the topics discussed, and the overall results are easily worth the cost of the sessions to the company. As was hoped, communication between participants improved, which will result in a smoother running, more efficient operation.

Robert Kerwin is manager of the Adaptive Techniques Department, Communications and Radar Division, Hughes Aircraft, Ground Systems Group, Fullerton, California.

31.
CREATIVITY

Dorothy Schaeffer

The secret to creative supervision is in making the familiar strange. This means more than just drawing charts, and revising policies and procedures. The creative manager is never afraid to explore the novel approach.

What is creativity? It is an illusive, subtle thing. If several people were asked to define creativity, they might call it "imagination, vision or ingenuity." Others might say that it is inspiration or genius. Until recently there was an acceptable belief by many that a person is born with this rare talent. Some authors describe it as the application of a person's mental ability and curiosity to discover something new. The act of relating previously unrelated things. Too deep? Think about it as being a way of looking at things through fresh eyes.

Whatever the definition may be, looking backward into history, we find the world's greatest thinkers suffering persecution, personal humiliation, even death for thinking ahead of their fellow men. They dared to use strange contexts to view familiar ideas and problems. The familiar was looked at in such a way that it became strange. An example occurred several centuries ago. Doctors believed that blood flowed from the heart to the body, surging through it like the tides of the sea. When a body of a fish was opened, the heart was seen acting like a pump. What had seemed to be familiar suddenly became strange to these men. Herein lies the secret to creativity—making the familiar strange.

Variety, as the adage goes, is the spice of life. None of us like to eat the same food all the time, read the same news stories. We wonder why advertisers don't realize we soon weary of seeing the same TV commercials. People are enthusiastic about novelties and new things. Every manager should recognize that this quirk of human nature gives numerous opportunities in business to use it as a stimulant to motivate employees.

So by knowing and understanding the traits and characteristics of creativity and the creative person, the manager can use it as another tool to improve performance and get results.

What is the description of a creative manager? He or she is a person who has a broad interest in life. These interests span many unrelated fields. This type of individual has a great need for independence, wanting to call the shots although respecting authority from a professional viewpoint.

He or she is motivated more by interesting, challenging work. Status and prestige are often secondary. This creates a highly mobile, independent personality who finds it difficult to be satisfied with the status quo. To others of less creative ability, this type of individual at times appears to rock the boat.

Many managers are so naive they envision themselves as being creative but confine this outlook to drawing charts and revising policies and procedures. The limit of creativity is often confined to technological creativity. We abound in technological innovations. What industry needs is innovation in the human sphere. Little if any thought is given to getting an employee to see the job in a different perspective.

Most creative managers spend more time on problem solving in the early stages. As was mentioned earlier, it involves application of a person's mental ability and curiosity to discover something new. He or she is never afraid to explore a novel approach, allowing the unusual to sift through the imaginative subconscious. This person recognizes he or she must be willing to make mistakes.

Since creativity can be stimulated by individuals in varying degrees, there are a number of ways managers can develop it in themselves and in their subordinates. One technique for group creativity is called brainstorming. Here a group gets together for not more than an hour. They are encouraged by the leader to throw out all their ideas on the subject. No one passes judgment regardless of how unusual or impractical an idea may appear to be. The leader has an individual outside of the group to record ideas as fast as they are suggested. This group interaction gives each member an opportunity to build on the ideas and thoughts of others.

Another technique uses the same principles but lets each individual work independently. If the persons are especially creative, this well may produce more profitable ideas than the group.

Great, you say. This sounds all well and good. As a manager, how am I supposed to apply all this theory to my job? I work in the real world. My company does have rules and regulations. I don't want to appear to be some kind of a nut.

The individual manager can apply creativity to any task if the axiom of making the familiar strange is applied.

What about monthly office meetings? Do your personnel stroll in with he same old "ho-hum" look on their face? The same old familiar place, faces, meeting and problems!

A second level manager in a large organization recently planned his quarterly results meeting using the following approach with his first level supervisors. Needless to say, they still remember it.

Each manager was told to report to a nearby shopping mall at exactly 1 p.m. No other details were given except they wouldn't be home until late that evening. In the parking lot they climbed aboard a rented bus and were taken to the city museum. They were shown the company's new products by a representative of the sales department in a small meeting room. After the meeting, refreshments were served, and a short tour of the museum was made. (Many had never been there although they had lived in the community most of their lives.)

The next stop was a local historical sight. Sitting around under huge oaks at picnic tables, the group's performance for the previous quarter was reviewed with handouts, discussions, etc. After the group left there, the plans and goals for the next quarter were discussed and finalized by the second level manager as he talked from the front of the bus.

The final destination turned out to be in the next town where the group was served refreshments and dinner.

Creativity? And then some! The managers could hardly wait for the next meeting. There could be no doubt in any person's mind talking with them that they were making every effort to reach the goals they had agreed upon to ensure their part of the continuation of such meetings. Was this the usual quarterly meeting? No way!

Another angle! What about the attendance discussion with the employee who is never off from work or the employee who can always be counted on to do a good job? The manager of this employee was overheard to say, "What am I expected to say to Bill? I told him last month how great he was and how much I appreciated his efforts."

So what! The creative manager might say, "Bill, let's go to the snack bar for a cup of coffee. Your attendance (work) is so good, I've run out of things to say to you. Let's spend the time letting you tell me about that fishing trip you made on your vacation." Bill has grown 10 feet tall. This is a discussion he will long remember. Far longer than the talk the supervisor might have had at his desk.

Within the restrictive boundaries of any organization, there is opportunity for creativity. Every assembly line supervisor or office manager can use it to improve performance and morale.

What about the tasks that are so routine it is hardly possible to provide any variety? These can be relieved by shifting assignments or jobs. Look at the group's schedules, goals, environment, surroundings. Will change help break the "burnout" that comes from boredom? Can objectives be original or different?

To sum up, a lack of creativity can be unwillingness to do something differently, not to make any waves. Putting it very bluntly, mentally and physically lazy. Creativity is a natural expression that each person has to the degree he or she wishes to exercise it. It has been said that human rights and creativity are part of the same coin. Without one, the other is impossible.

The individual payoff for creativity does not necessarily come in the paycheck but in the satisfaction of working in an environment where one can experiment and develop his or her full range of potential in meeting challenges. It is more than a fashionable addition to modern management. It is a requirement demanded by rapidly changing technology and human values.

32.
CREATIVITY, PROBLEM SOLVING AND DECISION MAKING

Jim G. Gillis

> Do certain individuals seem to have that gift of analytical prowess coupled with artistic creativity? Undoubtedly, this type of individual is headed into a high ranking executive position.

Look around you. Do you see certain individuals who seem to have that gift of analytical prowess coupled with artistic creativity? These individuals most likely follow basic steps when approaching a problem and use their imaginative creativity when decision making occurs. They seem to be able to draw on facts, ask the correct probing questions and use their ingenuity and people skills to identify the "not so obvious" or gray areas. Entrepreneurial charisma surrounds them and presents an aura of confidence to those dealing with them.

They are able to break down huge systems into smaller interrelated subsystems and determine how they function together. This gives them a "whole picture" framework to work with. Undoubtedly, this type of individual is headed into a high ranking executive position within the company. The three areas in which this all relates are:

- Creativity
- Problem Solving
- Decision Making

CREATIVITY

Try this test to find out how creative a person you are. Answer each item below either True or False.

209

Quiz

1. You were closer to your mother than
   to your father.   True [ ]   False [ ]
2. You have always been a good reader.   True [ ]   False [ ]
3. You usually daydream more than your
   friends do.   True [ ]   False [ ]
4. The more intelligent you are, the
   more imaginative and creative you
   are likely to be.   True [ ]   False [ ]
5. Since our I.Q.'s are limited, we
   cannot increase our problem
   solving ability.   True [ ]   False [ ]
6. It is always easier to solve a
   problem if you are eager to do so.   True [ ]   False [ ]
7. It's best to strongly focus all
   your attention on your problem
   and try to think it through.   True [ ]   False [ ]
8. It's best to be under some degree
   of stress when trying to solve
   a problem.   True [ ]   False [ ]
9. Building confidence through
   repeated success will always increase
   your ability to be a good problem
   solver.   True [ ]   False [ ]
10. To be creative we must apply
    consistent effort to our problems.   True [ ]   False [ ]

Answers and Explanations

In order to calculate your score, review the answers and explanations below, and award yourself one point for each correct answer.

1. TRUE Studies by psychologists J. Singer and R. Schonbar of Yale University in Connecticut show that those who identify with their mothers tend to be more creative thinkers, for some reason, than those who identify with their fathers. By the way, the researchers did not find the mothers to be more creative than the fathers, necessarily.

2. TRUE A study of over 500 suburban school children in Philadelphia, Pa., showed that reading skill and creative thinking ability go together. If you were a good reader as a child, you stand a better chance of being a creative person than if you were a poor reader.

3. TRUE Psychologist J. Singer, mentioned above, also found that daydreaming and creative thinking are correlated. One who is free to daydream is

also free enough to allow his imagination to work creatively towards the solution of a problem.

4. FALSE There is no connection between I.Q. and creative thinking. Creativity exists on different levels. Even a person of low intelligence can be creative within his or her own limits. By the same token, a very bright person may fail to be creative in day-to-day operations.

5. FALSE Productive thinking can be taught. Scientists M. Covington and R. Crutchfield of the University of California at Berkeley developed a program of imaginative thinking used by thousands of children. They say: "The basic idea is to teach them to use their minds in the manner of imaginative scientists, scholars, and detectives."

6. FALSE Although we should have some degree of interest in a problem, if our intensity of motivation is too high, it can hamper us. As our zeal increases, our effectiveness may also increase but only to an optimal point. Beyond that point, eagerness will be a deterrent to efficiency.

7. FALSE It is virtually impossible to force our minds to yield an answer to a troubling question. The European psychoanalyst Viktor Frankl discovered what he called "paradoxical intention." This means we should divert our attention away from our problem, take a break and forget it awhile. Later, when we return to the problem, we will see other aspects of it that were not noticeable before.

8. TRUE It may appear wise to relax and just allow the solution to come to you, but in actuality, this is not so. A small amount of pressure on us energizes our nervous systems enough to produce better quality thinking and memory.

9. FALSE There is such a thing as being overconfident. When we have a large number of successes behind us, we might form a "functional fixity," which means we become complacent, uncreative, and apply old solutions to new problems.

10. FALSE The solution to an enigma may often be available at an unconscious level, although we seldom tap this resource. When we sleep on a problem, we allow our unconscious mind to dwell on it. If practical, let a few days go by before you make an important decision. This incubation period may produce a creative solution.

What Your Score Means

After tallying your score, interpret it by reading the categories below.

7-10 correct—You are a creative thinker. You should be working in a job that offers you the chance to be an "idea person."

3-6 correct—You are among the vast majority of us who have average ability to generate imaginative solutions to problems.

0-2 correct—You are not at your best as an imaginative person. You would work best in tasks that require you to follow a set plan of action.

PROBLEM SOLVING

Managers have five methods by which they may approach problem solving. Here is a list of those five approaches.

1. *Traditional Problem Solving*
   This method is based on historical data and evidence. It will not enhance your ability and potential for advancement; however, it can be used in some cases.
2. *Rational Method*
   There are seven basic steps to traditional problem solving:
   a. An expected standard of performance which compares to an actual performance.
   b. A problem is a deviation from a standard of performance.
   c. A deviation from standard must be precisely identified, located and described.
   d. There is always something distinguishing that which has been affected by the cause, from that which is not affected.
   e. The cause is always a change that has taken place through some distinctive feature, mechanism or condition.
   f. The possible causes of a deviation are deduced from the relevant changes found in analyzing the problem.
   g. The most likely cause of deviation is one that exactly explains all the facts in the specification of the problem.
3. *Experimental Problem Solving*
   This method is basically done in labs, electronics, chemistry and mining.
4. *Creative Problem Solving*
   This appears to be the fastest growing method. This is basically done by brainstorming which applies to retail and advertising business nature.
5. *Quantitative Method*
   This method involves three areas:
   a. C.P.M.'s used especially in construction planning and monitoring.
   b. Breakeven analysis, which is a very powerful management tool.
   c. Inventory control in order to have the optimum quantities of stock on hand.

DECISION MAKING

There are seven basic steps to follow when attempting decision analysis.

1. The objects of the decision must be established first.
2. All objectives are classified in terms of importance.
3. Alternatives should be developed.

4. Alternatives are then evaluated against the established objectives.
5. Choice of the alternatives best able to achieve all the objectives represents the tentative decision.
6. The tentative decision is examined for possible future adverse consequences.
7. The effect of a final decision is controlled by taking other actions to prevent possible adverse consequences—make sure actions are carried out.

CONCLUSIONS

This article has presented three specific areas, in particular, Creativity, Problem Solving and Decision Making, which can be applied in daily operations and at every level within the organization.

By developing and maximizing your subordinates' skills, you will be enhancing your own at the same time. This kind of practice is just good fundamental management and leadership, which is so vital in any organization's success. If this is consistently applied, you win, your subordinates win, and your company wins.

Part V:
STIMULATING
NEW IDEAS

33.
HOW TO SPARK
NEW IDEAS

Sharon Nelton

> The most commonly mentioned obstacle to creativity is constraint. Constraint includes the absence of freedom in deciding what to do or how to do it, and lack of control over one's own ideas.

Consider what a creative breakthrough can do for a company. James Schlatter, a research chemist at G.D. Searle & Company, discovered aspartame and launched the pharmaceutical firm into the food business. Introduced nationally in 1982, NutraSweet, Searle's brand name for the low-calorie sweetener, brought the company $585 million last year.

Herman Miller, Inc., has been creating benchmarks in office furniture and environments since the 1930s. In 1968, the Zeeland, Mich., firm introduced the "Action Office," a concept of separating work spaces by shoulder-level dividers that has since become familiar in American offices. The firm is known for its Eames and Ergon chairs and last year came out the with the Equa chair, seating that adjusts to your body when you sit in it, and the Ethospace office, a complex of furniture and interior architecture aimed at humanizing and personalizing workspaces.

Its consistently creative output enabled Herman Miller to grow from a $30 million company with 500 employees in 1973 to over $400 million in sales and 3,000 employes in 1984.

Smaller companies know the value of creativity, too. Alan Canfield, senior vice president of A. J. Canfield Company, a regional beverage maker based in Chicago, wanted to develop a unique product to enter the diet soda market.

He came up with a formidable challenge for his chief chemist, Emanuel Wesber: Develop a diet soda that smelled and tasted like Fannie May fudge.

It took Wesber more than a year, but Canfield brought out Diet Chocolate Fudge Soda in the early 1970s. It enjoyed a modest success, and the company was ready when a series of events combined to send sales soaring.

One was the evolution of the fitness boom, which heightened the demand for diet drinks. Then came NutraSweet, which improved the taste but not the caloric content of such drinks. Canfield devised a way to cut distribution costs to offset the higher cost of the NutraSweet and launched a $350,000 television campaign. The effort received an extra push when nationally syndicated *Chicago Tribune* columnist Bob Greene wrote that the soda had helped him lose 22 pounds.

Canfield sold 30 million cans of its diet fudge soda in the first three months of 1985 alone, compared with 1 million in all of 1984. Instead of just four Midwestern states, the company now reaches 44 states.

The fudge soda and other innovations (such as a carbonated water that outsells Perrier in the Midwest) has helped the firm grow from 260 employees in the pre-diet-fudge days to nearly 500.

Call it creativity or innovation, the ability to come up with new ideas and make them work is, for most companies, the only way to stay alive. "An established company which in an age demanding innovation is not capable of innovation is doomed to decline and extinction," predicted management sage Peter F. Drucker a dozen years ago. "And a management which in such a period does not know how to manage innovation is incompetent and unequal to its task. Managing innovation will increasingly become a challenge to management, and especially to top management, and a touchstone of its competence."

How, then, can managers enhance creativity in their companies? The secret, many managers and experts agree, lies in developing a work environment in which creativity can flourish. While some chief executives bemoan the lack of creativity in their companies and blame employees, others hold themselves accountable for nourishing innovation.

"Responsibility for creative excellence starts at the top," says Norman W. Brown, president and CEO of Foote, Cone & Belding, the world's eighth largest advertising agency. "It is my primary responsibility."

Since creativity is central to the advertising business, Brown wanted to be sure that FCB was doing everything that could be done to support it. In late 1983, he set up a "creative strategy task force" representing the different disciplines and geographic areas of the Chicago-based company. For the next nine months, the team tracked ad campaigns, good and bad, back to their inception to find out what people and processes were used in their creation.

As a result of the task force findings, FCB adopted a set of principles called its "Strategic Creative Development Process." The principles appear in FCB's 1984 annual report. One of the most fundamental calls for "close collaboration between analyst and artist."

Traditionally, Brown explains, advertising campaign strategies have been devised by the advertising company's account executives working with managers from the client companies. Such executives, says Brown, are "left-brained" people, who rely primarily on the analytical left hemisphere of the brain and are logical, orderly and highly verbal. A strategy conceived that way was considered inviolate, and would then be turned over to the creative staff—writers and artists, for example—for implementation. "Their work would be evaluated precisely and often literally against that strategy."

But Brown says the task force learned that by themselves, left-brained people "articulate strategies in a closed way that tends to defeat the creative spirit rather than serve as a launching platform for creativity."

"What we found is that at its best, strategy itself is often a creative process. Logical, linear thinking only takes you so far and seldom makes the leap to truly brilliant, insightful strategy."

Now FCB brings the creative people—those who rely on the intuitive, artistic right hemisphere of the brain—into the process from the beginning, involving them in setting strategy as well as carrying it out. And once it is formulated, the strategy is no longer untouchable. Sometimes, says Brown, the work of the creative team will lead to an improvement in the strategy.

In a recent newsletter, Haley Associates, Inc., a New York executive recruiting firm, says it has noticed that more clients have begun to ask for candidates with creativity. But companies often make this request gingerly, "as if creativity were a rare and volatile gift for which they will have to pay too high a price. The unspoken plea is 'give us an innovative thinker, but please make him someone who can straighten his tie and get along with the staff.'"

Many managers are uncomfortable with creative people and do not regard themselves or their jobs as creative, according to Stanley S. Gryskiewicz, director of creativity development at the Center for Creative Leadership in Greensboro, N. C. As an early step in making their companies more innovative, he encourages managers to discard some old notions about creativity. Gryskiewicz, who defines creativity as "bringing something into existence for the first time," says some executives view creativity as something that is magical or mystical.

But Gryskiewicz says that everyone is creative, though styles of creativity may differ. "Innovators" challenge the definitions of problems to be solved and aim at doing things differently, while "adapters" accept problems as defined but work to do things better. Companies need both types, says Gryskiewicz.

And they need to look at creativity not as something mysterious but as a resource that can be developed. By taking that attitude, he says, "executives may be able to reconcile the need for innovation with the need for conservative, low-risk management styles."

When companies ask a recruiter to find creative managers, says Thomas H. Ogdon, Haley Associates executive vice president, they are looking for someone with "the ability to enter the problem-solving process with a fresher mind and come out with solutions that are unique." They want this quality combined with management and organizational skills.

The recruiting firm looks for an affirmative answer to three questions when it is evaluating a candidate: Does he look at a situation from several points of view? Does he resist snap judgments? Is there an absence of absolutes from his thinking?

Had he been put through the Haley screening process, Richard F. Wright probably would have filled the bill. Four years ago, Wright headed up an advanced product development team of six scientists and technicians at Mead Corporation, the paper products company headquartered in Dayton. He took an interest in the work of Fred Sanders, an inventor who was working in a different department at Mead and who was sneaking some experimental time for a new idea he had: a process for dry-developing color images on light-sensitive paper.

The company had done no imaging research, and there was little excitement about Sander's results, which, so far, were crude. But Wright, a chemist who had worked for Polaroid, saw the potential. He and his boss convinced Mead management to support research to develop the process further. Sanders (now retired) joined Wright's group, and the project was under way.

Today, the process is so advanced that the color images produced are of the quality found in better magazines. It is not on the market yet, however. Ultimately, the process will be linked with computers to make high-quality prints of images created on color screens at higher speed and lower cost than current technologies, such as ink jet and thermal transfer, permit.

While the Mead system is ready, the printer capable of linking the computer with that process is not. Wright's people are working with hardware manufacturers to help them develop a printer that would use the Mead light sensitive paper.

Last year, Mead Imaging, an out-growth of Wright's group, was formed as a separate division of Mead to commercialize the new technology. Wright, who expects that the system can be brought to market by 1988, is vice president of research and development of the new division. His original team of six has grown to 55, including 35 R&D scientists and technicians.

In the process of refining a new technology and making it marketable, Wright's high-performing group has filed nearly 40 patent applications. What kinds of management techniques did Wright use to bring about such a productive creative effort?

"The key idea came from an individual, as it almost always does, but it had to have a group of people to turn it into something useful," answers Wright. "One of the major factors in group creativity is focusing an individual's creative impulses on a group problem."

Wright uses the words "innovation" and "creativity" interchangeably. Having a "great new idea, period" is not enough. "In my view, something's got to happen," he says.

He practices "management by walking around," a Hewlett-Packard technique popularized by the book *In Search of Excellence*. "My style had always been one of spending most of my day walking around the halls talking to people and being aware of what is happening in the group," says Wright. "I do most of my work out in the hallways."

But he says a manager has "to walk a fine line between interfering in everybody's work and being supportive." He sees the role of the research and development manager not as one of controlling and manipulating employees but of being a leader. He also allows what he calls "creative meandering," permitting employees to set their own directions as long as they are focusing on the group objective.

Corporate culture and a physical environment that helps express that culture are key factors in nurturing creativity at Herman Miller, Inc.

"We're a research-driven product company, says David L. Armstrong, vice president of marketing. Instead of "surveying the market and making something to sell next year," he explains, the company's research subsidiary studies workplaces and tries to solve problems in work environments.

Herman Miller saw, for example, that most people did not make use of all the adjustments and knobs on office chairs that are supposed to make them more comfortable. They needed chairs that would be comfortable without manipulating knobs. "Therefore, we set out to design a chair to solve that problem," says Armstrong. The answer was the Equa chair, which is designed to flex in response to the person sitting in it and permits one to recline while keeping one's feet flat on the floor.

Another important aspect of the Herman Miller culture is that it is a "Scanlon Plan" company, adhering to principles developed years ago by labor leader Joseph Scanlon. Under the program, all employees participate in the management of the corporation by meeting in small groups to gather and share information about company performance, from the scrap rate to the percentage of shipments that are on time. Group representatives meet once a month with corporate officers to discuss performance and ways of improving it.

"I think the organization is by nature permission-giving," Armstrong says. "It gives permission to participate and understand. It also gives permission to make mistakes, be vulnerable and try new things. I think it sets up an atmosphere that's extremely active and productive in creative endeavors."

Just as Herman Miller is concerned with the workplaces of its customers, it gives attention to its own physical environment. While workspaces vary according to function and location of a given faculty, many are colorful and full of light, with windows opening onto green spaces. The company is known for the playful life-size sculptures of working people, by Stephen Hansen, that adorn the buildings. Armstrong calls it a "very work-rich environment" and finds it "extremely catalytic."

In recent research, Teresa M. Amabile, an assistant professor of psychology at Brandeis University and an associate of the Center for Creative Leadership, interviewed 46 research and development managers in over two dozen companies to learn which factors stimulate creativity and which ones inhibit it.

"Freedom" was the most commonly mentioned environmental stimulant for creativity. According to Amabile, this meant "freedom in deciding what to do or how to do it, a sense of control over one's ideas, a freedom from having to meet someone else's constraints, a generally open atmosphere."

It did not mean a complete absence of supervision, however. Usually, a project manager and higher-level supervisors played an important role in setting the direction of a project. "In those instances," says Amabile, "freedom came from the scientists' sense that their own ideas contributed in a major way to the day-to-day scientific conduct of their work."

The most commonly mentioned obstacle to creativity, according to the study, was constraint. "Constraint included an absence of freedom in deciding what to do or how to do it, a lack of control over one's own ideas," says Amabile.

The study supports the idea that broad goal setting is still necessary, however. Said one manager of a successful project: "I gave the people involved a clear idea of what the end product was going to be. I attempted to get each person involved in those aspects that were in their expertise, and I asked them how they would go about doing it. Beyond that, I let people set their own goals and manage their own business."

In contrast, another respondent said that a project suffered because not even broad goals were being set: "It's hard to work without certain goals in mind."

Effectively pursued, creativity is not only good for a company's bottom line, it is also good for the organization itself. According to Eugene Raudsepp, president of Princeton Creative Research, Inc., in Princeton, N.J., creativity spurs increased productivity by revitalizing employee motivation and generating effective team performance.

Managers everywhere are finding that they can plan for and nurture creativity. They can, in fact, take the mystery out of it and take steps to unleash and harness the good ideas that reside within subordinates—and within themselves. Together with psychologists, behavioral scientists and other experts on creativity, they have uncovered ways to help innovation flourish. Here are some of the best ideas:

Encourage Active Communication. Don't worry if subordinates spend a lot of time talking with each other, advises Mead's Richard Wright; you'll find out soon enough who's really wasting time. When people talk with each other often, they soon start sharing a lot of wild ideas, some of which will be good for the company.

"We don't have to structure meetings to do brainstorming," says Wright. "You can walk down the halls here and find brainstorming sessions going on across group lines almost constantly. Some of the most exciting things that happen in our group happen because these conversations take place."

Make Use of Diversity. That's what Foote, Cone & Belding did when it brought its analytical people together with its artistic people in developing ad strategies.

Creativity experts say that bringing together people with diverse backgrounds enhances the cross-fertilization process that is helpful in generating ideas. People from outside your field, for example, don't know that "something can't be done." They sometimes offer an entirely new—and workable—perspective.

Minimize Fear of Failure. "Act in a way that clearly demonstrates the attitude that if ideas are not adapted or do not work out, they are not wasted," counsels Eugene Raudsepp. "Regard errors and mistakes as opportunities for learning. Punitive action for every mistake or failure leads to excessive dependence on safe ways of doing things," he says.

Keep an Open Mind. Listen to all ideas, no matter how farfetched, and try to develop a capacity for recognizing a good idea when you see one—even if it is your own.

Denise Ertell, director of public affairs at Searle, says James Schlatter's discovery of aspartame came about by accident. He was heating a combination of amino acids and accidentally spilled some of the mixture on his fingers. Later on, he licked a finger to pick up a piece of filter paper and noticed a very sweet taste. He finally traced it back to the compound he was working with. He had the sense to recognize that the discovery might be useful—and so, says Ertell, did others in the company.

"Listening to your customers is the best way to make your business grow," contends Leonard A. Lauder, president and chief executive officer of Estee Lauder, Inc. In 1958, a cosmetic buyer for Neiman Marcus asked Lauder why the company didn't sell its product Youth Dew as a fragrance instead of a bath oil. That was how people were really using it, the buyer said.

Lauder tried it. "I made up a few hundred thousand samples as a perfume. I didn't change the formula. I simply put it in a bottle and said put it on your body rather than dump it into the bath."

When it was sold as a bath oil 17 years ago, Youth Dew sales were $50,000 a year. Last year, its sales as a fragrance were $150 million worldwide.

Embrace Fun. Many creative people believe that having fun is essential to the process of creating. A Herman Miller brochure even speaks of one of its designers, Bill Stumpf, as "just a big kid. Ergonomic design is his playground."

Budget Adequately for Innovation. Herman Miller spends just over 3 percent of its budget on R&D, and that is high for the industry. The results are worth it.

Instill a Positive Attitude. In group settings, for example, instead of trying to find the flaws in new ideas, encourage your people to find the pluses first and examine the negatives later. In such an atmosphere, people become more willing to suggest ideas; they need not fear being ridiculed.

Allow for Diversity in Personal Styles. Jack Pentes, an artist entrepreneur who founded Pentes Design in Charlotte, N.C., says he realized that he did some of his best thinking in the shower when he heard how often he started staff meetings with, "I had this idea in the shower this morning..."

Some people get their best ideas while walking on the beach or jogging, others during the relaxed moment just before sleep, and still others while on vacation.

Mead Corporation executive Richard Wright recalls that, as a young chemist at another company, he would frequently leave his work station to ponder problems while walking around the building, then feel guilty about being nonproductive. A boss told Wright, however, that he was doing fine and should continue to follow whatever style best suited him when it came to searching for new ideas.

Wright soon recognized the wisdom of that advice. An assignment relating to analysis of body fluids led to a walk along a river bank, where he worked out one of his best ideas toward the solution of the problem. He went back to the company, sat down in the cafeteria with a cup of coffee and wrote out the idea on a napkin.

The napkin, he says, is still in the company's files. Wherever it is, it is a symbol of two key factors in the proper approach to creativity: managers who recognize that different people need different types of environments in which to stretch their imaginations and workers who can take advantage of these environments, which can range from a well-equipped laboratory to a river bank.

34.
THE SEARCH FOR
GOOD IDEAS

William G. Kirkwood

Your search for good ideas will be more successful if you explore various definitions of the problem, separate identification and evaluation, build on available ideas, and avoid premature solutions.

In a time of dwindling natural resources, unpredictable interest rates, and increasingly tough challenges from foreign and domestic competitors, it's easy to conclude that all our problems could be solved with cheaper energy, more capital, or some other wave of an economic good fairy's magic wand. But in fact only one thing resolves the difficulties that confront individuals, organizations, and nations—good ideas. To be sure, being in the right place at the right time, fierce determination, and down-right good luck all contribute to success in business and other pursuits. But even these are worthless if they do not serve a sound idea. Thomas Edison may have been right when he remarked, "Genius is 1 percent inspiration and 99 percent perspiration," but without that critical 1 percent all the hard work in the world can't solve the difficult problems we face from time to time.

Perhaps Edison's comment has been cited so often because it is reassuring. We all know what hard work is, and we're all capable of it. However, inspired thinking is a much more mysterious and elusive commodity, seemingly one "you've either got or you don't." The how-to of inspiration is far from obvious, if there is any "how" to it at all. Where good ideas come from is sometimes plain enough after the fact, but when one's still searching for the solution to a difficult problem, even the most concerted efforts can seem aimless and futile.

Then what can be said about the search for good ideas? The ability to discover creative solutions to unusual and complex problems is indeed a rare talent. Nonetheless, the skills and attitudes that foster creativity can be consciously learned. A variety of slogans, aphorisms, tricks, and techniques for enhancing creative thinking have been offered by successful problem solvers, but it is possible to identify a few core principles that have applied in many successful problem-solving efforts. By making these principles a conscious part of our problem solving, we can discover good ideas with greater success, and we can help those who work or live with us to develop their own potential for sound thinking.

Here are the four principles that can make the search for good ideas more effective and more satisfying.

EXPLORING ALTERNATE DEFINITIONS

We all know there are many ways to solve a problem, but most of us believe that there is only one definition of the problem and the first step in problem solving is to state this definition. Nothing could be further from the truth. Indeed this fallacy is one of the most common barriers to inventive thinking. There are often several equally valid (but not equally obvious) ways of defining any problem, and the definition one settles on will determine the kinds of solutions to be considered.

Suppose we want to reduce unsightly and harmful litter in the nation's parks and recreation areas. What is the real problem? How to apprehend and punish litterers? How to persuade park visitors not to litter? How to better clean up inevitable litter? How to make litter less visible? Each definition is, in truth, the general statement of a potential solution to the problem. Rather than trying to determine which is "the right definition," the wise problem solver will view each definition as a sign post for a different avenue of thought. The individual will pick one definition and see where it leads, reserving the others for future reference if the first choice doesn't get results.

If you do the same, you will greatly increase your chances of identifying good ideas.

KEEPING IDEA IDENTIFICATION AND IDEA EVALUATION SEPARATE

Keeping idea identification and idea evaluation separate is often associated with brainstorming, a technique developed by advertising executive Alex Osborn. But the basic principle should be practiced in most problem solving situations, for the mental processes of idea invention and idea evaluation are incompatible.

Trying to search for possible solutions and judge them at the same time results in many ideas being rejected without being given a fair chance and the search being narrowed down to just a few possibilities. Also, it can discourage people from contributing their ideas. In group discussions there are some members who may be reluctant to voice their ideas because they will immediately be criticized by other group members. All this is not to say that evaluating ideas is undesirable, only that evaluation and inspiration should be separate activities, each performed in its own time. Doing so will improve the quality of both processes.

LEARN TO BUILD ON IDEAS, AS WELL AS CRITICIZE THEM

Imagine you've finally solved a perplexing problem after weeks or months of thought and someone asks, "How did you do it?" Would you trace all the false starts, wrong ideas, and vague suspicions you had along the way? Probably not. You'd only mention the highlights of the process. Years later, even these would no longer be recounted; the entire process would seem more like a historical event: "In 1983 Smith at last discovered a cure for the common cold."

Perhaps because successful problem-solving efforts are usually portrayed in an abbreviated form (and often with more than a little dramatizing), many believe great ideas lie dormant for some time in the mind of the thinker, then suddenly emerge full-grown and perfect in a moment of dazzling insight. Guided by this belief, their search for a good idea becomes a process of rejecting anything less than a perfect solution and waiting for that full-grown, unflawed idea to finally present itself.

Of course, it rarely happens that one's thinking takes a super-human leap from a total lack of insight to sudden awareness of an ideal solution. Quite the contrary. If we reject all the imperfect ideas we consider and wait for a totally satisfactory solution to arise, we soon tire of waiting and, faced with a growing pile of rejected ideas, conclude the problem just can't be solved. Or, ironically, having decided perfection isn't possible, we settle for a mediocre solution—far from what we could have achieved with a different approach.

So we recognize that perfect solutions, like perfect people, are rare—if not mythical—and even an obviously flawed idea probably has some strengths, or you wouldn't have thought of it in the first place. The wise problem solver knows great ideas are not born in a vacuum; they are the end-products of a building process in which appealing but flawed ideas are gradually patched up. We may imagine that creative thinkers are those who frequently experience sudden flashes of great insight, but the truth is that such thinkers know better than most how to turn a so-so idea into a really good one.

There are not tricks here. Just remember to actively look for the strengths in any idea you or others develop. As weaknesses become apparent, don't dismiss a concept altogether; seek ways to correct its flaws while retaining its strong points. This can be done using a three-step process.

When you wish to respond to an idea, first note its strengths. True, the idea might not be right in its present form, but are any parts of the concept useful? Are the goals of the idea positive, even if more work is needed to achieve them?

Does the philosophy that inspired the idea seem to be on the right track? Only after you've identified the concept's strengths should you address its short-comings. Last, for each weakness you see, develop a means to overcome the flaw while preserving positive features. By adhering to this sequence, you will remind yourself to accent the positive without overlooking critical difficulties. You will also be giving a real boost to those with whom you work if you high-light the strengths of their ideas before discussing the weaknesses. Wherever the ideas come from, building on available ones is the surest path from second-rate concepts to exceptional ones.

AVOID PREMATURE SOLUTIONS

Research on how people solve tough, unfamiliar problems suggests that the first solution considered is rarely as original or useful as the second or third. Why? The first idea that comes to mind will usually be the most obvious. Of course, if the problem we face is routine, this may be good enough. But when the task is difficult and unusual, obvious answers won't work. Until we get past the obvious, we are unlikely to meet the challenge. Success is even less likely if an individual skips the crucial step of problem definition in his or her eagerness to "get down to business" and avoid "wasting time on preliminaries."

The implications are clear: Avoid premature solutions. It takes time to use the principles cited earlier to develop one's thoughts into the best ideas poss-ible. So give the problem-solving process a chance to work. Often the differ-ence between rushing to a convenient, but mediocre, solution and developing a truly creative idea is only a matter of minutes or hours. While time pressures cannot be ignored, often one can easily afford to spend a bit more time explor-ing solutions other than the obvious. Indeed, one cannot afford not to do so.

In sum, then, your search for good ideas will be more successful if you explore various definitions of the problem, separate idea identification and evaluation, build on available ideas, and avoid premature solutions. Granted, these basic principles are easier to preach than to practice. But they do get results. Con-scientiously applied, they will help resolve the pressing needs that confront your organization. Even better, they will help you and your co-workers develop the skills and attitudes that are the keys to continuing personal and professional achievement.

William G. Kirkwood is Assistant Professor, Department of Communication, East Tennessee State University.

35.
BRIGHT IDEAS: "SPARKING"

Mary Miles

The process can foster a more spontaneous flow of creative ideas. Because it enhances positive "out-thinking," sparking can start a new trend for your business—one in which out-thinking the competition is a way of life.

Wanted: Fresh, new ideas; creative solutions to problems; achievement of company goals; *success*. Nothing too new or startling in these desires, right? Finding the best ways to fulfill them is a problem all managers face.

These days, many managers occasionally use some form of group think sessions to elicit ideas that will spell success. And the quality and quantity of these ideas is a reflection of the principles used in setting up and running the sessions.

One method used is NGT—the Nominal Group Technique—developed by Andre Delbecq and Andrew Van de Ven. NGT is a rather structured refinement of brainstorming. Members of a small group, guided by a leader, address a target problem by writing down ideas on paper; these ideas are later recorded on a master list, discussed separately, and rank-ordered by the participants.

One of the main advantages of this rather democratic process is that ideas can be presented in a free-flowing, yet nonthreatening, fashion. A group conclusion is reached through a tabulation of "scores." The entire routine is very controlled, very employee-involving, and often, very productive in terms of results and "team spirit."

IGNITING THE CREATIVE PROCESS

Another technique for making the most of brainstorming is "sparking." It was developed by Philomena D. Warihay and Daniel N. Kanouse, president and executive vice president of Take Charge Consultants, a Downingtown, Pennsylvania-based creativity and management-development concern.

Warihay and Kanouse, who are preparing a book on their methods, have a unique angle. They stress the importance of recognizing and fully engaging the powers of the brain's right hemisphere in achieving creative and innovative thinking. Their sparking process, used within a group, is freewheeling idea-making that is largely unhampered by traditional analytical, linear-type thought processes.

The left and right hemispheres of the brain perform two entirely different kinds of functions. The left handles repetitive, analytical, and sequential tasks; the right deals with more creative, emotional processes, like artistic expression, spatial awareness, finding problems, and creating images. You read a horror story using the skills learned and controlled through the left hemisphere; you imagine the chilling wind in the darkened graveyard, the creaking of the opening crypt, and the ghostly fingers closing around your throat via the right.

OUT-THINKING AND IN-THINKING

How is this knowledge important to a company, or manager in that company, seeking new approaches and solutions in the constant battle to get ahead? Warihay and Kanouse point to the familiar notion that a business succeeds by out-thinking the competition; but they have a very special definition for "out-thinking." For them, it means making maximum use of the right-hemisphere processes. To them, "out-thinking" is *creative* thinking.

"In-thinking," on the other hand, exhibits itself in conformance and uniformity. It's *safe* thinking. "What's the matter with this tactic?" an in-thinker might ask. "It's been working for 20 years, so why change it now?"

In a company characterized by in-thinking (and most are), novel and "far-out" ideas are apt to be frowned upon. In fact, say Warihay and Kanouse, in-thinking is "perpetuated through the modern-management model of systematic planning, organizing, and controlling—it contributes to administrative stability—it dictates 'business as usual.' In-thinking is reinforced and rewarded. Out-thinking is discouraged."

In-thinking is indeed necessary and valuable for some aspects of problem-solving. But the left side of the brain, which gives birth to in-thinking, has been overdeveloped at the expense of the right-side functions, according to Warihay and Kanouse.

WHERE ARE YOU?

It might be a good idea at this point to ponder what your initial reaction would be to an employee who came to you, eyes gleaming with excitement, and said, "Hey, Boss—know that problem we've been having in the order department? Well, I've just had the greatest idea! It may sound nutty at first, but I think I could really turn things around if..."

Would you hear doors slamming shut in your mind? ("Uh-oh, all I need now is to have this young guy shaking things up with his crazy ideas!") Or would you give him a chance? Most, it seems, would be irritated, on guard, threatened, bored, or uninterested.

Warihay and Kanouse think such reactions are wrong and non-productive. This is not to say that operating your department or company on sound principles of systematic, proven management procedures is unwise. It is to say, however, that the manager who closes his or her mind to innovation and the occasionally nonconventional—even revolutionary—idea can miss out on getting that extra edge, beating out those who do things by the book, out-thinking the competition and getting ahead.

How do you develop out-thinking in yourself and your subordinates? One way is to "abandon the myth that creativity is rare." For a group of people working out a problem, encouragement to deviate from traditional problem-solving techniques and permission to go as far as creativity and imagination will allow bring about a sort of igniting process. A free and unrestrained flow of ideas, unfettered by restrictive rules and boundaries, kindles more of the same—this is sparking.

Lest all this sound as if sheer license and chaos are being prescribed, Warihay and Kanouse do advocate some guidelines. We've already indicated that the secret of a successful sparking session lies in the assumption that everyone is capable of creative thinking, and in encouragement of such thinking by those who have put the group together. There must also be adequate definition of the problem; a dedication to resolutions; development of a proper "environment" for the session; and, last but not least, a skilled session leader. Skilled leadership, in fact, may be the key to generating out-thinking and culling from it sound conclusions that can be put to use.

THE BRAIN SYNDICATE

How does all this differ from ordinary brainstorming techniques? According to Warihay and Kanouse, "Sparking sessions bring together a group of people to relate to a specific problem or objective. To be highly creative, the group should comprise people having expertise related to the problem, but in different areas. This type of brain syndicate differs from traditional brainstorming groups in that each individual is knowledgeable in a uniquely relevant area and there is no overlap of disciplines."

Given a group of people with varying backgrounds and ideas, a specific problem to address, and the sparking of ideas generated by the rubbing together of lots of creative, right-hemisphere-type thinking, you can see that this technique must be unusually effective.

As in the Nominal Group Technique, the session leader must have a thorough knowledge of the issue at hand. But he or she must also be prepared to deal with a far less circumscribed process than the NGT leader encounters. Instead of writing down their ideas, participants in a sparking session vocalize them on the spot. This means that the group leader must be adept at guiding without controlling: providing feedback when necessary; reining in without suppressing or restraining; assimilating; and enhancing positive culmination of the session. The leader must have an excellent grasp of group dynamics, be able to keep things moving, provide reinforcement for members who need it, and keep more domineering members from taking over.

To free group members from left-hemisphere-oriented, linear, "logical" thinking habits, Warihay and Kanouse suggest the following guidelines for the session leader:

Set the Stage. This means providing participants with background, such as short questionnaire that "asks group members to view elements of a problem differently and to see improbable combinations and analogies...to ease their minds out of ruts." It also means providing members with an outline of the problem before the meeting. This "gets the problem into their subconscious minds, where it can percolate" awhile.

Frame the Problem. Good leaders must use their left hemispheres for this. It means systematically explaining the problem in "how-to" form to enable participants to address the issue as intelligently and creatively as possible. Warihay and Kanouse say that the statement "Develop a better mousetrap" is too general; the more specific "how to build a mousetrap that prevents the mouse from stealing the cheese" is preferred.

Create a Win/Win Situation. The leader has to establish several ground rules—namely, that all ideas are good ideas, and that no "killer" statements ("We've tried that before") will be allowed.

Don't Manipulate Group Members. The leader must allow members to be absolutely free in their brainstorming; if they are relaxed, feel no pressure, and are even having fun, the right hemisphere can operate at top form.

Structure Well to Generate Unstructured Responses. Here the leader must be superskilled. Unlike a random-search-oriented session, a sparking session must be carefully planned. (For a typical format, see Figure 1.)

CREATIVITY: A WHOLE-BRAIN PROCESS

With the sparking technique, you develop the potential of your business, as well as the creative talents of your personnel (that is, if each element—solid grasp of the target issue; selection of a good leader; generation of ideas; formula-

Figure 1.

Suggested Format for a Sparking Session

1. Welcome and informal introductions of leader and participants.
2. Review of operating norms (what is encouraged, what is discouraged).
3. Framing the problem.
4. Feedback to group members on their anonymous responses to a pre-session questionnaire.
5. Pen-and-pencil exercises to enhance awareness of the way the two hemispheres of the brain function.
6. Two or three specific activities aimed at generating creative responses to problems.
7. Group review of all solutions (in order to fit them into similar categories).
8. Preferencing—i.e., having several participants select a favorite solution for further exploration.
9. Teaming—further refinement of solution through paired teams. (This step is of great value in moving toward implementation.)

Adapted from a paper on the sparking technique by Philomena D. Warihay and Daniel N. Kanouse.

tion of new approaches, plans, and strategies that will send you forging ahead of the competition—is achieved). And everything is possible because of the powers of the right hemisphere, right? Wrong!

Though the right-brain aspects of creativity may be the "missing element" in many organizations' attempts to out-think the competition, let's not overlook the left hemisphere. Warihay and Kanouse, after all, stress that "creativity is a whole-brain phenomenon." Of the six well-known phases comprising the creative process, *illumination* and *incubation* are right-brain activities; *analysis* and *preparation* originate in the left hemisphere; and *interest* and *implementation* draw upon use of both sides.

The sparking-technique developers emphasize the importance of "teaching people how to balance left-brain thinking with right-brain thinking." Whole-brain thinking is viewed as a "cerebration"—a "cerebral celebration that keeps a company well ahead of its competitors."

Developing the sparking techniques for your own group has its cost. Warihay and Kanouse cite the possibility of creative people becoming frustrated as the process increases their awareness of problems. Perceiving problems is a function of the right-hemisphere—and "teaching people how to view the resolutions of problems differently also enhances their ability to see *potential* problems." This can be a heavy load.

Nor is creative thinking easy. It's hard work putting together a productive session—one that will bring forth solid, usable results instead of a chaotic morass of far-out ideas. To get 100 brainstorms that you think could make the earth move is one thing; to make them generate ever more fruitful ideas, and in a way that addresses issues specifically and constructively, is another.

And don't forget the risks. As Warihay and Kanouse put it, "New ideas require change. Change evokes resistance, and resistance can be trouble." But they also believe that the possible rewards of implementing the sparking process far outweigh the costs.

Like the Nominal Group Technique and traditional brainstorming methods, properly conducted sparking sessions can pull people together, make them more committed to company goals, and give them an increased sense of being part of a whole. The process can also foster a more spontaneous flow of creative ideas. And finally, because it enhances positive "out-thinking," sparking can start a new trend for your business—one in which out-thinking the competition is a way of life. And that is definitely good for your career.

Mary Miles, former managing editor of Computer Decisions, *is now a freelance writer based in Plymouth, Massachusetts.*

36.

100 WAYS TO SPARK YOUR EMPLOYEES' CREATIVE POTENTIAL

Eugene Raudsepp

Creativity, properly encouraged and directed, can be your company's greatest asset. A flexible attitude toward business procedures and employees' talents is key.

In our present corporate movement toward increased productivity and quality, creativity and innovation approaches have been relegated to the back seat, if not totally ignored. To be sure, creativity has moved from the after-dinner podium into the classroom, but it is rarely used systematically in the day-to-day corporate environment. Its conspicuous absence may mean that with all the approaches, processes, and interventions currently used to improve productivity and quality we may be mining sand instead of gold.

Creativity is directly linked to productivity and quality enhancement in that it:

- Increases the quality of solutions to organizational problems.
- Helps to bring about profitable innovations.
- Spurs increased productivity by revitalizing motivation.
- Upgrades personal skills.
- Catalyzes effective team effort.

This article provides insight into creating an organizational culture that would harness and focus people's energies to achieve innovative results. It offers 100 guidelines and interventions managers can use to improve organizational and personal innovation and achievement.

1. Take personal responsibility for the development of an organizational climate for innovation. Whereas subordinates may be supportive and encouraging of each other's creativity, they won't consistently sustain it unless they believe that their managers firmly support creative behavior.

2. Consciously experiment in new forms of organization, searching for suitable ways of maximizing the support that employees can give to one another with respect to creativity.

3. Concentrate efforts on those aspects of organizational culture—the traditional procedures and norms—that inhibit and stifle innovation.

4. Remember that innovative behavior does not happen spontaneously. You have to explicitly communicate that innovation is expected.

5. Create an open, interactive climate where your subordinates can stimulate greater awareness, excitement, and ideas in each other. The dominant mood in many corporations is one of isolation, frustration, apprehension, and vulnerability.

6. Free yourself from the hold of, and dependence on, traditional systems of governance. Do not over-direct, over-observe, or over-report.

7. Recognize that your change efforts will encounter the dead weights of inertia and resistance. By consistently and patiently demonstrating that you mean business and that you encourage creative behavior, the resistance will eventually lessen.

8. Formulate innovative objectives all your people can believe in and visualize. Communicate constantly on those objectives.

9. Dramatize particularly those problems to which creative solutions are now known to be needed.

10. Do merciless housecleaning of the "yesterday" products, services, and ventures that only absorb valuable resources and energy, but do not contribute to growth.

11. Budget time and resources adequately for innovation.

12. Encourage and train subordinates to develop greater psychological openness to new ideas and new experiences.

13. Recognize differences in individuals. Have a keen appreciation of the unique characteristics of each individual, his strengths and weaknesses. Treat each individual as a person of worth in his or her own right.

14. Match as much as possible project tasks and objectives with the true interests of each of the individuals involved.

15. Determine and act upon those aspects of each individual's motivation that most directly relate to his or her sense of self-confidence and desire to achieve.

16. Do everything possible to promote responsible individuality and maturity in your subordinates. Maturity is characterized by high motivation, autonomy, flexible behavior patterns, action orientation, and strong commitment to goals. Organizations may publicly contend that they support these qualities. Yet their policies are often designed to evoke the opposite qualities of immaturity and dependency.

Immature behavior results when people perceive that they have little or no control over their environment and are expected to behave in a conforming, passive, and subordinate manner. Rather than supporting individuals who

challenge assumptions and question the way things are run, organizations reward those who never question anything, who never rock the boat, who never
propose challenging ideas that would threaten the status quo or require some
restructuring and risk taking.

17.   Provide stimulating work which provides a feeling of personal and
professional growth. These are the strongest motivators for people and without
them they cannot get excited about their jobs.

18.   Provide projects and tasks that will bring a sense of accomplishment to
your subordinates and that satisfy their desire for development in a direction
that best matches their value system.

19.   Provide challenge by pitching assignments and projects just above individuals' known capabilities.

20.   Provide sufficient form and pattern in assignments to enable
subordinates to feel that the satisfactions they have enjoyed in the past will be
repeatable and will provide a secure springboard for takeoffs in new creative
directions.

21.   Help your subordinates to see problems as challenges. Instilling an attitude that there are opportunity potentials in problems helps them regard
problems in a more positive light. It also makes them more willing to overcome
the obstacles impeding progress toward project goals.

22.   Make known that employees' career success hinges on their creative
contributions.

23.   Allow diversity in personal styles. Don't let your own personality stifle
those who differ from your methods of doing things.

24.   Recognize that there is no single managerial style that is appropriate
and effective with all individuals. The creative manager is a situational stylist
and can select either participative, laissez-faire, or autocratic styles of managing, depending on circumstances and the individuals involved. The participative style, however, should be the favored style.

25.   Utilize resources, methods, and subordinates in more versatile ways to
achieve creative results.

26.   Focus potential and skills on goals, not roles. Excessive preoccupation
with roles saps creativity.

27.   Create a free-flow task environment that encourages getting the project
finished in the most creative way possible.

28.   Encourage and motivate subordinates to come back again and again to
the same problem until there is a creative breakthrough.

29.   Set high but reasonable standards, knowing that even the most lofty
ideas must eventually be subjected to the realistic technical and financial constraints of the organization. By setting high goals initially, you increase the
chances of some people coming through with breakthrough ideas.

30.   Instill an attitude that "thinks quality" at every stage of a project.

31.   While a measure of external structure and discipline has to be imposed,

ideally they should resonate with the individual's own sense of responsibility and self-discipline. As one manager stated, "Authentic discipline is internal, and is generated by absorption in inherently satisfying activity."

32.   Discover in what ways individuals think they are most creative or would like to be most creative, and what sort of creative contribution they would most like to make to the organization if they could. Almost every organization has a sizable number of people who could be creative enthusiastically, frequently, and naturally. Find out who they are and from special "brain trusts" to help produce creative solutions.

33.   Actively seek out, develop, and encourage individuals with special creative talents and aptitudes.

34.   Arrive at a sound problem statement and some vision of the desired end results. Make the appropriate decisions and set the initial directions. Zero in on the problem and really want to solve it in innovative ways. Involve people who can "own" the problem. Involve others who can offer their expertise, or who can be idea catalysts in the way they generate ideas, or who can represent the problem to others in unique ways.

35.   Lead and enthuse by suggestion and indirect persuasion, rather than by specification or command. Frame objectives in clear terms but allow freedom for development of diverse approaches.

36.   Initially define the problem rather broadly to allow maximum creative thinking. Broad definitions preclude the loss of potentially innovative solutions. Encourage more open-ended and less structured approaches to problem solving. For certain periods of time, tolerate messiness, complexity, and even disorder.

37.   Allow adequate time for ideas to develop and mature.

38.   Allow more freedom for individuals to guide their own work. At the very least, provide them with specific areas of self-direction, and increase these gradually whenever that's appropriate.

39.   Guard against your subordinates' over-involvement with putting out fires and coping with urgent, immediate problems.

40.   Make sure that the most promising people are not bogged down with specific tasks every moment of the day. Creative people need time to think, without having their thoughts tied exclusively to an activity or task.

41.   Make special organizational provisions for highly creative people and have them act as special task forces for the solving of complex, tough problems.

42.   Make sure subordinates have ready access to the resources, information, knowledge, and expertise they need in order to solve problems creatively.

43.   Allow free play and encourage openness. Freedom to play and toy in thinking, feeling, and imagination encourages creativity. An attitude that looks favorably on exploration and experiment helps creative experiences to come about. It also allows for the development of a more permissive and accepting "open system." This system is invigoratingly stimulating and allows a free interplay of differences among people. Moving from a closed to an open

system has the effect of changing influence relations to mutual relations where creativity and collaboration can be maximized.

44.   Train yourself and others to respond to what is positive in a proposed idea, rather than reacting negatively. As Charles F. Kettering so aptly put it: "The typical eye sees the 10 percent bad of an idea and overlooks the 90 percent good."

45.   Create situationally more facilitating conditions, more noncompetitive and nonevaluative contexts where mutual trust prevails.

46.   Reserve special rooms in the organization where people can go and "be creative."

47.   Encourage calculated risk taking because it is an important ingredient in growth and innovation.

48.   Develop greater frustration tolerance to mistakes and errors.

49.   Provide a safe atmosphere for failure. In many organizations the penalties for failure far exceed the rewards for success, which often is taken for granted. In some organizations the penalties for failure are even greater than the penalties for doing nothing. Even one failure can brand an individual as a loser. Reward success and ignore failure as much as possible.

50.   Reduce fear of failure and punishment if innovative ideas and recommendations do not pan out.

51.   Act in a way that clearly demonstrates the attitude that if ideas are not accepted, or do not work out, they are not wasted. Particularly those subordinates who are highly creative do not like to be associated with wasted effort for long.

52.   Regard errors and mistakes as opportunities for learning. Organizations place a heavy emphasis on the avoidance of errors and mistakes. This contributes to a sharp perception of any flaws or weaknesses in ideas and to a tendency to play it safe and to avoid punishment for adopting any but the safest, and often the least creative, ideas. We sorely need to reverse this attitude and focus on the "what's good about it" aspects, the "pros" in an idea. There will be plenty of time later to consider the idea's shortcomings.

Frequently, when the acceptable aspects are considered and strengthened, a way is found to modify the unacceptable particulars. If this cannot be accomplished satisfactorily, then it is obvious that the idea should be discarded. But it is absolutely mandatory that, initially, a positive stance be adopted, for if we give in to our natural tendency to focus on flaws and weaknesses right off the bat, we never really perceive all the implications of an idea. One technique is to consider or pretend that the idea is workable and to list and outline all the positive benefits of the idea. After this is done exhaustively, a switch can be instituted to reality testing and fault finding.

53.   Occasionally allow individuals to try out their pet ideas without any criticism whatsoever. Provide a reasonable margin for error. Punitive action for every mistake or failure leads to excessive dependence on safe ways of doing things.

54. Always use mistakes and setbacks positively, for these are learning opportunities.

55. Use even constructive criticism with caution and in small doses. Speak softly and carry a big carrot.

56. By your actions and attitudes show that you are for your people rather than against them. Be a catalyst rather than an obstacle. Many managers are so overburdened with requests that when someone comes up with a new idea or proposal, their negative mind-set confuses it with yet another annoying petition.

57. Encourage candor and frankness. Have the curiosity and ego-strength to find out how you yourself come across, how you are regarded, and how you can improve.

58. Help subordinates to develop greater self-reliance by doing what you can to reduce their fears, inhibitions, and defensiveness.

59. Create power by sharing power. Invent ways to create collaborative momentum.

60. Be a resource person rather than a controller or a boss.

61. Be loyal to your subordinates and know how to evoke loyalty from them. Loyalty cannot be created by gratitude, edict, or compulsion; it is the result of mutual respect and acceptance, which can be developed only through day-to-day interactions.

62. Be a sympathetic, friendly person who has high personal standards and integrity and is able to be either serious and sincere or humorous and relaxed, as the occasion demands. Truly listen to your people and laugh with them.

63. Know the difference between assertiveness and aggressiveness and act accordingly.

64. Act as a buffer between subordinates and outside problems and demands.

65. Make participative decision-making real, not symbolic, at all levels. Allow individuals to make more of their own decisions. As one highly creative manager put it, "A good deal of my time is spent trying to not make a decision. The best decisions are made by those closest to the problem, or those most affected by the decision."

66. Allow creative people to take as large a part as possible in overall decision making and in the formulation of long-term plans.

67. Increase delegation and the sharing of influence throughout the organization.

68. Encourage, develop, and release rather than inhibit initiative.

69. Make sure that subordinates know at all times where the organization is going and how their individual contributions are helping toward those corporate goals.

70. Upgrade and revamp both the tangible and intangible rewards and inducements for creative contributions. The time-honored incentives of increased power, status, and salaries encourage secretiveness, playing of politics,

jockeying for positions, conformity, and the desire to please superiors. This discourages innovative thinking.

71. Modify the seniority tradition so that individuals can be promoted from any level strictly on merit.

72. Use creativity-related performance dimensions in your performance appraisals.

73. Individuals should be given time off to reward them for unusual creative achievements.

74. Provide personal recognition for accomplishment. Emphasize the importance of the individual rather than his group or department.

75. Increase recognition of creative performance through formally established profit-sharing and similar programs, such as deferred compensation plans, cash or stock bonuses for outstanding individual contributions, patents, and royalties on inventions.

76. There should be letters of commendation and appreciation from the company president and other members of top management for important contributions. Honors and distinctions should be established that reflect admiration for creative excellence.

77. The company's public relations department should be assigned the responsibility of providing deserving individuals with special recognition and publicity. There should be press releases on individual achievements to newspapers, journals, and college alumni magazines.

78. Analyze the communication system—this is the way individuals get their perspective on the company and their source of stimulation or blockage on creativity.

79. Put creative people in communication with one another, particularly across interdisciplinary lines. Bring people with diverse knowledge and viewpoints together.

80. Create an educational situation in which small discussion groups, made up of people from management and operational areas, openly explore their problems and views together.

81. As critical incidents or success of failure in creativity occur, write them up and make use of them as subject matter for discussion and analysis. Develop your own curriculum materials in this field.

82. Optimize and expand subordinates' professional experience through relevant communication and exposure to experiences that would enrich their creativity.

83. Encourage open communications and the utilization of more people as resources.

84. Conduct meetings and face-to-face discussions about what opportunities could be exploited and arrive at a *commitment* to specific innovative goals.

85. The departmental structures should be made less rigid and encapsulated. This would encourage greater interdepartmental communication, and

this, in turn, would encourage heightened creativity. Eliminate the organizational "box mentality": "If you'll stay out of my organizational box, I'll stay out of yours."

86.   Although creative, highly motivated teams are exceedingly useful, also appreciate and find a place for the creative loner. Allow him or her freedom to follow leads that are contrary to group ideas.

87.   "Celebrate" the individual contributors and deemphasize the anonymity of group rewards and commendations.

88.   Welcome and encourage a diversity of ideas and opinions, no matter where they come from.

89.   Make people aware, through lectures and other special communications, of the pressures they bring on each other to conform.

90.   Import, for short periods of time, individuals who have a professional interest in teaching how to cultivate creativity. Provide creativity training and workshops.

91.   Locate individuals in the organization who have a capacity for helping others realize their creative potential. Let these individuals become tutors and mentors to those who show promise.

92.   Enhance your own creative ability through special workshop/seminars, specialized reading, and practice of creative exercises and games. This sets an excellent example subordinates will want to emulate. Enhanced creative ability also makes it easier for you to recognize and relate to the creativity of others.

93.   Encourage subordinates to offer ideas concerning not only their own jobs, but also problems outside their direct responsibility.

94.   Provide ready channels through which creativity converts into specific ideas, suggestions, and changes. You cannot simply wait for this to happen.

95.   Introduce formal mechanisms for the implementation of and follow-through on ideas.

96.   Make sure that innovative ideas are transmitted to your organization's top officials with your support, and insist on a feedback mechanism. Without this mechanism the flow of creative ideas dries up because the innovators feel that their ideas are not given a fair hearing or taken seriously enough. Make sure to get commitments from upper management to act on good ideas.

97.   Recommend and encourage more informal contact between top management and the individual contributors of ideas.

98.   Analyze the situations of subordinates in their first year of employment and those who are in their prime, near the top of their promotional possibilities.

99.   Analyze the situations surrounding subordinates who have gone stale, noting what they won't respond to and possible opportunities that might stimulate them.

100.   Do not consider creativity as a gimmick, but as an integral aspect of total organizational policy.

Eugene Raudsepp is president of Princeton Creative Research Inc., Princeton, New Jersey. An authority in the field of creativity and innovation training, he is author of numerous books, including Creative Growth Games, More Creative Growth Games, How Creative Are You?, How to Create New Ideas, *and* How To Sell New Ideas.

37.
GETTING BRIGHT IDEAS
FROM YOUR TEAM

Mary Miles

> The rather disciplined format of NGT makes it especially effective in eliciting and integrating ideas and information from a problem-solving group. One of NGT's primary strengths is that it encourages equal participation.

Making better decisions...improving productivity...generating new ideas...identifying and solving problems...defining and achieving goals... assessing effectiveness...formulating policies...integrating projects into the "big picture"...encourage team participation, commitment, loyalty.

To anyone in a management position, the goals listed above are most familiar. They are the table of contents, so to speak, of the management bible. Failure to continually address these concerns can spell ultimate failure for the individual executive—or for the entire company.

Any technique that can help all the members of a corporate team—from the top brass on down through the ranks—pull together to achieve the highest measure of success is worth its weight in microchips. The Nominal Group Technique (NGT), a refinement of brainstorming developed by Andrew Van de Ven and Andre Delbecq, is one such technique.

THE OLD WAY

Few modern businesses address issues in the old, autocratic manner whereby the Big Boss leaned back in his (never her!) chair, pressed his fingers together, and pontificated, sending all the subordinates scurrying to do his bidding. Today, the value of the group approach is well recognized. Among its advantages are the enthusiasm and sense of commitment engendered when employees feel they have meaningful input into the company's decision- and policy-making. And there is little doubt that "groups can achieve what individuals cannot," to quote Warihay and Kanouse. They continue, "Collective mind jogging generates energy that develops into commitment and produces results quite different from the achievement of any one individual."

In the 1930s, Alex Osborn, of the big advertising agency Batten, Barton, Durstine & Osborn, developed the now-familiar brainstorming technique, which *Webster's* defines as "the unrestrained offering of ideas or suggestions by all members of a conference to seek solutions to problems." The procedure calls for participants to throw any and all ideas into the pot, without holding back for fear of criticism or evaluation. It's the quantity, not the quality, of ideas that is the initial goal. Often, one idea generates another. When the ideas stop flowing the group evaluates, sifts, and attempts to come up with a fresh approach or solution. That worked fine for years, and still does in many circumstances. But there are attendant problems in old-style brainstorming; as a result, variations have been developed.

You've probably been a participant in a brainstorming session. Possibly it was a noisy free-for-all in which everyone talked at once and eventually the group so digressed from the original issue that nothing was really accomplished. When "a good time was had by all" is the best description of a brainstorming session, the company realizes little but enhanced camaraderie among the personnel.

Another problem is that the brainstorming meeting may not really be "free-for-all"—one or two individuals frequently take over a brainstorming session, effectively squelching less aggressive or vocal members and ramrodding their own ideas through.

Another potential problem is that if care isn't taken to include individuals who have sufficient knowledge about the issue, little will be accomplished. In any sort of group problem-solving session—whether it's a committee, a council, or a brainstorming workshop—it's important to involve people who can combine various kinds of relevant expertise to arrive at a logical and feasible solution.

Moreover, such a meeting must have a leader—one who is skilled at knowing when to direct when necessary, rein in when it's time for coming to conclusions, and guide the refining process that eventually leads to solutions and closure...all constructively and diplomatically.

Neither the Nominal Group Technique nor the sparking approach is exactly the same as brainstorming. NGT is a rather structured discussion method, ideally involving around 10 people. (In general, the larger the group, the more diluted the effectiveness of the process.)

What is an NGT session like? Andrew Van de Ven describes it in his book, *Group Decision-Making Effectiveness* (Kent State University Center for Business and Economic Research, 1974). Typically, seven to ten participants are gathered around a table. "However, they are not speaking. Instead, each individual is writing ideas on a pad of paper. At the end of 10 or 20 minutes, a very structured sharing of ideas takes place. Each individual, in round-robin fashion, provides one idea from his or her private list. This is written on a blackboard or flipchart in full view of the entire group.

"This round-robin listing continues until each member indicates that he or she has no further ideas to share. The output of this nominal process is the total set of ideas created by this structured process. Generally, spontaneous discussion then follows for a period...before 'nominal' voting...The selection of priorities, rank-ordering, or rating (depending on the group's decision rule) is done privately, and the group decision is the pooled outcome of the individual votes."

PREPARATION PAYS OFF

What are the difficulties you may encounter in implementing a fruitful NGT session? One, as we have noted, involves having a properly prepared and trained group leader, who knows precisely how the method works and has a sure fix on the issue to be addressed. (In such a forum, it's not necessarily best for the manager or boss to be the group leader.)

Another problem, one that exists for all group idea-generating conclaves, concerns the need for the participants to possess adequate level of knowledge about the targeted problem. Let's say you want to assess the feasibility of putting electronic mail capabilities into your operation. Your newest employee may have already exhibited fantastic capacity for solving problems in innovative ways, but he or she might not yet really be all that familiar with either company goals and procedures or electronic-mail. However, given a mini-course or a succinct report before the NGT session this person could utilize his or her creativity effectively.

Figure 1.

The Nominal Group Technique Session

These guidelines for conducting a Nominal Group Technique session were developed by Andrew Van de Ven and Andre Delbecq and provide a good resource for managers and group leaders.

Preparation

1. Select the NGT leader; make sure he or she knows exactly how the method works and completely understands the issue to be addressed.

2. Select the team members—usuallly from seven to ten participants (never fewer than five). Make sure they, too, understand how the technique works. Also, if necessary, prepare or make available materials so that participants will be properly educated on relevant aspects of the problem to be resolved. (Group members may be randomly chosen or assigned because of their specific talents.)

3. Select a meeting spot that will be available for one to two hours; it should be comfortable, private, and free from any possible distractions. Ideally, members should be seated around a table, where they can easily see one another, the leader, and the

chalkboard or flipchart. Paper and pencils are necessary for the participants' ideas, and 3 by 5 cards will be needed for the voting process.

The Meeting

1. The leader (not a group participant) reviews the NGT process and then hands out pencils and paper, at the top of which is printed the question under consideration.
2. Members write out their responses; 10 to 15 minutes should be allowed for this step.
3. The leader begins round-robin polling for each member's ideas, one at a time. As each idea is read, the leader records it on the flipchart. This procedure is continued around the table as many times as necessary until all the ideas have been recorded. (This generally takes about a half-hour.)
4. The group discusses each idea as listed, in sequence. No ideas are deleted, although they may be combined or expanded.
5. The leader hands out the 3 by 5 cards and instructs the group members to identify the five most important ideas on the master list and write them down on their cards. Then the members are asked to rank-order the ideas (5 points for the highest-ranked, down to 1 point for the lowest.)
6. The leader collects the cards and tabulates the scores on the master list.

ADVANTAGES

Its developers believe that the rather disciplined format of NGT makes it especially effective in eliciting and integrating ideas and information from a problem-solving group. Compared with other group methods, such as the old-time brainstorming session or the traditional committee approach, one of NGT's primary strengths is that it encourages equal participation. Each member formulates and writes down all his or her own ideas, undistracted and unthreatened by the ideas of others in the group. All ideas are entered in round-robin fashion on the board or flipchart—and reviewers of this technique point out that it's pretty difficult to keep track of who suggested what by the time all ideas have been recorded. The chance of anyone putting down or overriding someone else's thoughts is much lessened. A comprehensive "master list," thus formulated, looks impressive and gives all the participants a feeling that something positive is being accomplished.

Sequential discussion of the ideas on the master list maintains attention on the ideas, not on the individuals who proposed them: this reduces the chance of favoritism or sycophancy.

Rank-ordering of the individually favored solutions is also private, so the 'winning' ideas are determined democratically.

In today's fast-paced, complicated, and competitive business environment, the need to formulate goals and policies, identify and solve problems quickly, and make well-balanced, informed, and creative decisions is critical. The Nominal Group Techniques, representing a major modification of traditional group problem-solving methods, may well work for you.

Mary Miles, former managing editor of Computer Decisions, *is now a freelance writer in Plymouth, Massachusetts.*

38.

HOW TO MINE AND REFINE
NEW PRODUCT IDEAS

Caren Calish Gagliano

Success is never guaranteed, but it is more easily attained through
"planned growth." It's method, not magic, that brings creativity to new
product strategy. Here's how one tried-and-true method works.

Matching a company's capabilities to unfilled market needs requires a formal
search for new product ideas. Unfortunately, however, companies often rely on
the hope that somehow they'll stumble over "the great idea."

But few companies can afford that luxury in today's fast-paced markets. They
should instead promote a continuous flow of innovative ideas through a repeatable, renewable process that unearths opportunities a company can realistically
pursue. This article will examine a process for developing new product ideas
that efficiently taps wide ranging expertise from outside a company. And it will
show how that process worked for a manufacturer that needed to apply its existing technological capabilities to new products in new markets in order to survive.

Smit Nymegen Co., in Nijmegen, Holland, has been a leading European
transformer manufacturer for more than 70 years. But when the energy crisis of
the 1970s cut the growth in demand for electricity, Smit suffered a precipitous
sales decline. In the early 1980s, it tried to expand to non-European markets,
but those already were flooded with Western and Japanese competition.
Fortunately for the company and its 2,000 employees, management didn't
surrender. Instead, it actively sought ways to match its strengths and resources
to new markets and developed a viable position in a growing industry, superconducting magnetics.

Smit followed what can be call the "planned growth" approach to new
product development. It consists of four steps, the first three of which are emphasized in this article:

1. *Preparation:* developing criteria and identifying opportunities
2. *Creation:* identifying concepts

3. *Evaluation/qualification:* bridging the gap between ideas and commercialization
4. *Commercialization:* taking the product or service to market

Other companies have used the "planned growth" approach successfully. For example, a rolled steel company imperiled by cheap imports developed a new specialty steel laminate product. A building materials maker, faced with having to close a $40 million plant that used raw material declared unsafe, devised a way to use different materials to produce the same and new products in the same plant.

PHASE I: PREPARATION

During the first phase, management establishes criteria for introducing a new product or application and identifies areas of opportunity that are compatible with those parameters. Specific products are not identified at this point.

This process begins with daylong kickoff meetings attended by as many as eight people. Those officials—"growth problem owners"—should represent each of the company's or division's primary functional areas and should be expected to contribute to the solution.

Smit's kickoff meeting, for example, included the financial, production and engineering managers, as well as the head of design and a small cadre of technical specialists. To underscore the importance of their endeavors, the company's managing director also attended.

The responsibility of the task force is to develop a preliminary draft of criteria. Here's a possible agenda for such a group discussion:

1. Goal parameters: setting objectives for revenue/volume, return on investment, profit, general program and development time. Goal parameters also should include a company's individual needs and desires.
2. Implementation parameters: lists a company's assets and limitations. Leverageable company assets; investment/development/money available; technical/physical capabilities; marketing/distribution.
3. Policy parameters: how a company runs its business. Degree of proprietariness; corporate fit; quality/image; market; and unit economics— such as cost, price/volume, value added.

Criteria Review

Most kickoff meetings result in a mass of unorganized raw material with goals and objectives in no particular order. The group leader is responsible for organizing the material so the preliminary criteria can be reviewed.

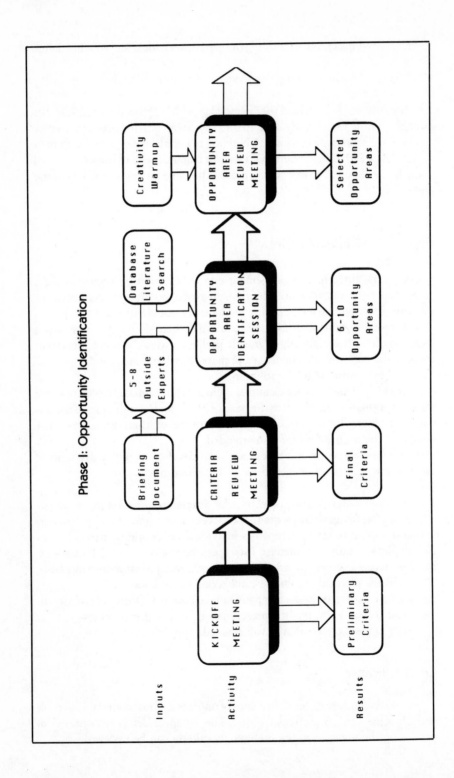

Phase I: Opportunity Identification

Inputs

Activity

Results

That review takes place at a subsequent meeting of the "growth problem owners" in which they review and ammend the criteria for the new product program. Criterion statements must be realistic, concise and specific and provide a framework for judging candidate ideas in terms of marketing, manufacturing, technological and financial practicality. Then statements must be rated and ranked according to their importance.

One of the best and simplest ways to rank each criterion is to assign a rating of "M" for must, "D" for desirable, or "B" for bonus.

Smit's team, for example, identified 24 criteria for considering opportunities. Here are the top 10.

- M1: Exploit Smit's present capabilities in its key technologies— electrical and/or magnetic fields, high-precision winding, high-current/high-voltage applications, magnetic core know-how.
- M2: First commercial sale should occur by mid-1986
- M3: Should generate a cumulative pretax profit of at least 3 million Dutch guilders by 1988.
- M4: Limit total investment to 6 million Dutch guilders
- M5: Limit "get smart" money—investment needed to investigate and research the new product concept once identified—to 750,000 Dutch guilders
- M6: Contribute to the continual employment of Smit's labor force
- M7: Have a minimum sales value/price of 100,000 Dutch gilders per unit
- D8: Should be manufactured utilizing Smit's existing production facilities
- D9: Can generate an additional sales volume of 20 million Dutch guilders
- D10: Should have a contribution margin above material and direct labor costs of at least 50%

Outside Expertise

Every company should be staffed to do today's business. But to grow into new businesses, companies usually need information and expertise they don't have. Thus, after the final criteria are agreed upon, a company should seek assistance from objective outside experts to help identify new product opportunities. Those outside panelists should be paid a modest honorarium and travel expenses. Before company officials ask for specific new product ideas, however, they should tap experts for market trends.

Each company is unique. Therefore, there are no rigid guidelines for selecting the panel of experts. But a company should look for "horizontal" experts: people with a broad overview of trends and activities in a specific area. Those experts usually are editors, academics, consultants, or industry and government workers. A company should research its choice in order to find and recruit the right people.

Smit, for example, assembled individuals from industry and academia, with credentials in a wide range of disciplines. Its panel included a designer of magnetic coils and coil systems, an internationally known science fiction writer, an expert in space vehicle propulsion, expert in electromagnetic devices, and the director of the applied superconductivity center at a major university.

Each panel member should receive a 10- to 15-page workbooklike "briefing document" about one week before the meeting. Members should be asked to read the document before the meeting to generate ideas. Moreover, they should be asked to bring in any written material related to the topic.

That document tells members as much as they need to know about the company, its customers and the task at hand. But it doesn't identify the company by name, to avoid any preconceptions. Exercises designed to draw out information and new ideas also are included. The completed briefing documents are collected at the meeting.

To stimulate thinking, the document should state that the objective is to identify changing events, situations, interest or trends that signal a need for new products or services. It also should pose probing questions to help attain that objective.

Smit's statement of purpose, for example, was identification for "present and changing applications for (large) electromagnetic fields."

A trained moderator can be used during the meeting to ensure that ideas are added to or built upon, not judged.

Participants will be excited, but exhausted, after the session. The people from a company's project team must debrief the session output the next day. Tape-recording the discussion makes that task simple.

All of the information from the briefing documents and the session tapes should be pulled together. That data must be studied and organized into "opportunity areas," which then can be examined by secondary research.

The output of the expert panel organized for Smit, for instance, identified the following areas of opportunity:

- fusion
- research applications
- separation/concentration
- propulsion
- storage/stabilization and
- high-energy physics

Program Strategy

For the final step of Phase I, the company team meets to evaluate the areas of opportunity identified by the panel of experts. The team enhances those ideas based upon their knowledge and expertise. Then they correlate them with the final criteria.

Secondary market research, user panels, etc. should be used to supplement those considerations. The same group of "growth problem owners" should be gathered for the strategy review meeting. A company should distribute to those participants:

- the finalized criteria (complete with "musts," "desirables" and "bonuses")
- the opportunity areas on which they are to concentrate their efforts
- an identification of expected trends and changes
- additional research results

PHASE II: CREATION

Once a company has selected the best area of opportunity, it should look for the most promising concept within it. That begins with a second meeting of outside experts. But this time, the expertise needed is *vertical* in nature. A company should remember, however, to select a team to "surround" the area of interest, not just hit it on the head.

Another briefing document should be used to prepare participants. That document should state the new objective and give some information on the company and current trends being considered. It should encourage members to generate ideas rather than conduct straight analysis. It also should use some creative technique to get the participants to think about the relationships of known elements. *Applied Imagination,* by Alex Osborn, is an excellent source of brainstorming. It's available from Charles Scribner & Sons Publishing Co., New York.

This second session follows the brainstorming principle of "never look for the best way: always look for 100 ways." Techniques to stimulate the imagination are used. For example, participants might be asked to make improbable comparisons with nature, relate two wildly dissimilar things, or imagine themselves as inanimate objects and then describe their thoughts and feelings. Participants should be told to relax and let their imaginations wander and to write down their ideas. The leader should be the only one who worries about parameters.

The purpose is to jolt the participants out of their conventional ways of thinking. In one interesting case, for example, a panel devoted a session to finding better ways to move logs downstream. The real problem was moving microscopic textile fibers before forming fabric.

Another interesting case involved designing protection for air cargo shipments that had to sit outdoors. Clear plastic doughnut lids sparked the idea for protective steel boxes.

Participants should write down ideas on 3-inch-by-5-inch cards to prevent them from getting lost. A morning's output usually falls into a dozen idea groups. After organizing raw ideas, the team should determine which ones need preliminary market research.

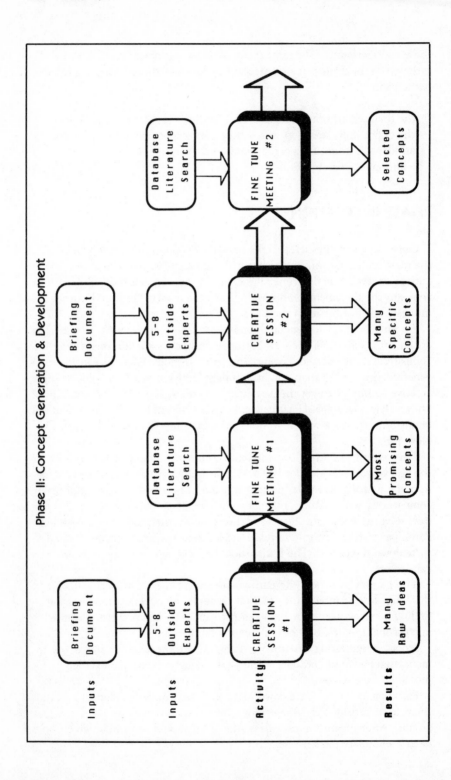

Phase II: Concept Generation & Development

Focusing on "separation and concentration," for example, Smit's creative panel determined that the following applications held particular promise. These ideas, however, were not tempered by research.

- magnetic separation in chemical processes
- U.S./world mineral separation
- prime/waste water treatment
- coal/dust particle separation
- recent advance in superconducting materials

The output of this second, more focused session also will need to be organized to present at yet another team meeting. At that meeting, inside experts should once again build on each other's ideas before those ideas are evaluated against the criteria.

PHASE III: EVALUATION/QUALIFICATION

Many people are involved in the third phase of the planned growth process. In this stage, the company team must evaluate the most promising new business, product or service ideas and decide which ones will be commercialized.

To make that decision, the company must investigate how commercially relevant the most promising ideas are. Results from feasibility studies, engineering studies, potential customer interviews and focus groups can help. Because Phase III ends with a new product concept, nothing should be left to chance.

A "minimeeting" attended by the company team kicks off Phase III. Various tasks are identified and responsibilities assigned. Tasks, of course, vary from company to company and from project to project, depending on what the company is trying to accomplish.

Here's a sample of some task assignments that might be made if the company is searching for a new product:

- Prepare renderings and/or models of the most promising new product ideas or new applications.
- Identify "authorities" in the appropriate fields, then gather opinions and recommendations through personal interviews and/or panel discussions.
- Set up individual or group interviews with potential customers.
- Begin engineering studies.
- Obtain relevant preliminary market information from available secondary data.
- Perform competitive analysis.
- For consumer products or services, obtain primary market data by conducting one or more focus groups drawn from relevant segments. For non-

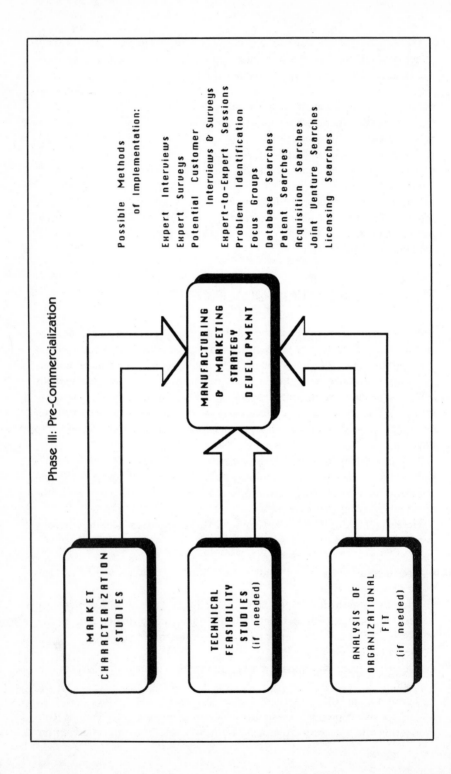

Phase III: Pre-Commercialization

Possible Methods
of Implementation:

Expert Interviews
Expert Surveys
Potential Customer
  Interviews & Surveys
Expert-to-Expert Sessions
Problem Identification
Focus Groups
Database Searches
Patent Searches
Acquisition Searches
Joint Venture Searches
Licensing Searches

MANUFACTURING
& MARKETING
STRATEGY
DEVELOPMENT

MARKET
CHARACTERIZATION
STUDIES

TECHNICAL
FEASIBILITY
STUDIES
(if needed)

ANALYSIS OF
ORGANIZATIONAL
FIT
(if needed)

consumer products, obtain primary market data from selected large prospective users and/or purchasers, either through phone interviews or through industrial focus groups.

If a company is searching for new applications for a material or technology, here are some typical task assignments:

- Prepare an outline/description for each of the most promising ideas.
- Identify and contact design engineers in leading firms in appropriate industries.
- Prepare a questionnaire asking for technical and market information to be mailed to design engineers.
- Identify pertinent trade and professional organizations and trade publications.

Those are only a sampling of the task assignments to be made. In addition to conducting home-based research and technical investigations, Smit personnel traveled through Europe and the United States to meet with prospective competitors and customers. Meetings, for example, were held with industrial scientists, government agencies, academic researchers, etc. Smit workers pursued pertinent facts, impressions and opinions.

Not all the necessary task assignments will be made at the kickoff meeting, of course. Other assignments, such as clarifying market data or confirming certain feasibility studies, inevitably will come up. Nevertheless, assignments made at the kickoff meeting must provide the company team with the information it needs to begin evaluating the best ideas.

While groups are terrific for generating new ideas, individuals make those ideas happen. Thus, at the beginning of Phase III, one person should be assigned to spearhead the activities and be responsible for turning the new idea into reality.

The Final Countdown

The company team should hold at least two additional meetings once the assigned tasks are completed. During those meetings, team members review and narrow down the available options.

That process should not be rushed. If more information is needed, additional task assignments should be made. And extra meetings should be scheduled, if necessary.

Evaluating good ideas is difficult. And sometimes when all other methods of evaluation fail, gut feelings are best. What's needed, therefore, are evaluation techniques that help clarify those gut feelings. Here are some tips:

1. All ideas should be collected and numbered sequentially: (I)
2. The top seven or eight factors should be selected to evaluate the ideas: (F)
3. Each idea should be rated against each factor by assigning it one of the following values.

3 = a good fit with F.
1 = I needs some modification to fit F.
0 = Can't decide.
-1 = I needs major refinement to fit F.

After evaluating each idea against each factor, a check should be put above any number that triggers a positive response, or gut feeling, for the idea it represents. Those ideas that scored well but did not win on gut feeling should be examined. Why weren't you as enthusiastic about them? What would make them more likable? The idea should be revised in accordance with these answers.

Also those factors where the idea fared poorly should be examined. How can it be improved? The same evaluation should be performed with ideas that won on gut feeling but elicited weak responses to one or more factors. What part of those ideas needs to be changed or modified? The idea should be revised to reflect your new insights.

Next, some of the "unusual" ideas that may have pulled very low scores for practical reasons should be looked at. Team members should try to identify what is likable about those ideas. If someone could find a way to adopt any part of it to something else, what would it be? Why is this adaptation appealing? The likable quality should be applied to another idea to see what happens. How could those ideas be made more practical without losing that quality or essence that makes each of them unique? Team members should try to revise some of those ideas without losing their essence.

These guidelines won't guarantee that evaluations will be completely correct. But are there any guidelines that can offer such a guarantee?

The most team members can hope for is that their evaluations will be accurate enough that the risks will be minimal when new products or services are introduced.

Many companies are fearful of entering unknown territories, such as putting a new product on the market. Planning a new product is one thing; investing a large amount of money in it is another. Many new products have died during the planning stage because of that last-minute fear of the unknown.

Making companies feel comfortable about the money they are investing, therefore, is the purpose of Phase III. Objective and credible information, such as market data and engineering studies, provides that comfort. The more hard information garnered, the more likely top management will be to take the plunge.

WHEN TO ACT

It's difficult to pinpoint the best time to act. The process, however, tends to drive itself home when information has been gathered and enough facts analyzed. The staff unites to fulfill the promise of the best ideas.

At Smit, this happened in stages. The company team elected to focus on water treatment and on the required superconducting magnetics technology that had proved to fit perfectly with its capabilities and resources. Research confirmed that focus and resulted in requests for bids for superconducting magnets from various universities and research laboratories. In short, the commercialization of the concept began during research stages.

Though Smit already had the technology to produce superconducting magnetic systems, its planned growth process directed it into the field of separation. It subsequently has entered into two joint ventures and is one of three bidders being considered by the U.S. high-energy physics community to furnish about $3 million worth of superconducting magnets for atomic particles research.

At the same time, the technology is being studied for possible medical applications, such as magnetic resonance imaging. In that case, Smit might serve as a subsupplier to system manufacturers.

It quickly became clear that Smit had a viable new direction almost completely compatible with its engineering and production capabilities. To take advantage of the new direction, the production manager quickly was made business manager of the company's new superconducting magnet systems department. Smit followed the process, and it worked.

CHAMPIONS OF PLANNED GROWTH

Appointing a project "champion" to take charge during the preparation and creative phases of the planned growth process is desirable. But it becomes essential during the evaluation/qualification stage.

At first glance, the chief executive officer might seem to be the best candidate. After all, he has the most clout. If he can't get people to follow through on their assignments, no one can.

But having the chief executive officer also take on the responsibilities of the project champion may be totally unrealistic. Chief executive officers must assume many roles—most of which involve time-critical problem-solving. They may not have the time to champion the project.

Instead, the project champion should be someone inside the company who does not have to learn how the company functions and who has secured the confidence of top management. Bringing in an outsider is unwise for two reasons. Firstly, that person must learn about the project and the company —two difficult jobs. Secondly, the outsider is an "unknown." And when there are two "unknowns"—the individual and the project—monitoring performance becomes difficult.

A better solution: Assign the known company performer to the unknown new opportunity, and the outsider to the known job—the one vacated by the insider chosen to be the project champion, for example.

Matching a technically oriented project to a technical person and a marketing-oriented project to a marketer can be beneficial. That isn't extremely important, however, because most projects involve both marketing and technical considerations. It's better to find a "doer" who can communicate and manage throughout the company.

It's most important that the champion be emotionally committed to the project and view it as an exciting career-growth opportunity. Project champions must be able to handle the many problems and disappointments that are inherent in any new product.

Phase the champion into the new job by constructing a timetable. Free the champion of 25% of his or her old responsibilities. Then gradually increase the champion's involvement in the new project until 100% of his or her time is devoted to it.

Needless to say, the project champion position isn't for everyone. Nor is it a job to which an individual should be appointed by executive command. The choice depends on the individual's personal commitment and enthusiasm. If he or she isn't willing or able to give 100%, the project may be doomed.

The planned growth process moves gradually, but steadily, from the general to the specific. Preliminary criteria become final criteria that can be matched against any new idea. The areas of opportunity evolve into a few promising new business ideas.

Each step provides additional information, or knowledge, to work with and refine. And outside experts and inside experts have the opportunity to add to that information. That process might break down if either side lacked expertise but, in reality, the company gets the best of both worlds.

There's no magic formula for ensuring success. About eight of 10 new products introduced today fail. But a company certainly can improve those odds by enlisting outside experts, proceeding systematically and carefully from one point to the next and by leaving little to chance. Success is never guaranteed, but it is more easily attained through planned growth.

Caren Calish Gagliano is Executive Vice President of Innotech Corporation, Trumbull, Conn., a manufacturing and consulting firm.

Part VI:
RECRUITING AND TRAINING A CREATIVE STAFF

39.

HOW TO FIND—AND
KEEP—CREATIVE PEOPLE

Michael Wolff

Finding creative people is difficult but it is even tougher to keep them stimulated once they've joined a research organization. Never lose sight of the fact that individuals create, not groups.

"The U.S. lags in scientific creativity. Our large industrial laboratories do not encourage creativity adequately. Our young scientists do not challenge established concepts as they once did. Few really new ideas are being developed. People are seeking the easy life rather than a life of study and hard work. As a result, creative output is declining."

While the above quote sounds like a voice from the present, it happens to be from an article Alfred E. Brown wrote 19 years ago, when he headed Gillette's Corporate Research Labs. Today, he is Director of Scientific Affairs for Celanese, and when he looks back on the 1960's they strike him as a relatively creative period for American industry! For this reason *Research Management* asked him how one finds creative people and—even tougher—keeps them stimulated once they've joined a research organization.

Brown begins by advising managers to look for people who are:

- Intellectually curious, continually probing with "Why?" and "What if?" questions.
- Flexible, with an open mind that is willing to accept new information. Creative people don't dismiss ideas on the grounds that "We tried that before and it won't work (one of the deadliest statements any R&D manager can make).
- Able, somehow, to put their finger on the real problem which others have missed, and then to define it accurately and clearly.
- Highly sensitive to needs, usually spotting them before anyone else.
- Able to see connections the average person has missed. They can put information together in many different ways and reach an acceptable solution.

- Unorthodox and anti-authoritarian, boldly questioning conventional ideas and established concepts.
- Mentally restless, intense, strongly motivated, and completely wrapped up in what they are doing.
- Problem-solvers rather than phenomenon-studiers. While the latter are valuable in the lab, where their analytical and investigative skills are obviously necessary, the truly creative problem-solver is normally goal-oriented rather than methods-oriented. He is obsessed with achieving an objective, and impatient with anything that gets in the way. He never limits himself to available methods, which often hinder new approaches to problem-solving.
- Not necessarily intelligent. People of average intelligence can be quite creative, Brown observes.

LOOK BY ASKING

For the research director selecting new people, the task is to recognize these characteristics. To some extent this can be done during an interview or by questioning others. Brown advises that if a candidate is just out of school ask his research professor if he has the above characteristics. "Because if he has them, he surely will have demonstrated them in his graduate thesis research."

Then question a few other professors along similar lines. And, of course, if the candidate has worked before, you had better ask these questions of his references, particularly references whom you know and can talk with frankly.

And what about creative people who may have been over-looked in your own labs? Brown is convinced that while no two people will agree on a definition of creativity, you will find enormous unanimity on recognizing creative people. He reports success with the following simple experiment.

Call everyone from the lab together and hand them blank slips of paper. Ask them to write down the names of the three most creative people in the lab. "I've done that in my own labs and in outside groups many times and found that you get a remarkable degree of agreement in recognizing the creative people in your midst."

STIMULATING CREATIVE TALENT

This is even harder than finding them, says Brown. The creative person will be quicker than the ordinary researcher to leave the company when he is unhappy, and while there is no proven formula for keeping creative people happily productive, Brown suggests that every organization try at least some of the following ideas in order to see which work best for its own situation.

- First of all, never lose sight of the fact that individuals create, not groups. And individuals tend to become dissatisfied and leave if they feel the organization does not recognize that they want to be recognized for their individual contributions.
- It is important to have creative leadership at the top. I have very seldom seen creative labs or R&D groups that didn't have a creative manager. I don't think the most creative person has to be in charge, but he's got to be more creative than the norm for the particular laboratory. And that applies to the chief executive too. The 3M Company, for instance, attributes its success to a heritage of creative leadership, where for years successive CEO's nurtured creative thinking and problem-solving. With a creative atmosphere at the top, you'll find more trust among research people, a lot less jealousy, and a willingness to discuss ideas openly rather than play them close to the chest. Information exchange will become a habit.
- For this reason, Brown strives to appoint the most creative people he can find who are interested in R&D management, to positions on the management ladder. While there are—or certainly should be—plenty of creative people on your technical ladder, he warns against selecting R&D managers, supervisors or project leaders who are uncreative, highly structured planner types. Although often excellent on formalized development projects, such people are prone not to allow their subordinates the necessary freedom to explore and find new ideas. "It is very difficult to stimulate scientists and engineers to be creative when they work under those who are not creative. The less creative person with long experience tends to know 'too much' about a situation. He knows why your idea 'can't work.' He lacks an open mind to someone else's new approach to a problem which he himself has worked on previously."
- Don't make the mistake of keeping a creative researcher in one little section or group forever. Expose your bright young graduates, and your older creative people, to the other creative minds in the laboratory by rotating people on a continuing basis. This also provides valuable exposure to different supervisors and styles of supervision.
- But don't rotate too often, Brown cautions. Insisting that creative people should have the chance to enjoy the fruits of their accomplishments, he feels that every couple of years should be about right. "It generally takes a person a year-and-a-half to solve the problem and finish the project. Studies have shown that when someone is put on a new project, he will have lots of ideas, stimulate (and be stimulated by) the others, and try many new things during the first six months. Afterwards, during the next six months or so, he will find solutions to the major problems and become less interested. That's the time to take him off the project and put him on a new team. The age of that team will then be one day, and you have the chance of getting a whole new creative surge."

- Use your most creative people on your toughest problems. Don't automatically turn to the resident expert, but recognize that creative people are problem-solvers in many different areas. "I call them the green thumb people; no matter what they plant, it always seems to come up. They are winners."
- Use your creative people to stimulate those who are less creative. They are very good at it. Arrange idea interchange sessions where they meet with good scientists and engineers on a regular basis and stimulate (and are, in turn, stimulated) by questioning established concepts and procedures.
- Similarly, when someone has a very tough problem and is searching for solutions, let him call one of these sessions with six or eight of your most creative people. After he has put forward his possible solutions and the others have put forward theirs, combinations of ideas will often result that nobody saw before.
- Give creative people lots of freedom. Don't let management hassle the individualist who likes to work in his office with the lights off, or with his shoes off, or at irregular hours. After all, lots of uncreative people break rules with impunity.
- But this doesn't mean there should be no pressure to produce. Brown is a great believer in maintaining urgency, or what the British call "dither," in a laboratory. "I have never yet found anyone buckling under time pressure. Of course, you don't apply pressure until the person has had time to define the problem and decide what he wants to do. But after that, pressure can be a great stimulus to creative research production."

    What kind of pressure? Pressure, says Brown, as simple as, "Come on, we've got to solve this problem soon or the company is going to be in trouble. Competition has a good product out there and timing is critical. Being ready with a product five years from now is no good."
- To stimulate creativity, it is important to convince people that you really want it. Putting creative people into high positions is one way, but equally important is to formally and publicly recognize creative contributions.

    Creative people are more interested in recognition, praise and under-standing than they are in salary alone, stresses Brown. That's why he recommends special rewards and incentives—everything from luncheons with top management where they are presented with facsimiles of their latest patent, to specific achievements publicized in the house organ, to introducing them to the CEO or president, when he tours the laboratory, and having them explain their work. "The creative person will glow at the recognition and his motivation will be strengthened once again."

40.
SYSTEM FOR INCREASING INVENTIVENESS

David S. Brown

> The visionaries in any culture are people capable of extending their
> perspective well beyond conventional ways of thinking.

Necessity, everyone seems to think, is the mother of invention. If so, who is
the father? This is what we need to know if we want to increase our inventiveness which, of course, we do.

If we are looking for a final and definitive answer, it may never be found.
Innovation occurs in many different ways in many different people. But a practical one is available which will work for the average citizen as it has for great
inventors, provided that we search hard enough for it. Paternity may
sometimes be difficult to determine but it's a lot easier than cloning.

The philosopher Alfred North Whitehead has confirmed this point. The
hundred years from 1800 to 1900 were one of the more creative periods of
history, giving us among other things the screw propelled ship, the lightbulb,
the automobile, the telegraph and telephone, the camera, the motion picture,
the phonograph, and many many innovations in the field of art, medicine,
warfare, government, and industry. Of this period, Whitehead writes that the
century's greatest invention, however, was "the invention of the method of
invention."

He neglects, however, to tell us precisely what it is, and even so successful an
inventor as Thomas Alva Edison did not specifically reveal the secret,
although it may be in part distilled from what he did. Certainly, other
successful inventors, whether logically or intuitively, divined it and put it to
their own use. The layman, meanwhile, incandescent light or not, has still
been very much in the dark. He need not be any longer.

THE SOURCES OF INVENTION

It is generally accepted that there are three major sources of invention. The
first of these is serendipity; the second, inspiration; and the third is system.

They are not as greatly different, however, as they may seem. If serendipity suggests chance—the finding of things of value when we are not actually looking for them—the finder must at least be sufficiently aware of the implications of his discovery to use it elsewhere. Edison invented the mimeograph while seeking something else. He had the good sense to realize he had come upon a discovery of importance and shortly found a use for it. Many others have done the same. Their inventiveness is merely channeled in a new direction.

It is useful to inquire why—and how—inspiration occurs. Too many people have reported that some of their better ideas are produced at night, after deep sleep, to suggest that this is purely a matter of chance—or even of revelation. We know that the brain works in mysterious ways even if we do not really know how it works, and are no longer surprised that problem solving sometimes occurs even in our dreams.

Inspiration reveals itself in other ways as well. We search diligently for an answer; then, suddenly in a flash, it comes to us. The fact that this happens more often in certain places, and under certain circumstances, than in others suggests that our thought processes are influenced whether we realize it or not by external factors. More will be said about this later.

Finally there is the matter of system. If one will observe how others go about a task they have been performing for some time or, better still, reflect upon how one goes about it oneself, it will usually be clear that there is method to it. There is method to inventing, also, and even if one cannot always say precisely what it is, it will often unconsciously be followed. This is undoubtedly what Whitehead was referring to. All great inventors have systems.

INVENTORS AND INNOVATORS

My search to identify the fatherhood of invention has involved me not only with the literature of creativity and invention but also with some of the better known names: Franklin, Whitney, Bell, Edison, Maxim, Morse, Lear, and others. But it is not limited to such as these.

There are other great innovators, although we usually do not think of them in these terms. They are the scientists, the artists, the educators, the industrialists, the financiers, the statesmen—yes, and even the generals and admirals—who have contributed so much to our civilization.

The history of nations is replete with examples of those who dared try something new, whether it was a new way of manufacturing shoes, a new system of teaching, a new art form, or a new military maneuver. Biography is better than history at explaining how such ideas evolved and how they were made acceptable.

Nor is ingenuity limited to the great or the near great. Most people are far more creative than they think, and if they ask the right questions and are sufficiently reflective with respect to the answers, they will often be able to indicate how and why they have produced some of the things they have.

One's profession or trade has much to do with it. Certain of these—artists, writers, engineers, managers, advertising people, mechanics, chefs, and the like—face a continuing need to be creative. Others—clerks, accountants, policemen, soldiers, factory hands, drivers, farmers, fishermen, and custodial employees—are much more likely to emphasize the routine. Certain sports, such as basketball and football, emphasize the innovative. Baseball has, in general, followed traditional patterns.

One's creativity is encouraged (or discouraged) by how one approaches a problem. If one is restricted to pre-determined conditions, as some lines of work automatically do, this will also limit solutions. Custom and habit are enemies of creativity.

We are also limited by the way we define the terms we use. The patenting process has emphasized the "thing" nature of inventions. Most of us think of an invention in terms of a gadget, a tool, or some other specific, but it can also be a contrivance, a process, or in fact a discovery which is different from what was before. Invention has many synonyms, among which are innovation, creativity, adaptation, stratagem, style, fabrication, design, and concept. In general, I have used the words interchangeably because the process they describe—that of devising something new or different—is fundamentally the same. Most people will go through life without ever holding a patent, but that does not keep them from discovering better ways of growing cucumbers, hanging pictures, filing papers, or writing love letters than they used before.

In seeking to understand the nature of this new "philosopher's stone," the key to fatherhood, I have put the question to 800 or so professional people over the past five years, asking them to reflect upon some of the things the have innovated, created, or devised and to try to recall the circumstances that produced them. While I have no statistics to share with my readers, these questions have revealed interesting and useful ideas. I have tried also to understand how I personally have come by the flashes of creativity I have had over my lifetime and have recorded some of the answers. They are not far off from what the great innovators have revealed of their systems.

A majority of the innovative ideas my subjects have had come from seven specific locations: the office, the workshop or laboratory, the kitchen, the yard, the bedroom, the car, and the bathroom. Some of these are places where problems most often occur, but the others are where we are most likely to be thinking about them.

The need established, we search—visually, first—for a solution. If we are in a kitchen and lacking a needed ingredient or faced with some mistake we have made, our eye scans what is available by way of remedy. The same is true in yard, shop, or laboratory.

Failing to find the answer, we enlarge the perimeters of our scan. We recall previous experience in similar, related, or, if we are practiced at it, even dissimilar circumstances. The bathroom, the bedroom, and car provide unconscious vehicles for doing this. There is a factor here not unlike that of Pavlov's dogs. The immersing of oneself in a tub or shower, or driving alone to work, is a signal to the mind to address the unanswered questions we have. It is surprising how many report this happening to them.

There are, of course, other more sophisticated ways of enlarging the perimeters of our vision, and it is a characteristic of the professional that these are planned and used. There is the literature search to see what others have suggested. This had been improved upon by the use of computers. Other people are directly involved in the process. One way is to ask them as individuals what they have to suggest. We assemble groups to increase the number of options. We bring in people with dissimilar backgrounds so that these options can be increased. Many cooks may spoil a porridge, but they increase the likelihood that a viable solution will be achieved—which is often more important than the porridge. What we are doing, of course, is increasing our line of sight by artificial means.

Edison is an excellent example of this. Long on memory, fertile of mind, curious by nature, willing to experiment, and impervious to failure, he ultimately acquired nearly 1100 patents and undoubtedly contributed in various ways to a great many more. That he harnessed the brains of others is obvious from the systems he developed to search out the solutions he had to have. This is emphasized by the many lawsuits, both as a plaintiff and defendant, in which he was involved over his lifetime. As one of his associates said of him, "Edison is in reality a collective noun and means the work of many men." Of himself, Edison said: "My business is thinking."

His thought pursued systematic patterns, much along the lines of those described earlier. His search for a viable carbon filament for what later became the light bulb involved him with the testing of hundreds of substances including cotton and silk thread, slivers of bamboo, and much else. Negative results, he once opined, are as important as positive ones because they show you what won't work.

One does not need to be original but one should be persistent. Daniel Lords, internationally known for his artistry with marionettes, says frankly: "Those ideas I don't steal from other sources you might call original." A designer, Robert Kulicke, in fact advocated taking hold of ideas wherever one finds them. He says:

> If you are a painter,...don't try to invent art. If you are a designer or a craftsman, don't try to reinvent the wheel; don't try to be original and don't try to express yourself!...If you really want to become good, then you must steal without shame from anyone in history who can do what you want to do.

If the word "steal" is a troubling one, a useful euphemism is "borrow." It is much the same. We all do it, whether innocently or intentionally. The public domain has much to offer, and imitation is rarely unwelcome and often enormously useful.

William J.J. Gordon, who was associated for a number of years with the

National Aeronautics and Space Administration's efforts to achieve the moon and who later went on to form his own consulting firm, has a name for the creative processes. He calls them *synectics*, which comes from the Greek and means "the joining together of different and apparently irrelevant elements." Not having what we want or need, we test other possibilities. Much of the time we do it mentally, but we have also developed ways of doing so institutionally.

One of the simplest of these is what is involved in the technique called brainstorming. But it is also involved in much more sophisticated ways in Operations Research. It is a systematic search for tools, techniques, and materials which, in one way or another, can be involved in the solution of the problems which vex us.

AND THE FATHER IS...

If necessity—the motivator—is the mother of invention, who is the father? Who indeed? And how do we use this knowledge to improve our own creativity?

Unlike other searchers for paternity, this one has many candidates. Surely, Curiosity is worth considering. All of the great inventors were of an inquisitive bent, and this had its reward. But innovation has been the reward also of many who were not particularly so.

The great French naturalist, Buffon, thought that genius was several parts Patience. There is strong support for this view. So also for Persistence and Conception. Invention, as some have suggested is nine parts Perspiration and one part Inspiration. These, however, tell us more of the quality the search requires than its nature.

Optimism and Single-Mindedness have their supporters. So also have Enthusiasm, Spirit, Insight, and Simplicity. The ideas they convey are useful ones. Some of life's more difficult riddles have turned out to have simple answers. Still, they do not resolve the problem.

The candidate with the most impressive blood lines clearly is Proximity. Experience shows that we look first for solutions in what is immediately available to us. All of us do this, not just the great inventors. If this does not suffice, we extend ourselves beyond. We raise our sights, we broaden our horizons, we magnify our "seeing power." We bring new ideas and objectives into perspective, into proximity to the problem. If the immediate environment does not satisfy, we replicate our surroundings and explore them for answers.

There are many ways of using the information we obtain from the eye- and brain-scans we undertake. Most of us have developed our own styles, some highly productive, for doing so. We have taught ourselves the value of free association, of cross-relating the information we have acquired, of analogy, and of analysis. Many have found the questioning of the obvious a fruitful way of proceeding. Most have learned the value of new and various points of view, and how they can be obtained. But these are merely systems for developing the relationships we are establishing. First, we must bring them close enough to us to make them usable at all.

The professionals are distinguished from layfolk by their skill in processing and manipulating the information thus acquired. They know the limitations of their own faculties and have learned to deal more aggressively and fruitfully with the organizational, cultural, emotional and—most important of all—perceptual/conceptual blocks to greater productivity.

The process begins by increasing the options we have. This is what Proximity has to offer—a reminder that we should systematically examine what is available to us, and if that is insufficient to our need, we should extend our inquiries beyond. The visionaries in any culture are just that—people capable of extending their perspective well beyond conventional ways of thinking. Determining the source of invention will, of course, always be debatable and each person will have his or her own ideas on the subject. If, however, Proximity is not the Father of Invention, it is certainly a member of the immediate family, and that in itself is an important revelation for those interested in both the genealogy of ideas and the encouragement of creativity.

Dr. David S. Brown is Professor of Management at George Washington University's School of Government and Business Administration.

41.

HOW TO NOURISH THE CREATIVE EMPLOYEE

Donald W. Myers

> The ability to channel employee ideas in a constructive manner requires
> an understanding of the care and feeding of the creative employee. This
> understanding involves the human and cultural aspects, the organization,
> and the management philosophy.

The best supervisor is not necessarily the one who tries singlehandedly to
come up with solutions to organizational problems. A more important quality
is the ability to channel employee ideas into the mainstream of the organization. To do that requires an understanding of the care and feeding of the creative employee.

The following quiz is a test of your capacity as a supervisor for managing
creativity. It is divided into four parts: the human elements of creativity, the
impact of the organizational environment, the effect of management philosophy, and the cultural aspects of creativity. Be honest with yourself in
answering the questions, and try not to look at the answers before giving your
opinion. Answer each question as true or false. The correct answers are explained beneath each question.

THE HUMAN ASPECTS OF CREATIVITY

1. Creativity and personal growth are interrelated.

TRUE. When employees are treated as adults who can creatively contribute
to the success of the organization, they mature as human beings. An environment conducive to creativity is a prerequisite for self-fulfillment since
creativity is in the main a personal expression of one's self. The individual
releases creative energies that provide personal fulfillment and satisfaction,
which according to Abraham Maslow is an indication of a "healthy
personality."

2. Employee creativity is the result of planned management action.

FALSE. Creativity will exist independent of management's actions. Management's role is to direct the creative behavior. As an example, one researcher found that where work methods were strictly prescribed, employees engaged in a variety of creative activities, including different types of games, purposeless antics, and singing. In this case, the creative behavior that was used to counter job monotony was harmless. Creativity can, however, have more harmful manifestations, including clever methods to restrict output, even sabotage. It is the nature of the frustrated employee either to withdraw by engaging in day-dreaming and absenteeism, or to exhibit aggressive behavior in overt violations of organizational rules.

3. There is no proven correlation between creativity and employee performance.

FALSE. Many managers feel that creativity has a detrimental effect upon productivity. They believe that employees who are thinking about ideas are wasting time that should be spent producing. But research conducted by myself and others shows a statistically significant correlation between employee creativity and job performance. Creative employees seem to have a zealous regard for long hours and hard work.

4. Creative problem-solving is a function of the left hemisphere of the brain.

FALSE. The right half of the brain controls the creative thought process used in solving problems. It is also the source of thought in initiating new programs and analyzing contingencies. The left half of the brain controls logic and decision making based on the routine and familiar. While right hemispheric thought leads to new hypotheses, it is the left side that verifies and rationally analyzes those hypotheses. Studies have shown that in the proper environment people can be induced to utilize the right half of their brains and thus develop their creative abilities.

5. Supervisors could be aided considerably if only there were some means of measuring creativity.

FALSE. There is already a considerable body of research regarding the measurement of creativity. The problem is putting those findings to work.

THE ORGANIZATION

6. Opportunities for employee creativity are limited in most organizations.

TRUE. The opportunities for creative expression are limited because organizations have not encouraged employees to tackle the myriad problems that every organization faces. Intel Vice-Chairman Robert N. Noyce, for one, believes that one of the reasons Japan is winning the competitive industrial battle with the United States is that U.S. manufacturers discourage innovation.

7. Extrinsic rewards like cash and praise are needed to arouse the creative abilities in employees.

TRUE. While intrinsic rewards are important, they cannot be the sole basis for encouraging creativity. Researchers have found that extrinsic reward systems have a significant impact on employees' creativity. The energies employees expend in creative efforts are a function of their desire for a particular reward and their expectation of receiving it. Employees value recognition in the form of money and praise (extrinsic rewards), as well as in the form of meaningful work assignments (intrinsic rewards) that allow them the freedom to choose methods and procedures in accomplishing tasks.

8. One of the principal deficiencies of the scientific management of Frederick W. Taylor is that it ignores the contribution of employee creativity.

FALSE. Taylor was perhaps the first person in management to recognize the creative efforts of employees to cooperatively reduce productive energies. The confusion about Taylor stems from the fact that he advocated scientifically determined methods of work. Consequently, he is criticized for having been insensitive to the human aspects of work and in favor of a more task-oriented approach to management. While some of the criticism may be valid, it cannot be said that he was unmindful of the effects of employee creativity on efficiency.

9. Creativity is an individual process that involves four stages of ideation—preparation, incubation, illumination, and verification.

FALSE. Elton Mayo, writing on the Hawthorne studies, noted that positive group creativity could be obtained by asking for group solutions to problems and by consulting the group about proposed changes. He also found that group involvement ensured commitment to the accomplishment of goals.

10. Inflexible organizations prevent employees from exhibiting their creative talents.

FALSE. Inflexible organizations require employees to be more creative in adapting. Gordo Allport has said that creativity is fundamental in personal adaptation to organizational life. The problem for management is the direction of creativity. Many arbitration cases testify to elaborate disciplinary procedures designed to coerce employee compliance to inflexible rules and procedures.

MANAGEMENT PHILOSOPHY

11. The creative potential of employees is limited.

FALSE. Your answer to the question reflects your philosophy of management. Douglas McGregor says that Theory X managers would answer true while Theory Y managers would say false, believing that creativity, like other human characteristics, is distributed in varying degrees among people. One of the paramount demands upon managers in the 1980s is to tap creative potential in employees.

12. Creativity can be developed in employees.

FALSE. While the answer to this one may seem tricky, the concept is not. Employees develop their creative talents, not management. Organizations can aid employees in their development of latent creative abilities, however, by providing an encouraging work environment. The proper atmosphere consists of a management philosophy that recognizes the value of creativity and nourishes ideas with job descriptions that are not tightly constraining, a reward system that is fair, and supervisors who communicate with employees.

13. Suggestion programs are necessary to ensure constructive creativity.

FALSE. While suggestion programs can be excellent for channeling creative energies, they do not guarantee constructive commitment. Systems like suggestion programs can promote employee creativity only if management demonstrates its willingness to recognize the importance of creative ideas. While both the system and the philosophy are important, the latter is more significant because it establishes the rationale for a system's existence. Mary Parker Follett said that people are not going to think creatively unless there is a reason for them to do so.

14. The objective of employee creativity is to obtain ideas that increase the efficiency of the organization.

FALSE. As many or more benefits result from the by-products of employee creativity than from the direct application of ideas. In my research, I have found that safety, for instance, can be improved when employees and managers are asked to focus their creative energies on finding ways to reduce accidents. A by-product is a heightened safety-consciousness among employees in their daily work. When employees are challenged to think creatively about their work, they seek to know more about their jobs and in the process become more competent and efficient. This self-development aspect of creativity is continuous as employees attempt to gain increasing amounts of knowledge to improve existing skills. This cyclical development can also promote adult personality development. Certainly the organization benefits from the direct application of ideas, but it profits to an even greater degree from the maturative process in which employees seek greater responsibility, become self-regulated, and develop as people.

15. The immediate supervisor determines the quality and quantity of employee creativity.

FALSE. Top management, through its organizational objectives, determines the quality of employee creativity. Supervisors only reflect the concerns of top management.

THE CULTURAL ASPECTS

16. Creativity and intelligence are related.

FALSE. In a study I conducted, there was no evidence of a difference in creativity between 100 mentally retarded employees and 100 non-retarded employees engaged in the same work and employed in the same organization. Other studies have also failed to indicate a correlation between intelligence and creativity.

17. Creative employees are usually long-haired types who are constantly dreaming up impractical schemes.

FALSE. There may be creative employees who fit that description but for the most part there's no point in trying to identify creative people by their physical features, personal attire, and so forth. The best way to tell is to ask employees for solutions to problems. Familiarity with workers will make their abilities clear enough—provided the organization really wants ideas, treats employees fairly, and gives them adequate recognition for their initiative.

18. Employees usually have little interest in using their creative abilities to help the organization.

TRUE. Researchers have noted that employees usually have little inclination to be constructively creative in their jobs. One of the principal reasons for this is the cultural pressure for conformity. Regimentation begins early in life at school and continues through the work career. During that time expressions of creativity are too often subjected to criticism and even ridicule. Not enough effort is made to stimulate and recognize creativity through intrinsic (meaningful work, opportunity for personal growth, and the like) rewards and extrinsic (money and praise) rewards. The result is inertia and apathy.

19. Research and development is the most appropriate function for creative employees.

FALSE. All organizational functions are appropriate for employee creativity. While there is a tendency to view research and development as the principal—even the sole—domain for creativity, experience has shown that for businesses to remain competitive, employee creativity is needed at all levels and in all functions. The most appropriate place for its use is where the need is greatest.

20. Managers do not appreciate the importance of employee creativity in organizational efficiency.

FALSE. Most modern-day managers realize that creativity is important. The problem is that they don't know what to do about it. As one manager said in a seminar I recently conducted, "I know all about creativity—you should hear the excuses I get from employees who show up late for work on Monday mornings." That's the negative side to creativity. Unfortunately, the positive side is not nearly so evident because employees are often frustrated in their creative efforts.

Donald W. Myers is Associate Professor of Management, School of Business Administration, Winthrop College.

42.
HIRING CREATIVE PEOPLE: THREE OPPORTUNITIES TO MAKE BETTER DECISIONS

Bernard Weiss

> Hiring a creative person is in itself a challenge. Hopefully, the suggestions presented here will lend themselves to creative adaptation in your organization to help you make better hiring decisions.

There's a special challenge in hiring creative persons, such as writers, art directors, photographers, designers, planners and certain engineers and scientists. The challenge isn't necessarily difficult to meet, yet many personnel directors are often uncomfortable when it comes to making decisions on job applicants for creative positions.

Why? Creative persons are not extraordinary people. They are, in fact, just ordinary people with some extraordinary gifts. They are subject to most of the same rules of employment that govern the rest of the population.

There are a few things about creative persons which require a slightly different approach to hiring. For example, many creative persons are not particularly verbal, and may not present themselves well during an employment interview. Unlike sales-persons, who are almost invariably at ease in a one-on-one business conversation, sensitive or introspective creative persons frequently are non-expressive when called upon to communicate verbally. They are not likely to volunteer much information about themselves or their special talent, even when urged to do so. Such persons need to be encouraged to talk about themselves so you can learn more about them.

After more than 20 years as both a creative employee and employer, I have learned a few lessons I want to share. There are three check-points during the hiring process which afford the opportunity to make decisions about creative persons. These checkpoints are the pre-employment interview, the employment review (or reference check) and the employment preview (trial) assignment.

THE PRE-EMPLOYMENT INTERVIEW

There are some things you can and should do to make the pre-employment interview more productive. There also are some things you should not do, or you may lose your best candidate without even realizing it. These suggestions are especially useful for line managers and supervisors and others who may not yet have developed the requisite interviewing skills.

Be attentive and sensitive to the individual. Employment interviews are likely to be stressful and anxiety-producing for many creative persons. You can relieve the tension by promoting the idea that you are really interested in the individual, as well as the talent. Minimize interruptions. Once the applicant has gotten down to the serious business of selling himself or herself to you, don't take telephone calls, don't rummage through the desk drawers and don't open mail.

Make it clear to others that you do not wish to be disturbed and give the job applicant the impression that for a few minuters, at least, he or she is the most important person in the world to you.

"Lubricate" the conversation. Compliment the candidate when he or she begins to speak of things about which you'd like to know more. Interject conversational asides and encourage full explanation and the development of detail.

Develop a facility for pausing and echoing. In an interview—indeed, in almost any conversation—most Americans are almost compelled by their cultural exposures to fill in pauses and awkward silences with additional (and usually elaborate) commentary. To take advantage of this tendency, develop the knack of simply looking expectantly at the candidate as he or she winds up an explanation or anecdote. Feeling slightly uncomfortable, the candidate will probably go on to tell you more details. As for echoing, merely repeat the last few words of the applicant's just concluded statement. Adding a slightly puzzled or questioning tone to your voice is even more likely to encourage additional explanatory remarks and comments.

TURNOFFS

When interviewing non-verbal job candidates, there are three pitfalls to be avoided. Experienced personnel managers don't make these mistakes, but less experienced line supervisors and managers frequently "turn off" applicants who aren't very expressive to begin with. These common errors are:

- Taking notes when the candidate is revealing sensitive, potentially damaging or personal information. It's best to wait for a change in the topic, or until the applicant is discussing something that he or she considers favorable or positive, before taking notes.

- Asking questions that may be answered "yes" or "no." With less verbal persons you'll need a list of leading questions, such as "What prompts you to consider leaving your present job?" or "What five things have you done that you are most proud of?"
- Conducting an inquisition. Although the interview is being conducted at your request, your quest should feel involved in a discussion, not an inquiry.

Don't ask all the questions on your list; it's not usually necessary. If your initial judgment about the applicant is positive, arrange for another interview later, an in-depth session with others in your company.

THE EMPLOYMENT REVIEW

From the job applicant's resume or application, note and confirm during the interview the name and telephone number of his or her former employer. This person must have been the previous immediate supervisor. In my experience, a conversation with the previous immediate supervisor is at least as rewarding as the interview with the job applicant. That supervisor probably knows more about the applicant's actual job performance and ability to meet creative challenge than anyone else.

When telephoning that supervisor, do not be side-tracked into a conversation with the personnel department, or with some friends or former colleagues. The personnel department usually is unable to answer the questions you'll be asking and often you won't be able to rely upon the answers of former friends or colleagues. You must speak directly with the former immediate boss.

First, confirm the information you've already learned about the applicant. Then ask about the applicant's strong points and professional assets. Since it's never difficult to enumerate someone's strong points, the former boss will probably speak freely. Because so much creative work is difficult to assess in terms of positive quality, some former employers will need specific questioning about the applicant's work history, such as "Did he or she advance original ideas?" "Is he or she a clear thinker?" "Does he or she merely adapt suggestions from others?" "Is he or she sensitive to criticism?"

WHOM TO BELIEVE

Ask next about the applicant's termination. The supervisor's explanation of the circumstances should be consistent with the explanation you got from the applicant. If there's any question, explore the matter carefully.

Your final question should be, "Would you re-hire the applicant?" This is the clincher, because the measure of an applicant's performance for a former employer was not in units of productivity, but contribution of abstract ideas and concepts. These are not easily measured and evaluated, but a former supervisor would want to hire back the applicant if his or her contributions were considered valuable—and that's what you're trying to find out.

Whatever answer you receive, try to qualify it. Be certain you understand circumstances leading to the severance of relations as well as the standards of performance by which employees are evaluated. For example, an applicant may have been discharged because he or she was habitually incorrect with data, smoked, insulted colleagues or had a fear of flying that restricted mobility for certain assignments. You can certainly relate to those problems; you may not want such an applicant in your company either.

But perhaps the applicant was dismissed because of an unusually artistic and highly unconventional work style, which a former employer did not appreciate. But that style may be just what you need to bring some life and excitement into your organization. The applicant may have felt restricted in his or her former spot; in this position, unlimited horizons may be realized.

You cannot, of course, devote a great deal of time checking out the employment history of all those who apply for creative jobs in your company. My suggestion is that you reserve this specific sort of reference checking for only the most highly regarded candidates—those few from among whom the final choice will be made. I also recommend that this employment review be delegated to the line manager or executive for whom the new applicant will be working; there are more insights to be gained when the future boss talks directly with a former boss.

THE EMPLOYMENT PREVIEW

Every time you hire a creative person, both you and the new employee enter the relationship with a set of expectations. These expectations are compounded by an overlay of anxiety regarding the job, performance level, creative challenge, company, others in the office and so forth. If these expectations prove unrealistic and false, or if the anxiety proves so great that it interferes with work, dissatisfaction and frustration set in. An early departure is the frequent result.

A work preview, or trial assignment, is one of the best methods for providing creative individuals with realistic job expectations and alleviating anxieties about the unknown. More important, it also gives you, the employer, an opportunity to evaluate a fresh sample of the individual's talent and creativity applied to your particular needs. Because there is so much variation in creative jobs, you'll have to develop your own trial assignments based on your special need for particular talent and skill. When you work up these trial assignments, however, remember that each one:

- Must be a realistic representation of the actual job to be performed, including a small but typical aspect of the job that is crucial to its successful achievement but that is difficult to explain or teach—creating a new design, for example.
- Should be performed under typical working conditions in the same office where the applicant will be working once hired.
- Must be assigned just as any other creative assignment would be assigned, with the same initial direction and assistance or supervision that might be expected under conditions now prevailing in that department.

If the job applicant is currently employed, ask the applicant to spend one or two evenings or a weekend on the trial assignment—just enough time to demonstrate what he or she can do for your organization.

Most serious candidates will welcome a chance to demonstrate in reality a creative talent that is difficult to appreciate in the abstract, especially if you offer a token fee of, say, $100 to $150 in return for a one- or two-day effort. The candidate will realize, as you do, that a trial assignment affords both parties a near-perfect opportunity to look each other over carefully with no long-term commitments.

PREVIEW SAMPLES

Here are some examples of realistic trial assignments in a Chicago publishing company with over 500 creative personnel. Editors there use these approaches. For a writing job, they provide transcripts of a series of interviews and ask applicants for suggested headlines, introductory paragraphs, an outline of the rest of the article and a list of suggestions for visual treatment.

For a graphic design or art director's job, they provide finished manuscript copy and a list of visual suggestions, plus recent issues of the magazine for which this manuscript was created. Applicants are asked for rough layouts and typed specs, with at least one or two pieces of artwork carried to semi-completion. For a job in the photography department applicants are given a shot list and a one-paragraph description of a project's visual objectives. Applicants are asked for black and white contact sheets and recommended prints.

The editors usually make themselves available for questions or discussion, and assign relatively tight deadlines. The actual trial assignments are evaluated by the editor for whom the job applicants will be working and all reports of completed assignments go back to the personnel department for inclusion in the various dossiers.

One caution: Beware the job applicant who gets back to you either too quickly or too slowly. Remember Weiss' adage: If you give a person five days to solve a problem creatively, that person should have spent the first three days thinking about it.

Among those you do hire, you will usually find yourself spending less time in an orientation. In my experience, applicants who are serious about a new job will have followed up the trial assignment with some extracurricular homework.

They will join your staff professionally prepared to make good on their initial favorable impression. Also, since they are on a psychic high, they will come up on the learning curve more quickly than others, saving you further training time.

One subtle but very important advantage of work previews is that they save time for employers. Applicants for creative jobs who aren't seriously interested in your company or your job will screen themselves out; they just won't execute the assignment. Others, upon getting a closer look at a realistic work sample, may disqualify themselves from further employment consideration. And, of course, the results of a work preview may, in your judgment, disqualify someone as being less than competent for the job. All of this contributes to fewer hiring mistakes.

CONCLUSION

I believe hiring creative persons is in itself a creative challenge. It represents a professional personnel problem that lends itself to creative solutions. It is hoped that the suggestions presented here will lend themselves to creative adaptation in your organization to help you make better hiring decisions.

Bernard Weiss is on the faculty of New York University and is president of Bernard Weiss & Associates, Stamford, Conn. He has written articles and conducts workshops and seminars for employers of creative staffs.

43.
YOU CAN BECOME MORE CREATIVE

H. A. Shearring

> The perfect creativity development system does not exist: there is always need for improvement, just as there is always hope that some undreamed-of breakthrough may be just over the horizon. Here is how a systems-integration approach will nourish creative talent.

A quarter of a century ago, good communications were going to solve all management's human problems. The new dawn was just around the corner. Unfortunately, before dawn became day, communications yielded pride of place to contentment. A happy worker was a productive worker. Hardly had managers settle down to shepherd herds of contented workers when the theme changed. Happy workers might be unproductive workers, and togetherness could lead to bankruptcy. But, other remedies were not lacking: Group Decision, Management by Objectives, Stress Reduction, Creativity Development, Y-Style Leadership, Job Enlargement, Democratic Participation, 9:9 Management, Transactional Analysis: a bewildering parade of rival techniques all claiming to be exactly what the manager should do.

All models and methods share two things. They all involve some sort of Remedial Intervention in the way People behave (RIP). Every RIP has a flavor of "Find out what the manager is doing and tell him to do it differently." It was almost a relief to turn to the prophets of computer power and find that the manager didn't need to change, but just to disappear.

Possibly the most ambitious of all the Remedial Interventions listed above is Creativity Development. It seems to promise the most. The new dawn is (again) just around the corner. If only we can release our creativity all will be well.

WHATEVER HAPPENED TO.....?

The various RIP approaches and techniques listed in the opening section do not always fail, but they do often fall short of hope and expectation, and of their genuine potential. It would take a library of books and dissertations to analyze the causes of the various successes and failures. For practical purposes there do seem to be significant links between results and the four questions which follow:

1. What sort of a problem diagnosis took place before a given RIP was adopted?
2. How far was the user organization in a fit state to benefit from the RIP?
3. How far was the RIP sold as a self-contained standard package, and how far was it adjusted to fit the buyer's situation?
4. How realistic were the vendor's claims?

1. What sort of problem diagnosis took place before a given RIP was adopted?

The first lesson one learns from running problem-solving courses is that the world is full of people acting on the basis of "Something must be done; this is something; let us therefore do it." Insurance policies are bought, payment schemes revised, factories opened and closed, organizations reshaped, computers installed—all without anyone asking, let alone answering, "Just what are you trying to remedy or achieve, and why do you think this is the way to do it?"

Purveyors and purchasers of RIP schemes are no exceptions to this misrule. Failure is especially likely when a package is bought because it is fashionable, or because management wants to be able to demonstrate to unions or government or shareholders that "something is being done"—regardless of relevance.

2. How far was the user organization in a fit state to benefit from the RIP?

RIPs are subject to the Sit-ups Principle. The Sit-ups Principle states: if a sixty-year-old executive can do twenty sit-ups without strain, that is good, but he doesn't need to do them. On the other hand, if he is so unfit that he cannot do two sit-ups without collapsing, then he desperately needs to be able to do twenty. The worse his condition, the more urgent it is to improve, and the harder it is. More, if he struggles directly to achieve the score now, he is likely to damage or destroy his entire system. As with individuals, so with organization. The more desperately they need a given RIP input, the less likely they are to be able to make it succeed, and the more trouble they are likely to meet as they try.

Management by Objectives (MBO) illustrates this. For MBO to succeed, at least one of two conditions must be present. The organization's atmosphere must be open: bosses and subordinates must communicate honestly enough. Failing that, management must work long and patiently to prepare people to accept and operate MBO before trying to launch it throughout the organization. MBO will fail in an organization where neither of these two conditions obtains. It is in those organizations which have the greatest need for it that MBO will degenerate into a paper-chase.

Buyers of an RIP must be prepared to prepare the ground. All too often they expect their new remedy to be too easy—a magical self-operating package. It is perhaps significant that some of these RIP systems are sold as packages—a term which suggest a self-contained entity. This gets people thinking in terms of the wrong model, that of a mechanical rather than of a living system. They think in terms of installing an obedient inanimate bit of equipment. A sounder model would be that of an organ transplant; at least that might prepare buyers to consider and take precautions against the risk of rejection by the rest of the system.

3. How far was the RIP sold as a self-contained standard package, and how far was it adjusted to fit the buyer's situation?

The "package" approach not only encourages the wrong mental set in the purchaser: it also tends to invalidate the package itself. Even so simple a thing as a report-writing course gets involved in many aspects of management style and organizational structure. It has to be related to a much wider context than might at first glance seem necessary.

This applies even more strongly to the explicitly interventionist RIPs. They can only succeed if they are put into context. They are not self-contained impermeable blocks but sub-systems influencing and being influenced by their host systems.

A clue to the absence of this system-integrated approach often comes from the experienced manager who comments "It's all very well in theory, but is won't work in practice." There are few things as practical as a valid theory. What he is often struggling to express is his intuitive awareness that the model behind the theory is unacceptable, incomplete, inappropriate, and not sufficiently mappable onto the complex reality it is designed to solve.

Such warnings should not be ignored, nor taken at face value. Instead the proponents of a given RIP should be brought together with its opponents to try to hammer out an understanding. Both should learn from the encounter, and any modified scheme that emerges will almost certainly be an improvement on the original version.

4. How realistic were the vendor's claims?

The more the exclusive attitude appears in the sales talk or documentation of any RIP, the more likely its results will be poor. When "the solution" replaces "a solution," when "it depends" becomes "absolutely," the signs are set for rigidity, the oversell and probably the over-price. The further the proponent of an RIP is from the original inventor, the more dogmatic and fundamentalist he or she tends to be. Loss of accuracy and loss of the spirit of the original source also increase with distance.

Transactional Analysis provides a current example. Eric Berne would hardly recognize, let alone acknowledge paternity of some of the more manipulative versions of his teachings now being marketed. A system for helping individuals free themselves from their own internal fetters has been devalued (in some quarters only) into a sort of one-upmanship.

CREATIVITY AND THE FOUR TEST QUESTIONS

All four of the questions in the previous section are relevant to Creativity Development schemes. In a "physician heal thyself" mode, problem diagnosis should not only be applied before buying a Creativity Development scheme: it should constitute part of the content of the scheme itself.

The Sit-ups Principle applies 100% to Creativity Development. The more uncreative the organization or individual, the harder it is to bring about improvement—and the harder it is to obtain any recognition of the need for improvement before disaster strikes. The system-integration approach is vital in any attempts to nourish creative talent. The fourth point, how vaild are the vendor's claims, naturally applies to Creativity as much as to any other RIP.

TOWARD A CONSUMER'S GUIDE

The four test questions need to be asked and satisfactorily answered before any purchase is made, whether of RIP or rowing boat, of personnel policy or perpetual motion machine. But they are too general.

It is reasonably certain that most readers of the *Journal of Systems Management* have never bought an elephant. Being intelligent people we could probably weed out the really decrepit and useless animals on offer at an elephant market, but beyond that we would be at a loss. "Caveat emptor" would help us a little as "Evaluate the animals' temperaments" or "Estimate the veracity of the rival mahouts' claims." Before one can buy elephants wisely one needs to have studied and bought elephants well.

Similar considerations apply to anyone thinking of adopting an RIP (MBO, Job Enrichment, Creativity Development, etc.) for himself or for his organization. He can obtain broad answers to the four general test questions. He can avoid ending up with a dead white elephant hanging round his neck. If he is a first-time buyer, he will be rather at a loss when he tries to evaluate the more specific strengths and weaknesses of any particular RIP program, and judge the plausibility of its claims.

The following five questions provide guidance to the first-time buyer of a Creativity Development Program (CDP):

1. How comprehensive is the program?
2. How wide-ranging are the techniques?
3. What attention is paid to external environments?
4. What attention is paid to the internal environment?
5. How does the program bridge over to everyday life?

You will find that as far as possible there is a lack of general advice on such things as the need to choose candidates wisely, the need to brief them before they go to a program, and to interview them for debriefing afterwards. All these are very necessary, but readers of this article are as likely to need this sort of general advice as they are to need warning against changing large checks for chance-met strangers in low-class bars.

1. How comprehensive is the program?

Ideally a program aimed at helping people develop their creativity will cover three inter-related themes. It will teach a range of specific techniques or drills for producing relevant new worthwhile ideas. Since ideas are neither generated nor implemented in an aseptic ivory tower, it will take into account the external environment (factory, home, country, etc.) and the forces operating there. Thirdly it will help members recognize the positive and negative forces within themselves that make for or against the exercise of creativity—the individual's internal environment. All three of these themes need to be covered if the full potential of Creativity Development is to be realized.

2. How wide-ranging are the techniques?

There are two main points to look for. First, does the program include elements designed to make its members identify and clearly define problems and opportunities before they start generating ingenious new solutions? There is little value in using a powerful problem-solving technique if it is directed at the wrong problem. This is a Creativity Development application of the earlier general test question "What sort of problem diagnosis took place before a given RIP was adopted?"

Second, does the program deal with one technique or approach or does it include a range of techniques? If a given program concentrates on one particular technique, by all means make use of it: but recognize that you have examined only one color in the spectrum and that for full enlightenment you need to supplement it with the others.

The fourth of the earlier general test questions asked "how realistic were the vendor's claims?" This question needs to be treated with common-sense. Do not reject a technique merely because its inventor makes sweeping claims on its behalf: it may still be useful even though it is not a universal solvent. For instance Morphological Analysis is a valuable tool for generating new ideas. It would be foolish to neglect it merely because at one point its inventor asserted its powers and virtues with an excess of parental fondness:

> I also claim that this approach leads us to the surest way to discovery of those human aberrations that are responsible for the ills of the world, and it will enable us to develop the means necessary for safe-guarding our existence, individually and collectively, as well as guide us on our way to cooperative action for the realization of a unified and stable world. (Fritz Zwicky, *Discovery, Invention, Research*. New York: Macmillan, 1966, pp. 30.)

You do not have to swallow all the claims of vegetarianism before you can enjoy and benefit from eating salads. Table 1 lists some basic techniques to look for in any *general* program purporting to develop creativity. It excludes such specialist elements as Delphi or Input/Output which have a narrower field of application.

Table 1.

Specification of Problems

Problem typologies
Techniques of identification and analysis
Establishing aim
Communication formats
Differentiations: symptoms/root causes
   generic/unique situations
   localized/system-wide situations

General Use Methods of Generating Solutions

Field Force Analysis
Morphological Analysis
Attribute Listing
Check Listing
Word Shifts
Brainstorming
Synectics

Minimal contents for Techniques Division of Creativity Development Program

---

There are various reasons for studying a range of techniques instead of just one or two. Basically these are "problem" reasons and "people" reasons. Different problems are likely to yield to different types of techniques. For that matter a single problem at different stages of its solution will often call for more than one method of attack. Brainstorming can be used to generate additional options in a thinly populated area of a morphological array. Morphology can help bring brainstorming ideas into focus. Field Force Analysis can help sell solutions as well as generate them. In brief, the various techniques supplement each other.

The people value of having a range of techniques is slightly less obvious. Partly it is because not all people think alike. Partly it is because we all tend to neglect one aspect or another of our mental faculties. There are many ways in which people think differently without thinking incompatibly. If you see the days of the week as colored and your colleague doesn't, this need cause no difficulties at work. But if you are by nature and nurture an innovator and he is an adaptor, then problems may follow. In the extreme case you will be frustrated by his "conformity" and "lack of vision"; he will be maddened by your "irresponsibility" and "lack of balance."

Some evidence now exists that the two hemispheres of the brain have rather different functions, paralleling this divergent/convergent emphasis. The right hemisphere is intuitive and combinatory: the left is predominantly logical and analytical. For effective creativity, both halves must work together. There is no one way to bring about this integration, of compensating whichever mode of thinking is underdeveloped, nor of enhancing understanding between the adaptors and innovators. A necessary, though by no means sufficient, condition is to learn and use problem-solving techniques which span the continuum. It is not enough for people to adopt the techniques with which they feel immediately comfortable: rather they should concentrate on those techniques which initially they find unattractive. And obviously this cannot be done in a program which presents only one type of technique.

3. What attention is paid to external environments?

It is a truism, but often neglected in practice, that getting a good idea represents only a first successful skirmish in the battle to solve a problem or develop an opportunity. Solution generating techniques are essential components in any program designed to make people more effectively creative; but those techniques by themselves do not make up a Creativity Development Program.

Table 2 lists some themes that need to be covered if the ideas which emerge from problem-solving sessions are to have a reasonable hope of survival.

Most of the terms in Table 2 are used in their everyday sense. However, "client" calls for some explanation. Formally, the client is the person who authorizes investigation of a problem or opportunity. He may run the investiga-

---

Table 2.

Selecting an Appropriate Solution

Principles of making decisions
Establishing criteria
Methods of evaluation
The need to identify the client(s)
Recognizing when the time is ripe for a particular innovation

Implementing the Solution

Principles of planning
User involvement
Techniques of presentation and persuasion
Monitoring and revision

The Influence of the Organization

The management climate: positive and negative elements
Patterns of organization
Basics of group dynamics
Resistance to change
Scanning for problems/opportunities

*Minimal contents for External Environment
Division of Creativity Development Program*

---

tion himself, or delegate it. If he does delegate it, then the subordinate must refuse to obey a brief which says, "There is the problem; come back in six months with the answer." Somehow or other the subordinate must keep the client in touch with the way the problem is being tackled, and must ensure that the client travels the same mental road as the problem-solver, at more or less the same time. Otherwise, after the original problem has been worked on, redefined, amended and so on, a solution found for the amended problem, the client will not even recognize the problem at the end of six months, let alone accept the solution. It is as if, after an interval of thirty years, a parent were to be expected to recognize a baby last seen in its cradle.

Informally, but powerfully, the client is also the person or collection of persons who can make or break the solution when implementation starts. This can be the office-boy, the minister, the chairman, the canteen staff, the union leader, the village elders, the production manager—or any combination of them. If they are to be involved in working whatever plan is devised by the creative problem-solvers, they must be involved or at the least kept in touch with its development. This is a simple lesson which not all research laboratories have yet learned, still less all international agencies.

4. What attention is paid to the internal environment?

When the author first drew up a Creativity Development Program, he imagined that one of the greatest difficulties would be persuading senior managers to mentally relax, to suspend disbelief, and to go off on the mental excursions and licensed craziness of brainstorming and synectics-type techniques.

In fact, this has presented few difficulties. It is easy enough to persuade people to play the problem-solving game according to the "let's be crazy" rule. Where the snag comes is in getting down from the stratosphere, descending from the dangling rope of fantasy to the solid ground of practical application. Especially, though not solely, when using methods toward the divergent end of the continuum, many people have shared the experience of kittens: it is easier to climb up a tree than to get down to earth again.

If people are not to misdirect their efforts, or waste time re-inventing the wheel, they must learn the mechanics of the various solution-generating techniques. But it is not enough to be able to go off on a synectics excursion, or set out a problem in any approved format, or lay out a morphological array; one must then perceive the new possibilities which they contain and conceal. The fantasy mists of far-out solution must be solidified into something tangible; the potential new mixes in any array must be distinguished; the significance of small clues must be discerned. This calls for mental flexibility: a readiness to see situations in a wider context than before; a readiness to think about thinking; a readiness to take mental risks. It may involve self-examination and self-confrontation, and these are uncomfortable processes.

Developing this mental flexibility, this readiness to break set, is the most important and the most difficult part of Creativity Development. It is often resisted or resented because it does involve patterns, abandoning old certainties. For people who want "quick results" and "cannot spare time," flexibility development is a ready candidate for sacrifice. This is as mistaken an approach as that of the boxer who rejects road work because it does not directly deliver knock-out blows, or the athlete who spurns general fitness training because it does not directly produce faster-moving feet.

Table 3 sets out some of the subjects that need to be dealt with in the part of a program dealing with this vital aspect of developing creativity. They cannot be covered in depth in the time usually available on a single formal training program, but at least they should be dealt with in sufficient detail for members to be able to go further under their own steam.

Table 3.

General Principles of Creative Thinking

Types of thinking
Elements common to all creative activity
Barriers to creativity
General approaches to overcoming barriers

Theoretical inputs and associated Practical Exercises

Basic systems thinking
Models, semantics, and their influence on mental operations
Principles of classification
Shifting between modes of perception
Transactional analysis
Self-recognition exercises
Relaxation drills

*Minimal contents for Internal Environment
Division of Creativity Development Program*

---

5. How does the program bridge over to every-day life?

Any interventionist technique runs the risk of being dealt with in isolation. This can be the isolation of one man being sent away on a program and then discouraged from applying it when he returns to his everyday environment. Or it can be a failure to relate program material to members' own real-life situations. Broadly speaking, an organization thinking of sending one solitary candidate to undergo Creativity Development Training should follow Mr. Punch's advice to young men about to get married: Don't! The main exception is the guinea-pig. It is reasonable to send one man to attend a program to see if it is worth using for other people. But the one man should be fairly senior—not some junior person with no authority to make his voice heard when he returns.

Two points can serve to indicate how well a Creativity Development Program is likely to transfer its teachings across to real life: whether members' own material is used; and whether there is any kind of follow-up.

CDPs naturally use a great deal of prepared material to get their points over. In addition they should work extensively on members' own problems. Otherwise there is a danger that people will learn to solve tidy cases but remain incapable of dealing with the messy situations which everyday life provides. In other words, the way to avoid a gap between program work and real-life work is to tackle the real-life work during the program. Once people have successfully used techniques on their own situations they will no longer feel or fear that "this just can't help me." An additional benefit of using real-life problems is that it will help people realize that genuine problem-solving is an untidy process—that there are blind alleys, false starts, and so on. This can be important in avoiding post-course discouragement. Without some such understanding the neophyte who has just thrown away his second attempt at a solution is more likely to give up in despair than to go for a walk and then come back for a post-incubation third attempt.

How to tell in advance whether this practical work will take place? Check to see if members are specifically required to bring with them details of at least two of their own current real-life problems. If they are not told to do this it is unlikely that this type of transfer is catered to, regardless of what may be said in the publicity material. Follow-up can take various forms—and its effectiveness often depends just as much on the client organization as on the instructing one.

Toward the end of the formal program each member should be required to draw up an Action Plan. This sets out exactly how he intends to apply and develop what he has learned. The plan must be specific, not full of woolly generalizations. It is then up to client organization to make sure that the proposed Action does not remain a mere hope but instead becomes a (probably modified) reality.

Again with the cooperation of the client organization, there are various possible activities to follow the initial formal Program. Follow-up sessions are an obvious example. Even if these are not practicable, members should be encouraged to keep in touch with their instructors and send them worked problems for evaluation. The combination of a planned series of post-course exercises and subsequent review and refresher meetings is the ideal.

Whatever the methods used, it should be made clear that the end of the formal part of a Creativity Development Program is merely the start of a life-long process of continuing growth. If this process is not encouraged the fault is as much with the client organization as with the training one.

TABLE D'HOTE OR A LA CARTE

A well-played violin solo is a beautiful thing to hear. The music of a solitary flute, the sound of unaccompanied human voices in a first-rate choir, the range and flexibility of the organ: all these have their charms. But the full splendor of music is only achieved when choir and full orchestra combine. Something similar applies to Creativity Development Programs. There is no reason not to use programs which teach one or two of the component parts of what has just been outlined as a desirable syllabus. But to achieve the full potential of Creativity Development, the client must carefully orchestrate the various parts. Over a period of two years he must ensure that all the components have been dealt with—and integrated into one whole.

It is almost certainly better to start with a comprehensive program if at all possible. After this the purchaser can go deeper into whichever aspects seem most valuable to himself or to his organization, and do this against an integrating framework. Otherwise the value of having diversity of viewpoints from a variety of instructors may be lost owing to the lack of a connecting theme.

Whether you choose to buy a la carte from a variety of sources or table d'hote from one, it is essential to recognize that in Creativity Development even more than in other RIPs there is never a time when you can say: we have arrived. There is always further to go.

IS CREATIVITY DEVELOPMENT DIFFERENT?

It all depends. Creativity Development has a greater potential than many other RIPs. This is partly because it encompasses many of them within itself, and partly because it makes a more fundamental intervention in individuals and organizations than do other approaches. It affects a wider range of behavior and applies to a wider range of situations. Its aims are more ambitious: it tries to free the individual so that he is able to achieve his potential at work or at play, alone or in a group. In organizations it aims at achieving full Organizational Development.

Bits and pieces of Creativity Development can be dealt with *in isolation*: this is not to be confused with a deliberate a la carte choice of a full program over a period of a couple of years. The isolation approach is that of the body builder who concentrates on building bulkier biceps or the health fan who drinks large amounts of Vitamin C. Biceps specialization and Vitamin C are all very well in their place; but they can do harm, and they certainly do not constitute a balanced Physical Development Program.

A balanced program of physical exercise, postural correction, diet, relaxation, plus a philosophy which makes positive sense out of the seeming chaos of life are all necessary components of a program aiming to bring about a fully developed human. Similarly a full range of inputs is needed if a Creativity Development Program is to deserve its name. At the very least it must include the items listed in Tables 1, 2 and 3. It is just because Creativity Development has so high a potential that it needs to be effectively taught. The greater the potential value, the greater the loss if that value is not attained. The man who refuses to visit Paris because he had been offended at Charles de Gaulle airport is losing much more than the man who refuses to visit Coney Island because his luggage has been mislaid at Kennedy.

ETC.

The perfect Creativity Development system does not exist: there is always need for improvement, just as there is always hope that some undreamed-of breakthrough may be just over the horizon. Any article on the subject needs to leave a heading "Etc." with a blank space beneath in which to insert whatever fresh ideas or developments emerge between the submission of an article and its publication.

Just as there is no perfect teaching system, so there can be no absolute success. Creativity Development cannot provide panaceas, not even for teaching Creativity Development. Stupidity, ignorance, error, failure, like the poor and colds in the head, are always with us. Yet, despite all the reservations, Creativity Development can greatly help individuals and organizations alike to grow nearer to their potential.

H. A. Shearring is President of International Management and Organizational Development Inc., London, England.

44.

THE IMAGINATION HARVEST: TRAINING PEOPLE TO SOLVE PROBLEMS CREATIVELY

Jerry Conrath

> Let's examine the six phases of creative problem solving and a number of
> exercises that you can use to fertilize your employees' imagination.

Imagination and creative thinking are scarce resources. Often you will have
to cultivate them in your employees before you can harvest effective solutions
to work problems.

Problem solving without creative thinking is a garden without seeds: only
slugs, thistles, compost, and finely turned soil. Creative thinking will plant a
mental garden, which can then be cultivated, weeded, nourished, and harves-
ted. And fortunately, creative thinking can be taught and applied to creative
problem solving. A solid one-day seminar spent training your employees
should be adequate if followed by much practice and persistent application.

Let's examine the six phases of creative problem solving and a number of
exercises that you can use to fertilize your employees' imagination.

WARMING UP

Phase One: Become Aware. Start by asking employees to list ten personal
achievements they consider creative. The initial lists you get will range from
"aw shucks" contributions by those who don't yet see themselves as creative to
poems by those who write for entertainment and expression. That's fine—your
interest at this point is in the process of creative thinking, not the product.
Your purpose at this point is to demystify the process of invention and intuitive
thinking. Your people need to realize they can think creatively if they allow
themselves to do it. This may take some convincing on your part. While some
people have had nourishment for their creative thoughts, most have not. Indeed, the rewards in life—school grades, parental praise, and job performance

appraisals—have usually come from following the rules and getting the "right" answers rather than from examining problems from many angles and exploring many answers. Creative thinking takes practice and by giving employees the opportunity to practice it, you will be raising their confidence. Then if you ask them to list more creative achievements, they will show such items as cooking stew, designing a new form for the office, saving money to buy a car, planning a garden with limited space, inventing stories for children, and bringing two hostile employees together.

Having whet their appetites for creative thinking you can now turn to developing their capacity for it.

Phase Two: Use Imagination and Invention. Teach them that they must never impose boundaries on themselves; but instead should think expansively, always pushing beyond the obvious, generating many ideas in order to end up with a few good ones, never judging ideas while generating them, and always trying new modes of thinking.

One way to get your employees to think expansively is by using the nine-dot exercise below. Ask staffers to link the nine dots with four interconnecting straight lines. When presented with a problem like this, people will typically impose boundaries on themselves, assuming that there's a rule requiring them not to draw lines outside the perimeter of the dots. Such thinking, however, makes solving the problem impossible (see the solution at the end of the article). Therefore, the message of this exercise is a powerful one: Imposing boundaries seriously limits your creative thinking and in some cases prevents problem solving.

If some of your staffers have already seen this problem or if you want to give them additional challenges, ask them to do the exercise with three lines or only with one line. The three-line solution takes miles of space, but it can be done by starting at the top of the upper left dot, passing through the center of the

Figure 1.
Nine Dot Exercise

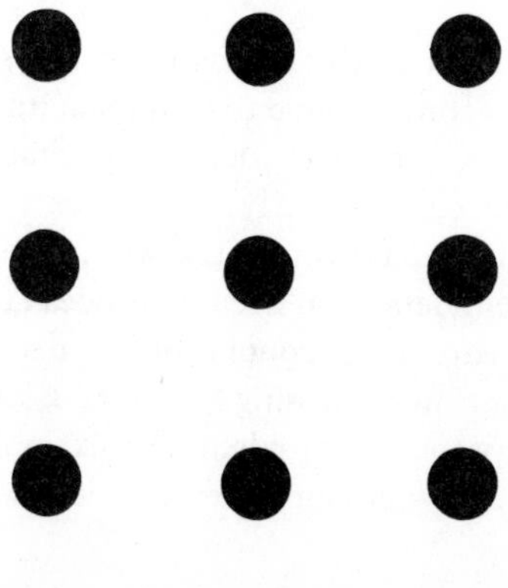

next one to the right, and touching the bottom of the third. Then you continue the line for about six miles and return through the middle row of dots, go another six miles and return through the last row of dots. There are also several one-line solutions. One is to take a paint brush and swoosh a line through all dots at once. Another is to cut the paper and line up all the dots in a row. Why not? Why impose boundaries that are not there?

You and your employees can read about this problem and the many creative solutions to it in *Conceptual Blockbusting* by James Adams.

EIGHT STEPS

Now you are ready to introduce your staffers to the creative problem-solving process itself. There are eight steps to follow: Define the problem, gather all relevant information, explore all possible options to solving the problem, analyze the advantages and disadvantages of each option, use intuition to help in the process before taking action, make a decision, fantasize the worst and the best that could happen with the decision, and implement and evaluate the decision.

Let's examine, in the next four phases, how to carry out this process.

Phase Three: Turn Irritants Into Problems. The first step, defining the problem, requires that employees take the following into consideration in order to develop a proper definition:

- Symptoms or information indicating that a problem exists must not be taken for the problem itself.
- A statement of an irritant or concern is not a definition of a problem and does not open the problem-solving process.
- A definition must open up the problem-solving process, not leap to a conclusion or decision.
- A definition must be specific to the solver and enable the individual to be involved in the problem-solving process through implementation.

To get your staffers through this difficult first step, ask them to list some irritants, frustrations, or concerns and to turn them into a problem statement. Then examine the results. Explain to your staffers: Statements such as "I'm too busy," "I need a new car," or "My typewriter is too old" are merely statements—not problem definitions. Likewise, "Should I have a cup of coffee?" is not a problem definition because it doesn't open up the problem-solving process but leaps to a conclusion or decision ("yes" or "no"). Furthermore, "This typewriter is missing 13 letters" is still not a problem definition but merely a symptom of a problem. An example of a proper problem definition you can give to your employees is, "How do I streamline my work habits in order to get the work done on time?" It opens up the problem-solving process, does not leap to a conclusion or decision, goes beyond making a simple statement of frustration, and is specific to the solver. Other examples of good definition are: "How do I save enough money to purchase a new car?" "How do I convince my manager that a new typewriter is necessary?"

Using these examples as guides, help your employees to work through their statements to design clear, open problem definitions.

Phase Four: Think Expansively. The second and third steps, gathering all relevant information and exploring all options to solving the problem, require staffers to go beyond the obvious. That demands that they have the self-confidence and self-discipline to push on even when they think they have completed the task. To help them, remind them that good ideas come from generating many ideas and that they must suspend judgment on these ideas to allow the creative process to work.

Give staffers some warm-up activities to help them get started. A good one is to ask them to think of as many possible uses as they can for some object in the room that they can all see. The goal is not to come up with only eight or ten uses but with 20 to 30. This will put staffers in the mind set of expansive, exploratory, creative thinking. Giggling should be allowed for we giggle when we warm up to jog, too. And remember: Success comes from quantity, not quality, at this step of the process.

Another good warm-up activity that will help employees go beyond the obvious is to count the squares (see below). What usually happens is that half the group settles on 17 squares, puts pens down, then waits impatiently for a halt to what appears to be a very simple task. When the supervisor walks around the room looking at answers and giving no feedback, pens are picked up again, exclamations of discovery are heard, and new numbers are added. After 10 to 12 minutes, about one-quarter of the group settles on 30 squares while

Squares Exercise

most people wrestle with 26, wondering what the big deal is. By the time the activity is stopped, some more people come up with 30. The reason: Training tells people there are 17 squares, because they were taught to count. Perception tells them there are more—that is, 30.

After performing this exercise, your employees should be ready to refocus on solving their problem. Arrange your staffers in groups of three or four and ask each to explain his or her problem definition and important information about the problem. Then have each group come up with as many options as possible to solving the member's problem. No one should be allowed to make such comments as: "My boss wouldn't let me do that," "It's too expensive," and "I've tried that before, it didn't work," for such judgments kill creative thinking. If adequately warmed up, your groups should buzz with ideas—solid, bizarre, routine, imaginative, funny, and traditional ones.

Phase Five: Synthesize and Analyze. The fourth step in creative problem solving is analyzing the advantages and disadvantages of each option. One way to develop employees' skill in this area is to have them practice synthesizing—combining the strengths of two different things to produce something new. For example, choose two items, such as a ballpoint pen and a clock, and ask employees to combine the strengths of each into a new invention. In one instance, someone came up with the idea of putting a timing device on a pen to record the time actually spent on a letter or a report.

Now have your staffers return to the list of options they previously developed and ask them to analyze the advantages and disadvantages of each potential solution.

For a one-day training seminar, it's sufficient to spend only a few minutes on step five (intuitive thinking), step six (decision making), and step seven (fantasizing the worst and best that could happen with a decision). Ask employees to take a break from analyzing their options and to try not to consciously make a decision based on them. Instead, tell them to let their intuition go to work—it will. Then, for example, if they have trouble choosing between two options, suggest that they flip a coin. If disappointment pops up over the result, tell them to go with the other option. Obviously, their intuition is telling them something their analysis did not reveal. Finally, tell them to make a tentative decision and quickly explore the worst and best consequences of that decision. It's helpful to prepare for the best and perhaps to rethink the decision if a worst possible case is too ugly.

Phase Six: Know Yourself Better. To help your staffers handle the eighth and last step, implementation, and overcome any barriers they may have to solving problems creatively, give them the following exercise: Ask them to list their creative thinking blocks and put a "p" next to those that are personal and an "o" next to those that are organizational. Then explore with them strategies for overcoming both types of barriers so that everyone will leave the session with a solution to an irritant-turned-into-a problem and some confidence and enthusiasm for implementing the decision.

Before concluding, see that all your subordinates leave with an individualized plan for discovering their unique pattern of creative thinking. One technique is to ask them to fill in a chart for at least a week, but preferably longer, indentifying each idea, when it came to them, and what they were doing when it came to them.

Patterns of time, place, companions (or the absence of them), and activities that spark creative thought should emerge. Instruct your employees to take note of them and to plan to increase those opportunities.

No individual has too many imaginative ideas, and no organization is burdened by too many idea people. Working ideas through the creative problem-solving process can turn seeds into nourishing gardens. So why not do your organization and employees a favor by helping staffers plant, weed, cultivate, and get ready for harvest?

Dot Exercise Solution

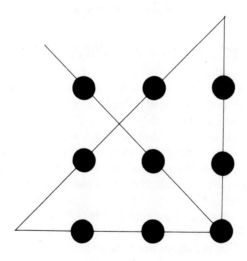

45.
A PERSONAL FILE OF STIMULATING IDEAS AND PROBLEM SOLVERS

Ted Pollock

Regardless of your specific responsibilities, your ability to think
—precisely, thoroughly, originally—represents the most valuable contribution you can make to your organization. Here are certain tested
strategies that enhance the mind's ability to produce ideas.

STRATEGIES FOR ENHANCING CREATIVITY

Given today's economic, competitive and technological environments,
regardless of your work, you need a steady stream of new ideas.

But where do ideas come from?

From minds that are trained to construct (or reconstruct) them.

Although no one pretends to understand fully how the human mind
operates, we know that there are certain tested strategies that enhance the
mind's ability to produce ideas. Here are some modes of thinking that may
prove fruitful for you:

Use Analogies. Analogies are similar situations in terms of things people
already know. For example, consider the many scientific products that have
been developed from analogous situations or principles of nature. Radar resulted from studying the uses of reflected sound waves among bats. Airplane cargo
doors were designed to work in the same way a clam shell opens. The built-in
seam weakness of the pea pod suggested an opening for cigarette packages that
has been adapted throughout the whole area of packaging. Analogous thinking
suggests many new associations that may lie untapped.

Build a Tolerance for Ambiguity by Setting Blocks or Goals. People learn from
problem situations. Lead a problem up to a certain unsolved point and then
stop, allowing time to toy with information, to be puzzled, intrigued, involved
or challenged. This is a technique that leads to more self-directed problem
solving.

Ask Provocative Questions. Recognize the difference between factual questions such as "How much?" "What if?" "Who?" and questions that require depth of comprehension: "How would you?" "Why?" or "How else?" Use many categories of questioning such as those which require translation, interpretation, extrapolation, identification, discovery, synthesizing and analyzing. Practice this skill by looking at a picture or advertisement and listing questions that can't be answered by looking at the picture. Use a checklist of question categories such as *longer, larger, shorter, smaller, adding, taking away, multiplying, changing, substituting, combining, reversing.* Make yourself as sensitive to question asking as you are to answer finding.

Allow Opportunities to Interact With Yourself and Your Knowledge. Provide opportunities to toy with information that is already known instead of continuing to acquire new information. Develop the skill of nurturing infant ideas by combining new associations out of what is already known. Use a multitude of experiences for doing something with facts and knowledge already possessed. Learn to use those skills that are highly developed, such as identifying, manipulating, exploring, being curious, using trial and error. Capitalize on these skills by practicing and using them instead of smothering or stifling them.

Be Receptive to Unexpected Responses and Their Significance. Be prepared to embellish, elaborate or embroider on information or knowledge. Realize how old information can be used in new ways by adding motion, color, light, movement, etc. Learn how to handle and capitalize on surprising responses whenever they occur. Take advantage of the significance of unusual, original or seemingly non-pertinent ideas.

Develop Skills in Reading Creatively. Read for usefulness as well as for inherent interest. Develop the skill of scanning. Acquire the knack of getting involved with what you read. Reorganize and rearrange information. Practice synthesizing, analyzing and recombining printed information. Make notes in the margins of printed materials, using language that helps you use the information you are reading. Understand the difference between reading as an information acquiring process and reading that leads to idea generation and development.

Learn to Listen Creatively. Bring a "What's-in-it-for-me?" attitude to everything you hear.

TOOT YOUR OWN HORN

The world being what it is, modesty is not always the surest road to success. Sometimes you have to let the world know exactly how good you are. You do this by telling your boss and co-workers about your department's accomplishments—how a tricky production problem was solved, how a tough customer was satisfied, how a crisis was averted.

Mention it when you can—in casual conversation, over lunch, in the car pool. You can get your message across tactfully if you share the credit and cite facts to back it up.

And when someone sends a compliment your way, don't blush and dig your toe into the dirt. Say "Thanks" or "We worked hard to accomplish that"—whatever is appropriate.

TO WIN COOPERATION EXPLAIN GOALS

Say, "Do this!" to a group of employees and a certain number will unquestioningly do what you want. A smaller number will think, "Sounds crazy, but if that's what you want, I'll do it." A still smaller number will think, "It's a dumb order, and I won't do it." Sometimes an employee is reluctant to cooperate because he remains unconvinced of the desirability, necessity or value of the goal you have set for him. Either you have not explained why he ought to do as you say or you have explained it poorly.

The remedy? Take whatever time may be necessary to explain the thinking behind your instructions. If you suspect the existence of mental reservations in an employee, sincerely invite him to question you. So simple an observation as "You don't seem convinced. What's troubling you?" may be enough to extract whatever objection is on the employee's mind.

Once you get it out of him, there are two possibilities: either you will persuade him that the goal is worth working for, in which case you will gain his cooperation; or he will persuade you that it is not worth pursuing, in which case you will be saved from making a mistake. Either way, you stand to gain.

HOW TO SHARPEN YOUR THINKING

Regardless of your specific responsibilities, your ability to think—precisely, thoroughly, originally—represents the most valuable contribution you can make to your organization. There are undoubtedly other men and women who can do what you do, perhaps not quite as well, but well enough to get the job done. But no one can duplicate precisely your thought processes. So anything you can do to improve your thinking ability is additional success insurance. Some ways to sharpen your thinking:

Be Precise. Most of us think in words, not pictures. But if the words you use are too general, imprecise or altogether wrong, your thinking will necessarily be sloppy. Suppose you say to yourself, "I can't depend on secretaries. "That's a sweeping statement and may not actually be what you mean. You may really be thinking of one particular instance of undependability. But in your haste or anger, you generalize. Result: impaired thinking. To think effectively you must use precise words.

Be Flexible. Rigidity is just as bad as generalizing. Beware of becoming too orderly in your thought processes. In order to think originally, you must be willing to allow your mind to wander, to strike out on its own, to go off on tangents, to play with various possibilities.

Talk It Over. Find someone with whom you can exchange views. In effect, you will be thinking out loud, and the opportunity to hear your thoughts sometimes provides new insights. The mere presence of another person tends to make you take a broader look at your approach.

Take Your Time. Nobody ever had a great idea in a hurry. Creative thinking is hard, demanding work. Ideas have to be critically assessed, reconsidered, modified, refined, tested. It's only human to overrate our own ideas, especially when we are keyed up over a problem. Time permitting, sleep on it, and see if it still looks like a winner in the morning.

GRIEVANCE CHECKLIST

The losses due to employee grievances have never been toted up, but you can be sure they are substantial. Quite aside from the obvious losses due to such things as strikes and slowdowns, consider the high cost of dissatisfaction, hostility, accidents, absenteeism and employee turnover.

Reasons for gripes range from personality clashes to poor working conditions. One thing is sure: there is always a reason, real or fancied. And each costs money and good human relations.

Are you unwittingly contributing to your people's grievances? Find out by scoring yourself on this checklist.

1. Do you let each person know how he is getting along at least twice yearly?
2. Do you *listen* to your people?
3. Do you try to get the complete story behind a complaint?
4. Do you check the record, investigate and get all the facts?
5. Do you carefully analyze the facts?
7. Are your decisions fair?
8. Do you explain to the person involved why your decision is a fair one?
9. Do you take full responsibility for the decision?

SHORTCUTS TO SELF-CONFIDENCE

Self-doubt afflicts most people at one time or another, but if you let it get the upper hand, it can paralyze initiative and sink a career before it gets off the ground. Next time you feel your self-confidence waning, ask—and answer—these questions:

- What failure in your past did you overcome and turn into a success?
- What was the proudest moment of your life?
- What was the toughest job you ever undertook in which you succeeded against all the odds?
- How did you sell yourself on sticking to it when the outlook was the bleakest?
- What was the greatest compliment anybody ever paid you?

See? You're quite a human being!

46.
STAFFING THE INNOVATIVE TECHNOLOGY-BASED ORGANIZATION

Edward B. Roberts
Alan R. Fusfeld

A creative, idea-generating scientist or engineer is a special kind of professional. This person needs to be singled out, cultivated, and managed in a special way.

This article examines the technology-based innovation process in terms of certain behavioral functions. These functions are usually informal, but they are critical. They can be the key to an effective organizational base for innovation. This approach to the innovation process is similar to that taken by early industrial theorists, such as Frederick W. Taylor, who focused on organizing efficiently the production process. However, examination of how industry has organized its innovation tasks—those tasks needed for product or process development and for responses to nonroutine demands—indicates an absence of comparable theory. Many corporations' attempts to innovate consequently suffer from ineffective management and inadequately staffed organizations. Yet, through studies conducted largely in the last fifteen years, we now know much about the activities that are requisite to innovation. We also know about the characteristics of the people who perform these activities most effectively.

THE INNOVATION PROCESS

The major steps involved in the technology-based innovation process are shown in Figure 1. Although the project activities do not necessarily follow each other in a linear fashion, there is more or less clear dermarcation between them. Each stage and its activities, moreover, require a different mix of "people" skills and behaviors to be carried out effectively.

Figure 1.

A Multi-stage View of a Technical Innovation Project

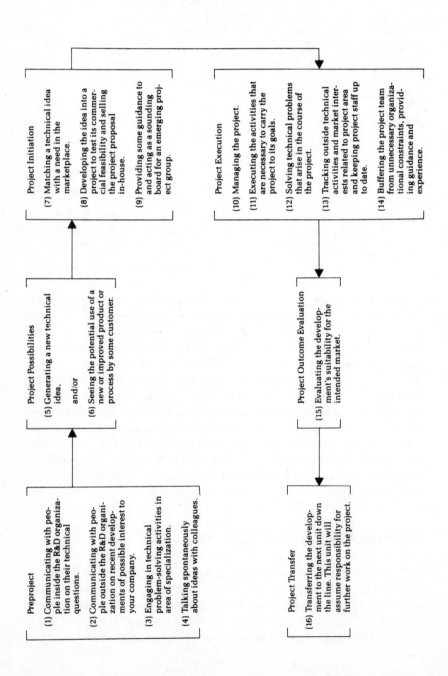

Preproject

(1) Communicating with people inside the R&D organization on their technical questions.

(2) Communicating with people outside the R&D organization on recent developments of possible interest to your company.

(3) Engaging in technical problem-solving activities in area of specialization.

(4) Talking spontaneously about ideas with colleagues.

Project Possibilities

(5) Generating a new technical idea,

and/or

(6) Seeing the potential use of a new or improved product or process by some customer.

Project Initiation

(7) Matching a technical idea with a need in the marketplace.

(8) Developing the idea into a project to test its commercial feasibility and selling the project proposal in-house.

(9) Providing some guidance to and acting as a sounding board for an emerging project group.

Project Execution

(10) Managing the project.

(11) Executing the activities that are necessary to carry the project to its goals.

(12) Solving technical problems that arise in the course of the project.

(13) Tracking outside technical activities and market interests related to project area and keeping project staff up to date.

(14) Buffering the project team from unnecessary organizational constraints, providing guidance and experience.

Project Outcome Evaluation

(15) Evaluating the development's suitability for the intended market.

Project Transfer

(16) Transferring the development to the next unit down the line. This unit will assume responsibility for further work on the project.

The figure portrays six stages as occurring in the typical technical innovation project. It also shows sixteen representative activities that are associated with innovative efforts. The six stages are identified as:

1. Preproject
2. Project possibilities
3. Project initiation
4. Project execution
5. Project outcome evaluation
6. Project transfer

These stages often overlap and frequently recycle.[1] For example, problems or findings that are generated during project execution may cause a return to project initiation activities. Outcome evaluation can restart additional project execution efforts. And, of course, project cancellation can occur during any of these stages, thus redirecting technical endeavors back into the preproject phase.

A variety of different activities are undertaken during each of the six stages. Some of the activities, such as generating new technical ideas, arise in all innovation project stages, from preproject to project transfer. Our research studies and consulting efforts in dozens of companies and government labs, however, have shown other activities to be concentrated in specific stages, as discussed below.

Preproject. Before formal project activities are undertaken in a technical organization, considerable technical work is done, which provides a basis for later innovation efforts. Scientists, engineers and marketing people find themselves involved in discussions that are internal and external to the organization. Ideas are discussed in rough-cut ways and broad parameters of innovative interest are established. Technical personnel work on problem-solving efforts to advance their own areas of specialization. Our discussions with numerous industrial firms in the U.S. and Europe suggest that from 30 to 60 percent of all technical effort is devoted to work outside of or prior to formal project initiation.

Project Possibilities. Specific ideas for possible projects arise from the preproject activities. They may be technical concepts for developments that are assumed to be feasible. They may also be perceptions of possible customer interests in product or process changes. Customer-oriented perspectives may originate with technical, marketing, or managerial personnel, who develop these ideas out of their own imaginations or from direct contact with customers or competitors. Recent evidence indicates that many of these ideas enter as "proven" possibilities inasmuch as these ideas have already been developed by the customers themselves.[2]

Project Initiation. As ideas evolve through technical and marketing discussions and exploratory technical efforts, the innovation process moves into a more formal project initiation stage. Activities occurring during this phase include attempts to match the directions of technical work with perceived customer needs. (Of course, such customer needs may exist either in the production organization or in the product marketplace.) Inevitably, a specific project proposal is written, proposed budgets and schedules are produced, and informal pushing as well as formal presentations are undertaken in order to sell the project. A key input during this stage is the counseling and encouragement that senior technical professionals or lab and marketing management may provide to the emerging project team.

Project Execution. When the project is approved formally, activities increase in intensity and focus. Usually, someone undertakes planning, leadership, and coordinating efforts. These efforts are related to the many continuing activities of the engineers and scientists assigned to the project. These activities include problem solving and the generation of technical ideas. Technical people make special attempts to monitor (and transfer in) the results of previous activity as well as relevant external information. Management or marketing people take a closer look at competitors and customers to be sure the project is appropriately targeted.[3] Senior people try to protect the project from being controlled too tightly or from being cast off prematurely. The project manager and other enthusiasts fight to defend their project's virtues (and budget). Unless cancelled, the project continues toward completion of its objectives.

Project Outcomes Evaluation. When the technical effort seems complete, most projects undergo another intense evaluation to see how the results compare with prior expectations and current market perceptions. If successful innovation is to occur, some further implementation must take place. The interim results are either transferred to manufacturing (where they are either embodied in the manufacturing process or produced in volume) or transferred to further stages of development. All such later stages involve heavier expenditures. The project outcome evaluation can then be viewed as a way to screen projects prior to their possible transfer into these later stages.

Project Transfer. If the project results survive this evaluation, transfer efforts take place (e.g., from central research to product department R&D, or from development to manufacturing engineering).[4] The project's details may require further technical documentation to facilitate the transfer. Key technical people may be shifted to the downstream unit to transfer their expertise and enthusiasm, since downstream staff members in the technical or marketing areas often need instruction to insure effective continuity. Within the downstream organizational unit, the cycle of stages may begin again, perhaps bypassing the earliest two stages and starting with project initiation or even project execution. This "pass down" continues until successful innovation is achieved, unless project termination occurs first.

NEEDED ROLES

Assessment of activities involved in the several-stage innovation process, as just described, points out that the repeated direct inputs of five different work roles are critical to innovation. The five roles arise in differing degrees in each of the several steps. Furthermore, different innovation projects obviously call for variations in the required role mix at each stage. Nevertheless, all five work roles must be carried out by one or more individuals if the innovation is to pass effectively through all six steps. The five critical work functions are:

- *Idea Generating*: Analyzing or synthesizing information about markets, technologies, approaches, or procedures, from which is generated an idea for a new or improved product or service, a new technical approach or procedure, or a solution to a challenging technical problem.[5] The analysis or synthesis may be implicit; the information may be formal or informal.
- *Entrepreneuring or Championing*: Recognizing, proposing, pushing, and demonstrating a new technical idea, approach, or procedure for formal management approval.[6]
- *Project Leading*: Planning and coordinating the diverse sets of activities and people involved in moving a demonstrated idea into practice.[7]
- *Gatekeeping*: Collecting and channeling information about important changes in the internal and external environments. Information gatekeeping can be focused on developments in the market, in manufacturing, or in the world of technology.[8]
- *Sponsoring or Coaching*: Guiding and developing less experienced personnel in their critical roles; behind-the-scenes support, protection, advocacy, and sometimes "bootlegging" of funds.[9]

Lest the reader confuse these roles as mapping one-for-one with different people, three points need emphasis: (1) some roles, e.g., idea generating, frequently need to be fulfilled by more than one person in a project team in order for the project to be successful; (2) some individuals occasionally fulfill more than one of the critical functions; (3) the role that people play periodically changes over their career with an organization. The latter two points will be discussed in more depth later in this article.

CRITICAL FUNCTIONS

These five critical functions represent the various roles that must be carried out for successful innovation to occur. They are critical from two points of view. First, each role is unique and demands unique skills. A deficiency in any one of the roles contributes to serious problems in the innovation effort, as we shall illustrate below. Second, each role tends to be carried out primarily by relatively few individuals, thereby making the critical role players even more unique. If any one of these individuals leaves, the problem of recruiting a replacement is very difficult. The specific qualities needed in the replacement usually depend on unstated role requirements. Most critical functions cannot be fulfilled by new recruits to an organization.

We must add at this point that another role clearly exists in all innovative organizations, but it is not an innovative role. "Routine" technical problem solving must be carried out in order to advance innovative efforts. Indeed, the vast bulk of technical work is probably routine. It requires professional training and competence, to be sure, but it is nontheless routine in character for an appropriately prepared individual. A large number of people in innovative organizations do very little critical functions work; others who are important performers of the critical functions also spend a good part of their time in routine problem-solving activity. Our estimate, supported now by data from numerous organizations, is that 70 to 80 percent of technical effort falls into this routine problem-solving category. But, the 20 to 30 percent that is unique and critical is the part we emphasize here.

Generally, the critical functions are not specified within job descriptions, since they tend to fit neither administrative nor technical hierarchies. But they represent necessary activities for R&D, such as problem definition, idea nurturing, information transfer, information integration, and program pushing. Consequently, these role behaviors are the underlying informal functions that an organization carries out as part of the innovation process. Beyond the five roles described earlier, different business environments may also demand that additional roles be performed in order to insure innovation.[10]

It is desirable for every organization to have a balanced set of abilities for carrying out these roles as needed. Unfortunately, few organizations have such a balanced set. Some organizations overemphasize one role (e.g., idea generating) and underplay another role (e.g., entrepreneuring). Technical organizations tend to assume that the necessary set of activities will somehow be performed. As a consequence, R&D labs often lack sensitivity to the existence and importance of these roles, which, for the most part, are not defined within the formal job structure. Yet, the way in which critical functions are encouraged and made a conscious part of technology management is probably an organization's single most important area of leverage for maintaining and improving effective innovation.

IMPACT OF ROLE DEFICIENCIES

Such an analytic approach to developing an innovative team has been lacking in the past. Consequently, many organizations suffer because one or more of the critical functions are not being performed adequately. Certain characteristic signs can provide evidence that a critical function is missing.

Idea generating is deficient if the organization is not thinking of new and different ways of doing things. However, when a manager complains of insufficient ideas, we commonly find the real deficiency to be that people are not aggressively entrepreneuring or championing ideas—either their own or others'. Pools of unexpected ideas that seldom come to managers' attention are evidence of an entrepreneuring deficiency.[11]

Project leading is suspect if schedules are not met, activities "fall through cracks" (e.g., coordinating with a supplier), people do not have a sense of the overall goal of their work, or units that are needed to support the work back out of their commitments. Projects leading is most commonly recognized by the formal appointment of a project manager. In research, as distinct from development, this formal role is often omitted.

Gatekeeping is inadequate if news of changes in the market, technology, or government legislation comes without warning. It is also inadequate if needed information is not passed along to people within the organization. If, six months after the project is completed, you suddenly realize that you have just succeeded in reinventing a competitor's wheel, your organization is deficient in needed gatekeeping! Gatekeeping is further lacking when the wheel is invented just as a regulatory agency outlaws its use.

Inadequate or inappropriate sponsoring or coaching often explains how projects are pushed into application too soon, and why project managers have to spend too much time defending their work. It also explains why personnel complain that they do not know how to "navigate the bureaucracy" of their organizations.

The importance of each critical function varies with the development stage of the project. Initially, idea generation is crucial. Later, entrepreneurial skill and commitment are needed to develop the concept into a viable activity. Once the project is established good project leadership is needed to guide its progress. Of course, the need for a critical function does not abruptly appear and disappear. Instead, the need grows and diminishes. Each function is the focus at some points, but it is of lesser importance at others. Thus, the absence of a function at a time when it is potentially important is a serious weakness, regardless of whether or not the role has been filled at an earlier, less crucial time. As a corollary, assignment of an individual to a project, at a time when the critical role that he or she provides is not needed, leads to frustration for the individual and to a less effective project team.

Frequently, we have observed that personnel changes that occur because of career development programs often remove critical functions from a project at a crucial time. Although these roles are usually performed informally, job descriptions are made in terms of technical specialties. Thus, personnel replacements are chosen on the basis of their technical qualifications rather than on their ability to fill the needs of the vacated critical roles. Consequently, the project team's innovative effectiveness is reduced, sometimes to the point of affecting the project's success.

CHARACTERISTICS OF THE ROLE PLAYERS

Compilation of several thousand individual profiles of staff in R&D and engineering organizations has demonstrated patterns in the characteristics of the people who perform each innovation function.[12] These patterns are shown in Table 1. The table indicates which persons are predisposed to be more interested in one type of activity than another and to perform certain types of activities well. For example, a person who is comfortable with abstractions and theory might feel more suited to the idea-generating function than would someone who is very practical. In any unit of an organization, people with different characteristics can work to complement each other. For instance, a person who is effective at generating ideas can be teamed with a colleague who is good at gatekeeping and with another colleague who has good entrepreneurial abilities. Of course, each person must understand his or her own expected role in a project and must appreciate the roles of others in order for the teaming process to be successful. As will be discussed later, some people have sufficient breadth to perform well in multiple roles.

Table 1 underlies our conclusions that each of the several roles required for effective technical innovation presents unique challenges and must be filled with different types of people. Each type must be recruited, managed, and supported differently and offered different sets of measures and controls. However, most technical organizations seem not to have grasped this concept. The result is that all technical people tend to be recruited, hired, supervised, monitored, evaluated, and encouraged as if their principal roles were those of creative scientists, or, worse yet, of routine technical problem solvers. In fact, only a few of these people have the personal and technical qualifications for scientific inventiveness and prolific idea generating. A creative, idea-generating scientist or engineer is a special kind of professional. This person needs to be singled out, cultivated, and managed in a special way. He or she is probably innovative, technically well educated, and enjoys working on advanced problems, often as a "loner."

The technical champion or entrepreneur is a special person, too. He or she shows creativity, but it is an aggressive form of creativity that is appropriate for selling an idea or product. The entrepreneur's drives may be less rational and more emotional than those of the creative scientists; he or she is committed to achieving but is less concerned about how to do so. This person is as likely to pick up and successfully champion someone else's original idea as to push something of his or her own creation. Such an entrepreneur may well have a broad range of interests and activities. He or she must be recruited, hired, managed, and stimulated very differently from the way an idea-generating scientist is treated in the organization.

The person who effectively performs project leading or project managing activities is yet a different kind of person. He or she is an organized individual, is sensitive to the needs of the several different people who are being coordinated, and is an effective planner. The ability to plan is especially important if long lead time, expensive materials, and major support are involved in the project development.

The information gatekeeper is a communicative individual and is the exception to the truism that engineers do not read (especially that they do not read technical journals). Gatekeepers provide links to sources of the technical information which flows into and within a research and development organization and which can enhance new product development or process improvement. But those who do research and development need market information as well as technical information: What do customers seem to want? What are competitors providing? How might regulatory shifts affect the firm's present or contemplated products or processes? For answers to questions such as these, research and development organizations need people we call the "market gatekeepers." These people are engineers, scientists, or possibly marketing people with technical backgrounds who focus on market-related information sources and communicate effectively to their technical colleagues. Such individuals read trade journals, talk to vendors, go to trade shows, and are sensitive to competitive information. Without them, many research and development projects and laboratories become misdirected with respect to market trends and needs.

Finally, the sponsor or coach is, in general, a more experienced, older project leader or former entrepreneur, who has a "softer touch" than when he or she was first in the organization. As a senior person, he or she can coach and help subordinates in the organization and can speak on their behalf to top management. This activity makes it possible for ideas or programs to move forward in an effective, organized fashion. Many organizations totally ignore the sponsor role, yet our studies of industrial research and development suggest that many projects would not have been successful were it not for the subtle and often unrecognized assistance of such senior people acting in the role of sponsors. Indeed, organizations are most successful when chief engineers or laboratory directors naturally behave in a manner consistent with this sponsor role.

The significant point here is that the staffing needed for effective innovation in a technology-based organization is far broader than the typical research and development director usually has assumed. Our studies indicate that many in-

Table 1.

Critical Functions in the Innovation Process

Critical Function	Personal Characteristics	Organizational Activities
Idea Generating	Expert in one or two fields. Enjoys conceptualization; comfortable with abstractions. Enjoys doing innovative work. Usually is an individual contributor. Often will work alone.	Generates new ideas and tests their feasibility. Good at problem solving. Sees new and different ways of doing things. Searches for the breakthroughs.
Entrepreneuring or Championing	Strong application interests. Possesses a wide range of interests. Less propensity to contribute to the basic knowledge of a field. Energetic and determined; puts self on the line.	Sells new ideas to others in the organization. Gets resources. Aggressive in championing his or her "cause." Takes risks.
Project Leading	Focus for decision making, information, and questions. Sensitive to the needs of others. Recognizes how to use the organizational structure to get things done. Interested in a broad range of disciplines and in how they fit together (e.g., marketing, finance).	Provides the team leadership and motivation. Plans and organizes the project. Insures that administrative requirements are met. Provides necessary coordination among team members. Sees that the project moves forward effectively. Balances the project goals with organizational needs.

Gatekeeping	Possesses a high level of technical competence. Is approachable and personable. Enjoys the face-to-face contact of helping others.	Keeps informed of related developments that occur outside the organization through journals, conferences, colleagues, other companies. Passes information on to others; finds it easy to talk to colleagues. Serves as an information resource for others in the organization (i.e., authority on who to see or on what has been done). Provides informal coordination among personnel.
Sponsoring or Coaching	Possesses experience in developing new ideas. Is a good listener and helper. Can be relatively objective. Often is a more senior person who knows the organizational ropes.	Helps develop people's talents. Provides encouragement, guidance, and acts as a sounding board for the project leader and others. Provides access to a power base within the organization—a senior person. Buffers the project team from unnecessary organizational constraints. Helps the project team to get what it needs from the other parts of the organization. Provides legitimacy and organizational confidence in the project.

effective technical organizations have failed to be innovative solely because one or more of these five quite different critical functions has been absent.

All of these roles can be fulfilled by people from multiple disciplines and departures. Obviously, technical people—scientists and engineers—might carry out any of the roles. But, marketing people also generate ideas for new and improved products, act as gatekeepers for information of key importance to a project (especially about use, competition, and regulatory activities), champion the idea, sometimes sponsor projects, and sometimes even manage new projects, especially for new product development. Manufacturing people periodically fill similar critical roles, as do general management personnel.

MULTIPLE ROLES

As indicated earlier, some individuals have the skills, breadth, inclination, and job opportunity to fulfill more than one critical function in an organization. Our data collection efforts with R&D staffs show that a few clusters explain most of these cases of multiple role playing. One common combination of roles is the pairing of gatekeeping and idea generating. Idea-generating activity correlates, in general, with the frequency of person-to-person communication, especially with that which is external to the organization.[13] Moreover, the gatekeeper, who is in contact with many sources of information, can often connect synergistically these bits into a new idea. This ability seems especially true of market gatekeepers who can relate market relevance to technical opportunities.

Another role couplet is between entrepreneuring and idea generating. In studies of formation of new technical companies, the entrepreneur who pushed company formation and growth was found in half the cases also to have been the source of the new technical idea underlying the company.[14] Furthermore, in studies of M.I.T. faculty, 38 percent of those who had ideas that they perceived to be of commercial value also took strong entrepreneurial steps to exploit their ideas.[15] The idea generating-entrepreneuring pair accounts for slightly less than one-half the entrepreneurs.

Entrepreneuring individuals often become project leaders. This progression is thought to be a logical organizational extension of the effort of effectively "selling" the idea for the project. Some people who are strong at entrepreneuring also have the interpersonal and plan-oriented qualities needed for project leading. The responsibility for managing a project, though, if often mistakenly seen as a necessary reward for successful idea championing. This mistake arises from a lack of attention to the functional differences between the two roles. One should not necessarily assume that a good salesman will be a good manager. If the entrepreneur can be rewarded appropriately and more directly for his or her own function, many project failures caused by ineffective project managers might be avoided. Perhaps giving the entrepreneur a prominent project role, while clearly designating a different project manager, might be an acceptable compromise.

Finally, sponsoring occasionally evolves into a takeover of any or all of the other roles, even though it should be a unique role. Senior coaching can degenerate into idea domination, project ownership, and direction from the top. This confusion of roles can become extremely harmful to the entire organization: Who will bring another idea to the boss once he steals some junior's earlier concept? Even worse, who can intervene to stop the project once the boss is running amok with his new pet?

The performance of multiple roles can affect the minimum size group needed for attaining "critical mass" in an innovative effort. To achieve continuity of a project, from initial idea all the way through to successful commercialization, a project group must effectively fill all five critical roles. It must also satisfy the specific technical skill requirements for project problem solving. In a new, high-technology company, this critical mass may sometimes be insured by as few as one or two cofounders. Similarly, an elite team—such as Cray's famed Control Data computer design group, Kelly Johnson's "skunk works" at Lockheed, or McLean's Sidewinder missile organization in the Navy's China Lake R&D center—may concentrate in a small number of select multiple-role players the staff needed to accomplish major objectives. But, the more typical medium-to-large company had better not plan on finding Renaissance persons or superstars to fill its job requirements. Staffing assumptions should more likely rest on estimates that 70 percent of scientists and engineers will turn out to be routine problem solvers only, and that even most critical role players will be single dimensional in their unique contributions.

CAREER-SPANNING ROLE CHANGES

We showed above how some individuals fulfill multiple critical roles concurrently or in different stages of the same project. Even more people are likely to contribute critically but differently at different stages of their careers. This difference over time does not reflect change of personality, although such changes do seem partly due to the dynamics of personal growth and development. The phenomenon also clearly reflects individual responses to differing organizational needs, constraints, and incentives.

For example, let's consider the hypothetical case of a bright, aggressive, young engineer who has just joined a company upon graduation. What roles can he play? Certainly, he can quickly become effective at solving routine technical problems and, hopefully, at generating novel ideas. But, even though he may know many university contacts and be familiar with the outside literature, he can't be an effective information gatekeeper, for he doesn't yet know the people inside the company with whom he might communicate. Nor can he lead project activities, since no one would trust him in that role. He can't effectively serve as entrepreneur, as he has no credibility as champion for change. And, of course, sponsoring is out of the question. During this stage of his career, the limited legitimate role options may channel the young engineer's productive energies and reinforce his tendencies toward the output of creative ideas.

Alternatively, if he wants to offer and do more than the organization will allow, this high-potential young performer may feel rebuffed and frustrated. His perception of what he can expect from the job and, perhaps more importantly, what the job will expect from him, may become set in these first few months on the job. Though he may remain with the company, he will "turn off" in disappointment from his previously enthusiastic desire to make multidimensional contributions. More likely, he will leave the company in search of a more rewarding job. He will perhaps be destined to find continuing frustration in his next one or two encounters. For many young professionals, the job environment moves too slowly from the stage of encouragement of idea generating to a time when entrepreneuring is even permitted.

The engineer's role options may broaden after two or three years on the job, however. Though routine problem solving and idea generating are still appropriate, some information gatekeeping may now also be possible as communication ties increase within the organization. Project leading may start to be seen as legitimate behavior, particularly on small efforts.[16] The young engineer's work behavior may begin to reflect these new possibilities. Nevertheless, his attempts at entrepreneurial behavior might still be seen as premature and sponsoring as still an irrelevant consideration.

After another few years at work, the role options are still wider. Routine problem solving, continued idea generating, broad-based gatekeeping (even bridging to the market or to manufacturing), responsible project managing, and project championing may become reasonable alternatives. Even coaching a new employee becomes a possibility. Though most people tend usually to focus on one of these roles (or on a specific multiple-role combination) during this mid-career period, the next several years can strengthen all these role options.

Losing touch with a rapidly changing technology may later narrow the available role alternatives as the person continues in his or her job. Technical problem-solving effectiveness may diminish in some cases, idea generating may slow down or stop, and technical information gatekeeping may be reduced. Market or manufacturing gatekeeping, however, may continue to improve with increased experience and outside contacts. Project managing capabilities may continue to grow as he or she tucks more projects under his or her belt. Entrepreneuring may be more important and for higher stakes. Sponsoring of juniors in the company may be more generally sought and practiced. This career phase is too often seen to be characterized by the problem of technical obsolescence, especially if the organization has a fixation on assessing engineering performance in terms of the narrow but traditional stereotypes of technical problem solving and idea generating. Channeling the engineer into a role that is more appropriate for an earlier stage in his or her career can be a source of mutual grief to both the organization and the individual. Such a role will be of little current interest and satisfaction to the more mature, broader, and now differently directed professional. An aware organization, thinking in terms of critical role differences, can instead recognize the self-selected branching in career paths that has occurred for the individual. Productive, technically trained people can carry out critical functions for their employers up to retirement if employers encourage the full diversity of vital roles.

At each stage of his or her evolving career, the individual can encounter severe conflicts between the organization's expectations and his or her personal work preferences. This conflict is especially likely if the organization is inflexible in its perception of appropriate technical roles. In contrast, if both the organization and the individual are adaptable in seeking mutually satisfying job roles, the engineer can contribute continuously and significantly to innovation. As suggested in this illustrative case, in the course of a productive career in industry, the technical professional may begin as a technical problem solver, spend several years primarily as a creative idea generator, and add technical gatekeeping to his or her repertoire while maintaining his or her earlier roles. He or she may then begin to serve as a project entrepreneur and lead projects forward. Gradually, he or she will develop greater market linking and project managing skills and eventually will assume senior sponsoring role, maintaining a position of project, program, or organizational leadership until retirement. This fully productive career would not be possible if the engineer were pushed to the side early as a technically obsolete contributor. The perspective taken here can lead to a very different approach to career development for professionals than is usually taken by industry or government.

MANAGING THE CRITICAL FUNCTIONS FOR ENHANCED INNOVATION

To increase organizational innovation, a number of steps can be taken to facilitate a balance of time and energy among the critical functions. These steps must be addressed explicitly or organizational focus will remain on the traditionally visible functions, such as problem solving, which produce primarily near-term incremental results. Indeed, the results-oriented reward systems of most organizations reinforce this short-run focus, causing the other, more significant activities to go unrecognized and unrewarded.[17] Implementation of the results, language, and concepts of a critical functions perspective is outlined below for the selected organizational tasks of manpower planning, job design, and selection of measurement and rewards. If managers thought in critical functions terms, other tasks, not dealt with here, would also be carried out differently. These tasks include R&D strategy, organizational development, and program management.

MANPOWER PLANNING

The critical functions concept can be applied usefully to the recruiting, job assignment, and development or training activities within an organization. In recruiting, for example, an organization needs to identify not only the specific technical or managerial requirements of a job, but also the critical function activities that the job implies, e.g., the organization needs to ask whether the job requires that less experienced personnel be coached and developed in order to insure the longer-run productivity of that area. If the job requires entrepreneuring, then the applicant who is more aggressive and has shown evidence of championing new ideas in the past should be preferred over the less aggressive applicant who has shown more narrow technically oriented interests in the past.

Industry, at best, has taken a narrow view of manpower development alternatives for technical professionals. The "dual ladder" concept envisions an individual rising along either scientific or managerial steps. Attempted by many but with only limited success ever attained, the dual ladder reflects an oversimplification and distortion of the key roles needed in an R&D organization.[18] As a minimum, the critical function concept presents "multiladders" of possible organizational contribution; individuals can grow in any or all of the critical roles, while benefiting the organization. Depending on an organization's strategy and manpower needs, manpower development along each of the paths can and should be encouraged. Furthermore, there is room for individual growth and development from one function to another, as people are exposed to different managers, different environments, and jobs that require different activities.

JOB DESIGN AND OBJECTIVE SETTING

Most job descriptions and statements of objectives emphasize problem solving and sometimes project leading. Rarely do job descriptions and objectives take into account the dimensions of a job that are essential for the performance of the other critical functions. Yet, the availability of unstructured time in a job, for example, can influence the performance of several of the innovation functions, and it needs to be designed into corresponding jobs. To stimulate idea generating, some slack time is necessary so that employees can pursue their own ideas and explore new and interesting ways of doing things. For gatekeeping to occur, slack time needs to be available for employees to communicate with colleagues and pass along information learned, both internal to and external to the organization. The coaching role also requires slack time, during which the "coach" can guide less experienced personnel.[19]

Essential activities for filling alternative roles also need to be included explicitly in a job's objectives. An important goal for a gatekeeper, for example, should be to provide useful information to colleagues. A person who has the attitudes and skills to be an effective champion or entrepreneur could be given responsibility for recognizing good new ideas. This person might have the charter to roam around the organization, talk with people about their ideas, and encourage their pursuit of these ideas. He could even pursue these ideas himself.[20]

PERFORMANCE MEASURES AND REWARDS

We all tend to do those activities that will be rewarded. If personnel perceive that idea generating will not be recognized but that idea exploitation will, they may withhold their ideas from those who can exploit them. They may try to exploit ideas themselves, no matter how unequipped or uninterested they are in carrying out the exploitation activity.

For this reason, it is important to recognize the distinct contributions of each of the separate critical functions. Table 2 identifies some measures relevant for each function, indicating both quantity and quality dimensions. For example, an objective for a person who has the skills and information to be effective at gatekeeping could be to help a number of people during the next twelve months. At the end of that time, his or her manager could survey the people whom the gatekeeper felt he or she had helped, and use the responses to assess the gatekeeper's effectiveness in communicating key information. In each organization, the specific measures chosen will necessarily be different.

Rewarding an individual for the performance of a critical function makes the function more manageable and open to discussion. However, what is perceived as rewarding for one function may be seen as less rewarding, neutral, or even negative for another function because of the different personalities and needs of those filling the roles. Table 2 presents some rewards that seem appropriate for each function. Again, organizational and individual differences will generate variations in the rewards selected. Of course, the informal positive feedback of managers in their day-to-day contacts is a major source of motivation and recognition for any individual performing a critical innovation function, or any job for that matter.

Salary and bonus compensation are not included here, but not because they are unimportant to any of these people. Financial rewards should be employed as appropriate, but they do not seem to be linked explicitly to any one innovative function more than to another.

PERFORMING A CRITICAL FUNCTIONS ASSESSMENT

The preceding sections demonstrate that the critical functions concept provides an important way to describe an organization's resources for effective

Table 2.

Measuring and Rewarding Critical Function Performance

Dimension of Management	**Critical Function** Idea Generating	Entrepreneuring or Championing	Project Leading	Gatekeeping	Sponsoring or Coaching
Primary contribution of each function for appraisal of performance	Quantity and quality of ideas generated.	Ideas picked up; percent carried through.	Project technical milestones accomplished; cost/schedule constraints met.	People helped; degree of help.	Success in developing staff; extent of assistance provided.
Appropriate rewards	Opportunities to publish; recognition from professional peers through symposia, etc.	Visibility; publicity; further resources for project.	Bigger or more significant projects; material signs of organization status.	Travel budget; key "assists" acknowledged; increased autonomy and use for advice.	Increased autonomy; discretionary resources for support of others.

innovation activity. To translate this concept into an applied tool, one needs to be able to assess the status of an R&D unit in terms of critical functions. Such an assessment potentially provides two important types of information: (1) inputs for management evaluations of the organization's ability to achieve goals and strategy; and (2) assistance to R&D managers and professionals in performance evaluation, career development, and more effective project performance.

METHOD OF APPROACH

The methodology chosen for a critical functions assessment is contingent on the situation. From experience gained with a dozen companies and government agencies in North America, the authors have found the most flexible approach to be a series of common questionnaires, which are developed from replicated academic research techniques on innovative contributors and modified as needed for the situation. Questionnaires are supplemented by a number of structured interviews or workshops. Data are collected and organized in a framework that represents: (a) the critical functions; (b) special characteristics of the organization's situation; (c) additional critical functions required in the specific organization; and (d) the climate for innovation provided by management. The results include a measure of an organization's current and potential strengths in each critical function; an evaluation of the compatibility of the organization's R&D strategy with these strengths; and a set of personnel development plans for both management and staff that support the organization's goals. This information is valuable for both the organization and the individual.[21]

SOME ACTIONS TAKEN IN ONE FIRM

As a result of a critical functions analysis in a company, multiple actions are usually taken. In order to consider some of the typical steps, we draw here from the outcomes implemented in one medium-sized R&D organization. The first action was that every first line supervisor and above, after some training, discussed with each employee the results of the employee's critical functions survey. (In other companies, employee anonymity has been preserved; data were returned only to the individual. In these companies, employees frequently have used the results to initiate discussions with their immediate supervisors regarding job fit and career development.) The purpose of the discussion was twofold: to look for differences in how the employee and his or her boss each perceived the employee's job skills; and to engage in developmental career planning. The vocabulary of the critical functions plus the tangible feedback gave the manager and the employee a meaningful, commonly shared basis for the discussion.

Several significant changes resulted from these discussions. A handful of the staff recognized the mismatch between their present jobs and skills. With the support of their managers, job modifications were made. Another type of mismatch that this process revealed was between the manager's perception of the employee's skills and the employee's own perception. Most of the time the manager was underutilizing his or her human resources.

In this particular firm, the data also prompted action to improve the performance of the project leading function. An insufficient number of people saw themselves performing this function. Moreover, they saw themselves as lacking skills in this area. As a result of these deficiencies, upper management conducted several "coaching" sessions, worked to further clarify roles, and showed increased support for project leadership efforts.

Important changes also were made in how the technical organization recruited. The characteristic strengths behind each critical function were explicitly employed in identifying the skills necessary to do a particular job. This analysis led to a useful framework for interviewing candidates. It helped determine how the candidates might fit into and grow within the present organization. Upper management also became conscious of the unintended bias in the recruiting procedure. This bias was introduced both by the universities at which the company recruited and by the recruiters themselves. (In this case, the senior researchers, who conducted most of the interviews, were primarily interested in idea generating.) As a result of the analyses, upper management was careful to have a mix of the critical functions represented by the people who interviewed job candidates.

The analyses led to other results that were less tangible than the above but equally important. Jobs were no longer defined solely in technical terms, i.e., in terms of required educational background or work experience. For example, if a job involved idea generation, the necessary skills and the typical activities for that critical function were included in the description of the job. Furthermore, the need for a new kind of teamwork developed since it was rare than any single person could perform effectively all five of these essential functions. Finally, the critical functions concept provided the framework for the selection of people and division of labor on the innovation team that became the nucleus for all new R&D programs.

CONCLUSION

We have examined the technology-based innovation process in terms of a set of informal but critical behavioral functions. Five critical roles have been identified within the life cycle of activities in an R&D project. These roles are idea generating, entrepreneuring or championing, project leading, gatekeeping, and sponsoring or coaching. In our surveys of numerous North American R&D and engineering organizations, we have made two key observations:

some unique individuals are able to perform concurrently more than one of the critical roles; and patterns of roles for an individual often change over the course of his or her productive work career.

These critical functions concepts have managerial implications in such areas as manpower planning, job design, objective setting, and performance measurement and rewards. They provide a conceptual basis for design of a more effective multiladder system to replace many R&D organizations' ineffectual dual ladder systems.

Several years of development, testing, and discussion of this critical functions perspective have also led to applications outside of R&D organizations. We have seen the perspective extended to such areas as computer software development and architectural firms. Recent discussions with colleagues suggest an obvious appropriateness for marketing organizations. A more difficult translation is expected in the area of finance and manufacturing. To the extent that innovative outcome rather than routine production is the output sought, we have confidence that the critical functions approach will afford useful insights for organizational analysis and management.

References

1. For a different and more intensive quantitative view of project life cycles, see E. B. Roberts, *The Dynamics of Research and Development* (New York: Harper & Row, 1964).
2. See E. van Hippel, "Users as Innovators," *Technology Review*, January 1978, 30-39.
3. For issues that need to be highlighted in a competitive technical review, see A. R. Fusfeld, "How to Put Technology into Corporate Planning," *Technology Review 80*.
4. For further perspectives on project transfer, see E. B. Roberts, "Stimulating Technological Innovation: Organizational Approaches," *Research Management*, (November 1979,) 26-30.
5. See D. C. Pelz and F. M. Andrews, *Scientists in Organizations* (New York: John Wiley & Sons, 1966).
6. See E. B. Roberts, "Entrepreneurship and Technology," *Research Management* (July 1968): 249-266.
7. See D. G. Marquis and I. M. Rubin, "Management Factors in Project Performance" (Cambridge, MA: M.I.T. Sloan School of Management, Working Paper, 1966).
8. T. J. Allen, *Managing the Flow of Technology* (Cambridge, MA: The MIT Press, 1977); R. G. Rhoades et al., "A Correlation of R&D Laboratory Performance with Critical Functions Analysis," *R&D Management*, October 1978, 13-17.
Our empirical studies have pointed out three different types of gatekeepers: (1)

technical—relates well to the advancing world of science and technology; (2) marketing—senses and communicates information relating to customers, competitors, and environmental and regulatory changes affecting the marketplace; and (3) manufacturing—bridges the technical work with the special needs and conditions of the production organization. See Rhoades et al. (October 1978).

9. See Roberts (July 1968): 252.

10. One role we have observed frequently is the "quality controller" who stresses high work standards in projects. Other critical roles relate more to organizational growth than to innovation, e.g., the "effective trainer" who could absorb new engineers productively into the company, seen as critical to one firm that was growing 30 percent per year.

11. One study that demonstrated this phenomenon is N. R. Baker et al., "The Effects of Perceived Needs and Means on the Generation of Ideas for Industrial Research and Development Projects," *IEEE Transactions on Engineering Management*, EM-14 (1967) 156-165.

12. Section VI describes a methodology for collecting these data.

13. See Allen, (1977).

14. See Roberts (July 1968).

15. See E. B. Roberts and D. H. Peters, "Commercial Innovations for University Faculty," *Research Policy*, in press.

16. One study showed that engineers who eventually became managers of large projects began supervisory experiences within an average of 4.5 years after receiving their B. S. degrees. See I. M. Rubin and W. Seelig, "Experience as a Factor in the Selection and Performance of Project Managers," *IEEE Transactions on Engineering Management*, EM-14, September 1967, 131-135.

17. For further perspectives on the consequences of this short-run view by U.S. managers, see R. H. Hayes and W. J. Abernathy, "Managing Our Way to Economic Decline," *Harvard Business Review*, July-August 1980, 67-77.

18. For a variety of industrial approaches to the dual ladder, see the special July 1977 issue of *Research Management* or, more recently, *Research Management*, November 1979, 8-11.

19. In a more macroscopic way, March and Simon observed years ago that innovation could only occur in the presence of organizational slack. See J. G. March and H. A. Simon, *Organizations* (New York: John Wiley & Sons, 1958).

20. For more details on various job design dimensions appropriate to the critical functions, see E. B. Roberts and A. R. Fusfeld, "Critical Functions: Needed Roles in the Innovation Process," in *Career Issues in Human Resources Management*, ed. R. Katz (Englewood Cliffs, N.J.: Prentice-Hall, forthcoming).

21. For samples of questionnaire items, more details on diagnostic uses of the resulting data, and numerical outputs from one company's assessment, see Roberts and Fusfeld (reference 20).

Edward B. Roberts is the David Sarnoff Professor of Management of Technology, M.I.T. Dr. Roberts holds the S.B. and the S.M. degrees in electrical engineering, the S. M. degree in management, and the Ph.D. degree in economics from M.I.T. Alan R. Fusfeld is Vice-president and Director of the Technology management group of Pugh-Roberts Associates, Inc. Mr. Fusfeld holds the B.E.S. degree from the Johns Hopkins University.

Part VII:
INNOVATE
OR PERISH

47.

HOW EFFECTIVELY ARE WE MANAGING INNOVATION?

Stanley Baran
Peter Zandan
John H. Vanston

> The managerial challenge is to translate the desire to innovate into the organizational environment. The survey results, however, suggest that the technical professionals are more interested in innovation than top management is.

Innovation is "in fashion" for American companies. For example, Transamerica's television and magazine ads tell us it is in the business of insurance, finance, manufacturing, transportation, and innovation. Hewlett-Packard "focuses on innovation." Pontiac's Fiero is "innovation at work," and True 100s cigarettes are simply promoted as "innovation."

This push for innovation has been well received and accepted by a corporate America that readily understands the contemporary economic environment—one characterized by rapid change, technological development, and keen competition. Indeed, companies operating in dynamic business environments must innovate to remain competitive. For this reason, corporations have been willing to commit greater financial and physical resources to research and development activities. This commitment to R&D stems from the belief that innovation does not just happen; it needs to be supported and managed to flourish.

Surprisingly, though, the professional and scholarly literature on innovation offers little evidence evaluating how organizations succeed or fail at managing innovation. If we assume that people, not "the system," develop new products and new market strategies, we should expect that management scientists would have thoroughly documented employees' attitudes toward innovation, the success of their superiors' experience in fostering positive attitudes toward innovation, and how those employees perceive their superiors' efforts and intent.

In the absence of empirical evidence, managers and other corporate executives have come to depend on a collection of intuitive and anecdotal knowledge. For example, the popular notion is that younger workers tend to be more innovative than their older counterparts and that those newer to an organization are more innovative than those with longer tenure. It is believed that those lower on the managerial ladder are more innovative than those higher up, those in high-technology organizations have an innovation advantage over people in "smoke stack" industries, and so on. This is not to say that the professional literature is devoid of well-reasoned observations and speculation. Numerous authors have eloquently emphasized the significance and effects of "corporate environment" on workers' ability to perform innovatively.[1] Yet, the attitudes of those working in those environments and under those designs, for the most part, have gone largely unexamined.

THE INNOVATION ASSESSMENT SURVEY

Designed to asses the "environment for innovation" in order to facilitate innovation improvement, an innovation assessment survey was administered to 249 managers and other technical professionals employed in the R&D and technical planning departments of more than 30 "Fortune 100" companies. They had been with their current companies for an average of 11 to 15 years; they were, on the average, between 36 and 40 years old; and the majority were second and third level managers. Data from the instrument, a self-administered questionnaire, were collected over an eight-month period spanning 1983 and 1984.

The survey defined innovation as "seeking new or better work methods, products, processes, or services." Respondents were asked how important "thinking innovatively and devoting time to innovative projects" were to their superiors' evaluation of their job performance, their personal satisfaction on the job, their status among their peers, their potential for advancement, the demands of their job, and the continuing success of their organization. In addition, four items were included that asked respondents to judge how often they were encouraged to innovate and/or discouraged from innovating. A number of open-ended questions asked for suggestions on how to "improve the level of innovative processes and products" and for the respondents' impressions of their organizations' strengths and weaknesses in encouraging innovation. Finally, a series of demographic items examined length of tenure with the organization, time spent in the current job, as well as age, management level, and company type.

WHAT WE FOUND

An examination of mean scores for the items dealing with the importance of innovation clearly demonstrates that the respondents personally value innovation more than they felt it was valued in their organizations. Means for the questions, "How important are thinking innovatively and devoting time to innovative projects in your personal job satisfaction" and "in the continuing success of your organization" were 4.3 and 4.2 respectively, out of a possible score of 5. This is what might be expected in today's innovation-conscious corporations. But what one might not foresee is the relatively low value that these same respondents see others in their environment placing on innovation. The importance of innovation to their superior's evaluation of their job performance ($x = 3.5$), their status among their peers ($x = 3.4$), their potential for advancement ($x = 3.4$), and the demands of their jobs ($x = 3.5$) are all lower than their own estimation of innovation's worth. *This implies that corporations are not doing a particularly good job of taking advantage of their employees' innovative fervor.* Employees find innovation personally satisfying and important to their companies' futures, but see themselves as "islands of innovation," with neither their bosses nor their peers recognizing their efforts. They see their organizations as unwilling to build innovation into the advancement timetable or into the specific demands of particular job assignments. Organizations may not be satisfying or meeting the potential for innovation that their employees seem to possess.

Responses to the questions about communication may hold some explanation. When asked how often they are "explicitly encouraged to approach (their) job responsibilities innovatively," only one-third of the respondents said frequently or always, while nearly the same number responded never or rarely. The mean response was 3.0, or "sometimes." Implicit encouragement was experienced somewhat more frequently ($x = 3.2$). Thirty percent of the respondents said that they were frequently encouraged toward innovation. This not only lends empirical support to the argument that informal communication is as important, if not more so, than formal communication; it may also help explain why employees (at least as they see it) place more importance on innovation than do their organizations. The implicit channels may be stoking the fires to a greater degree than the more visible official channels, leading to a belief that the organization is less interested in innovation.

DISCOURAGEMENT OF INNOVATION

This pattern is clearly visible when examining the discouragement of innovation. While only 48 percent of the sample said that they were frequently explicitly encouraged (none said always), 36 percent said that they were frequently implicitly discouraged from innovation (again, no one said always).

Responses to the open-ended questions helped highlight this phenomenon. Answers were analyzed in terms of their emphasis—that is, did they stress communication, organizational, educational, managerial, policy, or environmental concerns. The following Table lists the number of times each concern was raised in response to the question, "What do you think is your firm's greatest asset in encouraging innovation?" It demonstrates that when environmental and organizational factors are good, they are seen as important assets to a firm's innovative potential. When these factors are bad, they are seen as major inhibitors (along with management). What should be obvious here is that these employees see these organizational and environmental problems as a responsibility of management, and consider the eradication of these problems to be desirable. In spite of the common assumptions about demographic indicators of innovation that were mentioned earlier, only two variables—managerial level and length of time with the firm—showed any relationship with attitudes toward innovation. In fact, while statistically significant, these relationships were relatively weak. Managerial level was positively related to the importance of innovation in personal satisfaction and to the importance of innovation in the demands of their jobs. This seems reasonable in as much as the challenge of a particular position would be expected to increase with its height on the organizational ladder. Length of tenure with a firm was negatively related to the frequency of implicit encouragement toward innovation. The longer individuals were with their current organizations, the less frequently they experienced implicit encouragement. This may be due to the fact that their organizations were paying less attention to them as innovators.

	Greatest Strength for Encouraging Innovation	Greatest Weakness for Encouraging Innovation
Communication	7%	7%
Organization	18%	26%
Education	8%	1%
Management	12%	22%
Policy	6%	8%
Environment	24%	16%

What this demographic/innovation attitude relationship signifies is that organizational design and environment are keys to fostering innovation. This view is borne out in the company-by-company analysis of the data. Although there was no pattern suggesting that certain industries were better managers of innovation than others, individual companies did show unique "innovation profiles" that varied considerably from the picture drawn from the aggregate data. Specific corporate culture or climate is important for innovation. The firms that seemed most successful in the realm of innovation were those with a relatively high degree of internal competition to achieve and a willingness to experiment with and reward innovation. They offered their people a sense of personal involvement in innovative activities and made them feel appreciated for their efforts. They are companies that have made best use of informal channels to communicate about, reinforce, and reward innovation.

Returning to this study's overall data, however, it appears that management has generally not done as well as it would like in the realm of innovation. Business and government leaders, as well as the popular and professional press, have all expressed how important it is for companies to strongly support innovation. The managerial challenge is to translate that desire to innovate into an organizational environment. Our survey results, however, suggest that top management's stated commitment to innovation has yet to be successfully infused into organization structure and environment.

Reference

1. See for literature review, Abbey, Augustus, *Technological Innovation: The R&D Work Environment* (Ann Arbor: UMI Research Press, 1982).

Stanley Baran is a professor in the College of Communication at the University of Texas at Austin. He has written over 40 scholarly articles and three books, including Mass Communication and Everyday Life. *Peter Zandan is an adjunct professor in the College of Communication at the University of Texas at Austin. John Vaston is president of Technology Futures, Inc., a consulting, research, education firm specializing in effective management of technology and innovation.*

48.
STIMULATING TECHNOLOGICAL INNOVATION: NURTURING THE INNOVATOR

Bruce Merrifield

> The innovator must be encouraged to be both a generator of new in-
> itiatives and an opportunistic intervenor in each step of the innovation
> process. Innovators require sensitive management to maximize their
> potential.

There is nothing more important than an idea in the mind of man, and the effect of an individual invention can change and has changed the course of history. The printing press, for example, was the start of universal education; the simple cotton gin restructured the whole economy of the South; Bessemer's steel process provided the world with its most important construction material; and gunpowder ended the feudal system of the medieval world. All of these are examples of the power of invention.

But inventions are not always welcomed. Marconi's wireless made no impression on the British Admiralty, which preferred to have men waving flags at each other from hilltops. And many great ideas have taken decades to find utilitarian use. Consequently, it is helpful to think of innovation as at least a two-step process. The first is the invention itself, and the second is the long, costly, high-risk effort to convert that invention into a commercially viable product or process (Figure 1).

The innovation also can occur at other stages of the pipeline with both major and minor influence on the further course of the commercialization process. The role of the innovator, therefore, must be seen more broadly as both the generator of new initiatives, as well as an opportunistic intervenor into each step of the process. And no matter how elegant the facilities and the equipment, in the last analysis, it is the creative individual who generates both the original and the successor ideas which make an innovation possible. In fact, although the original invention might be so significant that it ultimately changes the course of history, its first practical use in society may require as

Figure 1.

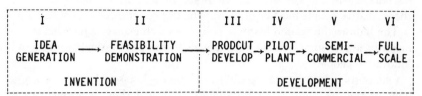

many as ten to twenty years of further innovative development time. Many individuals will be involved in the secondary innovations that make it commercially useful. These innovative people usually must be present at each stage of the pipeline. Without their creative contributions, the original invention might never see utility.

Since the power of this process is so great, support of technological innovation is of strategic importance to our society. A case can be made that the ascendancy of the industrial democracies is closely related to the management of innovation. In fact, it is a remarkable observation that the industrial democracies, which represent less than 10% of the world's population, have gained a commercial dominance that is out of all relationship to either their numbers or the antiquity of their civilizations. Moreover, 90% of our knowledge in the sciences has been generated in the last 40 years, and much of that in the United States. And although many other countries are now generating inventions, the U.S. has an unparalleled infrastructure of talent and skills which can rapidly reduce those inventions to commercial utility.

The impact on world history cannot be overestimated. This period in which we are now living will change the world and its ways of life beyond belief. And we who manage the innovative function hopefully can help guide this powerful force into positive and constructive channels. One key, of course, to the management of innovation is management of the innovator. History documents the power of great inventions and also the resistance to them. Management must recognize the creativity which exists in every person as it is expressed in unexpected ways and at unexpected times.

Innovative people exist in every R&D organization, although they often can go unrecognized. Creativity emerges in many forms, and sometimes it takes one innovator to recognize another. Research managers usually recognize that it is important to search actively for creative people and provide them with specialized attention and management.

Research managers also recognize that they must be especially tolerant of the creative individual whose creativity can be abrasive. Often the innovator is a strong individualistic person who finds conflict not only in the technology which he or she seeks to change, and the automatic resistance which change engenders, but also with other individuals who may feel threatened. And although the innovator tends to thrive on adversity, nevertheless, persistent discouragement can kill any creative thrust. In order to function effectively, these creative people must be given varying degrees of special consideration.

The Industrial Research Institute poll of research managers revealed that a majority employ some or all of the following techniques to stimulate or reward innovative people.

One of these is to provide flexibility in working hours and conditions; and 85% of the 200 companies responding indicated they do provide such flexibility. Characteristically, the innovator is enormously stimulated by work, becomes tremendously motivated by personal ideas and can work cruelly long hours, including weekends and holidays. An innovator's needs for access to facilities and resources, therefore, should be fulfilled if at all possible within safety limitations. More specifically, supervisors need to understand the importance to the innovator of a loyal, tolerant and supportive staff. Measures of this sort can clearly be at odds with an efficient organizational structure. Moreover, budgets, the review and evaluation procedure techniques for management by objectives, and strategic planning processes do not always accommodate to surprise innovations. Eighty-nine percent of the companies who responded either budget for unexpected developments or allow engineers and scientists to spend up to 10% of their time on investigations of their own choosing.

Special support services also are provided by about 63% of the companies reporting. These sometimes include assistance in market and financial analysis in order to better focus a new idea on the best commercial objectives; access to special skills, facilities or equipment in order to test the feasibility or further develop a new concept; access to information and to additional education if needed; and, particularly, in the reduction of red tape. Seventy-four percent of the companies reporting concurred in the need for reducing red tape, which produces time delays and tedious reporting procedures.

In addition, 75% also provide their outstanding innovators with various forms of special recognition. An innovator almost always is more than just a little interested in dollar rewards. Any tangible recognition of individual contributions is deeply satisfying and these people are often rewarded by special bonus considerations, title recognition and more frequent salary adjustments. However, only a few companies—about 10%—give the innovator "a piece of the action," usually in the form of a small royalty on sales. The innovator is often limited in opportunity for advancement unless he is able to switch to the administrative channels. Also, the very factors which contribute to originality, independence of thought, and critical analysis, often inhibit the innovator's ability to become submerged in a team effort or to be an effective team leader. Many companies (about 80%) have established a dual ladder so structured that a scientist can achieve salary grades equivalent to those associated with top management positions. However, a number of respondents pointed out that the concept is fine, but not always easy to administer; and in any case one leg of the ladder is shorter than the other.

Finally, about 95% of all respondents feel that continuing education is a vital component in nurturing the innovator. Companies use both structured and unstructured approaches. The structured approach involves attendance at technical meetings and symposia, short refresher or advanced topics courses, subsidy of advance degree work and both internal and external business and law programs. Informal educational programs revolve around seminars and consulting sessions with imported consultants, but in a number of companies also involve a structured and active flow of company information. Good communication of this type not only is seen as a valuable educational tool, but also fosters constant peer-group interactions which frequently lead to innovative iniatives. In large companies, red tape can swamp this process, and communications, therefore, have to be intentionally managed.

About a quarter of the companies responding have moved in recent years to a modified matrix management of the technical function. Matrix management enormously increases communication and rapid response to surprise events. However, it is a sophisticated management discipline which some research managers find difficult to master. Its use should increase, nevertheless, not only because of its value in potentiating the innovator and its effectiveness as an educational device, but also because it is more economical and maximizes specialized skills more effectively.

In conclusion, as we all know, ideas can have great consequences, and industrial survival in this rapidly changing era will become increasingly dependent, not only upon the innovative ideas that set off a chain reaction of development steps, but also upon the creative solutions to the many problems along the way which are required to convert an idea to a commercially viable product or process. Moreover, innovation in any field is primarily dependent upon the talent, the creativity and the persistence of trained and experienced individuals. This is our true capital. But innovators require sensitive management to maximize their potential. A process for identifying and conscientiously nurturing these people requires planning, structuring and constant reinforcement. Our ability to do just this has, indeed, been one of the great strengths of our industrial democracy. It will continue to be a keystone to commercial productivity and the extraordinary quality of life we have built over the last century. It is our responsibility to see that it does not wane, but is strengthened through ever more effective and professional management.

References

1. "Recognition and Awards for Industrial Innovation," Position Statement by the Industrial Research Institute, April 6, 1979.
2. Moore, D. C. and Davies, D. S. "The Dual Ladder—Establishing and Operating It," *Research Management*, Vol. XX, No. 4, July 1977, pp. 14-19.

3. Smith, J. J. and Szabo, T. T., "The Dual Ladder—Importance of Flexibility, Job Content, and Individual Temperament," *Ibid*, pp. 20-23.
4. Meisel, S. L., "The Dual Ladder—The Rungs and Promotion Criteria," *Ibid*, pp. 24-26.
5. Emmons, W. D., "The Dual Ladder—The Pioneering Research Approach," *Ibid*, pp. 27-29.
6. Cantrall, E. W., Manly, D. G., Schroeter, D. G., and Wakeham, H. R. R., "The Dual Ladder—Successes and Failures," *Ibid*, pp. 30-33.

Dr. Bruce Merrifield is vice president of technology of The Continental Group, Inc.

49.
CREATIVITY:
A PATH TO PROFIT

William D. Ellis

On-the-job creativity is everybody's property and many people have discovered it can make almost any line of work into an adventure and a career. It can pay to sit back and think of new methods of doing things.

Seventeen-year-old Lynn Hunt takes high school commercial courses mornings and works as a typist in downtown Cleveland, Ohio, afternoons. Recently, her office manager noticed she was tucking a slip of green paper behind the sandwich of carbon-treated invoices she was rolling into her typewriter. The slip had an odd-shaped window cut in it.

When Lynn was finished, the manager picked up the green slip and found an addressed envelope behind it. She smiled. "Beautiful! You can type addresses on the envelopes at the same time as the invoices!"

"Well," said Lynn hesitantly, "I...want to keep up."

"You will."

Adaptations of the window technique followed—sometimes it was a matter of tucking small, odd shapes of carbon paper behind a particular spot on the stack of letterheads.

Whatever the typing chore, Lynn learned to address the envelopes at the same time she typed the forms, and soon became the fastest worker in the office.

A small thing, perhaps, but on-the-job inventiveness speeded the entire office's typing practices—and earned her a raise.

Too often, we assume that creativity belongs to architects, artists, decorators and such, so we leave the field to them and dismiss our own ideas. This is backwards. While the card-carrying creative types are still painting the same bowl of fruit and designing the same glass-box skyscrapers, a harassed sales manager somewhere is figuring out a new way to move an overstock of galvanized iron, a tool-and-die maker is designing a power takeoff that will do three jobs simultaneously, an accountant is rescuing a small business.

FROM BROWN BAG TO BLUEPRINT

On-the-job creativity is everybody's property and many people have discovered it can make almost any line of work into an adventure and a career. One of these is a mechanic for a large manufacturing company. He knew the firm was planning to buy some very expensive machinery to speed up the manufacturing of automotive engine bearings. Eating his lunch under a tree one day, he suddenly envisioned a mechanical device that, installed on the present machines, would streamline the production as effectively as the new equipment.

He flattened his brown-paper lunch bag, diagramed his idea on it and dropped it into the company suggestion box. The company's engineers took the idea from the brown bag to blueprint form, then made a small model of the device. It worked. Under a company formula, the mechanic was rewarded with a bonus of $26,000.

He had read no books about the fine art of creativity. He was eating his lunch and he got an idea.

The main arena of creativity is the workaday world of people smack up against getting a job done.

For instance, Martha Driver, a librarian in East Cleveland, had the task of moving 60 tons of books to a new library building across town. The library board had budgeted for a professional moving job, but Martha preferred to save what money she could and put it into more books. She called on the local newspaper and persuaded the editor to publish a feature story headlining a special offer: "Unlimited Withdrawal Privileges. Draw Out All Your Summer Reading Now. Keep All Summer. Return Books in September—to the New Library."

Presto! The book-moving job was taken care of at considerably reduced cost.

The resources of large corporate research and development laboratories tend to discourage an individual from developing his own on-the-job ideas. But big R & D departments have two major handicaps: They are usually involved in big problems, and they don't have your knowledge of the problems—and possibilities—of your job. Noticing how many of the calculators and adding machines he sold were later stolen, salesman Paul Sander devised an economical lock and cable attachment for lashing office machines to desks. Then he formed his own company, J. O. Prague, of Wantagh, N. Y., to make and sell the device.

Frank Marino, an engineer at PVT Plastics in Brooklyn, N. Y., liked everything about his Volkswagen—except its nose. So he molded a plastic one that resembled a Rolls-Royce hood and put it on his little bug. It attracted so much admiration from passersby that his company now manufactures and sells them. About 5,000 of them are rolling the roads today.

Sometimes, the hardest place in which to be imaginative is a creative industry where customs, fads and competition freeze the options. In that case, think wild.

Knowing that young married couples have little money for furniture, Pittsburgh designers Eileen Pittler, 26, and George Brewer, 29, came up with the idea of stick-on furniture—life-size pictures of wall telephones, Tiffany lamps and Victorian brass bed headboards that could be gummed to the wall. The idea appealed to something whimsical in the young—enough to move 150,000 pieces of stick-on furniture in the first four months of production.

AN EYE FOR DETAILS

On-the-job creativity is often a matter of details.

A San Diego, Calif., cab driver has available for his customers a late newspaper, a sports magazine, chewing gum, a tourist map of the city. He keeps the cab interior sharp and sprays it with pine-scented aerosol. "Pays me to make the ride something they don't expect," he says. When he asks customers if they'd like to take the long route and see a specific landmark, "Half the time they say yes. I can make money on the worst days."

A service station located across from a businessman's lunch restaurant runs a perpetual tire sales contest among its employees. The fellow who usually wins goes over and inspects the tires in the restaurant parking lot. When he finds worn tires he leaves a hand-written note under the windshield wiper:

"I have a new four-ply steel radial for your left front. If you're here tomorrow leave your car across the street. I'll put it on while you eat.

"Mike-from-across-the-street."

Often, a good idea is merely a matter of imaginative combinations.

Three young employees of the Bronwen Corp., a Washington, D. C., brokerage firm, noticed that a lot of customers rushed in at noon to study the stock quotations and do their trading before going back to their own jobs. "They had neither time to eat nor time to trade," says partner Harry Hagerty. "We figured, why not put the two together?" The result is a restaurant called The Exchange Ltd., with a stock quotation board for scenery and phones for placing orders.

Undoubtedly the happiest ideas grow out of doing what you like to do. When Mabel Westberg's daughters married and moved out to the suburbs, she found herself doing much of their shopping for them in the big downtown Chicago, Ill., stores. She enjoyed it and it sparked a thought: There were, she realized, thousands of house-locked young mothers who, in order to go downtown for a $5 blouse, would end up paying for a baby-sitter, lunch, transportation—$15. Mrs. Westerberg, with the backing of her husband and family, took $5,000 out of her savings and began bringing things out to young mother's homes. Today, her home shopping service, know as Queen's Way to Fashion, is more than a $20-million-a-year business.

Creativity is sometimes reaching back and putting to work your fondest memories. Fifteen years ago, former semipro football player Harry Kimball was managing Rickeys Hotel in Palto Alto, Calif. Weekend business was way down. Then Harry got his winning idea—it occurred to him that Eastern coaches bringing their football teams West to play would have trouble keeping the boys in training when they stayed in San Francisco.

He called the coach of the Detroit Lions and offered to set up a training table any way he like it, and furnish special laundry service and transportation to the practice field at nearby Stanford University. The Lions took him up on the offer. So did the Cleveland Browns, the Green Bay Packers, the Chicago Bears, the Minnesota Vikings and a number of college teams. Word quickly spread across the country that Harry Kimball and his staff knew how to handle athletes. Today, while other hotels are still slow on weekends, Harry's, now known as Rickeys Hyatt House, is jumping.

Possibly the most important single element in bringing an on-the-job idea into being is simply believing in it—and hanging on to that belief. Matt Kiernan, an aggressive young salesman of business education courses for a New York management association, got his golden idea during his daily two-hour commute from Port Jefferson on the Long Island Rail Road—he proposed to his employer that they hire a railroad car and present their courses to the commuters.

Management couldn't see it "at that time." But every day, Matt watched all those people on the 6:42 sleeping, reading newspapers, wasting precious hours; the idea gnawed at him and he proposed it several more times.

Finally, he resigned his job, rented a railroad car, built two classrooms in it, and formed a company call "Edutran." Now he needed academic support, and he got it from Adelphi University, which supplied professors, books and curriculum as well as 55 commuting graduate students. As of this writing, Matt's programs has been expanded to two other Eastern railroads and 200 students, one of whom has received a master's degree. Fifteen more will do so in the near future.

BIRTHPLACE OF THE IDEA

Where do all these solid, creative ideas come from? For an answer, observe yourself.

Do you do your best thinking at your desk with pencil in hand, or by daydreaming when you're away from the job? Do your hunches tend to come at you in a flurry for several days at a time, then dry up for a month or so? (Many professional people find this so, and study and use these cycles.) Do your ideas jump out at you when you're driving on long trips? Respect that. Try pulling out of traffic (yes, emergency stopping—this is an emergency!) to write an idea down while the bloom is on it.

For some people, the stimulation of social conversation brings the big idea. Again, excuse yourself and make a few notes.

Some of the creativity tricks you'll discover about yourself may astonish you.

An industrial designer confides that when he's really stuck he walks through a war surplus store—he invariably finds some gadget there that helps break the idea jam. A sales promotion specialist walks through a variety store or the displays in an airport. A middle-management man confesses he pretends that he's president of the company—what would he change first?

Many men and women quit a good idea when they get hung up on a "missing link" they can't resolve. Professionals in creative jobs have the same gaps, but they leave them blank while they go on to work out the rest of the idea.

Few know that the late, great cartoonist Rube Goldberg was originally a highly successful design engineer. When he hit a gap he couldn't quickly solve he'd fill it with a gag: Cat (A), fishing for goldfish (B), dumps aquarium (C), which douses candle (D), which...Later, he'd go back and find the component which would bridge the gap (X) in the plan.

Whatever the problem, a good idea will keep burning a hole in the pockets of your mind. Let it. It's no bad thing to let an idea simmer. Your twin—the subconscious mind—keeps working on it and refining it while you're eating, sleeping, doing trivial chores. Your subconscious also keeps trying to apply everything new which you see, hear, learn or experience.

So the advice stands: Don't give up. Your hunches may be your future. As Lu Yockum, a man who has had a lot of jobs and is now a top executive of Westinghouse Electric Corp., recently said: "I never worried what job they gave me. If I didn't like it, I always changed it into one I did like. It isn't hard, if you learn to trust your own ideas."

50.
INNOVATION: THE ONLY HOPE FOR TIMES AHEAD?

Rosabeth Moss Kanter

> Integrative thinking that actively embraces change is more likely to take place in companies whose cultures and structures are also integrative, thereby encouraging the treatment of problems as "wholes" and considering the wider implications of actions.

As world events disturb the smooth workings of corporate machines and threaten to overwhelm us—from OPEC and foreign competition to inflation and regulation—the number of "exceptions" and change requirements increases, and companies must rely on more and more of their people to make decisions on matters for which a routine response may not exist. Thus, individuals actually need to count for more, because it is people within the organization who come up with new ideas, develop creative responses, and push for change before opportunities disappear or minor irritants turn into catastrophes. Innovations, whether in products, market strategies, technological processes, or work practices, are designed not by machines but by people.

After years of telling corporate citizens to "trust the system," today many companies must relearn instead to trust their people and encourage them to use neglected reactive capacities in order to tap the most potent economic stimulus of all—idea power.

THE THREAT OF FOREIGN COMPETITION

Foreign competition, which American businesses used to brush off easily, is now overtaking many of our major industries. The losers in World War II—Japan and West Germany—had to start fresh with new plants, equipment, and labor practices, and in many industries, they have begun to surpass even the technological leaders in the U.S. As little as ten years ago, Japan was known as the producer of cheap, plastic imitations. Now its cars, stereos, and consumer electronics set worldwide standards for quality. The business consequences are well known. For example, during the period from 1960 to 1980, sales of Japanese autos in the United States went from one-quarter of 1 percent to 22 percent of the market—a hundredfold increase. Overall, the United States lost 23 percent of its share of world markets in the 1970s.

International competitors were increasing in strength just as America's own economy was slowing down. While consumer prices nearly tripled in the last two decades, productivity decreased. Furthermore, the American edge in invention, our classic strength, was also declining. In the 1950s, the U.S. initiated more than 80 percent of the world's major innovations; today it is close to 50 percent, and foreigners are acquiring a much larger share of U.S. patents (now over a third).

THE RULES ARE CHANGING

Not only are competitive pressures intensifying in nearly every industry, but the rules of the game are changing. For example, financial services, air transportation, trucking, and telecommunications are four of the industries benefiting—or suffering—from deregulation. Ambitious new companies like People Express are ready with novel business concepts to capitalize on the giants' pratfalls. Even professional organizations like law firms face a new degree of competition as loosening regulations pave the way for innovative franchises, chains, and advertising. In this environment, there is no room for sluggishness, inertia, or strangulation in red tape. The game is being won by creative, fast-moving, opportunity-seizing corporations—companies peopled with "change masters" adept at innovation.

WHAT DOES INNOVATION MEAN?

The term "innovation" makes most people think first of technology—new products and new methods for making them. Typically, the word creates an image of an invention, a new piece of technical apparatus, or perhaps something of conventionally scientific character. When asked to list some of the major innovations of the last few years, most people mention microprocessors and computer-related devices. Few people mention new tax laws or the creation of enterprize zones, even though these too are innovations. Fewer still, if any, mention such innovations as quality circles or problem-solving task forces.

This situation is unfortunate, for our competitive world requires more social and organizational innovations. Indeed, by now it is virtually a truism that if technical innovation runs far ahead of our ability to use it because of lack of organizational change, we are simply wasting money (e.g., using expensive computers as typewriters because no one's changed the office system). The advanced technology incorporated in nuclear plants clearly needs more organizational innovation to prevent the frequent break-downs of both components and human controls. Even many "productivity improvements" rest, at root, on innovations that determine how jobs are designed or how departments are composed.

Innovation thus refers to the process of bringing any new, problem-solving or opportunity-addressing idea into use. Ideas for reorganizing, cutting costs, putting in new budgeting systems, improving communication, or assembling products in teams are also innovations.

THE NEED FOR "POWER TOOLS"

In doing the research for my book, *The Change Masters*, I examined more than 115 innovations in detail, including many with significant financial, strategic, or organizational implications. I explored developments as diverse as futuristic X-ray machines, computerized data libraries, new underwater sensing devices, and projects to improve office productivity. By comparing high innovation companies with low innovation ones, I saw how the skills of "corporate entrepreneurs" were allowed to flourish in companies producing more innovations of all kinds.

The results of my research lead me to conclude that what is needed to get people to turn a vague possibility or idea into a successful innovation are "power tools." These tools consist of information, support, and resources.

Information

The first essential ingredient for innovation is information to shape an idea—indications of needs, signs of opportunity, intriguing pieces of data. Early in the history of an innovation, potential innovators need to shift perspectives to get an unusual angle on a problem; later, they need the data to make it work.

Creative leaps of imagination are often made possible because people find themselves in situations where they encounter new information. So change masters like "Heidi Wilson" at the computer company I called by the pseudonym "Chipco" begin an assignment to reduce the cost of materials-handling across far-flung facilities by going outside their own department to get new perspectives on the issue.

"Open communication" patterns provide airwaves for innovation, the channels through which ideas can flow freely. In some business units at Wang Laboratories and General Electric, for example, there are rules banning closed meetings; anyone can theoretically attend any meeting. Hewlett-Packard keeps support staffs lean to reinforce the desire for face-to-face communication in "real time," that is, at the moment when the information is useful. One leading consumer products firm began a few years ago to share a remarkable amount of operation data right down to the shop floor, thereby finding that better-informed employees were also more resourceful at solving problems and exploring opportunities.

Recognizing the creativity produced by communicating across fields, the technical research group at Sohio hosts regular idea exchange conferences for its people to meet with other related staff groups and business line teams: five or six levels of the organization are represented. "Management by wandering around" is a slogan at Hewlett-Packard precisely because through encounters across all levels and specialities, good ideas are discovered.

Support

Once a project idea takes shape, potential change masters require a second "power tool"—support. They need go-ahead signs from key figures, "blessings" from above, the willingness of peers to cooperate, and the agreement of well-placed people to lend their names and reputations to the project.

It helps, although it is not enough, to have a boss who smiles upon innovation. If the idea cuts across organizational lines, then the support of other areas is necessary. An environment of collaboration and mutual support thus makes a critical difference in the degree of innovation possible. Indeed, higher management's promise of backing may be contingent on getting peers on board.

At General Electric Medical Systems, a service manager, "Sam Casey," approached his boss and his boss's boss to ask for a budget for a college recruitment and training program, which he had been supporting at a low level on his own. The executives agreed that they would provide a large budget if Casey could get his four peers to agree to support the project. Somewhat to the executives' surprise, he came back with his peers' support—he took his peers offsite for three days for a round of negotiations and planning.

Support is more readily available in organizations that encourage relationship-building across wide areas, make teamwork a common experience, and permit easy access to top executives, even in other fields. Change masters in these organizations also have sufficient stability and expectation of continued employment that people anticipate a future together.

The sheer volume of movement and contact in high innovation companies is striking. People's careers are likely to take them into a variety of areas. For example, multi-area conferences, meetings, and training programs in such organizations enable people to circulate and to get to know potential supporters and collaborators across corporate space. Digital Equipment makes it easy for mangers to meet face-to-face by running a regularly scheduled helicopter service to link Northeast facilities. This kind of arrangement made it possible for Heidi Wilson, the corporate manufacturing staff manager, to act on her idea for a rationalized materials flow system. For one thing, from her previous stint in an unrelated function, she had come to know managers in many plants who were ready to hear her out and introduce her to their bosses.

Nonetheless, people are unwilling to lend their support to a not-yet-proven idea if they fear that the person behind the idea will not be around to carry it out. Where an organization has been traumatized by poorly planned layoffs, support for innovation shuts down. In contrast, employment security and absence of cutthroat competition for future positions at Hewlett-Packard contribute to the availability of support for trying out new ideas.

Thus, long-standing relationships are often central to developing support for innovation. "Frank Jones," a chemical-process manager at Polaroid who was waiting for his chance to upgrade the department and develop new processes, gathered data about production that persuaded the plant manager was well as Jones's second boss, a chemical-operations manager, to help him sell top management on the idea of granting him the required large capital outlay. He easily developed staff support from a number of the functions in the plant, especially the technical specialists and production people, because he had worked side-by-side in production with some of them, and his long career had taken him through a number of the engineering areas. Over the years he had accumulated a bank of "relationship capital" from which to draw.

A "culture of pride" in the company's own people and products also makes support easier to acquire. Rather than turning to outsiders to bring in change and thus making long-term employees feel stagnant, as innovation-discouraging companies do, high-innovation organizations encourage people to stretch to meet new challenges and to respect each other's skills and competence. Their financial investments in people development reinforce this attitude. IBM and General Electric, for example, perhaps spend more on education per employee than any other U.S. company.

Indeed, one of the hallmarks of innovating companies is "praise abundance." Organizations like General Electric's medical operations help instill confidence in their people by fostering the feeling that "we're all winners." Similarly, change masters tend to make everyone involved in their innovation a "hero": everyone shares the credit and the glory. To go even one step further, the change master "Bob Smith," a district manager at an insurance company, dug into his own pockets and took up a collection from colleagues to raise a $2,000 bonus pool for the clerical workers whose efforts helped him reorganize the district in order to improve performance.

The trophies and wall plaques and letters of recognition and award breakfasts and late afternoon parking lot ceremonies in high innovation companies are all tools readily available to change masters to say thanks—and to motivate people to sign up for the next innovation.

Resources

The last key ingredient for a successful entrepreneurial effort is the resources to carry it out—the funds, staff time, space, equipment, or materials. Not all significant improvements involve large capital allocations, but even for small-investment prospects, the time and money have to be found, especially because innovations, almost by definition, are likely to go beyond a formal budget allocation. There are legendary stories, of course, of important innovations largely supported at first on "bootlegged" funds pulled creatively out of budget lines or by using after-hours labor: people at Xerox talk about its development of liquid crystal applications in this way. In tightly controlled systems where every paper clip has to be accounted for and spare hours become reasons for staff reductions, this might be the only option. But companies where innovation is common try to keep extra resources locally accessible, and there are likely to be many sources of uncommitted funds to tap.

At some high-tech firms, resources are accessible as a result of budgetary ambiguities. Staff or engineering managers at Chipco can go "tin-cupping," as they call it, to the product managers in their facility who have had big budgets, collecting a little bit of funding or a few extra personnel. This is how "Steve Talbot," an operating manager with a vague mandate to improve performance, funded a project to reorganize the sales force on a product basis, hired more salespeople, and tackled new markets, eventually doubling market share in the region.

Other companies find ways to make resources accessible outside the hierarchy, beyond normal budgetary channels. Companies like 3M have "innovation banks" to make "venture capital" available internally for development projects, a system supported by a project focus and an emphasis on small-scale operating units to keep approval points close to a manager's home base. Another high innovation company group has experimented with a top management steering committee to which any employee could bring proposals to fund a special project team. Having this additional way to seed innovations paid off. An engineer brought to the steering committee a proposal for a technical design project that was previously turned down by his boss because the department's own budget and staff allocation were too tight.

CONCLUSION

The entrepreneurial spirit producing innovation is associated with a particular way of approaching problems that I call "integrative": the willingness to move beyond received wisdom, to combine ideas from unconnected sources, to embrace change as an opportunity to test limits. To see problems integratively is to see them as wholes related to larger wholes, and thus challenging existing practices—rather than walling off a piece of experience and preventing it from being touched or affected by any new experience.

Entrepreneurs—and entrepreneurial organizations—always operate at the edge of their competence, focusing more of their resources and attention on what they do not yet know (e.g. investment in R&D) than on controlling what they already know. They measure themselves not by the standards of the past (how far they have come) but by visions of the future (how far they have yet to go). And they do not allow the past to serve as a restraint on the future; the mere fact that something has not worked in the past does not mean that it cannot be made to work in the future. Likewise, the fact that something has worked in the past does not mean that it should remain in the future.

Integrative thinking that actively embraces change is more likely to take place in companies whose cultures and structures are also integrative, thereby encouraging the treatment of problems as "wholes" and considering the wider implications of actions. Such organizations reduce rancorous conflict and isolation between organizational units; create mechanisms for exchange of information and new ideas across organizational boundaries; ensure that multiple perspectives will be taken into account in decisions; and provide coherence and direction to the whole organization. In these team-oriented cooperative environments, innovation flourishes.

If change masters have to be skilled at developing ideas and building coalitions to back them, it is equally true that the company environment in which they operate has to help clear the way. Where excessive segmentation drives wedges between departments, between levels, and simply between people, the circulation of information, support, and resources is discouraged, and innovators are cut off from needed power tools. But where there is a history of teamwork and cooperation, where multiple centers of resources exist, and where integrative sentiments prevail over territoriality, then the efforts of innovators are more likely to succeed.

Where America leads today in world markets, it is because of innovation. In certain vital, innovative industries, such as computers, pharmaceuticals, medical electronics, and telecommunications, the United States is even ahead of Japan. (Moreover, even though Japan is the world's number two exporter of large computers, a sizable share of them is made by IBM of Japan.) Thus, playing to national strengths means continuing to be innovative. Indeed, innovation may be the only hope for the times ahead.

Rosabeth Moss Kanter is Professor of Sociology and of Organization and Management at Yale University. She is also Chairman of the Board of Goodmeasure, Inc., a consulting firm in Cambridge, MA.

51.
BEING INNOVATIVE PAYS OFF

W. H. Weiss

> Enterprising companies see that innovation applies not only to new products or services, but also to new equipment, layouts, plants, organization and other functions.

Innovation is an essential ingredient for today's social and economic growth. It improves our quality of life, raises our standard of living and enables our organizations to grow and prosper. Innovation is creating and introducing new ways of doing things, better use of goods and more efficient services and systems.

Although many innovations are technological, they differ from inventions. Innovators get involved with systems and procedures, costs, jobs and the people who fill them. Innovators use knowledge and information. They make things happen and they bring about change.

In some circles, innovation is thought of only as it would pertain to new products or services. In reality, however, innovation may refer to new equipment, layouts, plants, organization and other functions.

Ideas are personal in that a new one always belongs to a person or a small group of people. But, to be of use, it has to progress through the minds of other people, be accepted, developed and implemented. Its success depends on the personalities of the people involved, the impersonal facts of tradition and the policy of the company where it originates.

THE INNOVATIVE PROCESS

Successful innovators say that ideas that pay off have gone through four steps of development, the first step being the conception of the idea. In the second step, more people become involved as the idea is discussed and examined. This step is considered the most critical to the idea's success since without acceptance in general, it will likely go no further.

The third step begins when the idea is publicized and everyone understands its nature and scope. At this time, people investigate its potential, measure its range and evaluate it economically. Much study may be required if the idea is complex or out of the ordinary. Various decisions relating to the idea become a part of the idea's development.

The fourth and final step of the innovation process consists of adopting the idea and putting it into practice.

ENVIRONMENT AS A FACTOR

Several human characteristics and tendencies affect the creation, development and implementation of ideas. The environment under which people work can act as a stimulant to bring out their innovativeness. The search for truth is a goal of the innovative mind. Inhibitions and misconceptions act as roadblocks. When people don't worry about making mistakes, even the timid and reticent ones may come up with some good ideas.

Aimless and undirected activity seldom brings about innovation. Endeavors must be planned and organized. A concerted effort is required if an innovation is to be fully developed and completely implemented. When management takes an early interest in a project, the company is more likely to benefit since misdirected activities will be righted much earlier, resulting in a saving of time and energy.

Enterprising companies see that the environment under which their employees work is conducive to innovation. This means that management provides the climate which rewards inquisitive minds and "we'll-find-the-answer" attitudes. When company objectives are pursued in this manner, unnecessary labor and superfluous procedures are eliminated. Such companies make the maximum use of their resources.

INCENTIVE TO INNOVATE

What are the ways by which innovation can be encouraged in today's society? There are several. For example, governments with future tax revenues in mind tend to believe that providing support to business and industry is a wise move. Unfortunately, however, many governments are willing to provide financial assistance only at research and development levels, believing that little else is required to ensure the commercialization of an idea. They fail to realize that the research investment is only a small portion of the total cost to create a new industry, bring out a new product or improve our standard of living. Within industry, the first step in providing the incentive is to make innovation one of the prime objectives of the company and to allocate resources in that direction. Then an organized search and identification of a profitable undertaking should be made from options available.

But the climate for innovation is not always favorable. This is not a fault of business and industry—it is simply a fact of life. All creative people continually buck conformity. Scientists and engineers need to recognize that within the structured confinement of their environment, the pressures for conformity and continuity will always be present. This often comes as a surprise to young, inexperienced employees who see their company asking them to be creative, inventive and innovative. Employees should recognize such pleas as merely expressions of corporate attitude or policy. In themselves, they are meaningless unless the company adopts the proper procedures to make the policy work. Without attention to these matters by management, employees may not willingly try to be creative and innovative.

Creative individuals and those who pride themselves on being innovative should be aware that every company has a limit to the number of new ideas it can consider and implement at any given time or within a time period. Often that limit is quite low, meaning that when it is reached, additional ideas must be put on the shelf unless they can be shown to have a very attractive payout time.

MOTIVATION FACTORS

Motivation is an essential requisite for successful innovation, and reward is the single most important motivator. People will go to great lengths to solve problems, but only if they know that their solutions will bring them recognition. Many companies promote and sponsor programs that are designed to bring out ideas from employees by giving special awards for those that are accepted. Some companies hand out recognition and token awards merely for the submission of an idea.

Although few of the ideas that employees submit may be acceptable for one reason or another, even those that seem worthless have some value. Any idea is important to the person who originated it. The fact that the person was given a chance to express it means much to him or her. Recognizing this, when any idea shows promise, slight that it may be, management should provide help, perhaps even suggesting a change in direction. The key to more and better innovation lies in not attempting to overcome inertia but rather in applying the principles of human motivation.

ROADBLOCKS TO INNOVATION

Management sometimes is guilty of putting roadblocks in the path of innovators. Lack of recognition of a problem and faulty reasoning as to how conditions could be improved are typical examples. A major obstacle looms when insufficient support is offered for programs which have all the qualifications for being profitable. Better technology doesn't come rapidly—it takes time and usually requires a fresh viewpoint, yet management may be slow to acquire people with that attribute.

Too many investment decisions are made with only cost reduction in mind. Also, changes may be made piecemeal rather than by wiping out an entire obsolete system and introducing an entirely new approach. Replacing old equipment and processes with new often cannot be cost-justified by traditional methods. However, such replacement could be cost-justified when money has to be spent anyway for capacity increases or diversification.

Another roadblock may be management's reluctance to plan for the long term. When new products are brought out, not enough time may be provided to confirm that the technology is right for the new process. A strategic plan for manufacturing would more clearly define the course of the company and enable an innovation to be more efficiently pursued.

HOW MANAGEMENT CAN HELP

The best way to promote innovation among employees is for managers to spend time in the production and engineering departments talking to employees and carefully listening to them. Nobody knows the problems of a process or the eccentricity of a machine better than the people who must operate and maintain it. Management can promote innovation with more success by limiting special assignments to the scientists and research and development people in the company. It is very difficult to be innovative when you're in strange waters and barely able to swim much less get to where you'd like to be.

Recognition and remuneration are important in prompting and sustaining innovation. People cannot be expected to develop their innovative skills if they believe their efforts will not be appreciated.

THE CHALLENGE OF INNOVATION

Encouraging employees to be innovative is going to be just as difficult in the future as it is today despite the fact that innovation is of vital importance to society in general and a company in particular. Contrary to the protestations of some of today's activists about the evils resulting from modern technology, history confirms that innovation almost always brings worthwhile benefits to business and industry. Even though major problems have arisen from innovation, our higher standard of living over other countries could not have been achieved without it.

Some scientists believe there is a slowing in the search for new knowledge in the natural sciences. Adding to this viewpoint are the many voices claiming that government regulations, laws and guidelines are discouraging our attempts to improve productivity. Business and industry are very much concerned about the cost of compliance with many of these regulations. Yet there has been very little progress made toward reducing them.

Regardless, although there may be less support for invention in the future, there is a continuing and increasing need for innovation. Everyone agrees that we must save what we have accomplished and that the quality of life can be improved further. Thus, the challenge of innovation remains with us.

W. H. Weiss is a consultant in industrial management. He has a MBA from Kent State University and has written four books, as well as many articles on human relations, management and engineering.

52.
PUT THAT "BETTER IDEA" TO WORK FOR YOU

Data Management

> People who have "made it" in management are usually individuals who have taken chances in their career. So don't be afraid to question the values of things, invest in new technologies or take political chances if you feel that you truly do have a "better idea."

That "great idea" you had last night is sure to make the company a million dollars. It will bring you instant fame and prestige—maybe even vault you into the executive suite.

The only problem is that you don't know how to put your brilliant idea into action. The real question is, "How am I going to 'sell' it to top management?"

"Once you have an idea, the place to begin is by examining your personal track record and behavioral aspects," says Don Berardo, a management counselor at the Meld Group, West Hartford, Conn.

"Also try to decide how your idea might effect the corporate profit mission. Consider what impact it will have on both you and the organization." In other words, besides helping you, will it really make money for the company?

"'Brainstorm' ideas are rarely novel," says Berardo. Therefore, it pays to be conservative and proceed with caution in order to protect your reputation within the organization.

Always check to see if your idea has been tested and tried before, by whom and its track record. If it hasn't been tried before, then it's best to proceed with caution.

After putting everything in perspective, if you still strongly feel that your idea will result in positive gains for your career and personal esteem, *and* the overall goals of your company, then proceed by talking to your boss.

If it is a good idea, your boss will probably want you to present your details to top management. Before such a meeting, be sure to keep the following in mind:

- Present an outline in abstract form that sums up your idea.
- Document all information—present valid facts and research.

- Use terms such as "profit," "savings" and "return on investment."
- Always consider potential political ramifications.

A brief oral and visual presentation is the best way to sell your idea to top management.

"The object of a presentation is to *persuade* people, and that's what a good presentation does," says Abbe Barker, editor of *Decker Communication Report*, San Francisco, Calif. "People will buy you before they buy your product (idea)."

A presentation will let you have plenty of eye-to-eye contact with top management. This allows you to see how you and your idea are being accepted or rejected, adds Barker.

The first step of any presentation is to request 10 to 15 minutes' time to direct your idea to top management. One possible opportunity would be either before or after the monthly planning session.

In any event, get your thoughts organized, and prepare your sales pitch ahead of time. Be sure to go into the meeting anticipating questions, and be ready to answer them. "It's important that you feel strongly for your idea," says Barker.

Be sure to use language that your audience will understand, and make it as vivid as possible. Also, use plenty of visual aids. "Most people will remember that more than a bunch of exact figures," says Barker.

Be careful that you don't give your audience *too much* information—this will only put them to sleep. For the best chance of selling your idea, consider the following tips:

- Use plenty of eye contact.
- Concentrate only on key points.
- Use overheads and flip charts.
- Don't put more than three ideas on a chart.
- If facts and figures are important, prepare them as handouts for distribution *after* your presentation.

According to management counselor Berardo, you shouldn't "fall in love with your idea." Don't become paranoid about it either, thinking that someone will steal your idea.

People who've "made it" in management are usually individuals who have taken chances in their career. So don't be afraid to question the values of things, invest in new technologies or take political chances if you feel you truly do have a "better idea."

53.

STIMULATING TECHNOLOGICAL INNOVATION: THE INNOVATIVE SPIRIT IN AN INDUSTRIAL SETTING

Lewis H. Sarett

To restore our innovative capacity and performance, stimuli and incentives are needed to unleash the creative talents of individuals and groups. The key factor in nurturing innovation has more to do with interpersonal relationships than with facilities or organizational services.

The literature and the dialogue over decades bespeak the interfaces between science, scientists, and scientific institutions on the one hand, and society and the agents of society (including governments) on the other. And in the last few years, there has been a marked crescendo in talk about innovation. Perhaps this has been because for too long innovation has been under-recognized and undervalued by those who make and influence national policy. Perhaps it has been because inflation- and publicity-imposed constraints of various kinds have caused investment in innovation to be increasingly suspect and the likelihood of success in innovation increasingly questionable. Perhaps it has been because our government has been fostering—both in Congress and in the Executive Branch—the concept of new science policies, reshaped and redirected, that could add to the innovative incentives and the innovative capacity of industry. For surely, as our leadership position in science and technology has gradually eroded, with consequent erosion of some of our economic, social, and political cornerstones, a key question—perhaps the key question—is what can be done to redress the imbalance, to restore our innovative capacity and performance.

In addressing this question, I will limit myself to the subject of nurturing innovation in the industrial research laboratory, with particular emphasis on the individual innovator. I take as my text some thoughts of Sir Francis Bacon. Writing in 1596 in an essay entitled—appropriately enough—"Of Innovations" he said:

As the births of living creatures, at first, are ill-shapen: So are all Innovations…yet not-withstanding, are commonly more worthy than most that succeed (follow): So the first Precedent (if it be good) is seldome attained by Imitation…It is true that what is settled by Custome though it be not good, yet at least is fit. And those things, which have long gone together, are, as it were, confederate within themselves. Whereas New Things peece not so well; But though they helpe by their utility yet they trouble by their Inconformity…They are like Strangers, more Admired and less Favoured.

What are some of the factors that help innovation, this ill-shapen "stranger," born into this world? Each will have his own set of factors, for they are different for each individual and for each research institution. I can only give you mine and those of my associates with whom I have discussed the matter at Merck—the research institution with which I have been identified since the 1940's. And I can only hope that you will find some parallels in your own experiences, or that when we and our institutions diverge, it will prove to be an interesting and productive divergence, which is the pattern and the strength of science.

When I think about nurturing innovation in an industrial research setting, I think first about the individual. We would all agree that innovation—in any field or in any setting—is primarily dependent on the talent, drive, enthusiasm, and creativity of trained and experienced individuals. We would all also agree, of course, that some of the characteristics I have enumerated can be encouraged by the surrounding professional and institutional context. But I persist in believing that in the absence of people with these innate qualities, innovative capacity cannot be caused to be present in a laboratory. One need search no further than Thomas Huxley to find the concept well expressed: "No delusion is greater than the notion that method and industry can make up for lack of motherwit." Of course the ability to recognize a creative individual is a unique talent. There are no rules to go by, and those who have the talent can't tell us about the extrasensory vibrations on which they rely. But certain it is that a few people can pick creative individuals with a remarkably high batting average—say 20%!

In my experience there has also been little correlation between ability to create new scientific concepts and ability to identify creative scientists. The person who can pull a great research team together is seldom the person who creates inventions. True, there are the Edwin Land and the Vannevar Bushes and the Max Tishlers who have created great research organizations and have been enormously innovative themselves in a scientific and technical sense. But they are the exceptions.

In collecting my thoughts for this article, I discussed the subject at some length with several of my colleagues with long experience at Merck. As you would expect, their views on what best creates a climate for innovation, or what most characterizes a successful innovator, were not identical. But the differences were more a matter of emphasis than of substance. We all agreed that innovators are: hard working, enthusiastic, persevering, highly motivated by personal recognition for their contributions, well prepared intellectually, and intuitive. We also agreed that each innovator is, above all, unique. Moreover, I have never encountered any productive laboratory, of any size, where the people were not only highly individualistic but also capable, somehow, of maintaining an often precarious balance in group effort toward common goals, even though it is sometimes through clenched teeth. This array of qualities makes them rare, and it is up to research management to direct such human resources wisely.

SELECTING CREATIVE PEOPLE

This means that the processes for selection of people may be the most important single determining factor for productivity in a laboratory. And one of the principal tasks of research management is to give recruitment top priority and personal attention, particularly in key positions, in which excellence begets excellence. Some of the most sensitive judgments relate to two aspects of recruitment: recruiting outside to fill a senior position and maintaining an appropriate flow of younger people with more recent training and new ideas into the laboratories. Somehow it never works out that modest growth and natural attrition provide enough vacancies for the young.

Another point to be made in this connection is the importance of selection from within and of scientific and career development programs. Too often we tend to look beyond what we have, and yet quality people are often there and will contribute in abundant measure to the productivity of the laboratories if only they are identified and developed. Such research laboratories as those of General Electric and Bell provide ample demonstration of the values derived from training and career development programs that supplement their skillful recruiting programs.

Those who manage research and development in industry and those who direct and own research-intensive corporations can foster innovation by providing a total context conducive to individual fulfillment. Such a context is made up of professional, institutional, and personal elements. I state them in that order because I believe that is their order of importance.

PROFESSIONAL AND INSTITUTIONAL INFLUENCES

A scientist is, above all, a professional. Thus the rewards and incentives and recognitions and stimuli that matter most are those which characterize and are visible in any setting where good science abounds. And good science abounds equally in academic, governmental, and industrial settings. But individuals in those settings do not necessarily perceive excellence in other settings, tending sometimes to feel that institutional purpose has an influence on the quality of science carried out there. Such narrow views are fortunately diminishing in frequency and in intensity.

The character of the institution in which industrial research laboratories are embraced has an great deal to do with innovation in the laboratories themselves. In the first place, if innovation is not complete until an idea is marketed, the laboratories must be surrounded by, and closely related to, development and testing, regulatory expertise, manufacturing, and especially marketing. Without them, and their successful and innovative performance, discovery and invention may not mean product and service. In the second place, the very kind of company influences research productivity, as do the nature and interest of top management. People in research don't need to feel that they are loved. But they do need to feel that they are understood and supported, and that that support is sustained instead of being a variable dependent on short-term business cycles. Clearly, innovation in a laboratory sense is more likely to occur when the whole company is innovative and research-dependent.

Most of us experienced the era of the 50's and 60's, when corporate thinking about research was simple and straightforward, and can be imagined as running along the following lines: "All research is good, and the more the better. Management will support research and automatically receive the blessings of new products and new processes which that investment will generate." The climate was propitious for the corporate entrepreneur. He took risks, and they paid off.

The environment had changed dramatically by the end of the 60's. The corporate managerial entrepreneurs had to a considerable extent disappeared, replaced by executives more adept at weighing and measuring and at trying to avoid the expensive traps which investment in research in a politically hostile environment could create. Naturally, this change has itself exacted a price. A corporate climate in which avoidance of mistakes is the top priority is not one in which research flourishes. Research after all is only a whole series of explorations with mostly disappointing outcomes—mistakes, if you will—relieved once in a great while by a dazzling success.

Let us hope that the forces at work today seeking to stimulate innovation and technological leadership will permit the return to a corporate environment in the U.S. that will be supportive of risk-taking once again, recognizing at the the same time that tomorrow's corporate processes will necessarily be more sophisticated than those that prevailed during the technological optimism of the 50's and 60's.

PROJECT SELECTION

Immediately on the heels of my first priority—that is, selection of talented and creative scientists—comes the second—the selection or "discovery" of great research projects. And because innovative people like to be where the action is, the selection of projects in turn reinforces the ability to attract and motivate creative scientists. Although we all recognize this activity as a key part of a productive R&D environment, the degree of effort and inspiration required for success is generally underestimated.

This problem of project selection does not necessarily apply to the small company started by an entrepreneur with a winning strategy. He can spin off enough ideas for refinements and improvements to keep his laboratories humming for a long time. But later on, after the entrepreneur has retired and a conventional business manager has taken over, difficulties may arise. Of course by this time the small company may have grown big enough to afford its own market research group, and they can help very considerably in the selection of research projects. Their major expertise, however, is usually directed to uncovering and evaluating new applications for in-line products and processes and to analyzing existing markets, rather than to imaginative leaps into totally new fields.

In pharmaceuticals, for example, it is no great trick to line up health problems in terms of their prevalence and to allocate research effort accordingly, taking into account technical feasibility as well. Indeed, judging from annual reports and other sources of intelligence, that is exactly what many companies around the world have done. The result is as predictable as it is unrewarding: Many look-alike cardiovascular beta-blockers awaiting approval of the FDA and other regulatory agencies; a host of antiinflammatory agents seeking regulatory attention; a number of pending antibiotics with comparable spectra of activity. The competition of similar products is not necessarily a bad thing. But if they are pursued at the expense of following promising new leads, true innovation suffers, as does the research prestige of the companies, prestige which nurtures the souls of their scientists and helps to attract new talent.

What is needed for really successful project selection is the inspired hunch which materializes into a whole new concept. And individuals are needed who bring talent to this task—individuals who have also accumulated the necessary experience to recognize opportunity when it arises, and who are eager to accept the drudgery of searching in the belief that such searching will eventually pay off. Such individuals are rare indeed. They usually stay in the lab and apply themselves to their research instead of making a career in the unrecognized and often unrewarded occupation of project selection. Yet, who among us wouldn't give his right arm for the kind of talent which decided to search for self-developing film for the camera, for a photocopying process to replace carbon paper, or for a revolutionary approach to gastric ulcer involving an unconventional type of histamine receptor?

ACADEMIC TIES

A third principal element in nurturing an environment for innovation is the maintenance of close academic ties. Our company, for one, has flourished through its cooperation with university researchers in the biomedical field. Our entry into the vitamin and antibiotic fields came about because we made ourselves useful partners with R. R. Williams, Thadeus Reichstein, E. C. Kendall, and other great academic investigators. After all, industrial laboratories are not naturally at the crossroads of science, where people meet to exchange ideas, discuss challenges, learn new points of view. But such interchange is important to the life of a laboratory; without it, the laboratory can wither. The counter-balances are simple and straightforward: Holding seminars on the laboratory campus, inviting distinguished and sometimes controversial people in to lecture, bringing people in from the four corners of the world to refresh and reinvigorate.

I recall an instance in steroid chemistry soon after the war. We invited Dr. Louis Feiser of Harvard to give a series of twenty lectures, open to anyone who wanted to attend. The lectures were after hours, in the cafeteria, and associated with dinner. The lectures were very well attended, serving quickly and painlessly to bring everybody up to speed. The same thing happened in molecular biology with Jacques Fesco of Princeton. In addition to their educational value, they instilled pride. They showed that everyone cared about having and using the latest knowledge and techniques in our research endeavors.

Many other ways have been found to establish ties with academia: Sabbaticals, either from a university to a company or the reverse; grants and consultantships; a board of academic advisors; and seminar programs.

It is interesting and heartening that the Domestic Policy Review of Industrial Innovation by the Department of Commerce is coming forth with specific recommendations on how to link academic and industrial research more closely—recommendations that appear to have met with virtually unanimous endorsement by the industrial community.

Every company necessarily has its own requirements related to publication. Our policy, for example, is to publish when patents appear. It does seem to me that the right course is to be as affirmative as possible within the inescapable limitations on publication—always testing to see why some data should not by published rather than the reverse. This is particularly important if a laboratory has something new and significant to say. Years ago we had such a body of data on the thiazides. We could have protected it. But, after agonizing a bit, we decided to publish, and—predictably—hastened competition in the process. However, the disclosures helped build Merck's reputation, and I wouldn't be surprised if in the long run they built us at the income line as well. Anyway, in perspective it was clearly the right thing to do.

THE PERSONAL SIDE

Then there is the personal side, by which I mean elements like salaries and benefits and incentive awards and all of the other factors that relate to comfort, convenience, standard of living and opportunity for promotion. Again on the basis of personal observation, I am convinced that nurturing innovation in an industrial laboratory is less related to such matters than to professional and institutional recognition. I wouldn't want to carry this too far. Obviously one expects wages and benefits and so on to be at, or close to, the level prevailing in the leading comparable laboratories. But I think "getting ahead" for the scientists is measured more in scientific than in economic terms. Certainly, the personal recognition to be gained by early publication of new knowledge is an important part of any benefits package.

Another important personal incentive is to bring the bench scientists into prominence instead of hiding him behind a screen of lab chiefs. We try to do this when we have meetings of our scientific advisors. We do it when we have our internal program reviews; we encourage the bench scientist to come in with research proposals—"bottom-up management." We even permit him to choose his own consultants instead of having them chosen for him.

And we have found that recognition of accomplishments counts. For our major scientific awards, for example, the Board of Directors makes up to $50,000 available for the individual to give a college or university in his name to further science, science training, or science communication. We make much of our awarded patents, display publications, celebrate new product launchings, applaud and exploit the awards our scientists receive—any and all things to convey how much importance we attach to excellence and accomplishment. We also believe in the values of a clearcut and well understood dual ladder—scientific and administrative—for advancement in the laboratories.

But perhaps the key factor in nurturing innovation has more to do with inter-personal relationships than with facilities and organizational services. Simply, it is this: High expectations on the part of corporate and research management tend to engender high self-expectations on the part of the individuals performing research. People tend to rise to the levels expected of them, and all of the facilities and services, the research environment, and the commitment to seeing a project through to completion reinforce the conviction that success will be—and must be—achieved.

In the final analysis, all kinds of stimuli and incentives are for the purpose of unleashing the talents of individuals and groups. One can't know for sure whether such programs will accelerate answers, or give the wanted answers, or even the right answers. One can know, however, that without such nurturing, the innovative spirit and, ultimately, the innovative capacity may wither and can even die.

The particular relevance of these thoughts in a broader context is this: Innovation may be laboratory-centered at the outset. But the innovative spirit must be characteristic of an organization as a whole if new ideas are to be converted into useful and widely used new products and services. Thus it can be argued that successful innovation is particularly important in industrial settings, through which advances in research and technology become advances toward the achievement of social and economic goals.

Dr. Lewis H. Sarett is senior vice president, science and technology at Merck & Co., Inc.

BIBLIOGRAPHY

Adams, J. K. *Secrets of the Trade* (New York: Viking, 1971).

Aragones, Sergio. *Mad Menagerie* (New York: Warner Books, 1983).

Arieti, Silvano. *Creativity: The Magic Synthesis* (New York: Basic Books, 1980).

Austin, James H. *Chase, Chance, & Creativity* (New York: Columbia University Press, 1978).

Baker, Paul. *Integration of Abilities: Exercises for Creative Growth* (New Orleans: Anchorage Press, 1977).

Barron, Frank. *Creative Person and Creative Process* (New York: Holt, Rhinehart and Winston, 1969).

Basil, Douglas. *The Management of Change* (Maidenhead, Berkshire, England: McGraw-Hill Ltd., 1974)

Beckett, John A. *Management Dynamics: A New Synthesis* (New York: McGraw-Hill, 1971).

Blakeslee, T. R. *The Right Brain* (New York: Doubleday, 1980).

Bosticco, M. *Creative Techniques for Management* (New York: International Publications Service, 1972)

Bransford, John D. and Stein, Barry S. *The Ideal Problem Solver: A Guide to Improving Thinking, Learning, and Creativity* (New York: W. H. Freeman, 1984).

Buzan, Tony. *Use Both Sides of Your Brain*, Revised Edition (New York: Dutton, 1983).

Cohen, Daniel. *Creativity: What Is It?* (New York: M. Evans and Company, 1977).

Crawford, Robert P. *The Techniques of Creative Thinking* (New York: Hawthorn Books, 1966)

Dauw, Dean C. and Fredian, Alan J. *Creativity and Innovation in Organizations* (Dubuque, IA: Kendall/Hunt Publishing Company, 1971).

Davis, Gray and Scott, Joseph. *Training Creative Thinking* (Melbourne, FL: R. E. Krieger Publishing Company, 1983).

Davis, Gray A. *Creativity Is Forever* (Dubuque, IA: Kendall/Hunt Publishing Company, 1983).

De Ropp, R. S. *The Master Game* (New York: Dell, 1974).

Di Cyan, E. *Creativity* (New York: Harcourt Brace & Jovanovich, 1978).

Dombroski, T. W. *Creative Problem Solving* (Hicksville, NY: Exposition Press, 1978).

Drucker, Peter F. *Technology, Management, and Society* (New York: Harper & Row, 1970).

Edwards, D. D. *How to Be More Creative* (Mountain View, CA: Occasional Productions, 1978).

Evans, J. R. *Get Your Act Together* (San Diego: Lane & Associates, 1979).

Flach, F. F. *Choices* (New York: Lippincott, 1977).

Fleming, Spencer. *How to Develop the Creative Powers of Your Imagination* (Alburquerque, NM: American Classical College Press, 1983).

Flesch, R. *The Art of Clear Thinking* (New York: Harper & Row, 1952).

Gardner, Howard. *Art, Mind, and Brain: A Cognitive Approach To Creativity* (New York: Basic Books, 1982).

Ghiselin, Brewster. *The Creative Process: A Symposium* (Berkeley, CA: University of California Press, 1985).

Glover, John A. *Becoming a More Creative Person* (Englewood Cliffs, NJ: Prentice-Hall, 1980).

Groch, J. *The Right to Create* (Boston: Little, Brown & Co., 1970).

Hare, A. P. *Creativity in Small Groups* (Beverly Hills, CA: Sage Publications, 1982).

Harman, Willis and Rheingold, Howard. *Higher Creativity* (Los Angeles: Jeremy P. Tarcher, 1984).

Hirschman, Elizabeth. *Creativity, Scheduling and the Future* (New York: State Mutual Books, 1980).

Karlson, Jon L. *Inheritance of Creative Intelligence* (Chicago: Nelson-Hall, 1978)

Koestler, Arthur. *The Act of Creation* (New York: Macmillan, 1964).

Kolenda, Konstantin. *Creativity and Openness: Essays in Honor of James S. Fulton* (Houston: Rice University Studies, 1976).

LeBoeuf, Michael. *Imagineering: How to Profit From Your Creative Powers* (New York: McGraw-Hill, 1980).

MacKinnon, Donald W. *In Search of Human Effectiveness: Identifying and Developing Creativity* (Buffalo, NY: Creative Education Foundation, State College at Buffalo, 1978).

Maier, N. R. F. *Problem Solving and Creativity in Individuals and Groups* (Monterey, CA: Brooks/Cole, 1970).

May, Rollo. *Courage to Create* (New York: W. W. Norton, 1975).

Middendorf, W. H. *What Every Engineer Should Know About Inventing* (New York: Marcel Dekker, 1981).

Moore, Edgar. *Creative Thinking* (Boston: Houghton-Miflin, 1984).

Osborn, Alex F. *Applied Imagination* (New York: Charles Scribner's Sons, 1952).

―――. *Your Creative Power* (New York: Charles Scribner's Sons, 1972).

Parnes, A. W. et al. *Creative Analysis* (New York: Dutton, 1978).

Perkins, D. N. *The Mind's Best Work* (Cambridge, MA: Harvard University Press, 1981).

Prince, George. *The Practice of Creativity* (New York: Harper & Row, 1970).

Raudsepp, Eugene. *How Creative Are You?* (New York: Putnam Publishing Group, 1981).

―――. *How to Sell New Ideas* (Englewood Cliffs, NJ: Prentice-Hall, 1981).

Raudsepp, E. and Hough, G. P. *Creative Growth Games* (New York: Harcourt Brace & Jovanovich, 1977).

Roslansky, John D. *Creativity* (Amsterdam: North-Holland Publishing Company, 1970).

Rosner, S. and Abt, L. E. *The Creative Experience* (New York: Grossman Publications, 1970).

―――. *Essays in Creativity* (Croton-on-Hudson, NY: North River Press, 1975).

Rothbart, Harold A. *Cybernetic Creativity* (New York: Robert Speller & Sons, 1972).

Rothenberg, A. *The Emerging Goddess* (Chicago: University of Chicago Press, 1979).

Rothenberg, Albert and Hausman, Carl R. *The Creativity Question* (Durham, NC: Duke University Press, 1976).

Seidel, George J. *Crisis of Creativity* (Notre Dame, IN: University of Notre Dame Press, 1966).

Slaatte, H. A. *The Creativity of Consciousness* (Lanham, MD: University Press of America, 1983).

Smith, Paul. *Creativity: An Examination of the Creative Process* (New York: Hasting House, 1959).

Stein, Morris. *Stimulating Creativity: Individual Procedures* (Orlando, FL: Academic Press, 1974).

Steiner, Gray A. *Creative Organization* (Chicago: University of Chicago Press, 1965).

Stockmyer, John and Williams, Robert. *Unleash the Right Brain* (West Allis, WI: Pine Mountain Press, 1985).

Talbot, David and Zheutlin, Barbara. *Creative Differences* (Boston MA: South End Press, 1978).

Taylor, C. W. *Climate for Creativity* (Elmsford, NY: Pergamon Press, 1972).

———. *Scientific Creativity* (Melbourne, FL: R. E. Krieger Publishing Company, 1975).

———. *Widening Horizons in Creativity* (New York: John Wiley, 1964).

Torrance, E. Paul. *Guiding Creative Talent* (Melbourne, FL: R. E. Krieger Publishing Company, 1962).

Upton, A. W. et al. *Creative Analysis* (New York: Dutton, 1978).

Utah Creativity Research Conference. *Scientific Creativity: Its Recognition and Development* (Melbourne, FL: R. E. Krieger Publishing Company, 1975).

Van Gundy, A. B. *108 Ways To Get a Bright Idea and Increase Your Creative Potential* (Englewood Cliffs, NJ: Prentice-Hall, 1983).

———. *Training Your Creative Mind* (Englewood Cliffs, NJ: Prentice-Hall, 1982).

Weinstein, Bob. *Twenty Ways to Be More Creative in Your Job* (New York: Simon & Schuster, 1983).

Whiting, Charles S. *Creative Thinking* (New York: Reinhold Publishing, 1958).

Zinker, J. C. *Creative Process in Gestalt Therapy* (New York: Random House, 1978).

INDEX